Lecture Notes in Computer Science 2670

Edited by G. Goos, J. Hartmanis, and J. van Leeuwen

Springer
Berlin
Heidelberg
New York
Barcelona
Hong Kong
London
Milan
Paris
Tokyo

Ricardo Peña   Thomas Arts (Eds.)

Implementation of Functional Languages

14th International Workshop, IFL 2002
Madrid, Spain, September 16-18, 2002
Revised Selected Papers

Springer

Volume Editors

Ricardo Peña
Universidad Complutense de Madrid
Facultad de Informática
Departamento Sistemas Informáticos y Programación
28040 Madrid, Spain
E-mail: ricardo@sip.ucm.es

Thomas Arts
IT-University in Gothenburg
Software Engineering and Management
Box 8718, 40275 Gothenburg, Sweden
E-mail: thomas.arts@ituniv.se

Cataloging-in-Publication Data applied for

A catalog record for this book is available from the Library of Congress.

Bibliographic information published by Die Deutsche Bibliothek
Die Deutsche Bibliothek lists this publication in the Deutsche Nationalbibliografie; detailed bibliographic data is available in the Internet at <http://dnb.ddb.de>.

CR Subject Classification (1998): D.3, D.1.1, F.3

ISSN 0302-9743
ISBN 3-540-40190-3 Springer-Verlag Berlin Heidelberg New York

Springer-Verlag Berlin Heidelberg New York
a member of BertelsmannSpringer Science+Business Media GmbH

http://www.springer.de

Printed in Germany

Typesetting: Camera-ready by author, data conversion by Olgun Computergrafik
Printed on acid-free paper SPIN: 10927458 06/3142 5 4 3 2 1 0

Preface

The International Workshops on the Implementation of Functional Languages (IFL) have been running for 14 years now. The aim of these workshops is to bring together researchers actively engaged in the implementation and application of functional programming languages to discuss new results and new directions of research. A non-exhaustive list of topics includes: language concepts, type checking, compilation techniques, (abstract) interpretation, automatic program generation, (abstract) machine architectures, array processing, concurrent/parallel programming and program execution, heap management, runtime profiling and performance measurements, debugging and tracing, verification of functional programs, tools and programming techniques.

The 14th edition, IFL 2002, was held in Madrid, Spain in September 2002. It attracted 47 researchers from the functional programming community, belonging to 10 different countries. During the three days of the workshop, 34 contributions were presented, covering most of the topics mentioned above.

The workshop was sponsored by several Spanish public institutions: the Ministry of Science and Technology, Universidad Complutense de Madrid, and the Tourism Office, Town Hall and Province Council of Segovia, a small Roman and medieval city near Madrid. We thank our sponsors for their generous contributions.

This volume follows the lead of the last six IFL workshops in publishing a high-quality subset of the contributions presented at the workshop in Springer's Lecture Notes in Computer Science series. All speakers attending the workshop were invited to submit a revised version for publication. A total of 25 papers were submitted. Each one was reviewed by four PC members and thoroughly discussed by the PC. The results of this process are the 15 papers included in this volume.

As a novelty this year, the PC awarded the best of the selected papers with the *Peter Landin Award.* This prize is being funded with the royalties, generously contributed by the authors, of the book *Research Directions in Parallel Functional Programming*, K. Hammond and G.J. Michaelson (eds.), Springer-Verlag, 1999. The prize is expected to run for the next few years and will surely be an added feature of future IFL workshops. The name of the winner of each edition will be published in the final proceedings. This year the awarded paper was *Towards a Strongly Typed Functional Operating System* by Arjen van Weelden and Rinus Plasmeijer. Congratulations to the authors.

The overall balance of the papers is representative, both in scope and technical substance, of the contributions made to the Madrid workshop, as well as to those that preceded it. Publication in the LNCS series is not only intended to make these contributions more widely known in the computer science community, but also to encourage researchers in the field to participate in future workshops. The next IFL will be held in Edinburgh, UK, during September 8–10, 2003 (for details see the page http://www.macs.hw.ac.uk/~ifl03).

This year we are saddened by the death of a beloved researcher in our community, Tony Davie, who passed away in January 2003. He was a long-standing contributor to the success of IFL through his knowledge, experience, and general support. He will be greatly missed by our community. We would like to remember him in the way he would have wished:

There was an FPer called Tony
whose persistence was not at all phony.
His limericks fine
made an excellent line
at dinners with mucho calzone.

We would like to thank the program committee, the referees, the authors, and the local organizing committee for the work and time that they devoted to this edition of IFL.

March 2003

Ricardo Peña
Thomas Arts

Program Committee

Peter Achten	University of Nijmegen, The Netherlands
Thomas Arts	Computer Science Laboratory, Ericsson, Sweden
Olaf Chitil	University of York, UK
Marko van Eekelen	University of Nijmegen, The Netherlands
Kevin Hammond	University of St. Andrews, UK
John Hughes	Chalmers University, Sweden
Rita Loogen	Philipps Universität-Marburg, Germany
Greg Michaelson	Heriot-Watt University, Edinburgh, UK
John O'Donnell	University of Glasgow, UK
Ricardo Peña	Universidad Complutense de Madrid, Spain
Doaitse Swierstra	University of Utrecht, The Netherlands
Phil Trinder	Heriot-Watt University, Edinburgh, UK
Tim Sheard	Oregon Graduate Institute, USA
Sven-Bodo Scholz	University of Kiel, Germany

Referees

Abyd Al Zain
Adam Bakewell
Andre Rauber Du Bois
Christophe Ringeissen
Clara María Segura
Clemens Grelck
Cristóbal Pareja Flores
Daan Leijen
Fabien Dagnat
Fernando Rubio
Frank Huch
Gabriele Keller
Hans-Wolfgang Loidl
Jan Henry Nystrom
João Saraiva
John van Groningen
Jurriaan Hage
Lex Augusteijn
Malcolm Wallace
Marc Feeley
Mikael Pettersson
Narciso Martí
Pablo Giambiagi
Pedro Vasconcelos
Pieter Koopman
Ralf Hinze
Robert Pointon
Simon Marlow
Tony Davie
Victor M. Gulías
Volker Stolz
Werner Kluge
Yolanda Ortega-Mallén

Sponsors

Table of Contents

Predictable Space Behaviour in FSM-Hume

Kevin Hammond[1] and Greg Michaelson[2]

[1] School of Computer Science
University of St Andrews, St Andrews, Scotland
kh@dcs.st-and.ac.uk
Tel: +44-1334-463241, Fax: +44-1334-463278
[2] Dept. of Mathematics and Computer Science
Heriot-Watt University, Edinburgh, Scotland
greg@macs.hw.ac.uk
Tel: +44-131-451-3422, Fax: +44-131-451-3327

Abstract. The purpose of the Hume language design is to explore the expressibility/decidability spectrum in resource-constrained systems, such as real-time embedded or control systems. It is unusual in being based on a combination of λ-calculus and finite state machine notions, rather than the more usual propositional logic, or flat finite-state-machine models. It provides a number of high level features including polymorphic types, arbitrary but sized user-defined data structures and automatic memory management, whilst seeking to guarantee strong space/time behaviour and maintaining overall determinacy. A key issue is predictable space behaviour. This paper describes a simple model for calculating stack and heap costs in *FSM-Hume*, a limited subset of full Hume. This cost model is evaluated against an example taken from the research literature: a simple mine drainage control system. Empirical results suggest that our model is a good predictor of stack and heap usage, and that this can lead to good bounded memory utilisation.

1 Introduction

Hume is a functionally-based research language aimed at applications requiring bounded time and space behaviour, such as real-time embedded systems. It is possible to identify a number of overlapping subsets of the full Hume language, increasing in expressive power, but involving increasingly complicated cost models. The simplest is the language that is studied here, FSM-Hume, which is restricted to first-order non-recursive functions and non-recursive data structures, but which supports a form of implicit tail recursion across successive iterations of a process. Despite its restrictions, FSM-Hume is still capable of expressing a variety of problems in the embedded/real-time systems sphere. One such problem, a simple mine drainage control system, is described in this paper. The paper defines a simple bounded space usage cost model for FSM-Hume and evaluates it against this sample application. We demonstrate that it is possible to produce good cost models for FSM-Hume and that these can be used to give good bounded space usage in practice.

R. Peña and T. Arts (Eds.): IFL 2002, LNCS 2670, pp. 1–16, 2003.

program ::=	$decl_1$; ... ; $decl_n$	$n \geq 1$
decl ::=	*box* | var *matches* | *datadecl* | *wiredecl*	
datadecl ::=	**data** id α_1 ... α_m = $constr_1$ | ... | $constr_n$	$n \geq 1$
constr ::=	con τ_1 ... τ_n	$n \geq 1$
wiredecl ::=	**wire** id *ins* *outs*	
box ::=	**box** *id* *ins* *outs* **fair/unfair** *matches*	
ins/outs ::=	$id_1, \ldots, id_n$	
matches ::=	⟨ match_1 , ... , match_n ⟩	$n \geq 1$
match ::=	⟨ pat_1 , ... , pat_n ⟩ → *expr*	
expr ::=	*int* | *float* | *char* | *bool* | *string* | var | *	
	| con exp_1 ... exp_n	$n \geq 0$
	| (exp_1 , ... , exp_n)	$n \geq 2$
	| **if** *cond* **then** exp_1 **else** exp_2	
	| **let** ⟨ $vdecl_1$, ..., $vdecl_n$ ⟩ **in** *expr*	
vdecl ::=	*id* = exp	
pat ::=	*int* | *float* | *char* | *bool* | *string* | var | _ | * | _*	
	| con var_1 ... var_n	$n \geq 0$
	| (pat_1 , ... , pat_n)	$n \geq 2$

Fig. 1. Hume Abstract Syntax (Simplified)

2 Boxes and Coordination

In order to support concurrency, Hume requires both computation and coordination constructs. The fundamental unit of computation in Hume is the *box*, which defines a finite mapping from inputs to outputs. Boxes are *wired* into (static) networks of concurrent processes using wiring directives. Each box introduces one process. This section introduces such notions informally. A more formal treatment is in preparation.

Boxes are abstractions of finite state machines. An output-emitting Moore machine has transitions of the form:

$$(\textit{old state, input symbol}) \rightarrow \quad (\textit{new state, output symbol})$$

We generalise this to:

$$\textit{pattern} \rightarrow \textit{function}(\textit{pattern})$$

where *pattern* is based on arbitrarily nested constants, variables and data structures and *function* is an arbitrary recursive function over *pattern* written in the *expression language*. By controlling the types permissible in *pattern* and the constructs usable in *function*, the expressibility and hence formal properties of Hume may be altered. Where types are sized and constructs restricted to non-conditional operations, Hume has decidable time and space behaviour. As construct restrictions are relaxed to allow primitive and then general recursion, so expressibility increases, and decidable equivalence and then decidable termination are lost. A major objective of our research is to explore static analyses that tell the programmer when decidable properties are compromised in particular programs, rather than placing explicit restrictions on the forms of all programs.

The abstract syntax of Hume is shown in Figure 1. A single Hume box comprises a set of pattern-directed rules, rewriting a set of inputs to a set of outputs, plus appropriate exception handlers and type information. The left hand side pattern of each rule defines the situations in which that rule may be active. The right hand side of each rule is an expression specifying the results of the box when the rule is activated. A box becomes active when any of its rules may match the inputs that have been provided. Hume expressions are written using a strongly-typed purely functional notation with a strict semantics. The functional notation simplifies cost modelling and proof. The use of strict evaluation ensures that source and target code can be directly related, thus improving confidence in the correct operation of the compilation system. Strong typing improves correctness assurances, catching a large number of surface errors at relatively low overall programmer cost, as well as assisting the required static cost/space analyses. Each expression is deterministic, and has statically bounded time and space behaviour, achieved through a combination of static cost analysis and dynamic timeout constructs, where the timeout is explicitly bounded to a constant time. Since the expression language has no concept of external, imperative state, such considerations must be encapsulated entirely through explicit communication in the coordination language.

2.1 Wiring

Boxes are connected using wiring declarations to form a static process network. A wire provides a mapping between inputs and outputs. Each box input must be connected to precisely one output. An output may, in principle, be connected to multiple inputs, but is normally connected to a unique input. The usual form of a wiring declaration specifies the input/output mappings for a single box. This is technically redundant in that the opposite mapping must also be specified in the boxes to which a given box is wired. It has the advantage from a language perspective of concentrating wiring information for a single box close to the definition of that box. It also allows boxes to be connected to non-box objects (external ports/streams, such as the program's standard input or output). It is possible to specify the initial value that appears on a wire. This is typically used to seed computations, such as wires carrying explicit state parameters.

2.2 Box Example

The Hume code for a simple even parity checking box is shown below. The inputs to the box are a bit (either 0 or 1) and a boolean value indicating whether the system has detected even or odd parity so far. The output is a string indicating whether the result should be even or odd parity. This box defines a single cycle.

```
type bit = word 1;  type parity = boolean;

box even_parity
in   ( b  :: bit,     p :: parity )
out  (p' :: parity, show :: string)
unfair
   ( 0, true  ) -> ( true, "true" )
 | ( 1, true  ) -> ( false, "false" )
 | ( 0, false ) -> ( false, "false" )
 | ( 1, false ) -> ( true, "false" );
```

The corresponding wiring specification connects the bit stream to the `input` source and the monitoring output to standard output. Note that the output `p'` is wired to the box input `p` as an explicit state parameter, initialised to `true`. The box will run continuously, outputting a log of the monitored parity.

```
stream input from "/dev/sensor";
stream output to "std_out";

wire even_parity
    ( input, even_parity.p' initially true )
    ( even_parity.p,output );
```

2.3 Coordination

The basic box execution cycle is:

1. check input availability for all inputs and latch input values;
2. match inputs against rules in turn;
3. consume all inputs;
4. bind variables to input values and evaluate the RHS of the selected rule;
5. write outputs to the corresponding wires.

A key issue is how input and output values are managed. In the Hume model, there is a one-to-one correspondance between input and output wires, and these are single-buffered. In combination with the fixed size types that we require, this ensures that communications buffers are bounded size, whilst avoiding the synchronisation problems that can occur if no buffering is used. In particular, a box may write an output to one of its own inputs, so creating an explicit representation of state, as shown in the example above.

Values for available inputs are latched atomically, but not removed from the buffer (consumed) until a rule is matched. Consuming an input removes the lock on the wire buffer, resetting the availability flag.

Output writing is atomic: if any output cannot be written to its buffer because a previous value has not yet been consumed, the box blocks. This reduces concurrency by preventing boxes from proceeding if their inputs could be made available but the producer is blocked on some other output. However, it improves strong notions of causality: if a value has appeared as input on a wire the box that produced that input has certainly generated all of its outputs.

Once a cycle has completed and all outputs have been written to the corresponding wire buffers, the box can begin the next execution step. This improves concurrency, by avoiding unnecessary synchronisation. Individual boxes never terminate. Program termination occurs when no box is runnable.

2.4 Asynchronous Coordination Constructs

The two primary coordination constructs that are used to introduce asynchronous coordination are to *ignore* certain inputs/outputs and to introduce *fair matching*. It is necessary to alter the basic box execution cycle as follows (changes are italicised):

1. check input availability *against possible matches* and latch *available* input values;
2. match *available* inputs against rules in turn;
3. consume *those inputs that have been matched and which are not ignored in the selected rule*;
4. bind variables to input values and evaluate the RHS of the selected rule;
5. write *non-ignored* outputs to the corresponding wires;
6. *reorder match rules according to the fairness criteria.*

Note that: i) inputs are now consumed after rules have been selected rather than before; ii) only some inputs/outputs may be involved in a given box cycle, rather than all inputs/outputs being required; and iii) rules may be reordered if the box is engaged in fair matching. This new model in which inputs can be ignored in certain patterns or in certain output positions can be considered to be equivalent to non-strictness at the box level.

We use the accepted notion of *fairness* whereby each rule will be used equally often given a stream of inputs that match all rules [1]. *Channel fairness* [1] is not enforced, however: it is entirely possible, for example, for a programmer to write a sequence of rules that will treat the input from different sources unfairly. It is the programmer's responsibility to ensure that channel fairness is maintained, if required.

For example, a fair merge operator can be defined as:

```
box merge
in  ( xs  :: int 32, ys :: int 32)
out ( xys :: int 32)
fair
  (x, *) -> x
| (*, y) -> y
;
```

```
for i = 1 to nThreads do
  runnable := false;
  for j = 1 to thread[i].nRules do
    if ¬ runnable then
      runnable := true;
      for k = 1 to thread[i].nIns do
        runnable &= thread[i].required[j, k] ⇒ thread[i].ins[k].available
      endfor
    endif
  endfor
  if runnable then schedule (thread[i]) endif
endfor
```

Fig. 2. Hume Abstract Machine Thread Scheduling Algorithm

The *-pattern indicates that the corresponding input position should be ignored, that is the pattern matches any input, without consuming it. Such a pattern must appear at the top level. Note the difference between *-patterns and wildcard/variable patterns: in the latter cases, successful matching will mean that the corresponding input value (and all of that value) is removed from the input buffer. For convenience, we also introduce a hybrid pattern: _*. If matched, such patterns will consume the corresponding input value *if one is present*, but will ignore it otherwise. Note that this construct cannot introduce a race condition, since the availability status for each input is latched at the start of each box execution cycle rather than checked during each pattern match. Ignored values can also be used as dynamic outputs. In this case no output is produced on the corresponding wire, and consequently the box cannot be blocked on that output.

2.5 Thread Scheduling

The prototype Hume Abstract Machine implementation maintains a vector of threads (*thread*), one per box, each with its own *thread state record*, containing state information and links to input/output wires. Each wire comprises a pair of a value (*value*) and a validity flag (*available*). used to ensure correct locking between input and output threads. The flag is atomically set to *true* when an output is written to the wire, and is reset to *false* when an input is consumed.

Threads are scheduled under the control of a built-in scheduler, which currently implements round-robin scheduling. A thread is deemed to be *runnable* if all the required inputs are available for any of its rules to be executed (Figure 2). A compiler-specified matrix is used to determine whether an input is needed: for some thread t, $thread[t].required[r, i]$ is true if input i is required to run rule r of that thread. Since wires are single-buffered, a thread will consequently block when writing to a wire which contains an output that has not yet been consumed. In order to ensure a consistent semantics, a single check is performed on all output wires immediately before any output is written. No output will be written until all the input on all output wires has been consumed. The check ignores * output positions.

constant	value (words)
$\mathcal{H}_{con}$	3
$\mathcal{H}_{tuple}$	2
$\mathcal{H}_{int32}$	2
$\mathcal{H}_{float32}$	2
...	...
$\mathcal{H}_{string}$	1

Fig. 3. Sizes of tags etc. in the prototype Hume Abstract Machine

3 A Space Cost Model for FSM-Hume

This section describes a simple cost model for space usage in FSM-Hume boxes. The model is defined with reference to the prototype Hume Abstract Machine [8], and provides a statically derivable upper bound on the space usage of FSM-Hume programs in terms of per-box stack and heap usage. The cost analysis is applied to the mine drainage example described in the previous section, and verified against the prototype Hume Abstract Machine Interpreter. A complete, formal description of the abstract machine and compiler can be found elsewhere [8]. The stack and heap requirements for the boxes and wires represent the only dynamically variable memory requirements: all other memory costs can be fixed at compile-time based on the number of wires, boxes, functions and the sizes of static strings. In the absence of recursion, we can provide precise static memory bounds on rule evaluation. Predicting the stack and heap requirements for an FSM-Hume program thus provides complete static information about system memory requirements.

3.1 Dynamic Memory in the Hume Abstract Machine

The Hume Abstract Machine is loosely based on the design of the classical G-Machine [3], restricted to strict evaluation and with extensions to manage concurrency and asynchronicity. Each box has its own dynamic stack and heap. All arguments to function calls, return values and box inputs are held on the stack as (1-word) heap pointers. All available box inputs are copied from the corresponding wire into the box heap at the start of each cycle. All other heap allocation happens as a consequence of executing some right-hand-side expression.

In the prototype implementation, all heap cells are *boxed* [15] with tags distinguishing different kinds of objects. Furthermore, tuple structures require *size* fields, and data constructors also require a *constructor tag* field. All data objects in a structure are referenced by pointer. For simplicity each field is constrained to occupy one word of memory. There is one special representation: strings are represented as a tagged sequence of bytes. These values are summarised in Figure 3. Clearly, it would be easy to considerably reduce heap usage using a more compact representation such as that used by the state-of-the-art STG-Machine [15]. For now, we are, however, primarily concerned with bounding and predicting memory usage. Small changes to data representations can be easily incorporated

$$\boxed{E \overset{\text{box}}{\vdash} \text{box} \Rightarrow \text{Cost}, \text{Cost}}$$

$$(1)\quad \frac{\forall i.\ 1 \le i \le n,\ \ E \overset{\text{type}}{\vdash} \tau_i \Rightarrow h_i \qquad E \overset{\text{body}}{\vdash} \text{body} \Rightarrow h, s}{E \overset{\text{box}}{\vdash} \textbf{box}\ \text{id}\ \textbf{in}\ (\ \text{id}_1 : \tau_1, \ldots, \text{id}_n : \tau_n\ )\ \textbf{out}\ \text{outs body} \Rightarrow \sum_{i=1}^{n} h_i + h, s}$$

$$\boxed{E \overset{\text{body}}{\vdash} \text{body} \Rightarrow \text{Cost}, \text{Cost}}$$

$$(2)\quad \frac{\begin{array}{c}\forall i.\ 1 \le i \le n,\ \ E \overset{\text{pat}}{\vdash} \text{ps}_i \Rightarrow sp_i \\ \forall i.\ 1 \le i \le n,\ \ E \overset{\text{space}}{\vdash} \text{exp}_i \Rightarrow h_i, s_i\end{array}}{\begin{array}{c}E \overset{\text{body}}{\vdash} (\ \textbf{fair} \mid \textbf{unfair}\ )\ \text{ps}_1 -> \text{exp}_1 \mid \ldots \mid \text{ps}_n -> \text{exp}_n \\ \Rightarrow \underset{i=1}{\overset{n}{max}}\ h_i,\ \underset{i=1}{\overset{n}{max}}\ (s_i + sp_i)\end{array}}$$

Fig. 4. Space cost axioms for boxes and box bodies

into both models and implementations at a future date without affecting the fundamental results described here, except by reducing absolute costs of both model and implementation.

3.2 Space Cost Rules

Figures 4–8 specify a space cost model for FSM-Hume boxes and declarations, based on an operational interpretation of the Hume abstract machine implementation. Heap and stack costs are each integer values of type Cost, labelled h and s, respectively. Each rule produces a pair of such values representing an independent upper bound on the stack and heap usage. The result is produced in the context of an environment, E, that maps function names to the space (heap and stack) requirements associated with executing the body of the function. This environment is derived from the top-level program declarations plus standard prelude definitions. Rules for building the environment are omitted here, except for local declarations, but can be trivially constructed.

Rules 1 and 2 (Figure 4) cost boxes and box bodies, respectively. The cost of a box is derived from the space requirements for all box inputs plus the maximum cost of the individual rule matches in the box. The cost of each rule match is derived from the costs of the pattern and expression parts of the rule. Since the abstract machine copies all available inputs into box heap from the wire buffer before they are matched, the maximum space usage for box inputs is the sum of the maximum space required for each input type. The space required for each output wire buffer is determined in the same way from the type of the output

$$\boxed{E \overset{\text{type}}{\vdash} \text{type} \Rightarrow \text{Cost}}$$

$$(3) \quad \frac{}{E \overset{\text{type}}{\vdash} \textbf{int } 32 \Rightarrow \mathcal{H}_{int32}}$$

...

$$(4) \quad \frac{\forall i.\ 1 \leq i \leq n,\ E \overset{\text{type}}{\vdash} \tau_i \Rightarrow h_i}{E \overset{\text{type}}{\vdash} (\ \tau_1\ ,\ \ldots\ ,\ \tau_n\ ) \Rightarrow \mathcal{H}_{con} + \sum_{i=1}^{n} h_i}$$

$$\boxed{E \overset{\text{data}}{\vdash} \text{data} \Rightarrow \text{Cost}}$$

$$(5) \quad \frac{\forall i.\ 1 \leq i \leq n,\ E \overset{\text{constr}}{\vdash} constr_i \Rightarrow h_i}{E \overset{\text{type}}{\vdash} \textbf{data} \text{ id } \alpha_1\ \ldots\ \alpha_m = \text{constr}_1 \mid \ldots \mid \text{constr}_n \Rightarrow \max_{i=1}^{n} h_i}$$

$$\boxed{E \overset{\text{constr}}{\vdash} \text{constr} \Rightarrow \text{Cost}}$$

$$(6) \quad \frac{\forall i.\ 1 \leq i \leq n,\ E \overset{\text{type}}{\vdash} \tau_i \Rightarrow h_i}{E \overset{\text{constr}}{\vdash} \text{con } \tau_1\ \ldots\ \tau_n \Rightarrow \mathcal{H}_{con} + \sum_{i=1}^{n} h_i}$$

Fig. 5. Heap cost axioms for types

value. Figure 5 gives representative costs for integers (rule 3) and tuples (rule 4), and rules 5–6 provide costs for user-defined constructed datatypes.

Figure 6 gives cost rules for a representative subset of FSM-Hume expressions. The heap cost of a standard integer is given by $\mathcal{H}_{int32}$ (rule 7), with other scalar values costed similarly. The cost of a function application is the cost of evaluating the body of the function plus the cost of each argument (rule 8). Each evaluated argument is pushed on the stack before the function is applied, and this must be taken into account when calculating the maximum stack usage. The cost of building a new data constructor value such as a tuple (rule 10) or a user-defined constructed type (rule 9) is similar to a function application, except that pointers to the arguments must be stored in the newly created closure (one word per argument), and fixed costs $\mathcal{H}_{con}$ and $\mathcal{H}_{tuple}$ are added to represent the costs of tag and size fields. The heap usage of a conditional (rule 11) is the heap required by the condition part plus the maximum heap used by either branch. The maximum stack requirement is simply the maximum required by the condition and either branch. Case expressions (omitted) are costed analogously. The cost of a let-expression (rule 12) is the space required to evaluate the value definitions (including the stack required to store the result of each new value

$$\boxed{E \overset{\text{space}}{\vdash} \text{exp} \Rightarrow \text{Cost}, \text{Cost}}$$

$$(7)\quad \frac{}{E \overset{\text{space}}{\vdash} n \Rightarrow \mathcal{H}_{int32}, 1}$$

...

$$(8)\quad \frac{E\ (\text{var}) = \langle h, s\rangle \qquad \forall i.\ 1 \le i \le n,\ E \overset{\text{space}}{\vdash} \text{exp}_i \Rightarrow h_i, s_i}{E \overset{\text{space}}{\vdash} \text{var}\ \text{exp}_1\ \ldots\ \text{exp}_n \Rightarrow \sum_{i=1}^{n} h_i + h,\ \max_{i=1}^{n}\ (s_i + (i-1)) + s}$$

$$(9)\quad \frac{\forall i.\ 1 \le i \le n,\ E \overset{\text{space}}{\vdash} \text{exp}_i \Rightarrow h_i, s_i}{E \overset{\text{space}}{\vdash} \text{con}\ \text{exp}_1\ \ldots\ \text{exp}_n \Rightarrow \sum_{i=1}^{n} h_i + n + \mathcal{H}_{con},\ \max_{i=1}^{n}\ (s_i + (i-1))}$$

$$(10)\quad \frac{\forall i.\ 1 \le i \le n,\ E \overset{\text{space}}{\vdash} \text{exp}_i \Rightarrow h_i, s_i}{E \overset{\text{space}}{\vdash} (\ \text{exp}_1,\ \ldots,\ \text{exp}_n\ ) \Rightarrow \sum_{i=1}^{n} h_i + n + \mathcal{H}_{tuple},\ \max_{i=1}^{n}\ (s_i + (i-1))}$$

$$(11)\quad \frac{E \overset{\text{space}}{\vdash} \text{exp}_1 \Rightarrow h_1, s_1 \quad E \overset{\text{space}}{\vdash} \text{exp}_2 \Rightarrow h_2, s_2 \quad E \overset{\text{space}}{\vdash} \text{exp}_3 \Rightarrow h_3, s_3}{E \overset{\text{space}}{\vdash} \textbf{if}\ \text{exp}_1\ \textbf{then}\ \text{exp}_2\ \textbf{else}\ \text{exp}_3 \Rightarrow h_1 + max(h_2, h_3), max(s_1, s_2, s_3)}$$

$$(12)\quad \frac{\begin{array}{c} E \overset{\text{decl}}{\vdash} \text{decls} \Rightarrow h_d, s_d, s'_d, E' \\ E' \overset{\text{space}}{\vdash} \text{exp} \Rightarrow h_e, s_e \end{array}}{E \overset{\text{space}}{\vdash} \textbf{let}\ \text{decls}\ \textbf{in}\ \text{exp} \Rightarrow h_d + h_e, max(s_d, s'_d + s_e)}$$

Fig. 6. Space cost axioms for expressions

definition) plus the cost of the enclosed expression. The local declarations are used to derive a quadruple comprising total heap usage, maximum stack required to evaluate any value definition, a count of the value definitions in the declaration sequence (used to calculate the size of the stack frame for the local declaratons), and an environment mapping function names to heap and stack usage (rule 19 – Figure 8). The body of the let-expression is costed in the context of this extended environment.

Finally, patterns contribute to stack usage in two ways (Figure 7): firstly, the value attached to each variable is recorded in the stack frame (rule 14); and secondly, each nested data structure that is matched must be unpacked onto the stack (requiring n words of stack) before its components can be matched by the abstract machine (rules 15 and 16).

$$\boxed{\mathrm{E} \overset{\text{pat}}{\vdash} \text{pat} \Rightarrow \text{Cost}}$$

$$(13)\quad \frac{}{\mathrm{E} \overset{\text{pat}}{\vdash} n \Rightarrow 0}$$

...

$$(14)\quad \frac{}{\mathrm{E} \overset{\text{pat}}{\vdash} \text{var} \Rightarrow 1}$$

$$(15)\quad \frac{\forall i.\ 1 \leq i \leq n,\ \ \mathrm{E} \overset{\text{pat}}{\vdash} \text{pat}_i \Rightarrow s_i}{\mathrm{E} \overset{\text{pat}}{\vdash} \text{con pat}_1 \ \ldots \ \text{pat}_n \Rightarrow \sum_{i=1}^{n} s_i + n}$$

$$(16)\quad \frac{\forall i.\ 1 \leq i \leq n,\ \mathrm{E} \overset{\text{pat}}{\vdash} \text{pat}_i \Rightarrow s_i}{\mathrm{E} \overset{\text{pat}}{\vdash} (\ \text{pat}_1,\ \ldots,\ \text{pat}_n\ ) \Rightarrow \sum_{i=1}^{n} s_i + n}$$

Fig. 7. Stack cost axioms for patterns

4 The Mine Drainage Control System

As a working example we have chosen a simple control application with strong real-time requirements. This application has previously been studied in the context of a number of other languages, including Ada with real-time extensions [5]. It was originally constructed as a realistic exemplar for control applications and comprises 750 lines of Ada or about 250 lines of FSM-Hume, of which the functional core is about 100 lines. We have also constructed a Java version.

The problem is to construct software for a simplified pump control system, which is to be used to drain water from a mine shaft. The system runs on a single processor with memory-mapped I/O. The pump is used to remove water that is collected in a sump at the bottom of the shaft to the surface. To avoid damaging the pump, it should not be operated when the water level in the sump is below a certain level. It must, however, be activated if the water rises above a certain level in order to avoid the risk of flooding. The main safety requirement is that the pump must not be operated when the concentration of methane gas in the atmosphere reaches a certain level. This is to avoid the risk of explosion. In order to ensure this, an environmental control station monitors information returned by sensors in the mine shaft, including the current methane level, the current level of carbon monoxide and the airflow. The pump is under the control of an operator who issues commands to turn the pump on and off subject to rules governing the pump operation. The operator may be overridden by their supervisor. All actions and periodic states of the sensors are logged.

$$\boxed{\mathrm{E} \overset{\text{decl}}{\vdash} \text{decl} \Rightarrow \text{Cost}, \text{Cost}, \text{Cost}, \mathrm{E}}$$

$$(17)\quad \frac{\mathrm{E} \overset{\text{space}}{\vdash} \exp \Rightarrow h, s}{\mathrm{E} \overset{\text{decl}}{\vdash} \text{id} = \exp \Rightarrow h, s, 1, \{\}}$$

$$(18)\quad \frac{\begin{array}{c} \forall i.\ 1 \leq i \leq n,\ \mathrm{E} \overset{\text{pat}}{\vdash} \text{pat}_i \Rightarrow sp_i \\ \forall i.\ 1 \leq i \leq n,\ \mathrm{E} \overset{\text{space}}{\vdash} \exp_i \Rightarrow h_i, s_i \\ \mathrm{E'} = \{\ \text{id} : \langle \max_{i=1}^{n} h_i,\ \max_{i=1}^{n} (s_i + sp_i)\}\rangle \end{array}}{\mathrm{E} \overset{\text{decl}}{\vdash} \text{id pat}_1 = \exp_1 \mid \ldots \mid \text{id pat}_n = \exp_n \Rightarrow 0, 0, 0, \mathrm{E'}}$$

$$\boxed{\mathrm{E} \overset{\text{decl}}{\vdash} \text{decls} \Rightarrow \text{Cost}, \text{Cost}, \text{Cost}, \mathrm{E}}$$

$$(19)\quad \frac{\begin{array}{c} \forall i.\ 1 \leq i \leq n,\ \mathrm{E} \overset{\text{decl}}{\vdash} \text{decl}_i \Rightarrow h_i, s_i, s'_i, \mathrm{E}_i \\ \mathrm{E'} = \mathrm{E} \overset{\rightarrow}{\oplus} \bigcup_{i=1}^{n} \mathrm{E}_i \end{array}}{\mathrm{E} \overset{\text{decl}}{\vdash} \text{decl}_1\ ;\ \ldots\ ;\ \text{decl}_n \Rightarrow \sum_{i=1}^{n} h_i,\ \max_{i=1}^{n} h_i, \sum_{i=1}^{n} (s_i + s'_i + \sum_{j=1}^{i-1} s'_j), \mathrm{E'}}$$

Fig. 8. Cost axioms for function and value declarations

Figure 9 shows the corresponding FSM-Hume process network. The primary processes are the pump controller, *pump*, the environment monitoring process, *environment* and the logging process *logger*. The *water*, *methane*, *carbon monoxide* and *airflow levels* are simulated, as are the *operator* and *supervisor*. Additional links between components to enable whole system monitoring through the logger are not shown but are present in the actual wiring. The application is fully described elsewhere [9].

4.1 Space Analysis of the Mine Drainage Example

The cost rules specified above have been extended to full FSM-Hume and implemented as a 200-line Haskell [14] module, which has then been integrated with the standard Hume parser and lexer and applied to the mine drainage control program. Figure 10 reports predicted and actual maximum stack and heap usage for 12,000,000 iterations of the box scheduler under the prototype Hume Abstract Machine Interpreter.

The results in Figure 10 show completely accurate cost predictions for the majority of boxes, with more serious variations for the heap usage of the *logger*,

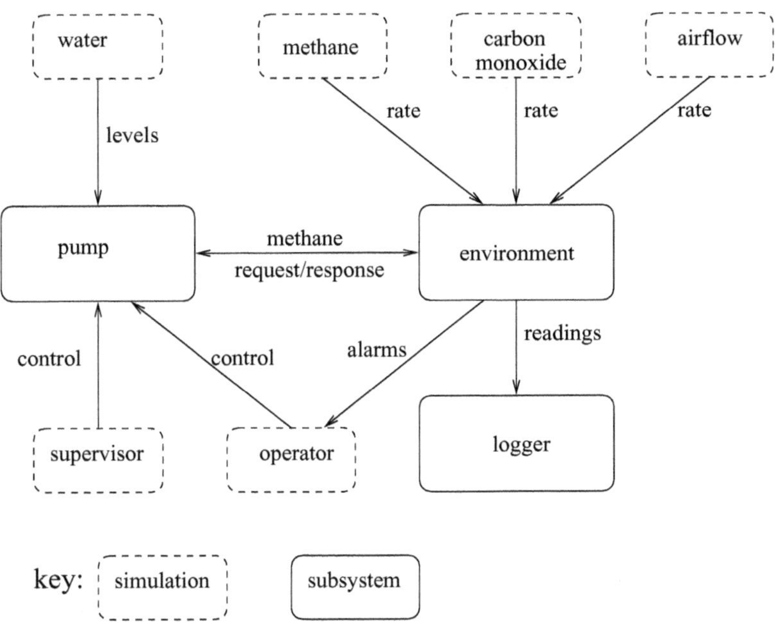

Fig. 9. Hume Processes for the Mine Drainage Control System

box	predicted heap	actual heap	excess	predicted stack	actual stack	excess
airflow	16	16	0	10	10	0
carbonmonoxide	16	16	0	10	10	0
environ	37	35	2	27	26	1
logger	144	104	40	25	25	0
methane	16	16	0	10	10	0
operator	38	29	9	23	23	0
pump	51	42	9	21	18	3
supervisor	29	29	0	20	20	0
water	54	54	0	20	20	0
(wires)	96	84	8	0	0	0
TOTAL	483	425	68	166	162	4

Fig. 10. Heap and stack usage in words for boxes in the mine drainage control system

operator and *pump* boxes. These three boxes are all relatively complex boxes with many alternative choices. Moreover, since these boxes are asynchronous, they will frequently become active when only a few inputs are available. Since unavailable inputs do not contribute to heap usage, the cost estimate will therefore be noticeably larger than the actual usage. The logger function also makes extensive use of string append. Since the size of the result will vary dynamically in some cases, the heap usage will consequently have been overestimated in some cases. Overall, the space requirements of the boxes have been overestimated by 72 words or 11% of the total actual dynamic requirement. Since precise figures may be undecidable in general (for example, where a possible execution path is never taken in practice), this represents a good but not perfect static estimate of dynamic space usage.

To verify that FSM-Hume can yield constant space requirements in practice, the pump application has been run continuously on a 1GHz Pentium III processor under RTLinux, kernel version 2.4.4. RTLinux [4] is a realtime microkernel operating system, which supports multiple realtime threads and runs a modified Linux system as a separate non-realtime thread. Realtime threads communicate with non-realtime Unix tasks using realtime FIFOs which appear as normal Unix devices, and which are the only I/O mechanism available to realtime threads other than direct memory-mapped I/O. The system guarantees a 15μs worst-case thread context-switch time for realtime threads.

Our measurements [8] show that the total memory requirements of the pump application, including heap and stack overheads as calculated here, *RTLinux operating system code and data*, Hume runtime system code and data, and the abstract machine instructions amount to less than 62Kbytes. RTLinux itself accounts for 34.4Kbytes of this total. Since little use is made of RTLinux facilities, and there is scope for reducing the size of the Hume abstract machine, abstract machine instructions, and data representation, *we conclude that it should be possible to construct full Hume applications requiring much less than 32Kbytes of memory, including runtime system support, for bare hardware as found in typical embedded systems.* This storage requirement is well within the capabilities of common modern parts costing $30 or less.

5 Related Work

Accurate time and space cost-modelling is an area of known difficulty for functional language designs [16]. Hume is thus, as far as we are aware, unique in being based on strong automatic cost models, and in being designed to allow straightforward space- and time-bounded implementation for hard real-time systems, those systems where tight real-time guarantees must be met. A number of functional languages have, however, looked at *soft* real-time issues [2,19,7,13], and there has been considerable recent interest both in the problems associated with costing functional languages [16,10,6,18] and in bounding space/time usage [11,17]. All of these approaches other than our own require programmer interaction in the form of cost control annotations.

6 Conclusions and Further Work

This paper has introduced the FSM-Hume subset of Hume, a novel concurrent language aimed at resource-limited systems such as real-time embedded systems. We have defined and implemented a simple cost semantics for stack heap usage in FSM-Hume, which has been validated against an example from the real-time systems literature, a simple mine drainage control system and implemented using the prototype Hume Abstract Machine interpreter. Our empirical results demonstrate that it is possible to define a concurrent functionally-based language with bounded and predictable space properties. Moreover, such a language can be remarkably expressive: the example presented here is representative of a range of real applications. We anticipate that it will be possible to build a full Hume implementation for a bare-bones system, such as a typical embedded systems application using less than 32KBytes of memory, including all code and data requirements. We are currently working on extensions to our cost model to cover recursion and higher-order functions [16]. In the longer term, we intend to demonstrate the formal soundness of our cost model against the Hume Abstract Machine and compiler.

References

1. K.R. Apt and E.-R. Olderog, *Verification of Sequential and Concurrent Programs*, 2nd Edition, Springer Verlag, 1997.
2. J. Armstrong, S.R. Virding, and M.C. Williams, *Concurrent Programming in Erlang*, Prentice-Hall, 1993.
3. L. Augustsson, *Compiling Lazy Functional Languages, Part II*, PhD Thesis, Dept. of Computer Science, Chalmers University of Technology, Göteborg, Sweden, 1987.
4. M. Barabanov, *A Linux-based Real-Time Operating System*, M.S. Thesis, Dept. of Comp. Sci., New Mexico Institute of Mining and Technology, June 97.
5. A. Burns and A. Wellings, *Real-Time Systems and Programming Languages* (Third Edition), Addison Wesley Longman, 2001, Chapter 17, pp. 653–684.
6. R. Burstall, "Inductively Defined Functions in Functional Programming Languages", Dept. of Comp. Sci., Univ. of Edinburgh, ECS-LFCS-87-25, April, 1987.
7. D.H. Fijma and R.T. Udink, "A Case Study in Functional Real-Time Programming", Dept. of Computer Science, Univ. of Twente, The Netherlands, *Memoranda Informatica 91-62*, 1991.
8. K. Hammond and G.J. Michaelson "An Abstract Machine Implementation for Embedded Systems Applications in Hume", `http://www.hume-lang.org/papers/HAM.ps`, January 2003.
9. K. Hammond and G.J. Michaelson "The Mine Drainage Control System in Hume", `http://www.hume-lang.org/examples/pump`, January 2003.
10. R.J.M. Hughes, L. Pareto, and A. Sabry. "Proving the Correctness of Reactive Systems Using Sized Types", *Proc. POPL'96 — ACM Symp. on Principles of Programming Languages*, St. Petersburg Beach, FL, Jan. 1996.
11. R.J.M. Hughes and L. Pareto, "Recursion and Dynamic Data Structures in Bounded Space: Towards Embedded ML Programming", *Proc. 1999 ACM Intl. Conf. on Functional Programming (ICFP '99)*, Paris, France, pp. 70–81, 1999.
12. J. McDermid, "Engineering Safety-Critical Systems", I. Wand and R. Milner(eds), *Computing Tomorrow: Future Research Directions in Computer Science*, Cambridge University Press, 1996, pp. 217–245.
13. J.C. Peterson, P. Hudak and C. Elliot, "Lambda in Motion: Controlling Robots with Haskell", *First International Workshop. on Practical Aspects of Declarative Languages (PADL '99)*, San Antonio, Texas, January 1999, Springer-Verlag LNCS No. 1551, pp. .91–105.

14. S.L. Peyton Jones (ed.), L. Augustsson, B. Boutel, F.W. Burton, J.H. Fasel, A.D. Gordon, K. Hammond, R.J.M. Hughes, P. Hudak, T. Johnsson, M.P. Jones, J.C. Peterson, A. Reid, and P.L. Wadler, *Report on the Non-Strict Functional Language, Haskell (Haskell98)* Yale University, 1999.
15. S. L. Peyton Jones, "Implementing Lazy Functional Languages on Stock Hardware: the Spineless Tagless G-Machine", *J. Funct. Prog.*, 2(2): 127–202, 1992.
16. A.J. Rebón Portillo, Kevin Hammond, H.-W. Loidl and P. Vasconcelos, "A Sized Time System for a Parallel Functional Language", *Proc. Intl. Workshop on Implementation of Functional Languages (IFL 2002)*, Madrid, Spain, Sept. 2002.
17. M. Tofte and J.-P. Talpin, "Region-based Memory Management", *Information and Control*, 132(2), 1997, pp. 109–176.
18. D.A. Turner, "Elementary Strong Functional Programming", *Proc. Symp. on Funct. Prog. Langs. in Education — FPLE '95*, Springer-Verlag LNCS No. 1022, Dec. 1995.
19. M. Wallace and C. Runciman, "Extending a Functional Programming System for Embedded Applications", *Software: Practice & Experience*, 25(1), January 1995.

When Generic Functions Use Dynamic Values

Peter Achten, Artem Alimarine, and Rinus Plasmeijer

Computing Science Department, University of Nijmegen
1 Toernooiveld, 6525 ED, Nijmegen, The Netherlands

Abstract. Dynamic types allow strongly typed programs to link in external code *at run-time* in a type safe way. Generic programming allows programmers to write code schemes that can be specialized *at compile-time* to arguments of arbitrary type. Both techniques have been investigated and incorporated in the pure functional programming language Clean. Because generic functions work on all types and values, they are the perfect tool when manipulating dynamic values. But generics rely on compile-time specialization, whereas dynamics rely on run-time type checking and linking. This seems to be a fundamental contradiction. In this paper we show that the contradiction does not exist. From any generic function we derive a function that works on dynamics, and that can be parameterized with a dynamic type representation. Programs that use this technique combine the best of both worlds: they have concise universal code that can be applied to any dynamic value regardless of its origin. This technique is important for application domains such as type-safe mobile code and plug-in architectures.

1 Introduction

In this paper we discuss the interaction between two recent additions to the pure, lazy, functional programming language Clean 2.0(.1) [5,10,13]:

Dynamic types Dynamic types allow strongly typed programs to link in external code (*dynamics*) *at run-time* in a type safe way. Dynamics can be used anywhere, regardless from the module or even application that created them. Dynamics are important for type-safe applications with *mobile code* and *plug-in* architectures.

Generic programming enables us to write general function schemes that work for any data type. From these schemes the compiler can derive automatically any required instance of a specific type. This is possible because of Clean's strong type system. Generic programs are a compact way to elegantly deal with an important class of algorithms. To name a few, these are *comparison*, *pretty printers*, *parsers*.

In order to apply a generic function to a dynamic value in the current situation, the programmer should do an exhaustive type pattern-match on all possible dynamic types. Apart from the fact that this is impossible, this is at odds with the key idea of generic programming in which functions *do* an exhaustive distinction on types, but on their finite (and small) structure.

R. Peña and T. Arts (Eds.): IFL 2002, LNCS 2670, pp. 17–33, 2003.

One would imagine that it is alright to apply a generic function to any dynamic value. Consider for instance the application of the generic equality function to two dynamic values. Using the built-in dynamic type unification, we can easily check the equality of the *types* of the dynamic values. Now using a generic equality, we want to check the equality of the *values* of these dynamics. In order to do this, we need to know at *compile-time* of which type the instance of the generic equality should be applied. This is not possible, because the type representation of a dynamic is only known at *run-time*.

We present a solution that uses the current implementation of generics and dynamics. The key to the solution is to guide a generic function through a dynamic value using an explicit type representation of the dynamic value's type. This guide function is predefined once. The programmer writes generic functions as usual, and in addition provides the explicit type representation.

The solution can be readily used with the current compiler if we assume that the programmer includes type representations with dynamics. However, this is at odds with the key idea of dynamics because these already store type representations with values. We show that the solution also works for conventional dynamics if we provide a low-level access function that retrieves the type representation of any dynamic.

Contributions of this paper are:

- We show how one can combine generics and dynamics in one single framework in accordance with their current implementation in the compiler.
- We argue that, in principle, the type information available in dynamics is enough, so we do not need to store extra information, and instead work with conventional dynamics.
- Programs that exploit the combined power of generics and dynamics are universally applicable to dynamic values. In particular, the code handles dynamics in a generic way without precompiled knowledge of their types.

In this paper we give introductions to dynamics (Section 2) and generics (Section 3) with respect to core properties that we rely on. In Section 4 we show our solution that allows the application of generic functions to dynamic values. An example of a generic pretty printing tool is given to illustrate the expressive power of the combined system (Section 5). We present related work (Section 6), our current and future plans (Section 7), and conclude (Section 8).

2 Dynamics in Clean

The Clean system has support for *dynamics* in the style as proposed by Pil [11,12]. Dynamics serve two major purposes:

Interface between static and run-time types: Programs can convert values from the statically typed world to the dynamically typed world and back without loss of type security. Any Clean expression e that has (verifiable or inferable) type t can be formed into a value of type `Dynamic` by: **dynamic** $e :: t$, or: **dynamic** e. Here are some examples:

```
toDynamic :: [Dynamic]
toDynamic = [e1, e2, e3, dynamic [e1,e2,e3]]
where  e1 = dynamic 50                  :: Int
       e2 = dynamic reverse             :: A.a: [a] → [a]
       e3 = dynamic reverse ['a'..'z'] :: [Char]
```

Any `Dynamic` value can be matched in function alternatives and case expressions. A 'dynamic pattern match' consists of an expression pattern *e-pat* and a type pattern *t-pat* as follows: (*e-pat*: : *t-pat*). Examples are:

```
dynApply :: Dynamic Dynamic → Dynamic
dynApply (f::a → b)(x::a)  = dynamic (f x) :: b
dynApply _         _       = abort "dynApply: arguments of wrong type."

dynSwap :: Dynamic → Dynamic
dynSwap ((x,y) :: (a,b))   = dynamic (y,x) :: (b,a)
```

It is important to note that *unquantified* type pattern variables (`a` and `b` in `dynApply` and `dynSwap`) do not indicate polymorphism. Instead, they are bound to (unified with) the offered type, and range over the full function alternative. The dynamic pattern match fails if unification fails.
Finally, *type-dependent* functions are a flexible way of *parameterizing* functions with the type to be matched in a dynamic. Type-dependent functions are overloaded in the `TC` class, which is a built-in class that basically represents all *type codeable* types. The overloaded argument can be used in a dynamic type pattern by postfixing it with ^. Typical examples that are also used in this paper are the packing and unpacking functions:

```
pack :: a → Dynamic | TC a
pack x = dynamic x::a^

unpack :: Dynamic → a | TC a
unpack (x::a^)  = x
unpack _        = abort "unpack: argument of wrong type."
```

Serialization: At least as important as switching between compile-time and run-time types, is that dynamics allow programs to *serialize* and *deserialize* values without loss of type security. Programs can work safely with data and code that do not originate from themselves.
Two library functions store and retrieve dynamic values in named files, given a proper unique environment that supports file I/O:

```
writeDynamic:: String Dynamic
                      *env → (Bool,*env)          | FileSystem env
readDynamic :: String *env → (Bool,Dynamic,*env) | FileSystem env
```

Making an effective and efficient implementation is hard work and requires careful design and architecture of the compiler and run-time system. It is not our intention to go into any detail of such a project, as these are presented in

[14]. What needs to be stressed in the context of this paper is that dynamic values, when read in from disk, contain a binary representation of a complete Clean computation graph, a representation of the compile-time type, and references to the related rewrite rules. The programmer has no means of access to these representations other than those explained above.

At this stage, the Clean 2.0.1 system restricts the use of dynamics to *basic*, *algebraic*, *record*, *array*, and *function* types. Very recently, support for polymorphic functions has been added. Overloaded types and overloaded functions have been investigated by Pil [12]. Generics obviously haven't been taken into account, and that is what this paper addresses.

3 Generics in Clean

The Clean approach to generics [3] combines the polykinded types approach developed by Hinze [7] and its integration with overloading as developed by Hinze and Peyton Jones [8]. A generic function basically represents an infinite set of overloaded classes. Programs define for which types instances of generic functions have to be generated. During program compilation, all generic functions are converted to a finite set of overloaded functions and instances. This part of the compilation process uses the available compile-time type information.

As an example, we show the generic definition of the ubiquitous equality function. It is important to observe that a generic function is defined in terms of *both* the type *and* the value. The signature of equality is:

```
generic gEq a :: a a → Bool
```

This is the type signature that has to be satisfied by an instance for types of kind $\star$ (such as the basic types `Bool`ean, `Int`eger, `Real`, `Char`acter, and `String`). The generic implementation compares the values of these types, and simply uses the standard overloaded equality operator `==`. In the remainder of this paper we only show the `Int`eger case, as the other basic types proceed analogously.

```
gEq{|Int|} x y = x == y
```

Algebraic types are constructed as sums of pairs – or the empty unit pair – of types. It is useful to have information (name, arity, priority) about data constructors. For brevity we omit record types. The data types that represent sums, pairs, units, and data constructors are collected in the module `StdGeneric.dcl`:

```
:: EITHER a b  = LEFT a | RIGHT b
:: PAIR a b    = PAIR a b
:: UNIT        = UNIT
:: CONS a      = CONS a
```

The built-in function type constructor $\rightarrow$ is reused here. The kind of these cases (`EITHER`, `PAIR`, $\rightarrow : \star \rightarrow \star \rightarrow \star$, `UNIT` $: \star$, and `CONS` $: \star \rightarrow \star$) determines the number and type of the higher-order function arguments of the generic function definition. These are used to compare the sub structures of the arguments.

```
gEq{|UNIT|}              UNIT          UNIT          = True
gEq{|PAIR|}     fx fy    (PAIR x1 y1)  (PAIR x2 y2)  = fx x1 x2 && fy y1 y2
gEq{|EITHER|}   fx fy    (LEFT x1)     (LEFT x2)     = fx x1 x2
gEq{|EITHER|}   fx fy    (RIGHT y1)    (RIGHT y2)    = fy y1 y2
gEq{|EITHER|}   _  _     _             _             = False
gEq{|CONS|}     f        (CONS x)      (CONS y)      = f x y
```

The only case that is missing here is the function type →, as one cannot define a feasible implementation of function equality.

Programs must ask explicitly for an instance of type T of a generic function g by: **derive** g T. This provides the programmer with a *kind-indexed* family of functions $g_{\star}$, $g_{\star\to\star}$, $g_{\star\to\star\to\star}$, ... The function g_κ is denoted as: g{|κ|}. The programmer can parameterize g_κ for any $\kappa \neq \star$ to customize the behaviour of g. As an example, consider the standard binary tree type `:: Tree a = Leaf | Node (Tree a) a (Tree a)` and let `a = Node Leaf 5 (Node Leaf 7 Leaf)`, and `b = Node Leaf 2 (Node Leaf 4 Leaf)`. The expression (`gEq{|`$\star$`|} a b`) applies integer equality to the elements and hence yields false, but (`gEq{|`$\star \to \star$`|} (\_ _ → True) a b`) applies the binary constant function true, and yields true.

4 Dynamics + Generics in Clean

In this section we show how we made it possible for programs to manipulate *dynamics* by making use of *generic* functions. Suppose we want to apply the generic equality function `gEq` of Section 3 to two dynamics, as mentioned in Section 1. One would expect the following definition to work:

```
dynEq :: Dynamic Dynamic → Bool      // This code is incorrect.
dynEq (x::a) (y::a) = gEq{|★|} x y
dynEq _ _           = False
```

However, this is not the case because at compile-time it is impossible to check if the required instance of `gEq` exists, or to derive it automatically simply because of the absence of the proper compile-time type information.

In our solution, the programmer has to write:

```
dynEq :: Dynamic Dynamic → Bool      // This code is correct.
dynEq x=:(_::a) y=:(_::a)   = _gEq (dynTypeRep x) x y
dynEq _ _                   = False
```

Two new functions have come into existence: `_gEq` and `dynTypeRep`. The first is a function of type `Type Dynamic Dynamic → Bool` that can be derived automatically from `gEq` (in Clean, identifiers are not allowed to start with `_`, so this prevents accidental naming conflicts); the second is a predefined low-level access function of type `Dynamic → Type`. The type `Type` is a special dynamic that contains a type representation, and is explained below. The crucial difference with the incorrect program is that `_gEq` works on the complete dynamic.

We want to stress the point that the programmer only needs to write the generic function `gEq` as usual *and* the `dynEq` function. All other code can, in principle, be generated automatically. However, this is not currently incorporated, so for the time being this code needs to be included manually. The remainder of this section is completely devoted to explaining what code needs to generated. Function and type definitions that can be generated automatically are *italicized.*

The function `_gEq` is a function that *specializes* `gEq` to the type τ of the content of its dynamic argument. We show that specialization can be done by a single function `specialize` that is parameterized with a generic function and a type, and that returns the instance of the generic function for the given type, packed in a dynamic. We need to pass types and generic functions to `specialize`, but neither are available as values. Therefore, we must first make suitable representations of types (Section 4.1) and generic functions (Section 4.2).

We encode types with a new type `(TypeRep` τ`)` and pack it in a `Dynamic` with synonym definition `Type` such that all values `(`t `:: TypeRep` τ`) :: Type` satisfy the invariant that t is the type representation of τ. We wrap generic functions into a record of type `GenRec` that basically contains all of its specialized instances to basic types and the generic constructors *sum*, *pair*, *unit*, and *arrow*. Now `specialize :: GenRec Type` $\rightarrow$ `Dynamic` (Section 4.3) yields the function that we want to apply to the content of dynamics, but it is still packed in a dynamic. We show that for each generic function there is a transformer function that applies this encapsulated function to dynamic arguments (Section 4.4). For our `gEq` case, this is `_gEq`.

In Section 4.5 we show that *specialization* is sufficient to handle all generic and non-generic functions on dynamics. However, it forces programmers to work with dynamics that are extended with the proper `Type`. An elegant solution is obtained with the low-level access function `dynTypeRep` which retrieves `Types` from dynamics, and can therefore be used instead (Section 4.6).

The remainder of this section fills in the details of the scheme as sketched above. We continue to illustrate every step with the `gEq` example. When speaking in general terms, we assume that we have a function g that is generic in argument `a` and has type `(`G `a)` (so $g =$ `gEq`, and $G =$ `Eq` defined as `:: Eq a :== a a` $\rightarrow$ `Bool`). We will have a frequent need for conversions from type `a` to `b` and vice versa. These are conveniently combined into a record of type `Bimap a b` (see Appendix A for its type definition and the standard bimaps that we use).

4.1 Dynamic Type Representations

Dynamic type representations are dynamics of synonym type `Type` containing values `(`t `:: TypeRep` τ`)` such that t represents τ, with `TypeRep` defined as:

```
:: TypeRep t
  = TRInt | TRUnit | TREither Type Type | TRPair Type Type | TRArrow Type Type
  | TRCons String Int Type
  | TRType [Type]          // [TypeRep a1,...,TypeRep an]
            Type           // TypeRep (T° a1 ... an)
            Dynamic        // Bimap (T a1 ... an) (T° a1 ... an)
```

For each data constructor (TRC $t_1 \ldots t_n$) ($n \leq 0$) we provide a n-ary *constructor* function tr$C$ of type `Type ...Type` $\rightarrow$ `Type` that assembles the corresponding alternative, and establishes the relation between representation and type. For basic types and the cases that correspond with generic representations (*sum*, *pair*, *unit*, and *arrow*), these are straightforward and proceed as follows:

trInt :: Type
trInt = **dynamic** *TRInt :: TypeRep Int*

trEither :: Type Type → Type
trEither tra=:(_::TypeRep a) trb=:(_::TypeRep b)
   = **dynamic** *(TREither tra trb) :: TypeRep (EITHER a b)*

trArrow :: Type Type → Type
trArrow tra=:(_::TypeRep a) trb=:(_::TypeRep b)
   = **dynamic** *(TRArrow tra trb) :: TypeRep (a → b)*

These constructors enable us to encode the structure of a type. However, some generic functions, like a pretty printer, need type specific information about the type, such as the name and the arity. Suppose we have a type constructor $T\ a_1 \ldots a_n$ with a data constructor $C\ t_1 \ldots t_m$. The `TRCons` alternative collects the *name* and *arity* of its data constructor. This is the same information a programmer might need when handling the `CONS` case of a generic function (although in the generic equality example we had no need for it).

trCons :: String Int Type → Type
trCons name arity tra=:(_:: TypeRep a)
   = **dynamic** *(TRCons name arity tra) :: TypeRep (CONS a)*

The last alternative `TRType` with the constructor function

trType :: [Type] Type Dynamic → Type
trType args tg=:(_::TypeRep t°) conv=:(_::Bimap t t°)
   = **dynamic** *(TRType args tg conv) :: TypeRep t*

is used for custom types. The first argument `args` stores type representations (`TypeRep` a_i) for the type arguments a_i. These are needed for generic dynamic function application (Section 4.5). The second argument is the type representation for the sum-product type $T^\circ\ a_1\ \ldots\ a_n$ needed for generic specialization (Section 4.3). The last argument *conv* stores the conversion functions between $T\ a_1\ \ldots\ a_n$ and $T^\circ\ a_1\ \ldots\ a_n$ needed for specialization.

The type representation of a recursive type is a recursive term. For instance, the Clean *list* type constructor is defined internally as `:: [] a = _Cons a [a] | _Nil`. Generically speaking it is a *sum* of: *(a)* the data *cons*tructor (`_Cons`) of the *pair* of the element type and the list itself, and *(b)* the data *cons*tructor (`_Nil`) of the *unit*. The sum-product type for list (as in standard static generics) is *:: List° a :== EITHER (CONS (PAIR a [a])) (CONS UNIT)* . Note that *List°* is not recursive: it refers to *[]*, not *List°*. Only the top-level of the type is converted into generic representation. This way it is easier to handle mutually recursive data types. The generated type representation, *trList*, for *List°* reflects its structure on the term level:

```
trList° :: Type → Type
trList° tra = trEither (trCons "_Cons" 2 (trPair tra (trList tra)))  (a)
                       (trCons "_Nil" 0 trUnit)                      (b)
```

The type representation for `[]` is defined in terms of *List°*; *trList* and *trList°* are mutually recursive:

```
trList :: Type → Type
trList tra=:(_::TypeRep a)
      =   trType [tra] (trList° tra) (dynamic epList :: Bimap [a] (List° a))
where     epList = { map_to = map_to, map_from = map_from }
          map_to [x:xs]                          = LEFT  (CONS (PAIR x xs))
          map_to []                              = RIGHT (CONS UNIT)
          map_from (LEFT   (CONS (PAIR x xs)))   = [x:xs]
          map_from (RIGHT (CONS UNIT        ))   = []
```

As a second example, we show the dynamic type representation for our running example, the equality function which has type `Eq a`:

```
trEq :: Type → Type
trEq tra=:(_::TypeRep a) = trArrow tra (trArrow tra trBool)
```

4.2 First-Class Generic Functions

In this section we show how to turn a generic function *g*, that really is a compiler scheme, into a first-class value `genrec`*g* `::` `GenRec` that can be passed to the specialization function. The key idea is that for the specialization function it is sufficient to know what the generic function would do in case of basic types, the generic cases *sum*, *pair*, *unit*, and *arrow*, and for custom types. For instance, for `Integers`, we need $g\{|\star|\}$ `::` *G* `Int`, and for *pairs*, this is $g\{|\star \to \star \to \star|\}$ `::` `A.a b: (G a) → (G b) → G (PAIR a b)`. These instances *are* functions, and hence we can collect them, packed as dynamics, in a record of type `GenRec`. We make essential use of dynamics, and their ability to hold polymorphic functions. (The compiler will actually *inline* the corresponding right-hand side of *g*.) The generated code for `gEq` is:

```
genrecgEq :: GenRec
genrecgEq = { genConvert   = dynamic convertEq (Section 4.3)
            , genType      = trEq              (Section 4.1)
            , genInt       = dynamic gEq{|*|}  :: Eq Int
            , genUNIT      = dynamic gEq{|*|}  :: Eq UNIT
            , genPAIR      = dynamic gEq{|* → * → *|}
                                :: A.a b: (Eq a) → (Eq b) → Eq (PAIR a b)
            , genEITHER    = dynamic gEq{|* → * → *|}
                                :: A.a b: (Eq a) → (Eq b) → Eq (EITHER a b)
            , genARROW     = dynamic gEq{|* → * → *|}
                                :: A.a b: (Eq a) → (Eq b) → Eq (a → b)
            , genCONS      = \n a → dynamic gEq{|* → *|}
                                :: A.a : (Eq a) → Eq (CONS a)
            }
```

4.3 Specialization of First-Class Generics

In Section 4.1 we have shown how to construct a representation t of any type τ, packed in the dynamic `(`t`::TypeRep` τ`)::Type`. We have also shown in Section 4.2 how to turn any generic function g into a record `genrec`g `:: GenRec` that can be passed to functions. This puts us in the position to provide a function, called `specialize`, that takes such a generic function representation and a dynamic type representation, and that yields $g :: G\ \tau$, packed in a conventional dynamic. This function has type `GenRec Type` $\rightarrow$ `Dynamic`. Its definition is a case distinction based on the dynamic type representation. The basic types and the generic *unit* case are easy:

```
specialize genrec (TRInt  :: TypeRep Int)    = genrec.genInt
specialize genrec (TRUnit :: TypeRep UNIT)   = genrec.genUNIT
```

The generic case for sums contains a function of type `(G a)` $\rightarrow$ `(G b)` $\rightarrow$ `G (EITHER a b)`. When specializing to `EITHER a b` (i.e. the type representation passed to `specialize` is `TREither tra trb`), we have to get a function of type `G (EITHER a b)` from functions of types `G a` and `G b` obtained by applying `specialize` to the type representations of `a` and `b`. Note that for recursive types the specialization process will be called recursively.

```
specialize genrec ((TREither tra trb) :: TypeRep (EITHER a b))
      = applyGenCase2  (genrec.genType tra) (genrec.genType trb)
                       genrec.genEITHER
                       (specialize genrec tra) (specialize genrec trb)
applyGenCase2 :: Type Type Dynamic Dynamic Dynamic → Dynamic
applyGenCase2  (trga :: TypeRep ga) (trgb :: TypeRep gb)
               (gtab :: ga gb → gtab) dga dgb
      = dynamic gtab (unwrapTR trga dga) (unwrapTR trgb dgb) :: gtab

unwrapTR :: (TypeRep a) Dynamic → a | TC a
unwrapTR _ (x :: a^) = x
```

The first two arguments of `applyGenCase2` are type representations for `G a` and `G b`. The following argument is, in this case, the generic case for `EITHER` of type `(G a)` $\rightarrow$ `(G b)` $\rightarrow$ `G (EITHER a b)`. The last two arguments are the specializations of the generic function to types `a` and `b`. Note, that `applyGenCase2` may not be strict in the last two arguments, otherwise it would lead to nontermination on recursive types, forcing recursive calls to `specialize`. In principle it is possible to extract the type representations (the first two arguments) from the last two arguments. However, in this case the last two arguments would become strict due to dynamic pattern match needed to extract the type information and, therefore, cause nontermination. Cases for products, arrows and constructors are handled analogously.

The case for `TRType` handles specialization to custom data types, e.g. `[Int]`. Arguments of such types have to be converted to their generic representations; results have to be converted back from the generic representation. This is done by means of bidirectional mappings. The bimap `ep` between a and a° needs to be lifted to the bimap between $(G\ a)$ and $(G\ a^\circ)$. This conversion is done by `convert`G below, and is also included in the generic representation of g in the `genConvert` field (Section 4.2). `dynApply2` is the 2-ary version of `dynApply`.

specialize genrec ((TRType args tra° ep) :: TypeRep a)
= dynApply2 genrec.genConvert ep (specialize genrec tra°)

The definition of `convert`G has a standard form, namely:

convertG :: (Bimap a b) → (G b) → (G a)
convertG ep = (bimapG ep).map_from

The function body of `bimap`G `a` is derived from the structure of the type term G `a` : `bimap`G `a` = $\langle G$ `a`$\rangle$ with $\langle\rangle$ defined as:

$$\begin{array}{lll}\langle x\rangle & = x & \text{(type variables, including } a\text{)}\\ \langle t_1 \rightarrow t_2\rangle & = \langle t_1\rangle \longrightarrow\!\!> \langle t_2\rangle & \\ \langle c\ t_1 \ldots t_n : \kappa\rangle & = \mathit{bimapId} & \textbf{if } a \notin \bigcup \mathit{Var}(t_i)(n \geq 0)\\ & = \mathit{bimapId}\{|\kappa|\}\ \langle t_1\rangle \ldots \langle t_n\rangle & \textbf{otherwise}\end{array}$$

Appendix A defines —> and `bimapId`; *Var* yields the variables of a type term. The generated code for `convertEq` and `bimapEq` is:

convertEq :: (Bimap a b) → (Eq b) → (Eq a)
convertEq ep = (bimapEq ep).map_from

bimapEq :: (Bimap a b) → Bimap (a → a → c) (b → b → c)
bimapEq ep = ep —> ep —> bimapId

4.4 Generic Dynamic Functions

In the previous section we have shown how the `specialize` function uses a dynamic type representation as a 'switch' to construct the required generic function g, packed in a dynamic. We now transform such a function into the function $\_g$ `:: Type` → `(`G `Dynamic)`, that can be used by the programmer. This function takes the same dynamic type representation argument as `specialize`. Its body invariably takes the following form (`bimapDynamic` and `inv` are included in Appendix A):

_g :: Type → G Dynamic
_g tr = **case** *specialize genrecg tr* **of**
(f :: G a) → convertG (inv bimapDynamic) f

As discussed in the previous section, `convert`G transforms a `(Bimap a b)` to a conversion function of type `(`G `b)` → `(`G `a)`. When applied to `(inv bimapDynamic) :: (Bimap Dynamic a)`, it results in a conversion function of type `(`G `a)` → `(`G `Dynamic)`. This is applied to the packed generic function `f::`G `a`, so the result function has the desired type `(`G `Dynamic)`.

When applied to our running example, we obtain:

_gEq :: Type → Eq Dynamic
_gEq tr = **case** *specialize genrecgEq tr* **of**
(f :: Eq a) → convertEq (inv bimapDynamic) f

4.5 Applying Generic Dynamic Functions

The previous section shows how to obtain a function $\_g$ from a generic function g of type (G a) that basically applies g to dynamic arguments, assuming that these arguments internally have the same type a. In this section we show that with this function we can handle all generic and non-generic functions on dynamics. In order to do so, we require the programmer to work with *extended* dynamics, defined as:

$:: DynamicExt = DynExt\ Dynamic\ Type$

An extended dynamic value (DynExt (v::τ) (t::TypeRep τ)) basically is a pair of a *conventional* dynamic (v::τ) *and* its dynamic type representation (t::TypeRep τ). Note that we make effective use of the built-in unification of dynamics to enforce that the dynamic type representation really is the same as the type of the conventional dynamic.

For the running example gEq we can now write an equality function on extended dynamics, making use of the generated function _gEq:

```
dynEq :: DynamicExt DynamicExt → Bool
dynEq (DynExt x=:(_::a) tx) (DynExt y=:(_::a) _) = _gEq tx x y
dynEq _ _                                          = False
```

It is the task of the programmer to handle the cases in which the (extended) dynamics do not contain values of the proper type. This is an artefact of dynamic programming, as we can never make assumptions about the content of dynamics.

Finally, we show how to handle *non-generic* dynamic functions, such as the dynApply and dynSwap in Section 2. These examples illustrate that it is possible to maintain the invariant that extended dynamics always have a dynamic type representation of the type of the value in the corresponding conventional dynamic. It should be observed that these non-generic functions are basically *monomorphic* dynamic functions due to the fact that unquantified type pattern variables are implicitly existentially quantified. The function wrapDynamicExt is a predefined function that conveniently packs a conventional dynamic and the corresponding dynamic type representation into an extended dynamic.

```
dynApply :: DynamicExt DynamicExt → DynamicExt
dynApply  (DynExt (f::a → b) ((TRArrow tra trb) :: TypeRep (a → b)))
          (DynExt (x::a) _)
    = wrapDynamicExt (f x) trb

dynSwap :: DynamicExt → DynamicExt
dynSwap (DynExt ((x,y)::(a,b)) ((TRType [tra,trb] _ _) :: TypeRep (a,b)))
    = wrapDynamicExt (y,x) (trTuple2 trb tra)

wrapDynamicExt :: a Type → DynamicExt | TC a
wrapDynamicExt x tr=:(_::TypeRep a^) = DynExt (dynamic x::a^) tr
```

4.6 Elimination of Extended Dynamics

In the previous section we have shown how we can apply generic functions to conventional dynamics if the program manages *extended* dynamics. We emphasized in Section 2 that every conventional dynamic stores the representation of all compile-time types that are related to the type of the dynamic value [14]. This enables us to write a low-level function dynTypeRep that computes the dynamic type representation as given in the previous section from any dynamic value. Informally, we can have:

```
dynTypeRep :: Dynamic → Type
dynTypeRep (x::t) = dynamic tr :: TypeRep t
```

If we assume that we have this function (future work), we do not need the extended dynamics anymore. The dynEq function can now be written as:

```
dynEq :: Dynamic Dynamic → Bool
dynEq x=:(_::a) y=:(_::a)     = _gEq (dynTypeRep x) x y
dynEq _ _                     = False
```

The signature of this function suggests that we might be able to derive dynamic versions of generic functions automatically as just another instance. Indeed, for type schemes G a in which a appears at an argument position, there is always a dynamic argument from which a dynamic type representation can be constructed. However, such an automatically derived function is necessarily a *partial* function when a appears at more than one argument position, because one cannot decide what the function should do in case the dynamic arguments have non-matching contents. In addition, if a appears only at the result position, then the type scheme is not an instance of G Dynamic, but rather Type → G Dynamic.

5 Example: A Pretty Printer

Pretty printers belong to the classic examples of generic programming. In this section we deviate a little from this well-trodden path by developing a program that sends a graphical version of any dynamic value to a user-selected printer. The generic function gPretty that we will develop below is given a value to display. It computes the bounding box (Box) and a function that draws the value if provided with the location of the image (Point2 Picture → Picture). Graphical metrics information (such as text width and height) depends on the resolution properties of the output environment (the abstract and unique type *Picture). Therefore gPretty is a state transformer on Pictures, with the synonym type :: St s a :== s → (a,s). Picture is predefined in the Clean Object I/O library [2], and so are Point2 and Box.

```
generic gPretty t :: t → St Picture (Box,Point2 Picture → Picture)
::  Point2  = { x     :: Int, y     :: Int }
::  Box     = { box_w :: Int, box_h :: Int }
```

The key issue of this example is how gPretty handles dynamics. If we assume that _gPretty is the derived code of gPretty as presented in Section 4 (that is either generated by the compiler or manually included by the programmer) then this code does the job:

```
dynPretty :: Dynamic → St Picture (Box,Point2 Picture → Picture)
dynPretty dx = _gPretty (dynTypeRep dx) dx
```

It is important to observe that the program contains no *derived* instances of the generic gPretty function. Still, it can display every possible dynamic value.

We first implement the gPretty function and then embed it in a simple GUI. In order to obtain compact code we use a monadic programming style [16]. Clean has no special syntax for monads, but the standard combinators return :: a → St s a and >>= :: (St s a) (a → St s b) → St s b are easily defined.

Basic values simply refer to the string instance that does the real work. It draws the text and the enclosing rectangle (o is function composition, we assume that the getMetricsInfo function returns the width and height of the argument string, proportional margins, and base line offset of the font):

```
gPretty{|Int|}      x = gPretty{|*|} (toString x)
gPretty{|String|}  s
    = getMetricsInfo s >>= \(width,height,hMargin,vMargin,fontBase) →
      let bound = { box_w=2*hMargin + width, box_h=2*vMargin + height }
      in  return  ( bound
                  , \{x,y} → drawAt {x=x+hMargin, y=y+vMargin+fontBase} s
                         o drawAt {x=x+1,y=y+1}
                                  {box_w=bound.box_w-2,box_h=bound.box_h-2}
                  )
```

The other cases only place the recursive parts at the proper positions and compute the corresponding bounding boxes. The most trivial ones are UNIT, which draws nothing, and EITHER, which continues recursively (poly)typically:

```
gPretty{|UNIT|}          _               = return (zero,const id)
gPretty{|EITHER|} pl pr (LEFT  x)    = pl x
gPretty{|EITHER|} pl pr (RIGHT x)    = pr x
```

PAIRs are drawn in juxtaposition with top edges aligned. A CONS draws the recursive component below the constructor name and centres the bounding boxes.

```
gPretty{|PAIR|} px py (PAIR x y)
    = px x >>= \({ box_w = wx, box_h = hx}, fx) →
      py y >>= \({ box_w = wy, box_h = hy}, fy) →
      let bound = { box_w = wx + wy, box_h = max hx hy }
      in  return ( bound, \pos → fy {pos & x=pos.x+wx} o fx pos )
gPretty{|CONS of {gcd_name}|} px (CONS x)
    = gPretty{|*|} gcd_name  >>= \({ box_w = wc, box_h = hc}, fc) →
      px x                   >>= \({ box_w = wx, box_h = hx}, fx) →
```

```
let bound = { box_w = max wc wx, box_h = hc + hx }
in  return  ( bound, \pos → fx (pos + {x=(bound.box_w-wx)/2, y=hc})
                         o fc (pos + {x=(bound.box_w-wc)/2, y=0 })
            )
```

This completes the generic pretty printing function. We will now embed it in a GUI program. The `Start` function creates a GUI framework on which the user can drop files. The program response is defined by the `ProcessOpenFiles` attribute function which applies `showDynamic` to each dropped file path name.

```
module prettyprinter

import StdEnv, StdIO, StdDynamic, StdGeneric

Start :: *World → *World
Start world = startIO SDI Void id
                [ ProcessClose closeProcess
                , ProcessOpenFiles (\fs pSt → foldr showDynamic pSt fs)
                ] world
```

The function `showDynamic` checks if the file contains a dynamic, and if so, sends it to the printer. This job is taken care of by the `print` function, which takes as third argument a `Picture` state transformer that produces the list of pages. For reasons of simplicity we assume that the image fits on one page.

```
showDynamic :: String (PSt Void) → PSt Void
showDynamic fileName pSt
    = case readDynamic fileName pSt of
          (True,dx,pSt) →  ( snd
                           o uncurry (print True False (pages dx))
                           o defaultPrintSetup
                           ) pSt
          (_, _, pSt)   →  pSt
where pages :: Dynamic PrintInfo → St Picture [IdFun Picture]
      pages dx _ = dynPretty dx >>= \(_,draw_dx) → return [draw_dx zero]
```

6 Related Work

The idea of combining generic functions with dynamic values was first expressed in [1], but no concrete implementation details were presented. The work reported here is about the implementation of such a combination.

Cheney and Hinze [6] present an approach that unifies dynamics and generics in a single framework. Their approach is based on explicit type representations for every type, which allows for *poor man's dynamics* to be defined explicitly by pairing a value with its type representation. In this way, a generic function is just a function defined by induction on type representations. An advantage of their approach is that it reconciles generic and dynamic programming right from start, which results in an elegant representation of types that can be used both for generic and dynamic programming. Dynamics in Clean have been designed and implemented to offer a *rich man's dynamics* (Section 2). Generics in Clean are schemes used to generate functions based on types available at compile-time. For this reason we have developed a first-class mechanism to be able to specialize generics at run-time. Our dynamic type representation is inspired by Cheney and Hinze, but is less verbose since we can rely on built-in dynamic type unification.

Altenkirch and McBride [4] implement generic programming support as a library in the dependently typed language OLEG. They present the generic specialization algorithm due to Hinze [9] as a function `fold`. For a generic function (given by the set of base cases) and an argument type, `fold` returns the generic function specialized to the type. Our `specialize` is similar to their `fold`; it also specializes a generic to a type.

7 Current and Future Work

The low-level function `dynTypeRep` (Section 4.6) has to be implemented. We expect that this function gives some opportunity to simplify the `TypeRep` data type. Polymorphic functions are a recent addition to dynamics, and we will want to handle them by generic functions as well. The solution as presented in this paper works for generic functions of kind $\star$. We want to extend the scheme so that higher order kinds can be handled as well. In addition, the approach has to be extended to handle generic functions with several generic arguments. The scheme has to be incorporated in the compiler, and we need to decide how the derived code should be made available to the programmer.

8 Summary and Conclusions

In this paper we have shown how generic functions can be applied to dynamic values. The technique makes essential use of dynamics to obtain first-class representations of generic functions and dynamic type representations. The scheme works for all generic functions. Applications built in this way combine the best of two worlds: they have compact definitions and they work for any dynamic value even if these originate from different sources and even if these dynamics rely on alien types and functions. Such a powerful technology is crucial for type-safe mobile code, flexible communication, and plug-in architectures. A concrete application domain that has opportunities for this technique is the functional operating system *Famke* [15] (parsers, pretty printers, tool specialization).

Acknowledgements

The authors would like to thank the anonymous referees for suggestions to improve the presentation of this paper.

References

1. Achten, P. and Hinze, R. Combining Generics and Dynamics. *Technical Report NIII-R0206*, July, 2002, Nijmegen Institute for Computing and Information Sciences, Faculty of Sciences, University of Nijmegen, The Netherlands.
2. Achten, P.M. and Wierich, M. A Tutorial to the Clean Object I/O Library - version 1.2. *Technical Report CSI-R0003*, February 2, 2000, Computing Science Institute, Faculty of Mathematics and Informatics, University of Nijmegen, The Netherlands.
3. Alimarine, A. and Plasmeijer, M. A Generic Programming Extension for Clean. In Arts, Th., Mohnen M., eds. *Proceedings of 13th International Workshop on the Implementation of Functional Languages (IFL2001)*, Selected Papers, Älvsjö, Sweden, September 24-26, 2001, Springer-Verlag, LNCS 2312, pp.168-185.
4. Altenkirch, T. and McBride, C. Generic Programming Within Dependently Typed Programming. To appear in *Proceedings Working Conference on Generic Programming*, Dagstuhl, Castle, Germany, July 11-12, 2002.
5. Brus, T., Eekelen, M.C.J.D. van, Leer, M.O. van, and Plasmeijer, M.J. Clean: A Language for Functional Graph Rewriting. In Kahn. G. ed. *Proceedings of the Third International Conference on Functional Programming Languages and Computer Architecture*, Portland, Oregon, USA, LNCS 274, Springer-Verlag, pp. 364-384.
6. Cheney, J. and Hinze, R. A Lightweight Implementation of Generics and Dynamics. In Chakravarty, M., ed. *Proceedings of the ACM SIGPLAN 2002 Haskell Workshop*, Pittsburgh, PA, USA, October 3, 2002, pp. 90-104.
7. Hinze, R. Polytypic values possess polykinded types. In Backhouse, R., Oliveira, J.N., eds. *Proceedings of the Fifth International Conference on Mathematics of Program Construction (MPC 2000), July 3-5, 2000*, LNCS 1837, Springer-Verlag, pp. 2–27.
8. Hinze, R. and Peyton Jones, S. Derivable Type Classes. In Graham Hutton, ed., *Proceedings of the Fourth Haskell Workshop*, Montreal, Canada, September 17, 2000.
9. Hinze, R. *Generic Programming and Proofs.* Habilitationsshrift, Universität Bonn, 2000.
10. Nöcker, E.G.J.M.H., Smetsers, J.E.W., Eekelen, M.C.J.D. van, and Plasmeijer, M.J. Concurrent Clean. In Aarts, E.H.L., Leeuwen, J. van, Rem, M., eds., *Proceedings of Parallel Architectures and Languages Europe*, June, Eindhoven, The Netherlands. LNCS 506, Springer-Verlag, pp. 202-219.
11. Pil, M.R.C., Dynamic types and type dependent functions. In Hammond, Davie, Clack, eds., *Proc. of Implementation of Functional Languages (IFL '98)*, London, U.K., Springer-Verlag, Berlin, LNCS 1595, pp.169-185.
12. Pil, M. *First Class File I/O*, PhD Thesis, *in preparation.*
13. Plasmeijer, M.J. and van Eekelen, M.C.J.D. *Functional Programming and Parallel Graph Rewriting*, Addison-Wesley Publishing Company, 1993.
14. Vervoort, M. and Plasmeijer, R. Lazy Dynamic Input/Output in the lazy functional language Clean. In Peña, R. ed. *Proc. of the 14th International Workshop on the Implementation of Functional Languages (IFL 2002)*, Madrid, Spain, September 16-18 2002, Technical Report 127-02, Departamento de Sistemas Informáticos y Programación, Universidad Complutense de Madrid, pp. 404-408.
15. van Weelden, A. and Plasmeijer, R. Towards a Strongly Typed Functional Operating System. In Peña, R. ed. *Proc. of the 14th International Workshop on the Implementation of Functional Languages (IFL 2002)*, Madrid, Spain, September 16-18 2002, Technical Report 127-02, Departamento de Sistemas Informáticos y Programación, Universidad Complutense de Madrid, pp. 301-319.

16. Wadler, Ph. Comprehending monads. In *Proceedings of the ACM Conference on Lisp and Functional Programming*, Nice, 1990, ACM Press, pp. 61-78.

A Bimap Combinators

A *(Bimap a b)* is a pair of two conversion functions of type $a \to b$ and $b \to a$. The trivial *Bimaps* `bimapId` and `bimapDynamic` are predefined:

```
::  Bimap a b    = { map_to :: a → b, map_from :: b → a }

bimapId :: Bimap a a
bimapId          = { map_to = id, map_from = id }

bimapDynamic :: Bimap a Dynamic | TC a
bimapDynamic     = { map_to = pack, map_from = unpack }        (Section 2)
```

The bimap combinator `inv` swaps the conversion functions of a bimap, `oo` forms the sequential composition of two bimaps, and `-->` obtains a functional bimap from a domain and range bimap.

```
inv :: (Bimap a b) → Bimap b a
inv { map_to, map_from } = { map_to = map_from, map_from = map_to }

(oo) infixr 9 :: (Bimap b c) (Bimap a b) → Bimap a c
(oo) f g =   { map_to     = f.map_to    o g.map_to
             , map_from   = g.map_from o f.map_from
             }

(-->) infixr 0 :: (Bimap a b) (Bimap c d) → Bimap (a → c) (b → d)
(-->) x y = { map_to      = \f → y.map_to    o f o x.map_from
             , map_from   = \f → y.map_from o f o x.map_to
             }
```

Fast Functional Lists

Phil Bagwell

Abstract. Since J. McCarthy first introduced Functional Programming, the Linked List has almost universally been used as the underpinning data structure. This paper introduces a new data structure, the VList, that is compact, thread safe and significantly faster to use than Linked Lists for nearly all list operations. Space usage can be reduced by 50% to 90% and in typical list operations speed improved by factors ranging from 4 to 20 or more. Some important operations such as indexing and length are typically changed from $O(N)$ to $O(1)$ and $O(lgN)$ respectively. In the current form the VList structure can provide an alternative heap architecture for functional languages using eager evaluation. To prove the viability of the new structure a language interpreter Visp, a dialect of Common Lisp, has been implemented using VList and a simple benchmark comparison with OCAML reported.

1 Introduction

Functional Programming, derived from Church's lambda calculus by J. McCarthy, has since its introduction almost exclusively used the Linked List as the underlying data structure. Today this implicit assumption remains and is manifested by the recursive type definition in the design of many modern functional languages. Although the Link List has proven to be a versatile list structure it does have limitations that encourage complementary structures, such as strings and arrays, to be used too. These have been employed to achieve space efficient representation of character lists or provide structures that support rapid random access but they do necessitate additional special operators and lead to some loss of uniformity. Further, operations that require working from the right to left in lists, *foldr* or *merge* for example, must do so using recursion. This often leads to stack overflow problems with large lists when it is not possible for optimizers to substitute iteration for recursion.

In the 1970's *cdr-coding* was developed to allow a *cons* cell to follow the *car* of the first. [7,3,4,8,6,9]. Flag bits were used to indicate the list status. More recently this idea was extended to allow k cells to follow the initial *car*, typically $k = 3$ *to* 7 and compiler analysis used to avoid most run-time flag checking. [1,2]. A different approach, based on a binary tree representation of a list structure, has been used to create functional random access lists based to give a $lg\ N$ indexing cost yet still maintain constant head and tail times. [5]

In this paper an alternative structure, the VList, is introduced. It can provide an alternative heap architecture for eagerly evaluated functional languages, combining the extensibility of a Linked List with the random access speed of an

R. Peña and T. Arts (Eds.): IFL 2002, LNCS 2670, pp. 34–50, 2003.

Array. It will be shown that lists can be built to have typically O(1) random element access time and a small, almost constant, space overhead.

To verify that this new structure could in fact form the basis for general list manipulations, such as *cons*, *car* and *cdr*, in a real language implementation, an experimental VList Lisp interpreter (Visp) was created. Based on a dialect of Common Lisp Visp was used to both test list performance and ensure there were no implementation snags through each stage from VList creation to garbage collection. The basic VList structure was adapted to support the common atomic data types, character, integer, float, sub-list and so on. Efficient garbage collection was a significant consideration. Visp then provided a simple framework for benchmarking typical list operations against other functional languages. Performance comparisons were made with the well-known and respected implementation of OCAML and are to be found in Section 2.9.

2 The VList

2.1 The Concept

Given a list defined as a sequence of elements having a head element and a tail containing the remaining elements. All list manipulations can then be considered to be constructed from the usual three special functions *cons*- add an element to the head of a list, *cdr* - return the tail of a list and *car* - return the head element of a list. Storing lists as individual elements but linked by means of a pointer provides an elegant and versatile memory structure. To *cons* an element to a list simply requires creating a new list node and linking it to the existing list. Finding the tail or *cdr* only requires following the link. The inherent conciseness of this approach is illustrated by the class implementation in section 2.6.

An alternative, the Vlist, is based on the simple notion of creating a linked set of memory blocks but rather than linking one at a time the size of each successive block grows by a factor 1/r to form a geometric series with ratio r, see Fig 1. The list is referenced by a pointer to the base of the last added block together with an offset to the last added entry in that block. At the base of each block a block descriptor contains a link to the previous smaller block Base-Offset, the size of the block and the offset of the last used location in the block, LastUsed.

Given the VList structure, *cdr* is accomplished by decrementing the offset part of the pointer. When this becomes zero, at a block boundary, the link to the next block Base-Offset is followed and the process continued. While *car* becomes an indirect load via the list pointer.

The list constructor *cons* requires a little more consideration. In Fig 2 a list has been created with the integers (8,7,6,5,4,3) then a new list has been formed by *consing* a (9) to the tail (6,5,4,3). During the *consing* of (9) the pointer offset is compared with the last used offset, LastUsed. If it is the same and less than the block size then it is simply incremented, the new entry made and LastUsed updated. This would have occurred as the integers (6), (7), (8) were added. If, on the other-hand, the pointer offset is less than the LastUsed a *cons* is being

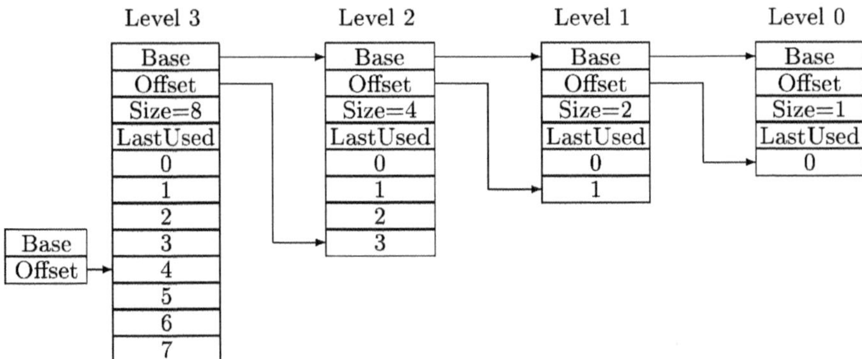

Fig. 1. A VList Structure

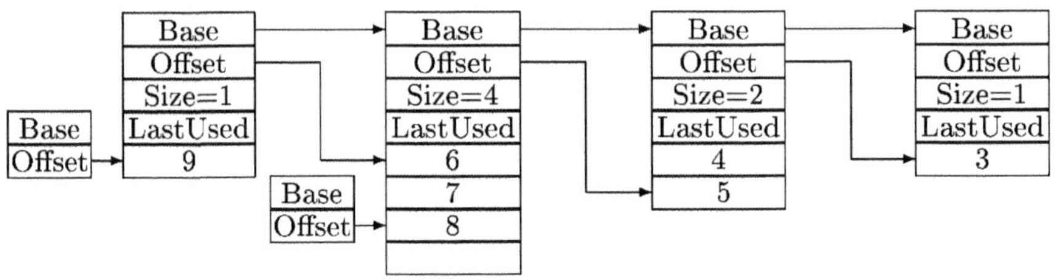

Fig. 2. A Shared Tail List

applied to the tail of a longer list, as is the case with the (9). In this case a new list block must be allocated and its Base-Offset pointer set to the tail contained in the original list. The offset part being set to the point in tail that must be extended. The new entry can now be made and additional elements added. As would be expected the two lists now share a common tail, just as would have been the case with a Linked List implementation. If the new block becomes filled then, just as before, a larger one by the factor $\frac{1}{r}$, is added and new entries continued.

As can be seen, the majority of the accesses are to adjacent locations yielding a significant improvement in the sequential access time and this locality makes efficient use of cache line loads.

Finding the length of a list or the nth entry of a list is a common requirement and most functional language implementations have in-built special functions such as *len* and *nth* to do so. However, a linked list structure implies that a typical implementation will traverse every element by a costly linear time recursive function. With the VList structure length and the nth element can be found quickly skipping over the elements in a block. Consider starting with a list pointer in Fig 1 then to find the nth element subtract n from the pointer offset. If the result is positive then the element is in the first block of the list at the calculated offset from the base. If the result is negative then move to the next block using the Base-Offset pointer. Add the Previous pointer offset to the negative offset.

While this remains negative keep moving onto the next block. When it finally becomes positive the position of the required element has been found. It will be shown that random probes to the nth element take a constant time on average and length determination proportional to lgN.

To compute the average access time notice that, for random accesses, the probability that the element is found in the first block is higher than in the second and higher still than in the third in proportions dependant on the block size ratio r chosen. Therefore, the time becomes proportional to the sum of the geometric series.

$$1 + r + r^2 .. \ or \ \frac{1}{1-r}, \ a \ constant$$

To compute the length of a list the list is traversed in the same way but the offsets are summed. Since every block must be traversed this will typically take a time proportional to the number of blocks. If, as is the case in Fig 1, r = 0.5 this would yield O(lg N), a considerable improvement over the O(N) time for a Linked List.

2.2 Refining the VList

The requirement to use two fields, base and offset, to describe a list pointer becomes cumbersome. Firstly there is the time penalty for two memory accesses during storage or retrieval and secondly the additional space required, twice that of a normal pointer. It would be more efficient if a single pointer could be used to represent the list. However, to achieve this it must be possible to recover the base of a list block from a simple list data element pointer, given that the data element itself may be an 8 bit character, 16 bit word or 32 bit integer.

This trick can be accomplished by breaking the list block into 16 byte sub-blocks, each one double word aligned in memory. The last 4 bytes in the sub-block are reserved for a 23 bit index(IX) that is the offset of the sub-block from the block base, a 4 bit integer (LU) that specifies the last used data byte in the sub-block, a 4 bit data type specifier and a 1 bit IsSingle flag (IS). With this arrangement the sub-block base is found by masking out the lower 4 bits of the pointer, the block base then being simply calculated from the sub-block index. Although the data type could be kept in the block descriptor it is repeated in each sub-block to avoid the additional memory reference when manipulations are confined to a sub-block. The other 12 bytes are available for data. See Fig 3.

The first sub-block in a block is a block descriptor. It contains the pointer to the previous block and the size of the current block.

To enable small lists to be represented efficiently the first block allocated to a new list is structured differently. It contains only two locations for data, the other being reserved for the Previous pointer. The flag IsSingle allows this type of block to be differentiated from the multiple entry one. With this arrangement the degenerate VList becomes a Linked List with the same overhead. It now becomes apparent why a 16 byte sub-block size has been chosen rather than for example a 32 or 64 byte one. The larger size would reduce the average overhead for large lists but have the consequence of a very high overhead on small lists. It

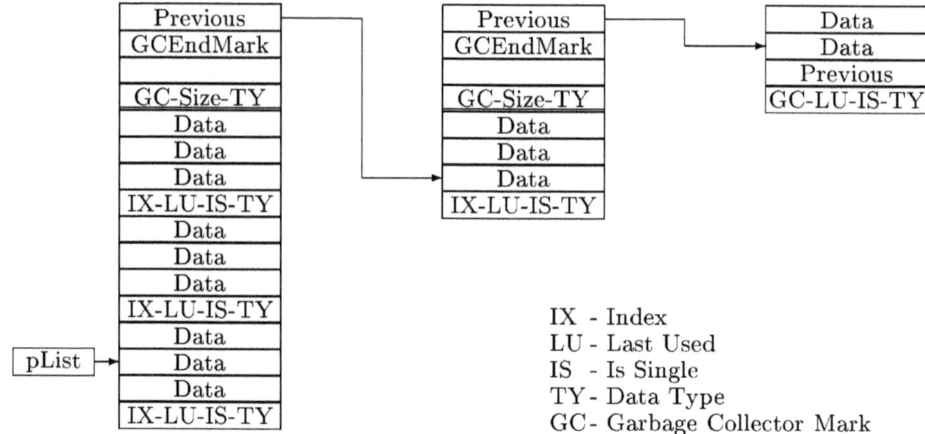

Fig. 3. VList With Single Pointer

is also clear that using the simpler structure of a base and offset would require the smallest single sub-block to be 32 bytes giving an unacceptable overhead for small lists.

2.3 Extending a VList with *cons*

Assume that a pointer references the head of a character VList and a new character element must be added. The sub-block base is recovered from the pointer by masking out the lower 4 bits. The data type size is recovered from the Element Type field, in this case a one byte character. The offset from the base to the pointer is calculated if this is less than 11 then the list pointer is incremented by one and the new element stored at the referenced location. The LastUsed field is updated and the new head of list pointer returned.

If the offset was equal to or greater than 11 the memory block size must be recovered from the block descriptor and compared with the current sub-block index. If there are more sub-blocks available then the list pointer is set to the beginning of the next sub-block and the new element added. If no more sub-blocks are available then a new memory block must be allocated and the element added at the beginning.

In static typed functional languages the lists are usually homogeneous while in dynamic typed languages such as LISP the lists are allowed to be hetrogeneous. Type mixing in one list is achieved by creating a new block whenever there is a change of type. This leads to a worst case degeneration to a simple Linked List if there is a type change on every extension of the list. The other degenerate case is when all *cons* operations are to the tail of a linked list which again could lead to a linked list of pairs of elements.

VLists can be made thread safe using a mutex, a Thread Lock (TL) bit in the sub-block. When a thread needs to update LastUsed it first uses an atomic

Table 1. Operation Times on VList and Linked List for given List Sizes

Size	VL cons	LL cons	VL cdr	LL cdr	VL len	LL len
1	0.95	0.75	0.06	0.05	0.07	0.05
2	1.01	1.51	0.06	0.06	0.07	0.06
3	1.05	2.29	0.07	0.09	0.07	0.08
4	1.09	3.07	0.08	0.14	0.07	0.11
5	1.13	3.98	0.15	0.23	0.07	0.16
10	2.53	7.63	0.29	0.42	0.15	0.43
20	3.10	15.16	0.40	0.84	0.15	0.83
50	5.99	37.86	0.90	6.30	0.29	7.16
100	10.21	76.22	1.61	11.59	0.49	12.22
200	18.26	152	4.13	21.70	1.06	22.95
500	38.96	406	10.70	51.91	2.05	53.19
1000	99.83	782	20.93	105.62	2.73	124.40
10000	975	7832	219.91	1030	4.14	1030

set-bit-and-test instruction to check the state of TL, normally zero. If the TL bit was set then the thread assumes conflict, adds a new block and points it back to the appropriate list tail in the sub-block being extended. Otherwise it is free to extend the list normally.

2.4 Performance Comparison of VLists and Link Lists

Table 2 compares the time to perform the same operations on VLists and Linked Lists for a range of character list sizes. For each list size 1000 lists were created using *cons* and then *cdr* used to move from the head to end of each list. Finally the length of each list was ascertained using *len*. All tests were performed on an Intel Pentium II(400Mz) and the entries report the average time in micro-seconds for the operation on a single list of that size.

The implementation code used for the tests are discussed in section 2.6. As would be expected the larger lists show a marked performance gain using VLists while it is important to note that small lists improve too. It is an obvious advantage to increase the performance of large list operations but it is reassuring to see that this has not been achieved by compromising small list manipulation speed since many applications are small list intensive.

2.5 Space Comparison of VLists and Link Lists

Table 2 details the number of bytes used to represent lists of different sizes for the two structures. The three columns designated "LL" tabulate the size of a corresponding linked list structure. With static typing a linked list will normally use 8 bytes per node while with dynamic typing 12 or 16 byte nodes are typically required. These are compared with the equivalent VList size based on the data type. With list sizes greater than 62 elements the VList is always smaller than an equivalent linked list.

Table 2. Space Use of VLists and Linked Lists

Size	LL 8	LL 12	LL 16	VL char(8)	VL int(16)	VL ptr/int(32)
1	8	12	16	16	16	16
2	16	24	32	16	16	16
3	24	36	48	16	16	16
4	32	48	64	16	16	48
5	40	60	80	16	16	48
6	48	72	96	16	48	48
7	56	84	112	16	48	112
8	64	96	128	16	48	112
9	72	108	144	16	48	112
10	80	120	160	48	48	112
11	88	132	176	48	48	112
12	96	144	192	48	112	112
13	104	156	208	48	112	112
14	112	168	224	48	112	112
15	120	180	240	48	112	112
16	128	192	256	48	112	240
17	136	204	272	48	112	240
18	144	216	288	48	112	240
19	152	228	304	48	112	240
20	160	240	320	48	112	240
62	496	744	992	112	240	496

For the majority of list sizes, a VList offers a considerable space saving when compared with an equivalent Linked List. For the test implementation, $r = 0.5$, each block added is twice the previous one. Recall, the first sub-block in a block is a block descriptor. Then, on average, for an 8 bit data type such as character there will be 33% overhead for the sub-block index and, on average, half of the last memory block allocated will be unused, a further 33% overhead for a total overhead of 80%, a significant reduction on those for statically typed Linked Lists. A Link List node must have space for a pointer and the associated character value therefore occupying two 32 bit words giving an overhead of 700% per character. For character lists the VList is almost an order of magnitude more space efficient and for other data types usually more than twice as efficient. If dynamic typing is used the efficiency improves further.

Note that the worse case space use degenerates to that of a linked list if every *cons* is to a VList tail.

2.6 Algorithm Complexity

The code examples that follow are those used to perform the statically typed character list tests reported in table 1. With some minor modification, they are primitives used to implement VISP. For simplicity the detail of the memory allocation, structure definition and list garbage collection have been omitted.

```
class CListLLE{
CListLLE *Prev; char chr;
public:
CListLLE *cdrchar()
  {
  if(this==NULL)return NULL;
  return Prev;
  }
CListLLE *conschar(char chr)
  {
  CListLLE *E;
  E=new CListLLE;
  E->chr=chr; E->Prev=this;
  return E;
  }
int lenchar()
  {
  CListLLE *L;
  if((L=this)==NULL)return 0;
  for(int Len=1;(L=L->Prev)!=NULL;Len++);
  return Len;
  }
};
```

Although the link list implementation is superficially simpler it does incur the cost of a memory access for each manipulation and of course a memory allocation for each *cons*. Since the *len* function must traverse every list element iteration has been chosen rather than the usual recursion to give the best possible benchmark performance.

The VList structure benefits from the data locality and the double word alignment implies that on most modern processors the whole sub-block will be loaded in one cache line. It is therefore cheap, with dynamic typing, to find the data type and thus the data type size for decrementing or incrementing in the *cdr* or *cons* operations respectively.

```
// VList class functions using fig 3 data structure
CListVLE *cdrchar()
  {
  if((int)this&0xF)return (CListVLE *)(((char *)this)-1);
  return Mcdrchar(this);
  }
CListVLE *Mcdrchar(CListVLE *LE)
  {
  if(!LE)return NULL;
  if(LE->IsSingle){
    if(LE->FI.Prev)return LE->FI.Prev;
    else return NULL;
    }
```

```
  if(LE->MU.Index)return (CListVLE *)(((char *)this)-5);
  return (LE-1)->DE.Prev;
  }

int lenchar()
  {
  CListVLE *LE,*L,*Next;
  int Length,LastUsedLen,LLen;
  if((L=this)==NULL)return 0;
  Length=0;
   do{
    LE=(CListVLE *)((int)(this)&0x7FFFFFF0);
    if (LE->IsSingle){
      Length+=((char *)L- (char *)LE)+1;
      Next=LE->FI.Prev;
      }
    else{
      LastUsedLen=((char *)L- (char *)LE) +1;
      LLen=LE->MU.Index*12+LastUsedLen;
      Length+=LLen;
      LE-=LE->MU.Index+1;
      Next=LE->DE.Prev;
      }
    }while(L=Next);
  return Length;
  }
```

A *cdr* operation on a linked list always requires a memory indirection while with the VList, in the majority of cases, a simple pointer decrement can be used. The implementation *cdr* exploits this, the first step forms the mask, test, decrement and function call to the second step. The initial step would typically be in-lined by a compiler leaving the less frequent sub-block boundary detection, end of list recognition and transitions to smaller blocks to the *Mcdrchar* function. Notice that the in-line part is a similar length to the equivalent in-line version of the link list *cdr* operation and should therefore give a negligible compiled code size change.

The advantage of the VList structure is readily illustrated by the *len* function. Notice how the sub-block index information allows the algorithm to accumulate the list length without visiting each element of the list. The *nth* function takes a similar form, while a *foldr* function can use the same index information to step to the end of a list typically maintaining only lgN stack entries for the reverse list traversal.

The VList *cons* operation is more complex than the equivalent linked list one. Some of the additional complexity directly follows from the need to cause branching when a *cons* is performed on the tail of a list. However, notice that a *cons* operation on a linked list always requires a memory allocation while this is infrequently the case with a VList. Most *cons* operations require just a pointer increment and indirect store. There are two main cases to consider; the initial created single blocks and the geometric series multiple sub-block blocks. The sample *cons* function implementation code that follows has been broken into these two parts.

```
CListVLE *conschar(char chr){
  CListVLE *LE,*B,*L;
  if(L=this){
    // extend current list
    LE=(CListVLE *)((int)(this)&0x7FFFFFF0);
    if(LE->IsSingle){
      // Single element
      if(((int)L&0xF)<7){
        if((char *)L - (char *)LE == LE->FI.LastUsed){
          // Increment and Store
          L=(CListVLE *)((char *)L+1);
          *(char *)L=chr;
          LE->FI.LastUsed++; return L;
          }
        else{
          LE=GetFree(0);
          LE->FI.Data[0]=chr;
          LE->FI.Prev=L;
          LE->EType=TCHAR;
          return LE;
        }
      }
      // No room so grow list
      B=GrowList(LE); // adds another block in geometric progression
      B->MU.Data[0]=chr;
      B->EType=TCHAR;
      return B;
      }

  // Continued below ...
```

Most of the time when a sub-block is filled in a large block there are more sub-blocks available. It is only necessary to test for this case, step over the reserved bytes and initialize the state data in the next sub-block. Eventually when all the sub-blocks have been filled a new, larger block will be added. An attempted *cons* on a tail will cause a branch and the new branch list will then follow the standard geometric progression starting from a single.

As mentioned previously it is a trivial matter to add a mutex to this process and support multi-threading.

```
  // ... Continued from above
else{  // Is a multiple sub-block
      if(((int)L&0xF)<11){
        if((char *)L - (char *)LE == LE->MU.LastUsed){
          // Increment and Store
          L=(CListVLE *)((char *)L+1);
```

```
          *(char *)L=chr; LE->MU.LastUsed++; return L;
          }
        else{  // Already used so must make a branch on tail
          LE=GetFree(0);
          LE->FI.Data[0]=chr;
          LE->FI.Prev=L;
          LE->EType=TCHAR;
          return LE;
        } }
      // Multi element
      B=LE-LE->MU.Index-1;
      if(1<<B->DE.Size!=LE->MU.Index+2){
        // More room in memory block
        LE->MU.LastUsed=15; // mark filled
        LE++; LE->MU.Load[0]=chr;
        LE->MU.LastUsed=0;LE->EType=TCHAR;
        LE->MU.Index=(LE-1)->MU.Index+1;
        LE->IsSingle=0; return LE;
        }
      else{  // No room so grow list
        B=GrowList(LE);
        B->MU.Data[0]=chr; B->EType=TCHAR;
        return B;
    } } }
  else{  // Empty List so create first element
    LE=GetFree(0);LE->FI.Data[0]=chr; LE->EType=TCHAR;
    }
  return LE;
  }
```

2.7 Garbage Collection

After a data set is no longer reachable by a program then it must be considered garbage and collectable as free memory. This is typically done as a mark, sweep and copy activity. With Linked Lists the GC algorithm must pass through each element of the list first marking it as potentially free, then ascertaining if it is reachable from the program roots and finally adding unreachable ones to the free list. Notice that with VLists for all types, except sub-lists, only the memory block descriptor need be inspected or marked during each step of this mark/sweep/copy cycle turning an O(N) process into an O(lg N) one, a significant advantage.

The VList as described does require that large blocks must be used which could be troublesome as a list is consumed. Allocating large memory blocks may become difficult when heap memory becomes fragmented, perhaps requiring costly de-fragmentation processes to be performed too frequently. Since the blocks will be allocated with the same size pattern it is quite likely that blocks will be used again with future function applications on a given list. Further keeping a list of each free block by size would ensure maximum reuse before garbage collection is forced.

2.8 Visp

The VList looks a promising data structure but it must be viable in a real functional language implementation. An experimental interpreter for a sub-set of Common Lisp was created and then benchmarked. The main departure from Common Lisp was allowing the use of infix operators. The details will not be covered, only the key design principles will be outlined.

Lisp programs are scanned by a simple parser and converted into VList structures directly reflecting the source structure. No optimizations are performed. For these benchmark tests the VLists are extended using $r = 0.5$, each block added to a list is twice the previous one in size. C++ functions, virtually identical to those illustrated above, were used to perform the fundamental list operations of *car*, *cdr*, *cons*, *reverse*, *length*, *nth* and so on. Arithmetic operations, flow control functions such as *if* and *while* and function definition *lambda* and *defun* were added. Finally the higher order function *foldr* written to enable the more common list operations to be simply benchmarked.

The low cost of indexing invited the inclusion of two native infix operators, "[" and "&[" with a small amount of syntactic dressing to allow writing "L [n]" meaning "nth L n" and "L &[n]" meaning return the tail starting at the nth position in the list.

The complete interpreter, including a garbage collector, was written as a set of C++ classes and a simple IDE provided to allow programs to be developed interactively. The look and feel of the developer interface is similar to that of OCAML.

2.9 BenchMarking

OCAML is a mature environment producing efficient native compiled code for standard list operations. VISP on the other hand is an interpreter using dynamic type checking and dynamic scoping. These naturally cause overhead in both the function call interpretation and the function argument validation. In order to gain some insight into the type of performance that may be expected by using VLists in a compiled native code environment these costs have been avoided for *clone*, *reverse* and *foldr* by adding them as primitives. Internally these functions are implemented by making calls to the *cons* and *cdr* primitives thereby side-stepping the interpreter overhead yet behave the same as a comparable compiled version. A few functions such as *len*, *create list* and *nth* explicitly use the novel structure of VLists to achieve low stack usage and better than the $(O)lgN$ typical execution times.

A set of simple benchmarks were written in OCAML and the Visp dialect, two code examples are listed in Fig 4. The OCAML versions were compiled with both the native and byte optimizing compilers. The Visp programs were run interactively via the IDE. A large list size was chosen to minimize the impact of the interpretive overhead and to highlight the advantage of the VList structure. Table 3 contains the benchmark results.

The standard Windows version of OCAML has a 10 milli-second time resolution and stack overflow limits the test lists to a length of around 40K items.

```
//filter OCAML
   let isodd n =  (n mod 2) == 1
   List.filter isodd x
// filter VISP
   defun filter(F L)(foldr(lambda(o i)(if(funcall F i)(o :: i)(o)))L NIL)
   defun isodd (x) (x % 2 == 1)
   filter #'isodd x
// Slow fib OCAML
   let rec fibslow n =
   if n < 2 then 1
   else (fibslow (n-1)) + (fibslow(n-2))
// Slow fib VISP
   defun fibslow(n)(if (n < 2)(1)(fibslow (n - 1) + (fibslow (n - 2))))
```

Fig. 4. Benchmark Code Examples

Table 3. Comparsion of OCAML with VISP (mS)

The Test	OCAMLN	OCAMLB	VISP
Create List	20	30	1
Create	20	30	73
Reverse	20	50	11
Clone	40	120	11
Append	80	90	12
Length	10	40	0.017
Filter Odd	60	170	139
Slow Fib	80	1110	7740
Calc	20	210	640
GC	10	60	0.011

Visp on the other hand will manipulate lists that fit in memory. A filter on a list of 100 million elements executes without error. All tests were performed on an Intel Pentium II(400Mz), times reported in milli-seconds.

The space used for the 40K integer list in OCAML is reported as 524Kb and in VISP as 263Kb. The 40K character list in OCAML is reported to take 524Kb and in VISP to take 66Kb. Entries in Table 3 are the benchmark results, time in milli-seconds, and is followed by a short description of each benchmark.

Create List. A 40K element list created with each element initialized to a common value. VISP uses the block structure of VLists and memory set primitives to fully exploit the VList structure.

Create. Also creates a 40K element list with each element initialized to a unique value. However in this case an interpreted VISP program *while* loop is used with *cons*. The slow down with interpretation is immediately obvious.

Reverse. The reverse of a 40K list. The primitive VISP *reverse* uses the *cdr* and *cons* operations in a loop to create the reversed list thus avoiding the interpretive overhead in this loop but using the standard primitives.

Clone. Creates an identical 40K list from an existing one. The primitive VISP *clone* is able to make use of the VList block structure to minimize stack while moving to the end of the source list and directly uses the primitive *cons* to create the new list thus avoiding the interpreter overhead. Using a block memory copy primitive would improve performance further.

Append. Append one 40K list to another. Similar approach to clone.

Length. Compute length of list. The primitive VISP *len* uses the size information stored in the blocks to compute the length. Since there are typically lgN blocks this operation is quickly accomplished.

Filter Odd. Returns a 20K list of all odd members in 40K list. This program is shown in figure 4 and can be seen to be a hybrid of the VLISP primitive *foldr* function with an interpreted *isodd* function. Since the inner loop contains the interpreted function the overall operation is slowed down by comparison to a fully primitive filter. However, the VList structure savings all but overcome the interpreter losses.

Slow Fib. Calculates Fibonacci numbers using an exhaustive search. This benchmark is included to demonstrate the overhead of the VISP interpreter. It uses no lists but is function call intensive. It is included to provide perspective on the interpreter call overhead. OCAML static typing and native code are definite advantages.

Calc. Evaluates a lengthy arithmetic intensive expression 100K times. This benchmark is included to demonstrate the overhead in VISP of interpreting and type checking arithmetic operations. No lists are involved and it is included simply for reference purposes. Again OCAML demonstrates the benefits of static typing and native code most clearly.

GC. The time to garbage collect the 40K element lists. Here the benefit of recovering blocks rather than individual link elements is apparent.

2.10 The n-dimensional VList

The time constant associated with random access to individual elements in a VList decreases as the growth ratio decreases. However, the size increment grows too and therefore the wasted space. Suppose, as the size grows, that at some point when the block size is s the new block is considered to be a two dimensional array of size s^2. Instead of the new block being arranged as one large block it is arranged as one block of s with pointers to s blocks containing data. This arrangement, depicted in Fig 5, has a negligible impact on *cons* and *cdr* operations while increasing random access times by a small constant time, one extra indirection.

As the list grows further, the next block required is considered to be a 3 dimensional array with s^3 entries, and so on. Thus each block is s times larger than the previous one so the random access time becomes

$$\frac{1}{1-\frac{1}{s}} + log_s N \ or \ \frac{s}{s-1} + log_s N$$

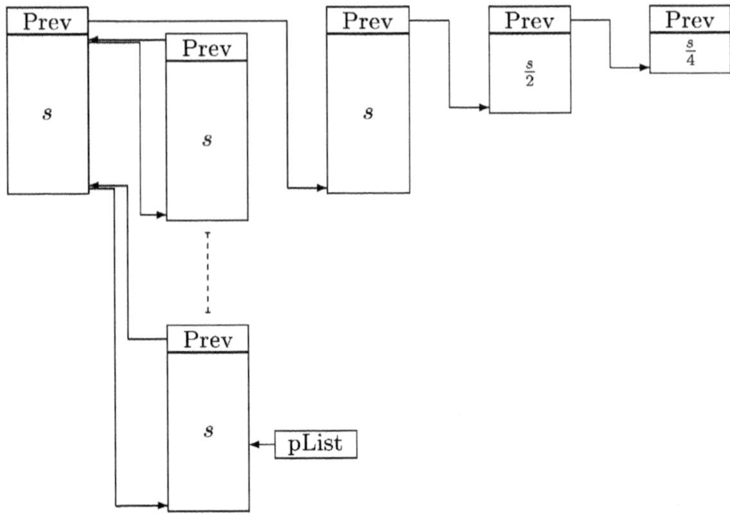

Fig. 5. The n-dimension VList

For a moderately large s this can be considered a constant for any practical memory size. Notice too that the average waste space also tends to a constant, namely $\frac{s}{2}$.

Recall that the Index in a sub-block was allocated 23 bits to allow the lists to become reasonably large. However, with the n-dimensional arrangement the Index could be restricted to only 7 bits allowing $s = 128$ sub-blocks and implying for integer data types that $3*2^7$ or 384 elements can be stored while for character data types this becomes $12 * 2^7$ or 1536. But there are now two more free bytes in a sub-block that can be used for data so the value can become $14 * 2^7$ or 1792 and overhead reduced to 15%. Note 1792^3 is over 4Gb so in a 32 bit environment n need not exceed 3.

Clearly the garbage collection and space allocation is helped by this arrangement. Blocks are a uniform size, and never greater than s reducing the problems of memory fragmentation but the log time for garbage collection has been relaxed. However, since most allocations are in 128 sub-block chunks garbage collection will still run a respectable $d * 2^7$, where d is data elements per sub-block, faster than an equivalent Linked List.

3 Conclusions

The VList proves to provide a promising alternative to the ubiquitous linked list that has for so long formed the defacto data structure for most functional languages. The VList core functions of *cons* and *cdr*, essential for all list manipulations, show very favourable benchmark results in a comparison with those for an equivalent Linked List structure. While other functions such as *len*, *nth* and *foldr* show significant speed and stack use improvements. Space efficiencies are indicated over a wide range of list sizes and the experimental VISP implementation has proven that the structure can be used to successfully implement a practical functional language together with the essential associated garbage collector.

It has not been necessary to add special data structures with their attendant special functions for arrays or strings to VISP. The VList constant random access time and the efficiency storage of character types obviate their need. Their absence removes some degree of complexity for the functional programmer and at the same time allows functions to be more generally applicable.

While the VList should be of interest to the functional language compiler community, in the simple form it can also provide an excellent solution for the more general problem of resizable arrays in other applications and the n-dimensional version yields constant wasted space while still achieving an O(1) average random access time. An improvement on the $\sqrt{N}$ waste space bound previously achieved. [10].

With such a fundamental change in the basic data structure for lists further research is needed to thoroughly understand overall performance. Future work includes the implementation of VLists in a compiled functional language and subsequent testing with a broad range of actual application programs to further validate the performance measurements and tune the garbage collection algorithm if needed. Developing a VList like structure for use in lazy evaluation and non-strict languages would be highly desirable too.

Acknowledgements

I would like to thank Prof. Martin Odersky and Christoph Zenger at the Labo. Des Methodes de Programmation (LAMP), EPFL, Switzerland for their review of the draft paper and valuable comments.

References

1. Zhong Shao and John H. Reppy and Andrew W. Appel : Unrolling Lists. Conference record of the 1994 (ACM) Conference on Lisp and Functional Programming (1994) 185–191
2. Zhong Shao: Compiling Standard ML for Efficient Execution on Modern Machines (Thesis) TR-475-94 (1994) 169
3. WJ Hansen: Compact list representation: definition, garbage collection and system implementation. Communications of the ACM (1969) 12/9, 499
4. D. W. Clark and C. C. Green: An empirical study of list structure in LISP. Communications of the ACM (Feb 1977) 20/2, 78–87
5. Chris Okasaki: Purely Functional Random-Access Lists. Functional Programming Languages and Computer Architecture (1995) 86–95
6. K. Li and P. Hudak: A new list compaction method. Software - Practice and Experience (Feb 1986) 16/2, 145–163

7. R Greenblatt: LISP Machine Progress Report memo 444 (Aug 1977) 169 A.I. Lab., M.I.T., Cambridge, Mass.
8. D.W. Clark: List Structure: Measurements, Algorithms, and Encodings, (Ph.D. Thesis Aug 1976) Dept. of Computer Science, Carnegie-Mellon University
9. D. G. Bobrow and D. W. Clark: Compact encoding of list structures. ACM Transactions on Programming Languages and Systems (Oct 1979) 1/2, 266–286
10. Andrej Brodnik and Svante Carlsson and Erik D. Demaine and J. Ian Munro and Robert Sedgewick: Resizable Arrays in Optimal Time and Space. Workshop on Algorithms and Data Structures (1999) 37-48

Fusion in Practice*

Diederik van Arkel, John van Groningen, and Sjaak Smetsers

Computing Science Institute
University of Nijmegen
Toernooiveld 1, 6525 ED Nijmegen, The Netherlands
{diederik,johnvg,sjakie}@cs.kun.nl

Abstract. Deforestation was introduced to eliminate intermediate data structures used to connect separate parts of a functional program together. Fusion is a more sophisticated technique, based on a producer-consumer model, to eliminate intermediate data structures. It achieves better results. In this paper we extend this fusion algorithm by refining this model, and by adding new transformation rules. The extended fusion algorithm is able to deal with standard deforestation, but also with higher-order function removal and dictionary elimination. We have implemented this extended algorithm in the Clean 2.0 compiler.

1 Introduction

Static analysis techniques, such as typing and strictness analysis are crucial components of state-of-the-art implementations of lazy functional programming languages. These techniques are employed to determine properties of functions in a program. These properties can be used by the programmer and also by the compiler itself. The growing complexity of functional languages like Haskell [Has92] and Clean [Cle13,Cle20] requires increasingly sophisticated methods for translating programs written in these languages into efficient executables. Often these optimization methods are implemented in an ad hoc manner: new language features seem to require new optimization techniques which are implemented simultaneously, or added later when it is noticed that the use of these features leads to inefficient code. For instance, type classes require the elimination of dictionaries, monadic programs introduce a lot of higher-order functions that have to be removed, and the intermediate data structures that are built due to function composition should be avoided.

In Clean 1.3 most of these optimizations were implemented independently. They also occurred at different phases during the compilation process making it difficult to combine them into a single optimization phase. The removal of auxiliary data structures was not implemented at all. This meant that earlier optimisations did not benefit from the transformations performed by later optimisations.

This paper describes the combined method that has been implemented in Clean 2.0 to perform various optimizations. This method is based on Chin's

* This work was supported by STW as part of project NWI.4411

R. Peña and T. Arts (Eds.): IFL 2002, LNCS 2670, pp. 51–67, 2003.

fusion algorithm [Chin94], which in its turn was inspired by Wadler's *deforestation algorithm* [Wad88,Fer88]. The two main differences between our method and Chin's fusion are (1) we use a more refined analysis to determine which functions can safely be fused, and (2) our algorithm has been implemented as part of the Clean 2.0 compiler which makes it possible to measure its effect on real programs (See Section 6).

The paper is organized as follows. We start with a few examples illustrating what types of optimizations can be performed (Section 2). In Section 3 we explain the underlying idea for deforestation. Section 4 introduces a formal language for denoting functional programs. In Section 5 we present our improved fusion algorithm and illustrate the effectiveness of this algorithm with a few example programs (Section 6). We conclude with a discussion of related work (Section 7) and future research (Section 8).

2 Overview

This section gives an overview of the optimizations that are performed by our improved fusion algorithm. Besides traditional deforestation, we illustrate so-called dictionary elimination and general higher-order function removal. We also indicate the 'pitfalls' that may lead to non-termination or to duplication of work, and present solutions to avoid these pitfalls.

The transformation rules of the fusion algorithm are defined by using a core language (Section 4). Although there are many syntactical differences between the core language and Clean we distinguish these languages more explicitly by using a sans serif style for core programs and a `typewriter` style for Clean programs.

2.1 Deforestation

Deforestation attempts to transform a functional program which uses intermediate data structures into one which does not. Note that these data structures can be of arbitrary type, they are not restricted to lists. These intermediate data structures are common in lazy functional programs as they enable modularity. For example, the function `any`, which tests whether any element of a list satisfies a given predicate, could be defined as:

```
any p xs = or (map p xs)
```

Here `map` applies `p` to all elements of the list `xs` yielding an intermediate list of boolean values. The function `or` combines these values to produce a single boolean result. This style of definition is enabled by lazy evaluation, the elements of the intermediate list of booleans are produced one at a time and immediately consumed by the `or` function, thus the function `any` can run in constant space. However this definition is still wasteful, each element of the intermediate list has to be allocated, filled, taken apart, and garbage collected.

If deforestation is successful it transforms the definition of `any` into the following efficient version:

```
any p []     = False
any p [x:xs] = p x || any p xs
```

The following example is given in both [Chin94] and [Wad88]. It elegantly shows that a programmer no longer needs to worry about annoying questions such as "Which of the following two expressions is more efficient?"

`append (append a b) c` or `append a (append b c)`

where `append` is defined as

```
append []     ys = ys
append [x:xs] ys = [x:append xs ys]
```

Experienced programmers almost automatically use the second expression, but from a more abstract point of view there seems to be no difference.

Deforestation as well as fusion will transform the left expression into the expression `app_app a b c` and introduce a new function in which the two applications of `append` are combined:

```
app_app []     b c = append b c
app_app [x:xs] b c = [x:app_app xs b c]
```

Transforming the right expression leads to essentially the same function as `app_app` both using Wadler's deforestation and by Chin's fusion. However, this saves only one evaluation step compared to the original expression at the cost of an extra function. Our fusion algorithm transforms the left expression just as deforestation or fusion would, but it leaves the right expression unchanged.

The major difficulty with this kind of transformation is to determine which applications can be fused (or deforested) safely. Without any precautions there are many situations in which the transformation will not terminate. Therefore it is necessary to formulate proper criteria that, on the one hand, guarantee termination, and on the other hand, do not reject too many fusion candidates. Besides termination, there is another problem that has to be dealt with: the transformation should not introduce repeated computations, by duplicating redexes. We will have a closer look at non-termination and redex duplication in Section 5.

2.2 Type Classes and Dictionary Removal

Type classes or ad-hoc polymorphism are generally considered to be one of the most powerful concepts of functional languages [Wad89]. The advantages are illustrated in the following example in which an instance of equality for lists is declared. Here we use the Clean syntax (deviating slightly from the Haskell notation).

```
instance == [a] | == a
where
    (==) []     []      = True
    (==) [x:xs] [y:ys]  = x == y && xs == ys
    (==) _      _       = False
```

With type classes one can use the same name (==) for defining equality over all kinds of different types. In the body of an instance one can use the overloaded operation itself to compare substructures, i.e. it is not necessary to indicate the difference between both occurrences of == in the right-hand side of the second alternative. The translation of such instances into 'real' functions is easy: Each *context restriction* (in our example `| == a`) is converted into a *dictionary* argument containing the concrete version of the overloaded class. For the equality example this leads to

```
eqList eq []     []     = True
eqList eq [x:xs] [y:ys] = eq x y && eqList eq xs ys
eqList eq _      _      = False
```

An application of == to two lists of integers, e.g. `[1,2] == [1,2]`, is replaced by an expression containing the list version of equality parameterized with the integer dictionary of the equality class, `eqList eqInt [1,2][1,2]`.

Applying this simple compilation scheme introduces a lot of overhead which can be eliminated by specializing `eqList` for the `eqInt` dictionary as shown below

```
eqListeqInt []     []     = True
eqListeqInt [x:xs] [y:ys] = eqInt x y && eqListeqInt xs ys
eqListeqInt _      _      = False
```

In Clean 1.3 the specialization of overloaded operations within a single module was performed immediately, i.e. dictionaries were not built at all, except for some rare, exotic cases. These exceptions are illustrated by the following type declaration (taken from [Oka98])

```
::  Seq a = Nil | Cons a (Seq [a])
```

Defining an instance of == for `Seq a` is easy, specializing such an instance for a concrete element type cannot be done. The compiler has to recognize such situations in order to avoid an infinite specialization loop.

In Clean 2.0 specialization is performed by the fusion algorithm. The handling of infinite specialization does not require special measures as the functions involved will be marked as unsafe by our fusion analysis. Moreover dictionaries do not contain unevaluated expressions (*closures*), so copying dictionaries can never duplicate computations. This means that certain requirements imposed by the fusion algorithm can be relaxed for dictionaries. In the remainder of the paper we leave out the treatment of dictionaries because besides this relaxation of requirements it very much resembles the way other constructs are analyzed and transformed.

2.3 Higher-Order Function Removal

A straightforward treatment of higher-order functions introduces overhead both in time and space. E.g. measurements on large programs using a monadic style of programming show that such overhead can be large; see section 6.

In [Wad88] Wadler introduces *higher-order macros* to elimate some of this overhead but this method has one major limitation: these macros are not considered first class citizens. Chin has extended his fusion algorithm so that it is able to deal with higher-order functions. We adopt his solution with some minor refinements.

So called accumulating parameters are a source of non-termination. For example, consider the following function definitions:

```
twice f x = f (f x)

f g = f (twice g)
```

The parameter of `f` is accumulating: the argument `twice g` in the recursive call of `f` is 'larger' than the original argument. Trying to fuse `f` with `inc` (for some producer `inc`) in the application `f inc` will lead to a new application of the form `f twice_inc`. Fusing this one leads to the expression `f twice_twice_inc` and so on.

Partial function applications should also be treated with care. At first one might think that it is safe to fuse an application `f (g E)` in which the arity of `f` is greater than one and the subexpression `g E` is a redex. This fusion will combine `f` and `g` into a single function, say `f_g`, and replace the original expression by `f_g E`. This, however, is dangerous if the original expression was shared, as shown by the following function `h`:

```
h    = z 1 + z 2
     where z = f (g E)
```

This function is not equivalent to the version in which `f` and `g` have been fused:

```
h    = z 1 + z 2
     where z = f_g E
```

Here the computation encoded in the body of `g` will be performed twice, as compared to only once in the original version.

2.4 Optimizing Generic Functions

Generic programming allows the programmer to write a function once and use it for different types. It relieves the programmer from having to define new instances of common operations each time he declares a new data type. The idea is to consider types as being built up from a small fixed set of type constructors and to specify generic operations in terms of these constructors. In Clean 2.0, for example, one can specify all instances of equality by just a few lines of fairly obvious code:

```
generic eq a :: a a -> Bool

eq{|UNIT|}                x         y               = True
eq{|PAIR|}    eqx eqy (PAIR x y)(PAIR x' y') = eqx x x' && eqy y y'
eq{|EITHER|} eql eqr (LEFT l)   (LEFT l')      = eql l l'
eq{|EITHER|} eql eqr (RIGHT r) (RIGHT r')     = eqr r r'
eq{|EITHER|} eql eqr _ _                          = False
```

Here `UNIT`, `PAIR` and `EITHER` are the fixed generic types. With the aid of this generic specification, the compiler is able to generate instances for any algebraic data type. The idea is to convert an object of such a data type to its generic representation (this encoding follows directly from the definition of the data type), apply the generic operation to this converted object and, if necessary, convert the object back to a data type. For a comprehensive description of how generics can be implemented, see [Ali01] or [Hin00].

Without any optimizations one obtains operations which are very inefficient. The conversions and the fact that generic functions are higher-order functions (e.g. the instance of `eq` for `PAIR` requires two functions as arguments, `eqx` and `eqy`) introduce a lot of overhead. The combined data and higher-order fusion is sufficient to get rid of almost all intermediate data and higher-order calls, leading to specialized operations that are usually as efficient as the hand coded versions. To achieve this, only some minor extensions of the original fusion algorithm were needed.

3 Introduction to Fusion

The underlying idea for transformation algorithms like Wadler's deforestation or Chin's fusion is to combine nested applications of functions of the form $F(\ldots, G\vec{E}, \ldots)$ [1] into a single application $F_i G(\ldots, \vec{E}, \ldots)$. This is achieved by performing a sequence of unfold steps of both F and G. An unfold step is the substitution of a function body for an application of that function, wheareas a fold step performs the reverse process. Of course, if one of the functions involved is recursive this sequence is potentially infinite. To avoid this it is necessary that during the sequence of unfold steps an application is reached that has been encountered before. In that case one can perform the crucial fold step to achieve termination. But how do we know that we will certainly reach such an application?

Wadler's solution is to define the notion of *treeless form*. If the above F and G are treeless it is guaranteed that no infinite unfolding sequences will occur. However, Wadler does not distinguish between F and G. Chin recognizes that the roles of these functions in the fusion process are different. He comes up with the so called producer-consumer model: F plays the role of *consumer*, consuming data through one of its arguments, whereas G acts as a *producer*, producing data via its result. Separate safety criteria can then be applied for the different roles.

[1] We write $\vec{E}$ as shorthand for $(E_1, \ldots, E_n)$

Although Chin's criterion indicates more fusion candidates than Wadler's, there are still cases in which it appears to be too restrictive. To illustrate these shortcomings we first repeat Chin's notion of safety: A function F is a safe consumer in its ith argument if all recursive calls of F have either a variable or a constant on the ith parameter position, otherwise it is *accumulating* in that argument. A function G is a safe producer if none of its recursive calls appears on a consuming position.

One of the drawbacks of the safety criterion for consumers is that it indicates too many consuming parameters, and consequently it limits the number of producers (since the producer property negatively depends on the consumer property). As an example, consider the following definition for `flatten`:

```
flatten []     = []
flatten [x:xs]  = append x (flatten xs)
```

According to Chin, the `append` function is consuming in both of its arguments. Consequently, the `flatten` function is not a producer, for, its recursive call appears on a consuming position of `append`. Wadler will also reject `flatten` because its definition is not treeless.

In our definition of consumer we will introduce an auxiliary notion, called *active arguments*, that filters out the arguments that will not lead to a fold step, like the second argument of `append`. If `append` is no longer consuming in its second argument, `flatten` becomes a decent producer.

Chin also indicates superfluous consuming arguments when we are not dealing with a single recursive function but with a set of mutually recursive functions. To illustrate this, consider the unary functions `f` and `g` being mutually recursive as follows:

```
f x = g x
g x = f (h x)
```

Now `f` is accumulating and `g` is not (e.g. `g`'s body contains a call to `f` with an accumulating argument whereas `f`'s body just contains a simple call to `g`). Although `g` is a proper consumer by Chin's definition, it makes no sense to fuse an application of `g` with a producer, for this producer will be passed to `f` but cannot be fused with `f`. Again no fold step can take place. Unfortunately, by considering `g` as consuming, any function of which the recursive call appears as an argument of `g` will be rejected as a producer. There is no need for that, and therefore we indicate both `f` and `g` as non-consuming.

4 Syntax

We shall formulate the fusion algorithm with respect to a 'core language' which captures the essential aspects of lazy functional languages such as pattern matching, sharing and higher-order functions.

Functional expressions are built up from applications of function symbols F and data constructors C. Pattern matching is expressed by a construction case ⋯ of ⋯. In function definitions, one can express pattern matching with respect to one argument at a time. This means that compound patterns are decomposed into nested ('sequentialized') case expressions. Sharing of objects is expressed by a let construction and higher-order applications by an @. We do not allow functions that contain case expressions as nested subexpressions on the right-hand side, i.e. case expressions can only occur at the outermost level. And as in [Chin94], we distinguish so called *g-type functions* (starting with a single pattern match) and *f-type functions* (with no pattern match at all).

Definition 1. (i) *The set of* expressions *is defined by the following grammar. Below, x ranges over variables, C over constructors and F over function symbols.*

$$\begin{array}{rl} E ::= & x \\ | & C(E_1, \ldots, E_k) \\ | & F(E_1, \ldots, E_k) \\ | & \mathsf{let}\ \vec{x} = \vec{E}\ \mathsf{in}\ E' \\ | & \mathsf{case}\ E\ \mathsf{of}\ P_1|E_1 \ldots P_n|E_n \\ | & E\ @\ E' \\ P ::= & C(x_1, \ldots, x_k) \end{array}$$

(ii) *The set of* free variables *(in the obvious sense) of E is denoted by* $\mathrm{FV}(E)$. *An expression E is said to be* open *if* $\mathrm{FV}(E) \neq \emptyset$, *otherwise E is called* closed.

(iii) *A* function definition *is an equation of the form*

$$F(x_1, \ldots, x_k) = E$$

where all the x_i's are disjoint and $\mathrm{FV}(E) \subseteq \{x_1, \ldots, x_k\}$.

The semantics of the language is call-by-need.

5 Fusion Algorithm

5.1 Consumers

We start by defining the supporting notions of active and accumulating.

We say that an occurrence of variable x in E is *active* if x is either a pattern matching variable (case x of ...), a higher-order variable (x @ ...), or x is used as an argument on an active position of a function. The intuition here is to mark those function arguments where fusion can lead to a fold step or further transformations. This definition ensures that for example the second argument of append is not regarded as consuming.

We define the notions of 'active occurrence' $actocc(x, E)$ and 'active position' $act(F)_i$ simultaneously as the least solution of some predicate equations.

Definition 2. (i) *The predicates actocc and act are specified by mutual induction as follows.*

$$
\begin{array}{lll}
actocc(x, y) & = true,\ if\ y = x \\
 & = false,\ otherwise \\
actocc(x, F\vec{E}) & = true,\ if\ for\ some\ i\colon E_i = x \wedge act(F)_i \\
 & = \bigvee_i actocc(x, E_i),\ otherwise \\
actocc(x, C\vec{E}) & = \bigvee_i actocc(x, E_i) \\
actocc(x, \mathsf{case}\ E\ \mathsf{of}\ \ldots P_i|E_i \ldots) & = true,\ if\ E = x \\
 & = \bigvee_i actocc(x, E_i),\ otherwise \\
actocc(x, \mathsf{let}\ \vec{x} = \vec{E}\ \mathsf{in}\ E') & = actocc(x, E') \vee \bigvee_i actocc(x, E_i) \\
actocc(x, E\ @\ E') & = true,\ if\ E = x \\
 & = actocc(x, E) \vee actocc(x, E'),\ otherwise
\end{array}
$$

Moreover, for each function F, defined by $F\vec{x} = E$

$$act(F)_i \Leftrightarrow actocc(x_i, E)$$

(ii) *We say that F is* active *in argument i if $act(F)_i$ is true.*

The notion of *accumulating parameter* as introduced by [Chin94] is used to detect potential non-termination of fusion as we could see in the example in section 2.3. Our definition is a slightly modified version to deal with mutually recursive functions as indicated in 3.

Definition 3. *Let $F_1, \ldots, F_n$ be a set of mutually recursive functions with respective right-hand sides $E_1, \ldots, E_n$. The function F_j is* accumulating *in its ith parameter if either*
(1) there exists a right-hand side E_k containing an application $F_j(\ldots, E'_i, \ldots)$ in which E'_i is open and not just an argument or a pattern variable, or
(2) the right-hand side of F_j, E_j, contains an application $F_k(\ldots, E'_l, \ldots)$ such that $E'_l = x_i$ and F_k is accumulating in l.

The first requirement corresponds to Chin's notion of accumulating parameter. The second requirement will prevent functions that recursively depend on other accumulating functions from being regarded as non-accumulating.

Combining the notions of active and accumulating leads to the notion of consuming, indicating that fusion is both interesting and safe for that parameter.

Definition 4. *A function F is* consuming *in its ith parameter if it is both non-accumulating and active in i.*

5.2 Producers

The notion of *producer*, indicating that fusion will terminate for such a function as producer, is also taken from [Chin94] here with a minor adjustment to deal with constructors. First we define *producer* for functions

Definition 5. *Let $F_1, \ldots, F_n$ be a set of mutually recursive functions. These functions are called* producers *if none of their recursive calls (in the right-hand sides of their definitions) occurs on a consuming position.*

Now we extend the definition to application expressions

Definition 6. *An application of S e.g. $S(E_1, \ldots, E_k)$ is a producer if:*

1. $\mathsf{arity}(S) > k$, *or*
2. *S is a constructor*
3. *S is a producer function*

5.3 Linearity

The final notion we require is that of *linearity* which is used to detect potential duplication of work. It is unchanged from the original definition as introduced by Chin.

Definition 7. *Let F be a function with definition $F(x_1, \ldots, x_n) = E$. The function F is* linear *in its ith parameter if*
(1) F is an f-type function and x_i occurs at most once in E, or
(2) F is a g-type function and x_i occurs at most once in each of the branches of the top-level case.

5.4 Transformation Rules

Our adjusted version of the fusion algorithm consists of one general transformation rule, dealing with all expressions, and three auxiliary rules for function applications, higher-order application, and for case expressions. The idea is that during fusion both consumer and producer have to be unfolded and combined. This combination forms the body of the newly generated function. Sometimes however, it appears to be more convenient if the unfold step of the consumer could be undone, in particular if the consumer and the producer are both g-type functions. For this reason we supply some of the case expressions with the function symbol to which it corresponds (case_F). Note that this correspondence is always unique because g-type functions contain exactly one case on their right-hand side.

We use $F_i S$ as a name for the function that results from fusing F that is consuming in its i_{th} argument, with producer S. Suppose F is defined as $F\vec{x} = E$. Then the resulting function is defined, distinguishing two cases

1. S is a fully applied function and F is a g-type function: the resulting function consists of the unfoldings of F and S. The top-level case is annotated as having come from F.
2. Otherwise the resulting function consists of the unfolding of F with the application of S substituted for formal argument i.

Note that each $F_i S$ is generated only once.

Definition 8. *Rules for introducing fused functions.*

$$
\begin{array}{ll}
F_i G(x_1,\ldots,x_{i-1},y_1,\ldots,y_m,x_{i+1},\ldots,x_n) & \\
\quad = \mathcal{T}[\![E[E'/x_i]]\!], & \textit{if } \mathsf{arity}(G) = m \textit{ and } F \textit{ is a g-type function} \\
 & \textit{where } G\vec{y} = E' \\
\quad = \mathcal{T}[\![E[G(y_1,\ldots,y_m)/x_i]]\!], & \textit{otherwise} \\
F_i C(x_1,\ldots,x_{i-1},y_1,\ldots,y_m,x_{i+1},\ldots,x_n) & \\
\quad = \mathcal{T}[\![E[C(y_1,\ldots,y_m)/x_i]]\!] &
\end{array}
$$

We use F^+ as a name for the function that results from raising the arity of F by one. The $\mathcal{R}$-rules raise the arity of an expression by propagating the application of the extra argument y through the expression E.

Definition 9. *Rules for arity raising*

$$
\begin{array}{l}
F^+(x_1,\ldots,x_n,y) \\
= \mathcal{T}[\![\mathcal{R}_y[\![E]\!]]\!] \\
\\
\mathcal{R}_y[\![\mathsf{let}\ \vec{x} = \vec{E}\ \mathsf{in}\ E']\!] \\
= \mathsf{let}\ \vec{x} = \vec{E}\ \mathsf{in}\ \mathcal{R}_y[\![E']\!] \\
\mathcal{R}_y[\![\mathsf{case}\ E\ \mathsf{of}\ \ldots P_i|E_i\ldots]\!] \\
= \mathsf{case}\ E\ \mathsf{of}\ \ldots P_i|\mathcal{R}_y[\![E_i]\!]\ldots \\
\mathcal{R}_y[\![E]\!] \\
= E\ @\ y
\end{array}
$$

The $\mathcal{T}$-rules recursively apply the transformation to all parts of the expression and invokes the appropriate auxiliary rules. These are the $\mathcal{F}$-rule for function applications which applies the safety criteria for fusion. The $\mathcal{H}$-rules for higher-order applications which replace higher-order applications by ordinary applications, using the arity-raised version of the applied function when necessary. And finally, the $\mathcal{C}$-rules for case expressions. The first alternative applies the fold-step where possible, the second alternative eliminates cases where the branch to be taken is known. The third alternative resolves nested cases by undoing the unfold step of F. A minor improvement can be obtained by examining the expression E_i', if this expression starts with a constructor it is better to perform the pattern match instead.

Definition 10. *Transformation rules for first and higher-order expressions*

$$
\begin{array}{ll}
\mathcal{T}[\![x]\!] & = x \\
\mathcal{T}[\![C\vec{E}]\!] & = C\mathcal{T}[\![\vec{E}]\!] \\
\mathcal{T}[\![F\vec{E}]\!] & = \mathcal{F}[\![F\mathcal{T}[\![\vec{E}]\!]]\!] \\
\mathcal{T}[\![\mathsf{case}\ E\ \mathsf{of}\ \ldots P_i|E_i\ldots]\!] & = \mathcal{C}[\![\mathsf{case}\ \mathcal{T}[\![E]\!]\ \mathsf{of}\ \ldots P_i|E_i\ldots]\!] \\
\mathcal{T}[\![\mathsf{let}\ \vec{x} = \vec{E}\ \mathsf{in}\ E']\!] & = \mathsf{let}\ \vec{x} = \mathcal{T}[\![\vec{E}]\!]\ \mathsf{in}\ \mathcal{T}[\![E']\!] \\
\mathcal{T}[\![E\ @\ E']\!] & = \mathcal{H}[\![\mathcal{T}[\![E]\!]\ @\ \mathcal{T}[\![E']\!]]\!] \\
\mathcal{T}[\![\vec{E}]\!] & = (\mathcal{T}[\![E_1]\!],\ldots,\mathcal{T}[\![E_n]\!])
\end{array}
$$

$$
\begin{array}{ll}
\mathcal{F}[\![F(E_1,\ldots,E_i,\ldots,E_m)]\!] & \\
 & = \mathcal{F}[\![F_iS(E_1,\ldots,E_{i-1},E'_1,\ldots,E'_n,E_{i+1}\ldots,E_m)]\!], \\
 & \quad \textit{if: for some } i \textit{ with } E_i = S(E'_1,\ldots,E'_n) \\
 & \quad \textit{1) } F \textit{ is consuming in } i \\
 & \quad \textit{2) } S(E'_1,\ldots,E'_n) \textit{ is a producer} \\
 & \quad \textit{3) } \mathsf{arity}(S) \neq n \\
 & \quad \textit{or} \\
 & \quad \textit{1) } F \textit{ is both consuming and linear in } i \\
 & \quad \textit{2) } \mathsf{arity}(F) = m \textit{ and } \mathsf{arity}(S) = n \\
 & \quad \textit{3) } S(E'_1,\ldots,E'_n) \textit{ is a producer} \\
 & \quad\quad \textit{or has a higher order type} \\
 & = F(E_1,\ldots,E_i,\ldots,E_m), \textit{ otherwise} \\
 & \\
\mathcal{H}[\![C(E_1,\ldots,E_k)\ @\ E]\!] & = C(E_1,\ldots,E_k,E) \\
\mathcal{H}[\![F(E_1,\ldots,E_k)\ @\ E]\!] & = \mathcal{F}[\![F(E_1,\ldots,E_k,E)]\!], \textit{ if } \mathsf{arity}(F) > k \\
 & = \mathcal{F}[\![F^+(E_1,\ldots,E_k,E)]\!], \textit{ otherwise} \\
 & \\
\mathcal{C}[\![\mathsf{case}_F G(E_1,\ldots,E_n) \text{ of } \ldots]\!] & \\
 & = \mathcal{F}[\![F(x_1,\ldots,x_{i-1},G(E_1,\ldots,E_n),x_{i+1},\ldots,x_n)]\!] \\
 & \quad \textit{where} \\
 & \quad\quad\quad F(x_1,\ldots,x_n) = \mathsf{case}\ x_i \text{ of } \ldots \\
\mathcal{C}[\![\mathsf{case}_F C_i(E_1,\ldots,E_n) \text{ of } \ldots C_i(x_1,\ldots,x_n)|E'_i\ldots]\!] & \\
 & = \mathcal{T}[\![E'_i[E_1/x_1,\ldots,E_n/x_n]]\!] \\
\mathcal{C}[\![\mathsf{case}_F(\mathsf{case}\ E \text{ of } \ldots P_i|E'_i\ldots) \text{ of } \ldots]\!] & \\
 & = \mathsf{case}\ \mathcal{T}[\![E]\!] \text{ of } \ldots P_i|E''_i\ldots \\
 & \quad \textit{where } E''_i = \mathcal{F}[\![F(x_1,\ldots,x_{i-1},\mathcal{T}[\![E'_i]\!],x_{i+1},\ldots,x_n)]\!] \\
 & \quad \textit{and} \\
 & \quad\quad\quad F(x_1,\ldots,x_n) = \mathsf{case}\ x_i \text{ of } \ldots \\
\mathcal{C}[\![\mathsf{case}_F x \text{ of } \ldots P_i|E_i\ldots]\!] & = \mathsf{case}_F x \text{ of } \ldots P_i|\mathcal{T}[\![E_i]\!]\ldots
\end{array}
$$

6 Examples

We now present a few examples of fusion using the adjusted transformation rules.

6.1 Deforestation

We start with a rather trivial example involving the functions Append, Flatten and Reverse. The first two functions have been defined earlier. The definition of Reverse uses a helper function with an explicit accumulator:

$$
\begin{array}{lll}
\mathsf{Reverse}(l) & = \mathsf{Rev}(l,\mathsf{Nil}) & \\
\mathsf{Rev}(l,a) & = \mathsf{case}\ l\ \mathsf{of} & \\
 & \quad \mathsf{Nil} & \mid a \\
 & \quad \mathsf{Cons}(x,xs) & \mid \mathsf{Rev}(xs,\mathsf{Cons}(x,a)) \\
\mathsf{test}(l) & = \mathsf{Reverse}(\mathsf{Flatten}(l)) &
\end{array}
$$

The result of applying the transformation rules to the function test is shown below.

$$
\begin{array}{ll}
\mathsf{test}(l) & = \mathsf{ReverseFlatten}(l) \\
\mathsf{ReverseFlatten}(l) & = \mathsf{RevFlatten}(l, \mathsf{Nil}) \\
\mathsf{RevFlatten}(l, r) & = \mathsf{case}\ l\ \mathsf{of} \\
 & \quad \begin{array}{l|l} \mathsf{Nil} & r \\ \mathsf{Cons}(x, xs) & \mathsf{RevAppendFlatten}(x, xs, r) \end{array}
\end{array}
$$

$$
\begin{array}{ll}
\multicolumn{2}{l}{\mathsf{RevAppendFlatten}(xs, l, r)} \\
 & = \mathsf{case}\ xs\ \mathsf{of} \\
 & \quad \begin{array}{l|l} \mathsf{Nil} & \mathsf{RevFlatten}(l, r) \\ \mathsf{Cons}(x, xs) & \mathsf{RevAppendFlatten}(xs, l, \mathsf{Cons}(x, r)) \end{array}
\end{array}
$$

One can give an alternative definition of Reverse using the standard higher-order *foldl* function. Transforming test then results in two mutually recursive functions that are identical to the auxiliary functions generated for the original definition of Reverse except for the order of the parameters.

Fusion appears to be much less successful if the following direct definition of reverse is used:

$$
\begin{array}{ll}
\mathsf{Reverseacc}(l) & = \mathsf{case}\ l\ \mathsf{of} \\
 & \quad \begin{array}{l|l} \mathsf{Nil} & \mathsf{Nil} \\ \mathsf{Cons}(x, xs) & \mathsf{Append}(\mathsf{Reverseacc}(xs), \mathsf{Cons}(x, \mathsf{Nil})) \end{array}
\end{array}
$$

Now Reverseacc is combined with Flatten but the fact that Reverseacc itself is not a producer (the recursive occurrence of this function appears on a consuming position) prevents the combination of Reverseacc and Flatten from being deforested completely. In general combinations of standard list functions (except for *accumulating* functions, such as Reverse), e.g. $\mathsf{Sum}(\mathsf{Map\ Inc}(\mathsf{Take}(n, \mathsf{Repeat}(1))))$ are transformed into a single function that generates no list at all and that does not contain any higher-order function applications.

6.2 Results

As a practical test of the effectiveness of the adjusted fusion algorithm we applied the fusion algorithm to several programs. The following test programs were used: `jpeg`[Fok95], `pseudoknot`[Har94] and the programs from [Har93], except `listcopy`. These programs were all ported to Clean 2.0. We computed the speedup by dividing the execution time without fusion by the execution time with fusion. Because the compiler does not support cross module optimisation, we copied frequently used standard list functions from the standard library to the module(s) of the program. The speedups for these programs are also shown in the table, but only if the speedup is not the same. In all cases specialization of overloaded functions was enabled. To show the effect of the specialization of overloaded functions we have run two small test programs: `mergesort` and `nfib`.

The optimisation of generic functions was tested with a small program converting arbitrary objects to and from the generic representation that has been used in [Ach02]. The largest test program is the Clean compiler itself. For the compiler the improvements were almost entirely caused by better optimization of a few modules that use a monadic style, and not by removal of intermediate data structures using deforestation. For this reason we have included the effect of fusion on these 'monadic' modules as a separate result. The results are summarized in the following table.

program	*speedup*	*added functions*	*speedup*
`jpeg`	1.34	`map,sum`	1.77
`pseudoknot`	1.11	`++, map`	1.14
`complab`	1.00		
`event`	1.19	`++, take`	1.44
`fft`	1.00	standard list functions	1.28
`genfft`	1.00	standard list functions	1.16
`ida`	1.16		
`listcompr`	0.84	`concat, ++`	1.18
`parstof`	1.19		
`sched`	1.00		
`solid`	1.01	`foldl`, combined `area.icl` and `Csg.icl`	1.17
`transform`	1.02	standard list functions	1.03
`typecheck`	1.11	`++, map, concat, foldr, zip2`	1.30
`wang`	1.00	standard list functions	1.04
`wave4`	1.40		
`mergesort`	1.91		
`nfib`	6.73		
`generic conversion`	71.00		
`compiler`	1.05		
`compiler-monads`	1.25		

Fusion not only influences execution speed but also memory allocation. It appears that the decrease in memory usage is roughly twice as much as the decrease in execution time. For instance, the compiler itself runs approximately 5 percent faster whereas 9 percent less memory was allocated relative to the non-fused compiler. More or less the same holds for other programs.

Compilation with fusion enabled takes longer than without. Currently the difference is about 20 percent, when the implementation stabilises we expect to improve on this.

In the most expensive module that uses a monadic style only 68 percent of the curried function applications were eliminated. This improved the execution speed 33 percent and the memory allocation 51 percent. It should however be possible to remove nearly all these curried function applications. The current algorithm is not able to do this, because some higher-order functions are not optimized because they are indicated as accumulating. This is illustrated in the following example:

```
f :: [Int] Int -> Int
f [] s = s
f [e:l] s = g (add e) l s
    where add a b = a + b
g :: (Int -> Int) [Int] Int -> Int
g h l s = f l (h s)
```

The argument `h` of the function `g` is accumulating because `g` is called with `(add e)` as argument, therefore `g` is not fused with `(add e)`. In this case it would be safe to fuse. This limitation prevents the compiler from removing nearly all the remaining curried function applications from the above mentioned module. However, if a call `f (g x)`, for some functions `f` and `g`, appears in a program, the argument of the function `f` does not always have to be treated as an accumulating argument. This is the case when the argument of `g` is always the same or does not grow in the recursion. By recognizing such cases we hope to optimize most of the remaining curried function applications. Or instead, we could fuse a limited number of times in these cases, to make the fusion algorithm terminate.

Another example of curried applications in this module that cannot be optimized are `foldl` calls that yield a higher order function. Such a higher order function occurs at an accumulating argument position in the `foldl` call, and can therefore not be fused.

7 Related Work

Gill, Launchbury, and Peyton Jones [Gil93] use a restrictive consumer producer model by translating list functions into combinations of the primitive functions fold (consumer) and build (producer). This idea has been generalized to arbitrary data structures by Fegaras, Sheard and Zhou [Feg94], and also by Takano and Meijer [Tak95]. The approach of the latter is based on the category theoretical notion of *hylomorphism*. These hylomorphisms are the building blocks for functions. By applying transformation rules one can fuse these hylomorphisms resulting in deforested functions. These methods are able to optimize programs that cannot be improved by traditional deforestation. In particular, programs that contain reverse-like producers, i.e. producer functions with accumulators as arguments. On the other hand, Gill ([Gil96]) also shows some examples of functions that are deforested by the traditional method and not by these techniques. However, the main problem with these approaches is that they require that functions are written in some fixed format. Although for some functions this format can be generated from their ordinary definitions it is unclear how to do this automatically in general.

Peyton Jones and Marlow give a solid overview of the issues involved in transforming lazy functional programs in their paper in the related area of inlining [Pey99]. Specifically they identify code duplication, work duplication, and the uncovering of new transformation opportunities as three key issues to take into account.

Seidl and Sørensen [Sei97] develop a constraint-based system in an attempt to avoid the restrictions imposed by the purely syntactical approach used in the treeless approach to deforestation as used by Wadler [Wad88] and Marlow [Mar95]. Their analysis is a kind of abstract interpretation with which deforestation is approximated. This approximation results in a number of conditions on subterms and variables appearing in the program/function. If these conditions are met, it is guaranteed that deforestation will terminate. For instance, by using this more refined method the example program at the end of section 6.2 would be indicated as being safe.

Deforestation is also implemented in the compiler for the logic/functional programming language Mercury. To ensure termination of the algorithm a stack of unfolded calls is maintained, recursive calls can be unfolded only when they are smaller than the elements on the stack. This ordering is based on the sizes of the instantation tree of the arguments of a call. Accumulating parameters are removed from this sum of sizes. For details see [Tay98]. Our fusion algorithm can optimize some programs which the Mercury compiler does not optimize, for example ReverseFlatten from section 6.1.

8 Conclusion

The original fusion algorithm has been extended and now combines deforestation together with dictionary elimination and higher-order removal. This adjusted algorithm has been implemented in the Clean 2.0 compiler allowing for tests on real-world applications. Initial results indicate that the main benefits are achieved for specialised features such as type classes, generics, and monads rather than in 'ordinary' code.

Further work remains to be done in the handling of accumulating parameters. Marlow presents a higher-order deforestation algorithm in his PhD thesis [Mar95] which builds on Wadler's original first-order deforestation scheme. A full comparison with the algorithm presented here remains to be done. Finally a formal proof of termination would be reassuring to have.

References

Ach02. P. Achten, A. Alimarine, R. Plasmeijer. *When Generic Functions Use Dynamic Values.* Post-workshop submission: 14th International Workshop on the Implementation of Functional Languages, IFL 2002, Madrid, Spain, September 2002.

Ali01. A. Alimarine and R. Plasmeijer. *A Generic Programming Extension for Clean.* In: Arts, Th., Mohnen M., eds. Proceedings of the 13th International Workshop on the Implementation of Functional Languages, IFL 2001, Selected Papers, Älvsjö, Sweden, September 24–26, 2001, Springer-Verlag, LNCS 2312, pages 168–185.

Chin94. W.-N. Chin. *Safe fusion of functional expressions II: Further improvements* Journal of Functional Programming, Volume 6, Part 4, pp 515–557, 1994.

Cle13. R. Plasmeijer, M. van Eekelen. *Language Report Concurrent Clean. Version 1.3.* Technical Report CSI R9816, NIII, University of Nijmegen, June 1998. Also available at `www.cs.kun.nl/~clean/contents/contents.html`

Cle20. R. Plasmeijer, M. van Eekelen. *Language Report Concurrent Clean. Version 2.0. DRAFT!*, NIII, University of Nijmegen, December 2001. Also available at `www.cs.kun.nl/~clean/contents/contents.html`

Feg94. L. Fegaras, T. Sheard, and T. Zhou. *Improving Programs which Recurse over Multiple Inductive Structures.* In Proc. of ACM SIGPLAN Workshop on Partial Evaluation and Semantics-Based Program Manipulation, Orlando, FL, USA, June 1994

Fer88. A. Ferguson and P. Wadler. *When will Deforestation Stop.* In Proc. of 1988 Glasgow Workshop on Functional Programming, pp 39–56, Rothasay, Isle of Bute, August 1988.

Fok95. J. Fokker. *Functional Specification of the JPEG algorithm, and an Implementation for Free*, In Programming Paradigms in Graphics, Proceedings of the Eurographics workshop in Maastricht, the Netherlands, september 1995, Wien, Springer 1995, pp102–120.

Gil96. A. Gill. *Cheap Deforestation for Non-strict Functional Languages*,PhD Thesis, Department of Computing Science, Glasgow University, 1996.

Gil93. A. Gill, S. Peyton Jones, J. Launchbury. *A Short Cut to Deforestation*, Proc. Functional Programming Languages and Computer Architecture (FPCA'93), Copenhagen, June 1993, pp223–232.

Har93. P. Hartel, K. Langendoen. *Benchmarking Implementations of Lazy Functional Languages*, In Proc. of Functional Programming Languages and Computer Architecture, 1993, pp341–349.

Har94. P. Hartel, *et al. Pseudoknot: A Float-Intensive Benchmark for Functional Compilers*, 6th Implementation of Functional Languages, School of Information Systems, University of East Anglia, Norwich, UK, 1994, pp13.1–13.34.

Has92. P. Hudak, S. Peyton Jones, P. Wadler, B. Boutel, J. Fairbairn, J. Fasel, K. Hammond, J. Hughes, Th. Johnsson, D. Kieburtz, R. Nikhil, W. Partain, J. Peterson. *Report on the programming language Haskell*, In ACM SigPlan Notices, 27 (5): 1–164. May 1992.

Hin00. R. Hinze and S. Peyton Jones. *Derivable Type Classes.* In Graham Hutton, editor, Proceedings of the Fourth Haskell Workshop, Canada, 2000.

Mar95. S. Marlow.*Deforestation for Higher-Order Functional Programs* PhD Thesis, Department of Computer Science, University of Glasgow, 1995.

Pey99. S. Peyton Jones, S. Marlow. *Secrets of the Glasgow Haskell Compiler inliner* Workshop on Implementing Declarative Languages, 1999.

Oka98. C. Okasaki. *Purely Functional Data Structures* Cambridge University Press, ISBN 0-521-63124-6, 1998.

Sei97. H. Seidl, M.H. Sørensen. *Constraints to Stop Higher-Order Deforestation* In 24th ACM Symp. on Principles of Programming Languages, pages 400–413, 1997.

Tak95. A. Takano, E. Meijer. *Shortcut to Deforestation in Calculational form*, Proc. Functional Programming Languages and Computer Architecture (FPCA'95), La Jolla, June 1995, pp 306–313.

Tay98. S. Taylor.*Optimization of Mercury programs* Honours report, Department of Computer Science, University of Melbourne, Australia , November 1998.

Wad88. P. Wadler. *Deforestation: Transforming Programs to Eliminate Trees* Proceedings of the 2nd European Symposium on Programming, Nancy, France, March 1988. Lecture Notes in Computer Science 300.

Wad89. P. Wadler, S. Blott. *How to make ad-hoc polymorphism less ad hoc* In Proceedings 16th ACM Symposium on Principles of Programming Languages, pages 60–76, 1989.

Proving Make Correct: I/O Proofs in Haskell and Clean

Malcolm Dowse, Glenn Strong, and Andrew Butterfield

Trinity College, Dublin University
{Malcolm.Dowse,Glenn.Strong,Andrew.Butterfield}@cs.tcd.ie

Abstract. This paper discusses reasoning about I/O operations in the languages Haskell and Clean and makes some observations about proving properties of programs which perform significant I/O. We developed a model of the I/O system and produced some techniques to reason about the behaviour of programs run in the model. We then used those techniques to prove some properties of a program based on the standard `make` tool. We consider the I/O systems of both languages from a program proving perspective, and note some similarities in the overall structure of the proofs. A set of operators for assisting in the reasoning process are defined, and we then draw some conclusions concerning reasoning about the effect of functional programs on the outside world, give some suggestions for techniques and discuss future work.

1 Introduction

In [2] we presented some preliminary work describing reasoning about the I/O-related properties of programs written in functional programming languages. Only tentative conclusions could be drawn from that study because of the relatively simple nature of the program under consideration. In this case study the program combines I/O and computation in essential and non-trivial ways. The results of the previous study were encouraging regarding the ease of reasoning about I/O operations on functional languages, but more work was required. There are, therefore, a number of issues to be addressed:

Question 1. How do the reasoning techniques used in [2] scale when applied to more complex programs which perform arbitrary I/O actions?

Our aim is to reason about the side-effects of a program on its environment. It is therefore an essential property of our reasoning system that it enables us to discuss I/O actions in a functional program in terms of their side effects. Since we are interested in both Haskell[5] and Clean[8] we require I/O system models which can accommodate both languages. The differences between the two I/O systems raises another question:

Question 2. Do the different I/O systems used by Haskell and Clean lead to any significant differences in the proofs developed for each program, and if so do these differences correspond to differences in ease of reasoning?

R. Peña and T. Arts (Eds.): IFL 2002, LNCS 2670, pp. 68–83, 2003.

2 Make

A standard programming utility is the `make` tool[6] which automates certain parts of program compilation. The essential features of `make` are:

1. It controls all necessary compilation to ensure that the most up-to-date sources are used in the target program,
2. It ensures that no *unnecessary* compilations are performed where source files have not changed.

To facilitate our case study we produced two programs from an abstract specification of the standard `make` utility: one written in the functional programming language Haskell, and one in the functional programming language Clean. Each program implemented the specification for `make` but used the native I/O system for the language (Haskell uses a monadic I/O system[10] while Clean uses a system based on unique types[9]).

For this study we can observe that the I/O `make` performs is limited to:

1. Reading the description of the program dependencies from a text file (the "makefile"),
2. Checking these dependencies against the filesystem to determine what compilation work needs to be done,
3. Executing external commands as detailed in the makefile in order to bring the target program up to date.

The I/O performed in the first point is of little interest from a reasoning point of view (being essentially a parsing problem) and so we consider our make program only from the position where the dependencies have been read and examined. These dependencies can be represented by a tree-like data structure where there is a root node representing a goal (a file to be built) and a number of sub-trees representing dependencies. Each node in the tree has an associated command to be run when the goal at that node should be rebuilt.

In this paper we are only interested in certain contexts, which we will refer to as "reasonable" uses of `make`: we will allow, for instance, only certain kinds of commands to be used in the makefile (see Sect. 3). We make these restrictions as we are interested in `make` only as a tool to assist in exploring the issues which arise in reasoning about the side-effects of programs.

3 The Possibility of I/O Proofs

An obvious concern is the possibility or practicality of doing any kind of formal proofs involving I/O, which accompanies a concern regarding the lack of concurrency in our model. The gist of the argument is as follows:

> On a real machine with a real OS there are many other processes running concurrently, so the I/O model needs to deal with these. In any case, some other process may make arbitrary changes to the filesystem while

`make` is running so it becomes impossible to give a formal proof of any property, even in the unlikely event of having a complete formal model covering all possible concurrent processes.

We first address the issue of the impossibility/impracticality of doing formal proofs of the I/O behaviour of `make` (or any other similar program). First, consider the reaction of a `make` user if someone was to replace their make program with a broken version, or even go to such extremes as to substitute a completely different program (renaming `cat` to `make`, for example). The user would rapidly become aware that something was up. The point is, in typical uses of the make program, users have reasonable expectations for its behaviour, which are generally met, by and large. The main reason is that most users rely on an operating system to ensure that there aren't arbitrary and destructive changes to the collection of files being manipulated by `make`. Despite the theoretical possibility of concurrent processes making arbitrary changes to a user's files, the common practical use of `make` occurs in a much more controlled environment.

If informally we know what to expect of `make`, then it is possible to consider formal proofs of its properties. If arbitrary concurrent behaviour elsewhere in the system makes it impossible to reason formally about its behaviour, then it is just as impossible to reason informally about its behaviour, and its behaviour in that context will appear arbitrary.

In this case-study we have adopted an abstraction which ignores concurrent changes to the file system — we assume such changes occur to parts of the filesystem beyond the scope of any particular use of `make`. This is the normal mode of use for this program. We have also ignored the fact that makefiles can specify arbitrary commands to be run, instead assuming that all commands are "well-behaved", by which we mean that their net effect is to create their target if absent or modify it so that its timestamp becomes the most recent in the system. Just as arbitrary concurrent processes make it impossible to reason about `make`, either formally or informally, so does the use of arbitrary commands in makefiles (consider, as a particularly perverse example, a command which invokes another instance of `make` with a different makefile containing a completely different dependency ordering over the same collection of files!). As `make`'s sole concern is with examining timestamps and running commands to bring targets up-to-date, this abstraction suffices to capture the behaviour for which the make program can reasonably be held responsible. The informal descriptions of `make` do not make any reference to concurrent processes, so we need not consider them. In any case, what could the program documentation say about other processes, other than issue a warning that the program's behaviour is not guaranteed in the presence of arbitrary destructive concurrent processes? It is important to note that we are not advocating a position that states that reasoning about I/O in general need not consider concurrency issues. In general such issues are important and will be the subject of future case studies. However, in the case of the make program they are a distraction.

A final comment is also required about the perception that formal proof is useless unless it is somehow "complete", i.e. covering every aspect of the system being modelled. This view was encouraged by early formal methods research which sought to produce systems which were completely verified "head-to-toe" (e.g. [11]). However formal proof is much more practical when it focuses on aspects of interest (usually safety critical), by exploiting suitable choices of abstractions. In this case-study we discuss formal reasoning about I/O activities of versions of `make` implemented in Haskell and Clean, in an environment where no concurrent processes affect the files under consideration, and all makefile commands behave like "`touch`" from the perspective of make. Furthermore, the main aim of this case-study is to compare the effects of the distinct I/O approaches (monads vs. uniqueness-typing) on the ease of reasoning formally about I/O in such programs.

4 Behaviour of Make

There are six principal theorems relating to the implementation of `make`. The proofs are contained in [4], and for brevity we will give only an informal statement of each theorem before discussing the proof tactics in more depth. Each of these theorems is true under the simplifying assumptions of the I/O model and program abstractions performed on the original programs.

- Theorem 1 states that files whose names do not appear in the makefile will not have their modification times changed by running make.
- Theorem 2 states that directly after executing the command for a file, that file will be newer than any other file in the file system.
- Theorem 3 states that after executing make the modification time of a file will be no earlier than it was before running make.
- Theorem 4 states that following an execution of make the topmost dependency in the tree will be newer than all of the dependencies under it.
- Theorem 5 states that if the top dependency in the tree has not changed following an execution of make, then all of the dependencies under it will also be unchanged,
- Theorem 6 states that following an execution of make that Theorem 4 holds recursively through the tree.

These theorems form the specification of `make`'s behaviour, and are the basis for the implementations.

5 Implementation of Make

We use a simple algebraic datatype to represent the dependency tree. There are additional constraints on the construction of the tree: the tree must be finite, and when names are repeated in different parts of the tree they must contain identical subtrees (see Sect. 8).

```
type Name = FilePath
type Command = String
data Target = Target Name Command [Target] | Leaf Name
```

The recursive portion of the make algorithm is (in Haskell):

```
make :: Target -> IO FileTime
make (Leaf nm) = do
  mtime <- getFileTime nm
  if (mtime==NoFileTime)
    then error ("can't make "++nm++"!")
    else return mtime

make (Target nm cmd depends) = do
  mtime <- getFileTime nm
  ctimes <- update_deps depends
  if (mtime <= (newest ctimes))
    then do
      exec nm cmd
      getFileTime nm
    else
      return mtime

update_deps = mapM make
```

Similar implementations in Clean are provided, highlighting the different programming style encouraged by the Clean I/O system. In order to provide a fully operational implementation in Clean it was necessary to provide the implementation details of the `exec` function using Clean's foreign language interface.

```
make :: Target *World -> (FileTime, *World)
make (Leaf n) w = make` (filedate n w)
     where make` (NoFileTime, w) = abort ("No rule for"+++n)
           make` (FileTime t, w) = (FileTime t, w)

make (Target n c depends) w
     # (times,w)                     = update_deps depends w
     # (this_time,w)                 = filedate n w
     | this_time <= (maxList times) = filedate n (exec c w)
     | otherwise                     = (this_time,w)

update_deps [] w = ([],w)
update_deps [x:xs] w # (t,w)  = make x w
                     # (ts,w) = update_deps xs w
                     = ([t:ts],w)
```

Both implementations of `make` contain error handling code that is not significant to normal execution. In order to simplify the proof process we produce *abstracted* forms of these programs which eliminate the error handling clauses. When proving properties of these abstracted programs we will supply suitable preconditions so that the proofs become, in effect, statements that hold for all cases where errors do not occur. In this way we can simplify the production of the proofs (we intend exploring programs with error cases in future work).

6 The I/O Model

To facilitate the proofs we provide a model of I/O that covers all the operations used by the make implementations. Times can be represented as integers (from some suitable zero-moment).

$$t \in \mathit{EpochTime} = \mathbb{Z}$$

Each file can have a time associated with it; we also provide a value to represent the lack of a file time (associated with a missing file). We also represent names, commands and the target dependency tree in the obvious way:

$$f \in \mathit{FileTime} = \text{FILETIME}\ \mathit{EpochTime} \mid \text{NOFILETIME}$$

The filesystem is represented as a map from (file)names to times. We can represent the complete world that the program operates in as the product of a filesystem and a universal clock:

$$\phi \in \mathit{FS} = \mathit{Name} \xrightarrow{m} \mathit{EpochTime}$$
$$\mathcal{W}, (\phi, \tau) \in \mathit{World} = \mathit{FS} \times \mathit{EpochTime}$$

The level of abstraction chosen for this case study is high enough to eliminate any need to model the contents of files, or any filesystem operations other than touching a file to update the modification time. This operation corresponds to the notion of updating a file, without committing to any specific notion of what the update involves. The operation will ensure that after the action the named file exists with an "up to date" file time, regardless of the state of the file before the action was performed.

We provide an ordering on times where the "missing" time is older than all other possible times, and times are ordered sequentially otherwise. This is a convenient representation for make as it allows us to view missing files as being older than all other files and therefore eternally out of date.

$$\text{NOFILETIME} \preceq f = \mathit{True}$$
$$(\text{FILETIME}\ t_1) \preceq (\text{FILETIME}\ t_2) = t_1 \leq t_2$$

We provide two operations on the filesystem. The first allows us to look up the value associated with a given file name, which will be the file's modification time. We do not advance the clock in this operation.

$$\text{getFileTime} : \mathit{Name} \to \mathit{World} \to \mathit{FileTime}$$
$$\text{getFileTime}[n](\phi, \tau) \mathrel{\widehat{=}} n \in \mathtt{dom}\ \phi \ \to\ \text{FILETIME}\ \phi(n)\ ,\ \text{NOFILETIME}$$

The second important operation is to execute command 'cmd'. We assume here that the execution of a command c with associated filename n will have exactly the effect of updating the associated file date in the filesystem and advancing the universal clock.

$$\begin{aligned} \text{exec} &: \mathit{Name} \rightarrow \mathit{Command} \rightarrow \mathit{World} \rightarrow \mathit{World} \\ \text{exec}\, n\, c\, (\phi, \tau) &= (\phi \dagger \{n \mapsto \tau + 1\}), \tau + 1) \end{aligned}$$

This assumption allows us to reason effectively about the "exec" operation which would otherwise be capable of performing any arbitrary transformation on the world model. The intention of this definition of "exec" is to model a particular case of program execution by make, which corresponds to running a simple compiler. We use the operator †, called override, to introduce and replace bindings in a map. The notation $\phi \dagger \{n \mapsto \alpha\}$ indicates that in the map ϕ, the value n should mapped to the value α in the resultant map.

It is clear from this model that we are only interested in modelling "reasonable" uses of `make`. As described in Sect. 3, a full implementation of `make` (such as GNU Make [3]) can contain arbitrary system commands, shell scripts and calls to arbitrary programs which we do not attempt to model.

7 Semantics

We use a natural semantics for the functional languages, and a notation for the I/O model which resembles the functional languages under consideration. The intention here is to simplify the presentation of the results by working in a notation which matches closely the original programs, but with the reasoning steps justified by the IVDM[13][14] semantics provided. In effect we are using a functional syntax with IVDM semantics.

In [2] both functional programs were rewritten in a common syntax to facilitate a comparison of the reasoning steps in the proofs, and the proofs were performed on that common syntax. In this paper we have chosen to work at a level closer to the original languages since there is no clear advantage to syntactically sugaring the programs into a neutral form in this case.

For the Clean semantics this essentially consists of a model of the world containing a filesystem and clock:

```
:: FS :== [(Name,EpochTime)]
:: World :== (FS,EpochTime)
```

Implementations of the I/O operations used in the program are provided in terms of their effect on this `World` value. These implementations reflect the embedding of the I/O model of Sect. 6 into the semantics of the language. Note that in a Clean implementation the `World` value requires uniqueness attribution, which is not required here since we are safely in the domain of the language semantics. Indeed, the I/O model does not have a direct equivalent to this attribute. We note, however, that the use of the `World` value remains single-threaded.

For the Haskell semantics we take a particular view of the IO monad and include an explicit representation of the world in the program so that we can directly state the required properties. The World type is defined as above, and a new IO type is wrapped around it to represent the IO monad.

```
:: IO a = IO (World -> (World, a))
```

The usual set of monadic operators ("bind", "seq" and "return") are provided, along with rules for a desugaring of Haskell's idiomatic do notation that will allow the Haskell program to be rewritten in terms of this IO monad definition.

```
return v = retf where retf = IO (\w -> (w,v))

(IO f1) >>= ac2 = IO bindf
      where bindf w =
              let (w1,v) = (f1 w)
                  (IO f2) = (ac2 v)
              in  (f2 w1)
```

Note that we choose a model for the monad that introduces an explicit state value (here called "World"). We do this in order to allow explicit statements to be made regarding the world state.

The implementation we have chosen is a standard representation of a monad which manages state, as used in [12], [10]. It satisfies the necessary laws to be considered a monad in the Haskell sense.

This choice of an implementation for the IO monad should not be taken as a limitation of the proofs. The only properties we require are that the sequencing be correct (as required by the monad laws), so that there is an unambiguous state available at the necessary points in the proof, and that the state be preserved between I/O actions. It seems most convenient to maintain this state explicitly within the monad so that it is directly available when required.

We introduce the usual set of map manipulation operations (such as override) and give semantics to the necessary I/O operations. For instance:

```
exec nm cmd = IO (\(p,k) -> ((override nm (k+1) p, k+1),()))
```

This operation `override` corresponds to the † operator introduced earlier, and indicates that the map `p` is having its mapping from `nm` replaced.

In the Haskell proof the use of the monadic operators (`>>=`, `>>` and `return`) presents a problem. These operators are used to enforce the single threading of the world value by disallowing any other function access to the explicit world value. This single threading is a necessary property of any implementation, but when attempting to produce our proofs it is necessary to refer directly to that value and inspect it. This is necessary because the properties that we wish to establish via the proofs are properties of that world value, and it will be necessary to trace the transformations applied to the world in order to verify that the property holds. One solution to this problem is to carefully unwrap the monadic value each time the world must be inspected, and re-wrap it again before the next proof step is taken. While possible, this approach requires an inconvenient degree of mechanical work. Instead, we provide a number of new operators related to the standard monadic combinators. These operators can be used to lift a world value out of a monadic computation so that it can be inspected and manipulated in a proof. The three most interesting of these operators are:

- `>=>`, called "after", an operator which applies a monadic `IO` action to a world value, effectively performing the requested action and producing a new world. The function can be trivially defined:

  ```
  (>=>) :: World -> (IO a) -> (World, a)
  w >=> (IO f) = (f w)
  ```

- `>->`, called "world-after", an operator which transforms a world value using an IO action. The result of this operation is a new world value which represents the changes made.

  ```
  (>->) :: World -> (IO a) -> World
  w >-> act = fst (w >=> act)
  ```

- `>~>`, called "value-after", the corresponding operator to `>->`, which transforms a value but does not retain the new world value that was produced.

  ```
  (>~>) :: World -> (IO a) -> a
  w >~> act = snd (w >=> act)
  ```

These operators can be seen in action in section Sect. 8.1 where they are used to make statements about the before- and after-execution state of the world. Note that we can safely define and use these operators in our *proof* since we are working with a type correct program, which is therefore safely single-threaded. These operators would not be safe if added into a functional language, but are appropriate for reasoning.

8 Proofs About Make

The subjects of the proofs performed can be placed into five distinct categories (the proof numbering scheme is taken from [4]):

1. Proofs relating to `pre_make`, the general precondition for make. `pre_make` states a number of simple properties about the world (for instance, that the clock maintained in the world state has a later time than any of the files in the filesystem) and the dependency tree. This precondition captures several assumptions which are not expressed in the I/O specification itself. The proofs in this category mostly show that once `pre_make` holds, it continues to hold under various transformations.
2. Proofs relating to the structure of the dependency tree. The `pre_make` precondition requires the dependency tree used in `make` to maintain certain properties, which these proofs establish (for instance, the property that if two targets are equal then their subtrees are also equal. This proof effectively states that whenever a filename appears more than once in a makefile the dependencies must be the same both times). The proofs in this category are solely tree manipulation proofs and do not use the I/O model of section Sect. 6.

3. Proofs which make general statements regarding the I/O model and the operation of `make` in that world (for instance, a proof that if a filename "n" does not appear in the dependency tree then running make will not affect that file). These proofs establish invariants and theorems for `make`.
4. Proofs related to the sequencing of I/O operations over the execution lifetime of `make`; for instance, the proof that after running `make` files will age or remain unchanged (they will not get younger).
5. Proofs of high-level properties (in a sense, the interesting properties) of `make`, for instance the proof that following a run of `make` none of the dependencies will be older than the target.

We make a number of assumptions in order to simplify the process of reasoning about the programs, most of which are captured in a predicate `pre_make` which is used as a precondition. A few assumptions are also encoded in the model of the I/O system. The essential assumptions are:

- The dependency graph is a directed acyclic graph with the special property that all nodes with repeated names also share identical subtrees (that is, cycles have been converted into duplications, and filenames are not repeated any other way).
- At the start of the program, the world-clock is later than any of the times in the filesystem (that is, no file has a future date). This property is required only to make the expression of various properties more elegant, as they would otherwise require additional side-conditions to eliminate postdated files.
- Program execution, as performed by exec, has no observable effect on the filesystem other than updating the time of a single, specifically named file.

In general the proofs will require that the precondition `pre_make` is true, and are expressed as consequences of that condition.

8.1 Formal Statement of Properties

In order to commence the proof a formal statement of the property to be proved is produced, generally in terms of application of `make` to some arbitrary world (although some proofs are statements of general properties of the dependency trees and do not involve the world value).

Haskell formulations of two formal statements, along with natural language descriptions of the properties, are:

1. `(pre_make t w) ==> (deps_older (w >-> make t) t)`
   Following an invocation of `make` the target will be newer (or at least will have the same time) as its dependencies.
2. ```
   (pre_make t w) && (n `notElem` (allnames t)) ==>
       (filesSame [n] w (w >-> make t))
   ```
   If a given file is not mentioned in the makefile (and therefore in the dependency graph) then it will remain unchanged following an invocation of `make`.
   ```

The function `filesSame` used in that definition states that a sequence of files have not had their modification times changed between two worlds:

```
filesSame :: [Name] -> World -> World -> Bool
filesSame ns w1 w2 = all fileSame ns
 where fileSame n = (w1 >~> getFileTime n)==(w2 >~> getFileTime n)
```

The Clean language expressions of the formal statements are very similar to the Haskell statements with suitable changes to reflect the different I/O system. For example, the first property listed above is expressed as

```
(pre_make t w) ==> (deps_older (snd (make t w)) t)
```

in the Clean proofs, and the second is

```
(pre_make t w) && (notElem n (allnames t)) ==>
   (filesSame [n] w (fst (make t w)))
```

Note that the operators `>->`, etc. are needed in the Haskell theorems to introduce the worlds over which we are quantifying, but in Clean the world appears explicitly as a variable and so no special machinery is needed in order to refer to it. Nevertheless, it is sometimes convenient to introduce definitions for these operators in Clean; see the definition on page 81. Some implications of the syntactic and semantic correspondences between Clean and Haskell are discussed in Sect. 8.2.

8.2 Sketches of Sample Proofs

In general the proof bodies are too large to be included here, and can be found in [4]. For consistency we use the proof numbering scheme of that document when it is necessary to refer to proofs. We show a representative proof and discuss the general approaches taken, in order to support the conclusions.

The proofs generally proceed by rewrites of the statements using the formal semantics of the appropriate language referred to in Sect. 7, and a number of the basic proofs are used to "bootstrap" more sophisticated reasoning techniques (**HL.2.13**, for instance, is concerned with proving the validity of a form of induction). We show here an outline of the critical lemma required by Theorem **H.1**, which establishes that files which are not mentioned in the makefile will not be affected by runs of `make`. As indicated by the prefix **H**, this is a proof about the Haskell program (Clean proofs and lemmas are prefixed by the letter **C**). We begin with the formal statement of the required property:

```
(pre_make t w) && (n `notElem` (allnames t)) ==>
  (filesSame [n] w (w >-> make t))
```

We proceed by structural induction on `t`, starting as usual with the base case:

Base Case: `t = (Leaf n1)`
  ⟨ defn. of `make` on leaves (**HL.4.1.2** ⟩
`(w >-> make (Leaf n1)) == w`

⇒ ⟨ **HL.5.1** (`filesSame` is an equivalence relation) ⟩

```
(filesSame [n] w (w >-> make (Leaf n1)))
```

⇒ ⟨ adding pre-condition ⟩

```
(pre_make t w) && (n 'notElem' (allnames t)) ==>
  (filesSame [n] w (w >-> make t))
```

Inductive Case: `t = (Target n1 m ts)` We proceed then to the inductive case:
⟨ Inductive hypothesis ⟩

```
all (\t1->FORALL w1: (pre_make t1 w1)&&(n 'notElem' (allnames t1))
   ==> (filesSame [n] w1 (w1 >-> make t1))) ts
```

⇒ ⟨ Firstly, let `ws` = `trace make ts w`. Then, instantiating all `w1` in the inductive hypothesis ⟩

```
all (\(t1,w1) -> (pre_make t1 w1) &&  (n 'notElem' (allnames t1))
    ==> (filesSame [n] w1 (w1 >-> make t1))) (zip ts ws)
```

The trace structure referred to in the hint is introduced by `trace` which will repeatedly apply `make`, but returns not only the final `World` value which results, but all intermediate `World` values as well; this allows us to reason about the individual applications of make. The appropriate definition of `trace` for the Haskell proof is:

```
trace :: (a -> IO b) -> [a] -> World -> [World]
trace a [] w = [w]
trace a (p:ps) w = (w : (trace a ps (w >-> a p)))
```

The proof continues:
⇒ ⟨ Assuming local `pre_make` pre-condition, and using **HL.3.4** ⟩

```
all (\(t1,w1) -> (n 'notElem' (allnames t1))
    ==> (filesSame [n] w1 (w1 >-> make t1))) (zip ts ws)
```

⇒ ⟨ Also, since `((allnames t1) 'subset' (allnames t))`, assuming the second local pre-condition yields: ⟩

```
all (\(t1,w1) -> (filesSame [n] w1 (w1 >-> make t1))) (zip ts ws)
```

= ⟨ rewriting, using `trace` properties. ⟩

```
all (\(w1,w2) -> filesSame [n] w1 w2)) (zip ws (tail ws))
```

⇒ ⟨ Since `filesSame` is an equivalence relation (**HL.5.1**): ⟩

```
(filesSame [n] w (last ws))
```

= ⟨ **HL.3.4.2** (`trace` properties) ⟩

```
(filesSame [n] w (w >-> update_deps ts))
```

⇒ ⟨ Adding `make` defn. (**HL.4.1.3**) ⟩

```
(w >-> make t) ==  (w >-> do {
    ctime <- getFileTime n1; mtimes <- update_deps ts;
    if (ctime >= (newest mtimes)) then do {exec n1 m;
                                            getFileTime n1}
                                   else return ctime;})
&& (filesSame [n] w (w >-> update_deps ts))
```

If `(ctime >= (newest mtimes))`

```
(w >-> make t) == (w >-> do {
    ctime <- getFileTime n1;
    mtimes <- update_deps ts;
    exec n1 m;
    getFileTime n1;})
&& (filesSame [n] w (w >-> update_deps ts))
```

= ⟨ `getFileTime` defn. ⟩

```
(w >-> make t) == (w >-> do {update_deps ts;exec n1 m})
&& (filesSame [n] w (w >-> update_deps ts))
```

⇒ ⟨ and, since from initial `filesSame` pre-condition, `n/=n1` ⟩

```
(w >-> make t) == (w >-> do {update_deps ts;exec n1 m})
&& (filesSame [n] w (w >-> update_deps ts))
&& (filesSame [n] (w >-> update_deps ts)
   (w >-> do {update_deps ts;exec n1 m}))
```

⇒ ⟨ **HL.5.1** ⟩

```
(filesSame [n] (w >-> make t))
```

If `(ctime < newest mtimes):`

```
(w >-> make t) ==
  (w >-> do {
    ctime <- getFileTime n1;
    mtimes <- update_deps ts;
    return ctime;})
&& (filesSame [n] w (w >-> update_deps ts))
```

= ⟨ `getFileTime` defn., monad properties ⟩

```
    (w >-> make t) ==
      (w >-> update_deps ts)
    && (filesSame [n] w (w >-> update_deps ts))
```

⇒ ⟨ substitution ⟩

```
    (filesSame [n] (w >-> make t))
```

End-If

⟨ Adding assumed pre-conditions ⟩

```
(pre_make t w) && (n `notElem` (allnames t)) ==>
  (filesSame [n] w (w >-> make t))
```

In order to prove the same property for the Clean program we produce a similar statement of the required property:

```
(pre_make t w) ==> (deps_older (snd (make t w)) t)
```

and proceed inductively as we did for the Haskell proof. There are some minor syntactic differences in the Clean proof, for instance the case analysis in the inductive case is produced by guarded equations in the body of make (rather than an `if-` expression), giving:

```
letb (times,w) = update_deps depends w in
  letb (this_time,w) = filedate n w in
    filedate n (exec c w)
```

in place of the monadic body offered in the Haskell program (here `letb` refers to a "let-before" structure which semantically matches the Clean hash-let notation). Despite this superficial difference the structure of the reasoning in the Clean proof is essentially identical to the structure of the Haskell proof. Provision of suitable definitions of some of the reasoning operators such as:

```
(>->) :: World (World -> (World,a)) -> World
(>->) w f = fst (f w)

(>~>) :: World (World -> (World,a)) -> a
(>~>) w f = snd (f w)
```

can make the proofs textually similar (and in some cases, identical).

9 Conclusions

Our first conclusion is that reasoning about I/O systems is made much easier by the provision of suitable domain-specific models of the I/O system. The simple model of the filesystem used in this study is well suited to establishing various interesting properties of `make` and does not include any unnecessary or distracting details about file contents. It is likely that similar domain specific models for other programs can be derived from richer I/O system models by filtering the models based on the I/O primitives that are used in solving a specific problem.

We also observed that the provision of a suitable set of mathematical tools which represent either commonly performed program actions, or common reasoning patterns in the proof, simplify the proof process. In particular, the apparent need to manipulate the structured IO monad during proofs that need to inspect the action of side-effects on the world value can be removed by the provision of suitable operators, such as `>->` and `>=>`. By removing the need to manipulate the IO monad directly these operators simplify the production of proofs about the effects of programs. Furthermore these operators represent basic abstractions for I/O-performing programs, such as "world after execution" and semantically equivalent operations can be provided for I/O systems other than the monadic. This means that proofs expressed in terms of these operators will sometimes be reusable when establishing properties of programs in other systems. This means that a suitable set of reasoning operators can provide a unifying framework for reasoning about I/O in various I/O systems.

In [2] we explored a program which manipulated a small part of the world filesystem component, namely a single file. This lead us to a tentative conclusion that the explicit environment passing style of Clean programs was easier to reason about because (i) we could confine our attention to the small portion of the world state under consideration, and (ii) because we did not have the small overhead of unwrapping the monad.

However, the case study presented here differs crucially in that (i) the program involves the state of the entire filesystem at every step, and (ii) we have developed a set of operators which simplify the proofs in both paradigms. We can conclude that for this case study, the differences in reasoning overhead between the two paradigms are too small to be of any concern.

As to the question of how the reasoning techniques of [2] scale when applied to larger programs, it is clear to us that as the programs become more complex some new techniques are required to deal with the additional complexity, for instance, the `trace` operation, but that the basic approach works well.

9.1 Future Work

We intend investigating further the potential of reasoning about side-effects performed by functional programs, with the intention of proving correctness properties of the programs. It will also be necessary to perform further case studies on suitably sized programs to establish how general the properties found here are, and to determine how the proof approaches taken here generalise.

The production of a more complete I/O model with techniques for filtering out aspects of that model that are not required for specific proofs will probably be a requirement of further case studies.

The identification of more reasoning operators and proof abstraction techniques will be required to simplify the production of proofs which are currently quite lengthy. It will also be important to produce more sophisticated mechanisms for modelling the error handling techniques used (particular the exception based approach of Haskell).

One technique to manage the length of the more complex proofs would be machine assistance. Embedding a functional definition of the I/O model being used, such as that described in Sect. 6, into a theorem prover suited to reasoning about functional programs (for example, Sparkle [7]) would be an interesting exercise and may help to make the size of more complex proofs tractable.

Acknowledgements

The authors wish to thank the delegates of IFL2002 and the members of the Foundations and Methods group at TCD, whose comments and suggestions have greatly improved the quality of this paper.

References

1. Andrew Butterfield and Glenn Strong. Comparing i/o proofs in three programming paradigms: a baseline. Technical Report TCD-CS-2001-28, University of Dublin, Trinity College, Department of Computer Science, August 2001.

2. Andrew Butterfield and Glenn Strong. Proving correctness of programs with i/o — a paradigm comparison. In Markus Mohnen Thomas Arts, editor, *Proceedings of the 13th International Workshop, IFL2001*, number LNCSn2312 in Lecture Notes in Computer Science, pages 72–87. Springer–Verlag, 2001.
3. Richard M. Stallman and Roland McGrath. *GNU Make: A Program for Directing Recompilation, for Version 3.79.* Free Software Foundation, 675 Mass Ave, Cambridge, MA 02139, USA, Tel: (617) 876-3296, USA, 2000.
4. Malcolm Dowse, Glenn Strong, and Andrew Butterfield. Proving "`make`" correct: I/o proofs in two functional languages. Technical Report TCD-CS-2003-03, Trinity College, Dublin, 2003. http://www.cs.tcd.ie/publications/tech-reports/reports.03/TCD-CS-2003-03.pdf.
5. Paul Hudak, Simon L. Peyton Jones, and Philip Wadler (editors). Report on the programming language haskell, a non-strict purely functional language (version 1.2). *SIGPLAN Notices*, Mar, 1992.
6. Stuart I. Feldman. Make-a program for maintaining computer programs. *Software - Practice and Experience*, 9(4):255–65, 1979.
7. Maarten de Mol, Marko van Eekelen, and Rinus Plasmeijer. Sparkle: A functional theorem prover. In Markus Mohnen Thomas Arts, editor, *Proceedings of the 13th International Workshop, IFL2001*, number LNCS2312 in Lecture Notes in Computer Science, page 55. Springer–Verlag, 2001.
8. Rinus Plasmeijer and Marko van Eekelen. Concurrent clean version 2.0 language report. `http://www.cs.kun.nl/~clean/`, December 2001.
9. Erik Barendsen and Sjaak Smetsers. Uniqueness typing for functional languages with graph rewriting semantics. *Mathematical Structures in Computer Science*, 6(6):579–612, 1996.
10. Philip Wadler. Monads for functional programming. In M. Broy, editor, *Program Design Calculi: Proceedings of the 1992 Marktoberdorf International Summer School.* Springer-Verlag, 1993.
11. He Jifeng, C. A. R. Hoare, M. Fränzle, M. Müller-Ulm, E.-R. Olderog, M. Schenke, A. P. Ravn, and H. Rischel. Provably correct systems. In H. Langmaack, W.-P. de Roever, and J. Vytopil, editors, *Formal Techniques in Real Time and Fault Tolerant Systems*, volume 863, pages 288–335. Springer-Verlag, 1994.
12. Andrew D. Gordon. *Functional Programming and Input/Output.* PhD thesis, University of Cambridge, August 1992.
13. Mícheál Mac an Airchinnigh. *Conceptual Models and Computing.* PhD thesis, University of Dublin, Trinity College, Department of Computer Science, 1990.
14. Arthur Hughes. *Elements of an Operator Calculus.* PhD thesis, University of Dublin, Trinity College, Department of Computer Science, 2000.

Gast: Generic Automated Software Testing

Pieter Koopman, Artem Alimarine, Jan Tretmans, and Rinus Plasmeijer

Nijmegen Institute for Computer and Information Science, The Netherlands
{pieter,alimarin,tretmans,rinus}@cs.kun.nl

Abstract. Software testing is a labor-intensive, and hence expensive, yet heavily used technique to control quality. In this paper we introduce Gast, a fully automatic test tool. Properties about functions and datatypes can be expressed in first order logic. Gast automatically and systematically generates appropriate test data, evaluates the property for these values, and analyzes the test results. This makes it easier and cheaper to test software components. The distinguishing property of our system is that the test data are generated in a systematic and generic way using generic programming techniques. This implies that there is no need for the user to indicate how data should be generated. Moreover, duplicated tests are avoided, and for finite domains Gast is able to prove a property by testing it for all possible values. As an important side-effect, it also encourages stating formal properties of the software.

1 Introduction

Testing is an important and heavily used technique to measure and ensure software quality. It is part of almost any software project. The testing phase of typical projects takes up to 50% of the total project effort, and hence contributes significantly to the project costs. Any change in the software can potentially influence the result of a test. For this reason tests have to be repeated often. This is error-prone, boring, time consuming, and expensive.

In this paper we introduce a tool for automatic software testing. Automatic testing significantly reduces the effort of individual tests. This implies that performing the same test becomes cheaper, or one can do more tests within the same budget. In this paper we restrict ourselves to *functional testing*, i.e. examination whether the software obeys the given specification.

In this context we distinguish four steps in the process of functional testing: 1) *formulation of a property* to be obeyed: what has to be tested; 2) *generation of test data*: the decision for which input values the property should be examined, 3) *test execution*: running the program with the generated test data, and 4) *test result analysis*: making a verdict based on the results of the test execution.

The introduced Generic Automatic Software Test system, Gast, performs the last three steps fully automatically. Gast generates test data based on the types used in the properties, it executes the test for the generated test values, and gives an analysis of these test results. The system either produces a message that the property is proven, or the property has successfully passed the specified number of tests, or Gast shows a counterexample.

R. Peña and T. Arts (Eds.): IFL 2002, LNCS 2670, pp. 84–100, 2003.

GAST makes testing easier and cheaper. As an important side-effect it encourages the writing of properties that should hold. This contribute to the documentation of the system. Moreover, there is empirical evidence that writing specifications on its own contributes to the quality of the system [16].

GAST is implemented in the functional programming language CLEAN[14]. The primary goal is to test software written in CLEAN. However, it is not restricted to software written in CLEAN. Functions written in other languages can be called through the foreign function interface, or programs can be invoked.

The properties to be tested are expressed as functions in CLEAN, they have the power of first order predicate logic. The specifications can state properties about individual functions and datatypes as well as larger pieces of software, or even about complete programs. The definition of properties and their semantics are introduced in Section 3.

Existing automatic test systems, such as QuickCheck [3,4], use random generation of test data. When the test involves user-defined datatypes, the tester has to indicate how elements of that type should be generated. Our test system, GAST, improves both points. Using systematic generation of test data, duplicated tests involving user-defined types do not occur. This makes even proofs possible. By using a generic generator the tester does not have to define how elements of a user-defined type have to be generated. Although GAST has many similarities with QuickCheck, it differs in the language to specify properties (possibilities and semantics), the generation of test data and execution of tests (by using generics), and the analysis of test results (proofs). Hence, we present GAST as a self–contained tool. We will point out similarities and differences between the tools whenever appropriate.

Generic programming deals with the universal representation of a type instead of concrete types. This is explained in Section 2. Automatic data generation is treated in Section 4. If the tester wants to control the generation of data explicitly, he is able to do so (Section 7).

After these preparations, the test execution is straightforward. The property is tested for the generated test data. GAST uses the code generated by the CLEAN compiler to compute the result of applying a property to test data. This has two important advantages. First, there cannot exist semantic differences between the ordinary CLEAN code and the interpretation of properties. Secondly, it keeps GAST simple. In this way we are able to construct a light-weight test system. This is treated in Section 5. Next, test result analysis is illustrated by some examples. In Section 7 we introduce some additional tools to improve the test result analysis. Finally, we discuss related work and open issues and we conclude.

2 Generic Programming

Generic programming [7,8,1,6] is based on a universal tree representation of datatypes. Whenever required, elements of any datatype can be transformed to and from that universal tree representation. The generic algorithm is defined on this tree representation. By applying the appropriate transformations, this generic algorithm can be applied to any type.

Generic programming is essential for the implementation of GAST. However, users do not have to know anything about generic programming. The reader who wants to get an impression of GAST might skip this Section on first reading.

Generic extensions are currently developed for Haskell [10] and CLEAN [14]. In this paper we will use CLEAN without any loss of generality.

2.1 Generic Types

The universal type is constructed using the following type definitions [1][1].

```
:: UNIT        = UNIT                 // leaf of the type tree
:: PAIR    a b = PAIR a b             // branch in the tree
:: EITHER a b = LEFT a | RIGHT b // choice between a and b
```

As an example, we give two algebraic datatypes, `Color` and `List`, and their generic representation, $\texttt{Color}_g$ and $\texttt{List}_g$. The symbol `:==` in the generic version of the definition indicates that it are just type synonyms, they do not define new types.

```
::Color = Red | Yellow | Blue // ordinary algebraic type definition
::Color_g :== EITHER (EITHER UNIT UNIT) UNIT // generic representation

::List a = Nil | Cons a (List a)
::List_g a :== EITHER UNIT (PAIR a (List a))
```

The transformation from the user-defined type to its generic counterpart are done by automatically generated functions like[2]:

```
ColorToGeneric :: Color -> EITHER (EITHER UNIT UNIT) UNIT
ColorToGeneric Red    = LEFT (LEFT UNIT)
ColorToGeneric Yellow = LEFT (RIGHT UNIT)
ColorToGeneric Blue   = RIGHT UNIT

ListToGeneric :: (List a) -> EITHER UNIT (PAIR a (List a))
ListToGeneric Nil          = LEFT UNIT
ListToGeneric (Cons x xs) = RIGHT (PAIR x xs)
```

The generic system automatically generates these functions and their inverses.

2.2 Generic Functions

Based on this representation of types one can define generic functions. As example we will show the generic definition of equality[3].

```
generic gEq a   :: a a -> Bool
gEq{|UNIT|}           _          _          = True
gEq{|PAIR|}    fa fx (PAIR a x) (PAIR b y) = fa a b && fx x y
gEq{|EITHER|} fl fr (LEFT x)    (LEFT y)    = fl x y
gEq{|EITHER|} fl fr (RIGHT x)   (RIGHT y)   = fr x y
gEq{|EITHER|} _  _  _           _           = False
gEq{|Int|}            x          y          = x == y
```

[1] CLEAN uses additional constructs for information on constructors and record fields.

[2] We use the direct generic representation of result types instead of the type synonyms $\texttt{Color}_g$ and $\texttt{List}_g$ since it shows the structure of result more clearly.

[3] We only consider the basic type `Int` here. Other basic types are handled similarly.

The generic system provides additional arguments to the instances for PAIR and EITHER to compare instances of the type arguments (a and b in the definition).

In order to use this equality for Color an instance of gEq for Color must be derived by: derive gEq Color. The system generates code equivalent to

```
gEq{|Color|} x y = gEq{|EITHER|} (gEq{|EITHER|} gEq{|UNIT|} gEq{|UNIT|})
                   gEq{|UNIT|} (ColorToGeneric x) (ColorToGeneric y)
```

The additional arguments needed by gEq{|EITHER|} in gEq{|Color|} are determined by the generic representation of the type Color: $\texttt{Color}_g$.

If this version of equality is not what you want, you can always define your own instance of gEq for Color, instead of deriving the default.

The infix version of this generic equality is defined as:

```
(===) infix 4 :: !a !a -> Bool | gEq{|*|} a
(===) x y = gEq{|*|} x y
```

The addition |C a to a type is a class restriction: the type a should be in class C. Here it implies that the operator === can only be applied to type a, if there exists a defined or derived instance of gEq for a.

This enables us to write expressions like Red === Blue. The necessary type conversions form Color to $\texttt{Color}_g$ need not to be specified, they are generated and applied at the appropriate places by the generic system.

It is important to note that the user of types like Color and List need not be aware of the generic representation of types. Types can be used and introduced as normally; the static type system also checks the consistent use of types as usual.

3 Specification of Properties

The first step in the testing process is the formulation of properties in a formalism that can be handled by GAST. In order to handle properties from first order predicate logic in GAST we represent them as functions in CLEAN. These functions can be used to specify properties of single functions or operations in CLEAN, as well as properties of large combinations of functions, or even of entire programs.

Each property is expressed by a function yielding a Boolean value. Expressions with value True indicates a successful test, False indicates a counter example. This solves the famous *oracle problem*: how do we decide whether the result of a test is correct.

The arguments of such a property represent the universal variables of the logical expression. Properties can have any number of arguments, each of these arguments can be of any type.

In this paper we will only consider well-defined and finite values as test data. Due to this restriction we are able to use the *and*-operator (&&) and *or*-operator (||) of CLEAN to represent the logical operators *and* ($\wedge$) and *or* ($\vee$) respectively.

Our first example involves the implementation of the logical or-function using only a two-input nand-function as basic building element.

```
or :: Bool Bool -> Bool
or x y = nand (not x) (not y) where not x = nand x x
```

The desired property is that the value of this function is always equal to the value of the ordinary or-operator, `||`, from CLEAN. That is, the `||`-operator serves as specification for the new implementation, `or`. In logic, this is:

$$\forall x \in Bool \,.\, \forall y \in Bool \,.\, x||y = or\, x\, y$$

This property can be represented by the following function in CLEAN. By convention we will prefix property names by `prop`.

```
propOr :: Bool Bool -> Bool
propOr x y = x||y == or x y
```

The user invokes the testing of this property by the main function:

```
Start = test propOr
```

GAST yields `Proof: success for all arguments after 4 tests` for this property. Since there are only finite types involved the property can be proven by testing.

For our second example we consider the classical implementation of stacks:

```
:: Stack a :== [a]

pop :: (Stack a) -> Stack a
pop [_:r] = r

top :: (Stack a) -> a
top [a:_] = a

push :: a (Stack a) -> Stack a
push a s = [a:s]
```

A desirable property for stacks is that after pushing some element onto the stack, that element is on top of the stack. Popping an element just pushed on the stack yields the original stack. The combination of these properties is expressed as:

```
propStack :: a (Stack a) -> Bool | gEq{|*|} a
propStack e s = top (push e s) === e && pop (push e s) === s
```

This property should hold for any type of stack-element. Hence we used polymorphic functions and the generic equality, `===`, here. However, GAST can only generate test data for some concrete type. Hence, we have to specify which type GAST should use for the type argument `a`. For instance by:

```
propStackInt :: (Int (Stack Int) -> Bool)
propStackInt = propStack
```

In contrast to properties that use overloaded types, it actually does not matter much which concrete type we choose. A polymorphic property will hold for elements of any type if it holds for elements of type `Int`. The test is executed by `Start = test propStackInt`. GAST yields: `Passed after 1000 tests`. This property involves the very large type integer and the infinite type stack, so only testing for a finite number of cases, here 1000, is possible.

In `propOr` we used a reference implementation (`||`) to state a property about a function (`or`). In `propStack` the desired property is expressed directly as a relation between functions on a datatype. Other kind of properties state relations between the input and output of functions, or use model checking based properties. For instance, we have tested a system for safe communication over unreliable channels by an alternating bit protocol with the requirement that the sequence of received messages should be equal to the input sequence of messages.

The implication operator, $\Rightarrow$, is often added to predicate logic. For instance $\forall x. x \geq 0 \Rightarrow (\sqrt{x})^2 = x$. We can use the law $p \Rightarrow q = \neg p \vee q$ to implement it:

```
(===>) infix 1 :: Bool Bool -> Bool
(===>) p q = ~p || q
```

In Section 7.1 we will return to the semantics and implementation of $p \Rightarrow q$

In first order predicate logic one also has the existential quantifier, $\exists$. If this is used to introduce values in a constructive way it can be directly transformed to local definitions in a functional programming language, for instance as: $\forall x. x \geq 0 \Rightarrow \exists y. y = \sqrt{x} \wedge y^2 = x$ can directly be expressed using local definitions.

```
propSqrt :: Real -> Bool
propSqrt x = x >=0 ===> let y = sqrt x in y*y == x
```

In general it is not possible to construct an existentially quantified value. For instance, for a type *Day* and a function *tomorrow* we require that each day can be reached: $\forall day. \exists d.\ tomorrow\ d = day$. In GAST this is expressed as:

```
propSurjection :: Day -> Property
propSurjection day = Exists \d = tomorrow d === day
```

The success of the `Exists` operator depends on the types used. The property `propSurjection` will be proven by GAST. Also for recursive types it will typically generate many successful test case, due to the systematic generation of data. However, for infinite types it is impossible to determine that there does not exists an appropriate value (although only completely undefined tests are a strong indication of an error).

The only task of the tester is to write properties, like `propOr`, and to invoke the testing by `Start = test propOr`. Based on the type of arguments needed by the property, the test system will generate test data, execute the test for these values, and analyze the results of the tests. In the following three sections we will explain how GAST works. The tester does not have to know this.

3.1 Semantics of Properties

For GAST we extend the standard operational semantics of CLEAN. The standard reduction to weak head normal form is denoted as $whnf\,[\![\ e\ ]\!]$. The additional rules are applied after this ordinary reduction. The implementation will follow these semantics rules directly. The possible results of the evaluation of a property are the values **Suc** for success, and **CE** for counterexample. In these rules $\lambda\, x.p$ represents any function (i.e. a partially parameterized function, or a lambda-expression). The evaluation of a property, $Eval\,[\![\ p\ ]\!]$, yields a list of results:

$$Eval\,[\![\ \lambda\, x.p\ ]\!] = [r | v \leftarrow genAll; r \leftarrow Eval\,[\![\ (\lambda\, x.p)\, v\ ]\!]\,] \quad (1)$$

$$Eval\,[\![\ \mathbf{True}\ ]\!] = [\,\mathbf{Suc}\,] \quad (2)$$

$$Eval\,[\![\ \mathbf{False}\ ]\!] = [\,\mathbf{CE}\,] \quad (3)$$

$$Eval\,[\![\ e\ ]\!] = Eval\,[\![\ whnf\,[\![\ e\ ]\!]\ ]\!] \quad (4)$$

To test property p we evaluate $Test\,[\![\ p\ ]\!]$. The rule $An\,[\![\ l\ ]\!]\,n$ analysis a list of test results In rule 5, N is the maximum number of tests. There are three possible test results: **Proof** indicates that the property holds for all well-defined values of the argument types, **Passed** indicated that the property passed N tests without finding a counterexample, **Fail** indicates that a counterexample is found.

$$Test\,[\![\ p\ ]\!] = An\,[\![\ Eval\,[\![\ whnf\,[\![\ p\ ]\!]\ ]\!]\ ]\!]\,N \tag{5}$$
$$An\,[\![\ [\,]\ ]\!]\,n = \mathbf{Proof} \tag{6}$$
$$An\,[\![\ l\ ]\!]\,0 = \mathbf{Passed} \tag{7}$$
$$An\,[\![\ [\,\mathbf{CE} : rest\,]\ ]\!]\,n = \mathbf{Fail} \tag{8}$$
$$An\,[\![\ [\,r : rest\,]\ ]\!]\,n = An\,[\![\ rest\ ]\!]\,(n-1), \text{if}\, r \neq \mathbf{CE} \tag{9}$$

The most important properties of this semantics are:

$$Test\,[\![\ \lambda x.p\ ]\!] = \mathbf{Proof} \Rightarrow \forall v.(\lambda x.p)v \tag{10}$$
$$Test\,[\![\ \lambda x.p\ ]\!] = \mathbf{Fail} \Rightarrow \exists v.\neg(\lambda x.p)v \tag{11}$$
$$Test\,[\![\ p\ ]\!] = \mathbf{Passed} \Leftrightarrow \forall r \in (take\,N\,Eval\,[\![\ p\ ]\!]\,).r \neq \mathbf{CE} \tag{12}$$

Property 10 state that GAST only produces **Proof** if the property is universal valid. According to 11, the system yields only **Fail** if a counter example exists. Finally, the systems yields **Passed** if the first N tests does not contain a counterexample. These properties can be proven by induction and case distinction from the rules 1 to 9 given above. Below we will introduce some additional rules for $Eval\,[\![\ p\ ]\!]$, in such a way that these properties are preserved.

The semantics of the `Exists`-operator is:

$$Eval\,[\![\ \mathbf{Exists}\ \lambda\,x.p\ ]\!] = One\,[\![\ [r|v \leftarrow genAll; r \leftarrow Eval\,[\![\ (\lambda\,x.p)\,v\ ]\!]\,]\,]\!]\,M \tag{13}$$
$$One\,[\![\ [\,]\ ]\!]\,m = [\,\mathbf{CE}\,] \tag{14}$$
$$One\,[\![\ l\ ]\!]\,0 = [\,\mathbf{Undef}\,] \tag{15}$$
$$One\,[\![\ [\,\mathbf{Suc} : rest\,]\ ]\!]\,m = [\,\mathbf{Suc}\,] \tag{16}$$
$$One\,[\![\ [\,r : rest\,]\ ]\!]\,m = One\,[\![\ rest\ ]\!]\,(m-1), \text{if}\, r \neq \mathbf{Suc} \tag{17}$$

The rule $One\,[\![\ l\ ]\!]$ scans a list of semantic results, it yields success if the list of results contains at least one success within the first M results. As soon as one or more results are rejected the property cannot be proven anymore. It can, however, still successfully test the property for N values. To ensure termination also the number of rejected test is limited by an additional counter. These changes for $An\,[\![\ l\ ]\!]$ are implemented by `analyse` in Section 6.

4 Generating Test Data

To test a property, step 2) in the test process, we need a list of values of the argument type. GAST will evaluate the property for the values in this list.

Since we are testing in the context of a referentially transparent language, we are only dealing with pure functions: the result of a function is completely determined by its arguments. This implies that repeating the test for the same arguments is useless: referential transparency guarantees that the results will be identical. GAST should prevent the generation of duplicated test data.

For finite types like `Bool` or non-recursive algebraic datatypes we can generate all elements of the type as test data. For basic types like `Real` and `Int`, generating all elements is not feasible. There are far too many elements, e.g. there are 2^{32} integers on a typical computer. For these types, we want GAST to generate some common border values, like 0 and 1, as well as random values of the type. Here, preventing duplicates is usually more work (large administration) than repeating the test. Hence, we do not require that GAST prevents duplicates here.

For recursive types, like list, there are infinitely many instances. GAST is only able to test properties involving these types for a finite number of these values. Recursive types are usually handled by recursive functions. Such a function typically contains special cases for small elements of the type, and recursive cases to handle other elements. In order to test these functions we need values for the special cases as well as some values for the general cases. We achieve this by generating a list of values of increasing size. Preventing duplicates is important here as well.

The standard implementation technique in functional languages would probably make use of classes to generate, compare and print elements of each datatype involved in the tests [3]. Instances for standard datatypes can be provided by a test system. User-defined types however, would require user-defined instances for all types, for all classes. Defining such instances is error prone, time consuming and boring. Hence, a class based approach would hinder the ease of use of the test system. Special about GAST is that we use generic programming techniques such that one general solution can be provided once and for all.

To generate test data, GAST builds a list of generic representations of the desired type. The generic system transforms these generic values to the type needed. Obviously, not any generic tree can be transformed to instances of a given type. For the type `Color` only the trees `LEFT (LEFT UNIT)`, `LEFT (RIGHT UNIT)`, and `RIGHT UNIT` represent valid values. The additional type–dependent argument inserted by the generic system (see the `gEq` example shown above) provides exactly the necessary information to guide the generation of values.

To prevent duplicates we record the tree representation of the generated values in the datatype `Trace`.

```
:: Trace = Unit | Pair [(Trace,Trace)] [(Trace,Trace)]
         | Either Bool Trace Trace | Int [Int] | Done | Empty
```

A single type `Trace` is used to record visited parts of the generic tree (rather than the actual values or their generic representation), to avoid type incompatibilities.

The type `Trace` looks quite different from the ordinary generic tree since we record *all* generated values in a single tree. An ordinary generic tree just represents *one* single value.

New parts of the trace are constructed by the generic function `generate`. The function `nextTrace` prepares the trace for the generation of the next element from the list of test data.

The function genAll uses generate to produce the list of all values of the desired type. It generates values until the next trace indicates that we are done.

```
genAll :: RandomStream -> [a] | generate{|*|} a
genAll rnd = g Empty rnd
where g Done rnd = []
      g t    rnd = let (x, t2, rnd2) = generate{|*|} t rnd
                       (t3, rnd3)    = nextTrace t2 rnd2
                   in [x: g t3 rnd3]
```

For recursive types, the generic tree can grow infinitely. Without detailed knowledge about the type, one cannot determine where infinite branches occur. This implies that any systematic depth-first strategy to traverse the tree of possible values can fail to terminate. Moreover, small values appear close to the root of the generic tree, and have to be generated first. Any depth–first traversal will encounter these values too late. A left-to-right strategy (breath–first) will favor values in the left branches and vice versa. Such a bias in any direction is undesirable.

In order to meet all these requirements, nextTrace uses a random choice at each Either in the tree. The RandomStream, a list of pseudo random values, is used to choose. If the chosen branch appears to be exhausted, the other branch is explored. If both branches cannot be extended, all values in this subtree are generated and the result is Done. The generic representation of a type is a balanced tree, this guarantees an equal distribution of the constructors if multiple instances of the type occur (e.g. [Color] can contain many colors).

The use of the Tree prevents duplicates, and the random choice prevents a left–to–right bias. Since small values are represented by small trees the will occur very likely soon in the list of generated values.

An element of the desired type is produced by genElem using the random stream. Left and Right are just sensible names for the Boolean values.

```
nextTrace (Either _ tl tr) rnd
    = let (b, rnd2) = genElem rnd in
      if b  (let (tl‘, rnd3) = nextTrace tl rnd2 in
             case tl‘ of
               Done     = let (tr‘, rnd4) = nextTrace tr rnd3 in
                          case tr‘ of
                            Done = (Done, rnd4)
                            _    = (Either Right tl tr‘, rnd4)
               _        = (Either Left tl‘ tr, rnd3))
            (let (tr‘, rnd3) = nextTrace tr rnd2 in
             case tr‘ of
               Done     = let (tl‘, rnd4) = nextTrace tl rnd3 in
                          case tl‘ of
                            Done = (Done, rnd4)
                            _    = (Either Left tl‘ tr, rnd4)
               _        = (Either Right tl tr‘, rnd3))
```

The corresponding instance of generate follows the direction indicated in the trace. When the trace is empty, it takes a boolean from the random stream and creates the desired value as well as the initial extension of the trace.

```
generic generate a :: Trace RandomStream -> (a, Trace, RandomStream)
generate{|EITHER|} fl fr Empty rnd
  = let (f,rnd2) = genElem rnd in
    if f (let (l,tl,rnd3) = fl Empty rnd2
          in  (LEFT  l, Either Left  tl Empty, rnd3))
         (let (r,tr,rnd3) = fr Empty rnd2
          in  (RIGHT r, Either Right Empty tr, rnd3))
generate{|EITHER|} fl fr (Either left tl tr) rnd
  | left = let (l,tl2,rnd2) = fl tl rnd
           in  (LEFT  l, Either left tl2 tr, rnd2)
         = let (r,tr2,rnd2) = fr tr rnd
           in  (RIGHT r, Either left tl tr2, rnd2)
```

For `Pair` the function `nextTrace` uses a breath–first traversal of the tree implemented by a queue. Two lists of tuples are used to implement an efficient queue. The tuple containing the current left branch the next right branch, as well as the tuple containing the next left branch and an empty right branch are queued.

4.1 Generic Generation of Functions as Test Data

Since CLEAN is a higher order language it is perfectly legal to use a function as an argument or result of a function. Also in properties, the use of higher order functions can be very useful. A well-known property of the function `map` is:

```
propMap :: (a->b) (b->c) [a] -> Bool | gEq{|*|} c
propMap f g xs = map g (map f xs) === map (g o f) xs
```

In order to test such a property we must choose a concrete type for the polymorphic arguments. Choosing `Int` for all type variables yields:

```
propMapInt :: ((Int->Int) (Int->Int) [Int] -> Bool)
propMapInt = propMap
```

This leaves us with the problem of generating functions automatically. Functions are not datatypes and hence cannot be generated by the default generic generator. Fortunately, the generic framework provides a way to create functions. We generate functions of type `a->b` by an instance for `generate{|(->)|}`. First, a list of values of type `b` is generated. The argument of type `a` is transformed in a generic way to an index in this list. For instance, a function of type `Int -> Color` could look like `\a = [Red,Yellow,Blue] !! (abs a % 3)`. Like all test data, `genAll` generates a list of these functions. Currently GAST does not keep track of generated functions in order to prevent duplicates, or to stop after generating all possible functions. Due to space limitations we omit details.

5 Test Execution

Step 3) in the test process is the test execution. The implementation of an individual test is a direct translation of the given semantic rules introduced above. The type class `Testable` contains the function `evaluate` which directly implements the rules for $Eval[\![p]\!]$.

```
class Testable a where evaluate :: a RandomStream Admin -> [Admin]
```

In order to be able to show the arguments used in a specific test, we administrate the arguments represented as strings as well as the result of the test in a record called `Admin`. There are three possible results of a test: undefined (`UnDef`), success (`Suc`), and counter example found (`CE`).

```
:: Admin = {res::Result, args::[String]}
:: Result = UnDef | Suc | CE
```

Instances of `TestArg` can be argument of a property. The system should be able to generate elements of such a type (`generate`) and to transform them to string (`genShow`) in order to add them to the administration.

```
class TestArg a | genShow{|*|}, generate{|*|} a
```

The semantic equations 2 and 3 are implemented by the instance of evaluate for the type `Bool`. The fields `res` and `arg` in the record `ad` (for administration) are updated.

```
instance Testable Bool
where evaluate b rs ad = [{ad & res=if b Suc CE, args=reverse ad.args}]
```

The rule for function application, semantic equation 1, is complicated slightly by administrating function arguments.

```
instance Testable (a->b) | Testable b & TestArg a
where evaluate f rs admin
        = let (rs, rs2) = split rs  in  forAll f (gen rs) rs2 admin
forAll f list rs ad
 = diagonal [  evaluate (f a) (genRandInt s) {ad&args=[show a:ad.args]}
            \\ a<-list & s<-rs]
```

The function `diagonal` takes care of a *fair* order of tests. For a 2-argument function f, the system generates two sequences of arguments, call them $[a, b, c, ..]$ and $[u, v, w, ..]$ respectively. The order of tests is $f\,a\,u, f\,a\,v, f\,b\,u, f\,a\,w, f\,b\,v, f\,c\,u, ..$ rather than $f\,a\,u, f\,a\,v, f\,a\,w, .., f\,b\,u, f\,b\,v, f\,b\,w, ...$

6 Test Result Evaluation

The final step, step 4), in the test process is the evaluation of results. The system just scans the generated list of test results as indicated by $An [\![\, l \,]\!]$. The only extension is the showing of the number and arguments of the current test before the test result is evaluated. In this way the tester of GAST is able to identify the data causing an runtime error or taking a lot of time. A somewhat simplified version of the function `test` is:

```
test :: p -> [String] | Testable p
test p = analyse (evaluate p RandomStream newAdmin) maxTests MaxArgs
where analyse :: [Admin] Int Int -> [String]
      analyse [] n m = ["\nProof: success for all arguments"]
      analyse l  0 m = ["\nPassed ",toString maxTests," tests"]
      analyse l  n 0 = ["\nPassed ",toString maxArgs," arguments"]
      analyse [res:rest] n m
        = [blank,toString (maxTests-n+1),":":showArgs res.args
           case res.res of
             UnDef  = analyse rest n (m-1)
             Suc    = analyse rest (n-1) (m-1)
             CE     = ["\nCounterexample: ": showArgs res.args []]]
```

7 Additional Features

In order to improve the power of the test tool, we introduce some additional features. These possibilities are realized by combinators (functions) that manipulate the administration. We consider the following groups of combinators: 1) an improved implication, $p \Rightarrow q$, that discards the test if p does not hold; 2) combinators to collect information about the actual test data used; 3) combinators to apply user-defined test data instead of generated test data.

QuickCheck provides a similar implication combinator. Our collection of test data relays on generic programming rather than a build–in `show` function. QuickCheck does not provide a similar generation of user–defined test data.

7.1 Implication

Although the implication operator `===>` works correctly, it has an operational drawback: if p does not hold, the property $p \Rightarrow q$ holds and is counted as a successful test. This operator is often used to put a restriction on arguments to be considered, as in $\forall x.x \geq 0 \Rightarrow (\sqrt{x})^2 = x$. Here we wants only to consider tests where $x \geq 0$ holds, in other situations the test should not be taken into account. This is represented by the result *undefined*. We introduce the operator `==>` for this purpose.

$$Eval\,[\![\,\mathbf{True} ==> p\,]\!] = Eval\,[\![\,p\,]\!] \tag{18}$$

$$Eval\,[\![\,\mathbf{False} ==> p\,]\!] = [\,\mathbf{Rej}\,] \tag{19}$$

If the predicate holds the property `p` is evaluated, otherwise we explicitly yield an undefined result. The implementation is:

```
(==>) infixr 1 :: Bool p -> Property | Testable p
(==>) c p
    | c = Prop (evaluate p)
        = Prop (\rs ad = [{ad & res = Undef}])
```

Since `==>` needs to update the administration, the property on the right-hand side is a datatype holding an update–function instead of a Boolean.

```
:: Property = Prop (RandomStream Admin -> [Admin])

instance Testable Property
where evaluate (Prop p) rs admin = p rs admin
```

The operator `==>` can be used as `===>` in `propSqrt` above. The result of executing `test propSqrt` is `Counter-example found after 2 tests: 3.07787e-09`. The failure is caused by the finite precision of reals.

7.2 Information about Test Data Used

For properties like `propStack`, it is impossible to test all possible arguments. The tester might be curious to known more about the actual test data used in a test. In order to collect labels we extend the administration `Admin` with a field `labels` of type `[String]`. The system provides two combinators to store labels:

```
label    ::      l p -> Property | Testable p & genShow{|*|} l
classify :: Bool l p -> Property | Testable p & genShow{|*|} l
```

The function `label` always adds the given label; `classify` only adds the label when the condition holds. The function `analyse` is extended to collect these strings, orders them alphabetically, counts them and computes the fraction of tests that contain this label. The label can be an expression of any type, it is converted to a string in a generic way (by `genShow{|*|}`).

These functions do not change the semantics of the specification, their only effect is the additional information in the report to the tester.

$$Eval\,[\![\ \textbf{label}\ l\ p\ ]\!] = Eval\,[\![\ p\ ]\!]\ \text{ adds } l \text{ to the administration} \quad (20)$$
$$Eval\,[\![\ \textbf{classify True}\ l\ p\ ]\!] = Eval\,[\![\ \textbf{label}\ l\ p\ ]\!] \quad (21)$$
$$Eval\,[\![\ \textbf{classify False}\ l\ p\ ]\!] = Eval\,[\![\ p\ ]\!] \quad (22)$$

We will illustrate the use of these functions. It is possible to view the exact test data used for testing the property of stacks by

```
propStackL :: Int (Stack Int) -> Property
propStackL e s = label (e,s) (top (push e s)===e && pop (push e s)===s)
```

A possible result of testing `propStackL` for only 4 combinations of arguments is:

```
Passed 4 tests
(0,[0,1]): 1 (25%)
(0,[0]): 1 (25%)
(0,[]): 1 (25%)
(1,[]): 1 (25%)
```

The function `classify` can, for instance, be used to count the number of empty stacks occurring in the test data.

```
propStackC e s = classify (isEmpty s) s (propStack e s)
```

A typical result for 200 tests is:

```
Passed 200 tests
[]: 18 (9%)
```

7.3 User-Defined Test Data

GAST generates sensible test data based on the type of the arguments. Sometimes the tester is not satisfied with this behavior. This occurs for instance if very few generated elements obey the condition of an implication, cause enormous calculations, or overflow.

The property `propFib` states that the value of the efficient version of the Fibonacci function, `fibLin`, should be equal to the value of the well-known naive definition, `Fib`, for non-negative arguments.

```
propFib n = n>=0 ==> fib n == fibLin n

fib 0 = 1
fib 1 = 1
fib n = fib (n-1) + fib (n-2)
```

```
fibLin n = f n 1 1
where f 0 a b = a
      f n a b = f (n-1) b (a+b)
```

One can prevent long computations and overflow by limiting the size of the argument by an implication. For instance:

```
propFib n = n>=0 && n<=15 ==> fib n == fibLin n
```

This is a rather unsatisfactory solution. The success rate of tests in the generated list of test values will be low, due to the condition many test results will be undefined (since the condition of the implication is false). In those situations it is more efficient if the user specifies the test values, instead of letting the GAST generate it. For this purpose the combinator `For` is defined. It can be used to test the equivalence of the Fibonacci functions for all arguments from 0 to 15:

```
propFibR = propFib For [0..15]
```

Testing yields `Proof: success for all arguments after 16 tests.`

The semantics of the `For` combinator is:

$$Eval [\![\lambda x.p \textbf{ For } list]\!] = [r|v \leftarrow list; r \leftarrow Eval [\![(\lambda x.p)\, v]\!]] \qquad (23)$$

The implementation is very simple using the machinery developed above:

```
(For) infixl 0 :: (x->p) [x] -> Property | Testable p & TestArg x
(For) p list = Prop (forAll p list)
```

Apart from replacing or combining the automatically generated test date by his own tests, the user can control the generation of data by adding an instance for his type to `generate`, or explicitly transform generated data-types (e.g. lists to balanced trees).

8 Related Work

Testing is labor-intensive, boring and error-prone. Moreover, it has to be done often by software engineers. Not surprisingly, a large number of tools has been developed to automate testing. See [15] for an (incomplete) overview of existing tools. Although some of these tools are well engineered, none of them gives automatic support like GAST does for *all* steps of the testing process. Only a few tools are able to generate test data for arbitrary types based on the types used in properties [2].

In the functional programming world there are some related tools. The tool QuickCheck [3,4] has similar ambitions as our tool. Distinguishing features of our tool are: the generic generation of test data for arbitrary types (instead of based on a user-defined instance of a class), and the systematic generation of test data (instead of random). As a consequence of the systematic generation of test data, our system is able to detect that all possible values are tested and hence the property is proven. Moreover, GAST offers a complete implementation of first order predicate logic.

Auburn [13] is a tool for automatic benchmarking of functional datatypes. It is also able to generate test data, but not in a systematic and generic way. Runtime errors and counterexamples of a stated property can be detected.

HUnit [9] is the Haskell variant of JUnit [11] for Java. JUnit defines how to structure your test cases and provides the tools to run them. It executes the test defined by the user. Tests are implemented in a subclass of `TestCase`.

An important area of automatic test generation is testing of reactive systems, or control-intensive systems. In these systems the interaction with the environment in terms of stimuli and responses is important. Typical examples are communication protocols, embedded systems, and control systems. Such systems are usually modelled and specified using some kind of automaton or state machine. There are two main approaches for automatic test generation from such specifications. The first is based on Finite State Machines (FSM), and uses the theory of checking experiments for Mealy-machines [17]. Several academic tools exist with which tests can be derived from FSM specifications, e.g., PHACT/THE CONFORMANCE KIT [18]. Although GAST is able to test the input/output relation of an FSM (see Section 3), checking the actual state transitions requires additional research.

The second approach is based on labelled transition systems and emanates from the theory of concurrency and testing equivalences [19]. Tools for this approach are, e.g., TGV [20], TESTCOMPOSER [21], TESTGEN [22], and TORX [23,24]. State-based tools concentrate on the control flow, and cannot usually cope with complicated data structures. As shown above GAST is able to cope with these data structures.

9 Discussion

In this paper we introduce GAST, a generic tool to test software. The complete code, about 600 lines, can be downloaded from `www.cs.kun.nl/~pieter`. The tests are based on properties of the software, stated as functions based on first order predicate logic. Based on the types used in these properties the system automatically generates test data in a systematic way, checks the property for these generated values, and analyzes the results of these tests.

One can define various kind of properties. The functions used to describe properties are slightly more powerful than first order predicate logic (thanks to the combination of combinators and higher order functions) [5]. In our system we are able to express properties known under names as black-box tests, algebraic properties, and model based, pre- and post-conditional. Using the ability to specify the test data, also user-guided white-box tests are possible.

Based on our experience we indicate four kinds of errors spotted by GAST. The system cannot distinguish these errors. The tester has to analyze them.

1. Errors in the implementation; the kind of mistakes you expect to find.
2. Errors in the specification; in this situation the tested software also does not obey the given property. Analysis of the indicated counter example shows that the specification is wrong instead of the software. Testing improves the confidence in the accuracy of the properties as well as the implementation.
3. Errors caused by the finite precision of the computer used; especially for properties involving reals, e.g. `propSqrt`, this is a frequent problem. In general

we have to specify that the difference between the obtained answer and the required solution is smaller than some allowed error range.

4. Non-termination or run-time errors; although the system does not explicitly handle these errors, the tester notices that the error occurs. Since GAST lists the arguments before executing the test, the values causing the error are known. This appears to detect partially defined functions effectively.

The efficiency of GAST is mainly determined by the evaluation of the property, not by the generation of data. For instance, on a standard PC the system generates up to 100,000 integers or up to 2000 lists of integers per second. In our experience errors pop up rather soon, if they exist. Usually 100 to 1000 tests are sufficient to be reasonably sure about the validity of a property.

In contrast to proof-systems like SPARKLE [12], GAST is restricted to well-defined and finite arguments. In proof-systems one also investigates the property for non-terminating arguments, usually denoted as $\perp$, and infinite arguments (for instance a list with infinite length). Although it is possible to generate undefined and infinite arguments, it is impossible to stop the evaluation of the property when such an argument is used. This is a direct consequence of our decision to use ordinary compiled code for the evaluation of properties.

Restrictions of our current system are that the types should be known to the system (it is not possible to handle abstract types by generics); if there are restrictions on the types used they should be enforced explicitly; and world access is not supported. In general it is very undesirable when the world (e.g. the file system on disk) is effected by random tests.

Currently the tester has to indicate that a property has to be tested by writing an appropriate `Start` function. In the near future we want to construct a tool that extracts the specified properties from CLEAN modules and tests these properties fully automatically.

GAST is not restricted to testing software written in its implementation language, CLEAN. It is possible to call a function written in some other language through the foreign function interface, or to invoke another program. This requires an appropriate notion of types in CLEAN and the foreign languages and a mapping between these types.

Acknowledgements

We thank Marko van Eekelen, Maarten de Mol, Peter Achten, Susan Evens and the anonymous referees for their contribution to GAST and this paper.

References

1. A. Alimarine and R. Plasmeijer *A Generic Programming Extension for Clean.* IFL2001, LNCS 2312, pp.168–185, 2001.
2. G. Bernot, M.C. Gaudel, B.Marre: *Software Testing based on Formal Specifications: a theory and a tool*, Software Engineering Journal, 6(6), pp 287–405, 1991.

3. K. Claessen, J. Hughes. *QuickCheck: A lightweight Tool for Random Testing of Hasskell Programs*. International Conference on Functional Programming, ACM, pp 268–279, 2000. See also `www.cs.chalmers.se/~rjmh/QuickCheck`.
4. K. Claessen, J. Hughes. *Testing Monadic Code with QuickCheck*, Haskell Workshop, 2002.
5. M. van Eekelen, M. de Mol: *Reasoning about explicit strictness in a lazy language using mixed lazy/strict semantics*, Draft proceedings IFL2002, Report 127-02, Computer Science, Universidad Complutense de Madrid, pp 357–373, 2002.
6. R. Hinze and J. Jeuring. *Generic Haskell: Practice and Theory*, Summer School on Generic Programming, 2002.
7. R. Hinze, and S. Peyton Jones *Derivable Type Classes*, Proceedings of the Fourth Haskell Workshop, Montreal Canada, 2000.
8. Hinze, R. *Polytypic values possess polykinded types*, Fifth International Conference on Mathematics of Program Construction, LNCS 1837, pp 2–27, 2000.
9. HUnit home page: `hunit.sourceforge.net`
10. S. Peyton Jones, J. Hughes: *Report on the programming language Haskell 98 – A Non-strict, Purely Functional Language*, 2002 `www.haskell.org/onlinereport`.
11. JUint home page: `junit.sourceforge.net`
12. M. de Mol, M. van Eekelen, R. Plasmeijer. *Theorem Proving for Functional Programmers,* , LNCS 2312, pp 55–72, 2001. See also `www.cs.kun.nl/Sparkle`.
13. Graeme E. Moss and Colin Runciman. *Inductive benchmarking for purely functional data structures*, Journal of Functional Programming, 11(5): pp 525–556, 2001. Auburn home page: `www.cs.york.ac.uk/fp/auburn`
14. Rinus Plasmeijer and Marko van Eekelen: *Concurrent Clean Language Report (version 2.0)*, 2002. `www.cs.kun.nl/~clean`.
15. Maurice Siteur: *Testing with tools–Sleep while you are working*. See also `www.siteur.myweb.nl`.
16. J. Tretmans, K. Wijbrans, M. Chaudron: *Software Engineering with Formal Methods: The development of a storm surge barrier control system–revisiting seven myths of formal methods*, Formal Methods in System Design, 19(2), 195–215, 2001.
17. D. Lee, and M. Yannakakis, M *Principles and Methods for Testing Finite State Machines– A Survey*, The Proceedings of the IEEE, 84(8), pp 1090-1123, 1996.
18. L. Feijs, F. Meijs, J. Moonen, J. Wamel *Conformance Testing of a Multimedia System Using PHACT* in *Workshop on Testing of Communicating Systems 11* pp 193–210, 1998.
19. E. Brinksma, J. Tretmans *Testing Transition Systems: An Annotated Bibliography*", in *Modeling and Verification of Parallel Processes–*4th *Summer School MOVEP 2000* LNCS 2067, pp 186-195, 2001.
20. J. Fernandez, C. Jard, T. Jéron, C. Viho *Using On-the-Fly Verification Techniques for the generation of test suites*, LNCS 1102, 1996.
21. A. Kerbrat, T. Jéron, R. Groz *Automated Test Generation from SDL Specifications*, in *The Next Millennium–Proceedings of the* 9th *SDL Forum*, pp 135–152, 1999.
22. J. He, K. Turner *Protocol-Inspired Hardware Testing*, in *Int. Workshop on Testing of Communicating Systems 12* pp 131–147, 1999.
23. A. Belinfante, J. Feenstra, R. Vries, J. Tretmans, N. Goga, L. Feijs, S. Mauw, L. Heerink *Formal Test Automation: A Simple Experiment*, in *Int. Workshop on Testing of Communicating Systems 12* pp 179-196, 1999.
24. J. Tretmans, E. Brinksma *Côte de Resyste – Automated Model Based Testing*, in *Progress 2002 –* 3rd *Workshop on Embedded Systems*, pp 246–255, 2002.

Lazy Dynamic Input/Output in the Lazy Functional Language Clean*

Martijn Vervoort and Rinus Plasmeijer

Nijmegen Institute for Information and Computing Sciences
Toernooiveld 1, 6525 ED, Nijmegen, The Netherlands
{martijnv,rinus}@cs.kun.nl

Abstract. In this paper we explain how dynamics can be communicated between independently programmed Clean applications. This is an important new feature of Clean because it allows type safe exchange of both data and code. In this way mobile code and plug-ins can be realized easily. The paper discusses the most important implementation problems and their solutions in the context of a compiled lazy functional language. The implemented solution reflects the lazy semantics of the language in an elegant way and is moreover quite efficient. The resulting rather complex system in which dynamics can depend on other dynamics, is effectively hidden from the user by allowing her to view dynamics as "typed files" that can be manipulated like ordinary files.

1 Introduction

The new release of the Clean system [11] offers a hybrid type system with both static and dynamic typing. Any statically typed expression can in principle be converted into a dynamically typed expression i.e. a dynamic, and backwards.

The type stored in the dynamic, i.e. an encoding of the original static type, can be checked at run-time via a special pattern match after which the dynamic expression can be evaluated as efficiently as usual.

In this paper we discuss the storage and the retrieval of dynamics: any application can read a dynamic that has been stored by some other application. Such a dynamic can contain unevaluated function applications, i.e. closures, functions and types that are unknown to the receiving application. The receiving application therefore has to be extended with function definitions. Dynamics can be used to realize plug-ins, mobile code and persistency in a type safe way without loss of efficiency in the resulting code.

The integration of strongly typed lazy dynamic I/O in a compiled environment with minimal changes to the existing components of the system while maintaining efficiency and user-friendliness, requires a sophisticated design and implementation. This paper presents the most interesting problems and their solutions by means of examples.

* This work was supported by STW as part of project NWI.4411

R. Peña and T. Arts (Eds.): IFL 2002, LNCS 2670, pp. 101–117, 2003.

This work is based on earlier work by Cardelli [1] who introduced the theoretical foundations of dynamics. Marco Pil has extended and adapted it for Clean. In contrast to his work [9] and [10], this paper addresses the I/O aspects of dynamics. Dynamic I/O is the input and output of dynamics by appropriate extensions of the compilation environment and its run-time system.

Our contribution is that we have designed and implemented an efficient extension of the Clean compilation environment and its run-time system to support lazy dynamic I/O. The presented solution can also be applied to other lazy functional programming languages such as Haskell [5].

The outline of this paper is as follows. In section 2 we introduce the elementary operations of dynamics: packing and unpacking. In section 3 we introduce I/O of dynamics: dynamic I/O. The requirements and the architecture are presented in section 4. For reasons of efficiency, dynamics are divided into pieces. This is explained in section 5. This splitting up of dynamics can cause sharing problems. These are solved in section 6. In section 7 we explain how we have managed to hide the resulting complexity of the system from the user. The paper concludes with related work, conclusions and future work.

2 Elementary Language Operations on Dynamics

A dynamic basically is a typed container for an ordinary expression. The elementary operations on dynamics are packing and unpacking. In essence these elementary operations convert a statically typed expression into its dynamically typed equivalent and vice versa.

2.1 Packing a Typed Expression into a Dynamic

A dynamic is built using the keyword `dynamic`. Its arguments are the expression to be packed into a dynamic and, optionally, the *static* type `t` of that expression. The actual packing is done lazily. The resulting dynamic is of static type `Dynamic`. A few examples are shown below:

```
(dynamic True    :: Bool              ) :: Dynamic
(dynamic fib 3                        ) :: Dynamic
(dynamic fib     :: Int -> Int        ) :: Dynamic
(dynamic reverse :: A.a: [a] -> [a] ) :: Dynamic
```

A dynamic should at least contain:

- The expression to be packed, which is called the *dynamic expression* for the rest of this paper.
- An encoding of its static type `t` (either explicitly specified or inferred), which is called the *dynamic type* for the rest of this paper.

2.2 Unpacking a Typed Expression from a Dynamic

Before a dynamically typed expression enclosed in a dynamic can be used, it must be converted back into a statically typed expression and made accessible. This can be achieved by a run-time dynamic pattern match.

A dynamic pattern match consists of an ordinary pattern match and a type pattern match. First, the type pattern match, on the dynamic type is executed. Only if the type pattern match succeeds, the ordinary pattern match on the dynamic expression is performed. If the ordinary pattern match succeeds, the right hand side of an alternative is executed. Otherwise, evaluation continues with the next alternative. A small example is shown below:

```
f :: Dynamic -> Int
f (0 :: Int) = 0
f (n :: Int) = n * n + 1
f else       = 1
```

The dynamic pattern match of the first alternative requires the dynamic type to be an integer type and the dynamic expression to be zero. If both conditions are met, zero is returned. The second alternative only requires the dynamic type to be an integer. The third alternative handles all remaining cases.

The example below shows the dynamic version of the standard apply function:

```
dyn_apply :: Dynamic Dynamic -> Dynamic
dyn_apply (f :: a -> b) (x :: a) = dynamic (f x) :: b
dyn_apply else1         else2    = abort "dynamic type error"
```

The function takes two dynamics and tries to apply the dynamic expression of the first dynamic to the dynamic expression of the second. In case of success, the function returns the (lazy) application of the function to its argument in a new dynamic. Otherwise the function aborts.

The multiple occurrence of the type pattern variable `a` effectively forces unification between the dynamic types of the two input dynamics. If the first alternative succeeds, the application of the dynamic expression `f` to the dynamic expression `x` is type-safe.

3 Dynamic I/O: Writing and Reading Typed Expressions

Different programs can exchange dynamically typed expressions by using dynamic I/O. In this manner, plug-ins and mobile code can be realized. To achieve this, the system must be able to store and retrieve type definitions and function definitions associated with a dynamic. Among other things, this requires dynamic linking.

3.1 Writing a Dynamically Typed Expression to File

Any dynamic can be written to a file on disk using the `writeDynamic` function of type `String Dynamic *World -> *World`. In the producer example below a dynamic is created which consists of the application of the function `sieve` to an infinite list of integers. This dynamic is then written to file using the `writeDynamic` function.

Evaluation of a dynamic is done lazily. As a consequence, the application of `sieve` to the infinite list, is constructed but not evaluated because its evaluation is not demanded. We will see that the actual computation of a list of prime numbers will be triggered later by the consumer.

```
producer :: *World -> *World
producer world = writeDynamic "primes" (dynamic sieve [2..]) world
where
    sieve :: [Int] -> [Int]
    sieve [prime:rest] = [prime : sieve filter ]
    where
        filter = [ h \\ h <- rest | h mod prime <> 0 ]
```

More information than the dynamic expression and its type have to be stored at run-time, if the dynamic is to be used as a plug-in by applications other than its creating application. We also need:

- The function definitions required for the evaluation of the dynamic expression. A severe complication here is that these function definitions have been compiled to native machine code. When the dynamic is used, these compiled function definitions have to be added to the running application.
- The type definitions required for matching the dynamic type against the type pattern specified in the dynamic pattern. The type definitions are needed because different Clean applications may have different definitions of equally named types. A type definition check is only needed to check that equally named types are indeed equivalent.

In general this information is already known at compile-time, but it should be made accessible at run-time.

3.2 Reading a Dynamically Typed Expression from File

Any dynamic can be read from disk using the `readDynamic` function of type `String *World -> (Dynamic,*World)`. This `readDynamic` function is used in the consumer example below to read the earlier stored dynamic. The dynamic pattern match checks whether the dynamic expression is an integer list. In case of success the first 100 elements are taken. Otherwise the consumer aborts.

```
consumer :: *World -> [Int]
consumer world
    # (dyn, world) = readDynamic "primes" world
    = take 100 (extract dyn)
```

```
where
    extract :: Dynamic -> [Int]
    extract (list :: [Int]) = list
    extract else            = abort "dynamic type check failed"
```

To turn a dynamically typed expression into a statically typed expression, the following steps need to be taken:

1. Unify the dynamic type and the type pattern of the dynamic pattern match. If unification fails, the dynamic pattern match also fails.
2. Check the type definitions of equally named types from possibly different applications for structural equivalence provided that the unification has been successful. If one of the type definition checks fails, the dynamic pattern match also fails. Equally named types are equivalent iff their type definitions are syntactically the same (modulo α-conversion and the order of algebraic data constructors).
3. When evaluation requires the now statically typed expression, construct it and add the needed function definitions to the running application.

The addition of compiled function definitions and type definitions referenced by the dynamic being read is handled by the dynamic linker.

4 Architecture for Dynamic I/O

The architecture based on requirements listed in this section, is presented. The context it provides is used by the rest of this paper.

4.1 Requirements

Our requirements are:

- *Correctness.* We want the system to preserve the language semantics of dynamics: storing and retrieving an expression using dynamic I/O should not alter the expression and especially not its evaluation state.
- *Efficiency.* We want dynamic I/O to be efficient.
- *Preservation of efficiency.* We do not want any loss of efficiency compared to ordinary Clean programs not using dynamics, once a running program has been extended with the needed function definitions.
- *View dynamics as typed files.* We want the user to be able to view dynamics on disk as "typed files" that can be used without exposing its internal structure.

4.2 Architecture

For the rest of this paper, figure 1 provides the context in which dynamic I/O takes place.

The Clean source of an application consists of one or more compilation units. The Clean compiler translates each compilation unit into compiled function definitions represented as symbolic machine code and compiled type definitions. The compiled function and type definitions of all compilation units are stored in the application repository.

Application 1 uses the `writeDynamic` function to create a dynamic on disk. The dynamics refers to the application repository.

Application 2 uses the `readDynamic` function to read the dynamic from disk. If the evaluation of the dynamic expression is required after a successful dynamic pattern match, the dynamic expression expressed as a graph is constructed in the heap of the running application. The dynamic linker adds the referenced function and type definitions to the running application. Then the application resumes normal evaluation.

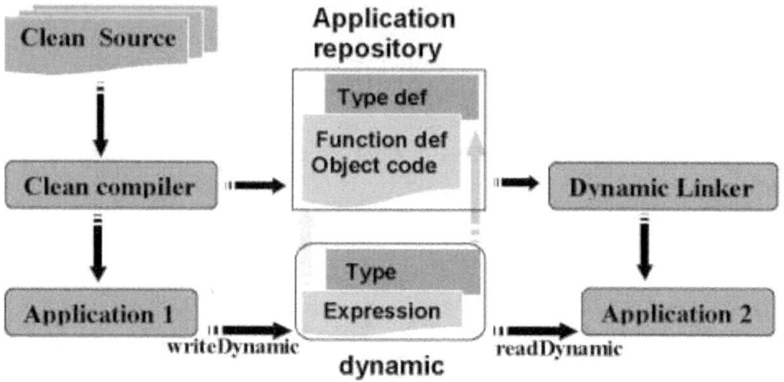

Fig. 1. Architecture of dynamic I/O

Some of the requirements are already (partially) reflected in the architecture:

- *Efficiency.* The figure shows that the dynamic expression and its dynamic type can be identified separately from each other. Therefore the rather expensive construction of the dynamic expression can be postponed until its dynamic type is successfully pattern matched. The next sections refine this *laziness* even more.
  The figure also shows that a dynamic does not contain the compiled function and type definitions. The dynamic merely *refers to* the repository which means that dynamics can share repositories and especially function definitions that have already been compiled. This *sharing* reduces the expensive cost of linking function definitions.
- *Preservation of efficiency.* As the figure shows *compiled* function definitions are used by dynamics. The very same function definitions are also used by ordinary Clean programs not using dynamic I/O. Therefore after dynamic I/O completes, the program is resumed at normal efficiency.

5 Partitions: Dynamic in Pieces

In this section, we explain that dynamics are not constructed in their entirety but in smaller pieces called *partitions*. This is sensible because often the evaluator does not need all pieces of a dynamic. As a consequence the expensive linking process of function definitions is postponed until required.

5.1 Dynamics are Constructed Piece by Piece

Up until now, we have implicitly assumed that dynamics are constructed in their entirety. But only the following steps need to be taken, to use a dynamic expression (nested dynamics may contain more dynamic expressions):

1. Read a dynamic type from file.
2. Decode the type from its string representation into its graph representation.
3. Do the unifications specified by the dynamic pattern match.

Only after successful unifications:

4. Read the dynamic expression from file.
5. Decode the expression from its string representation into its graph representation.

We have decided to construct a dynamic piece by piece for reasons of efficiency. In general the construction of a dynamic in its entirety is both unnecessary and expensive. For example when a dynamic pattern match fails, then it is unnecessary to construct its dynamic expression. Moreover, it is even expensive because it would involve the costly process of linking the compiled function definitions.

As a consequence, a dynamic which is represented at run-time as a graph, must be partitioned. The (nested) dynamic expressions and the dynamic types should be constructible from the dynamic by its partitions.

5.2 Partitions

Partitions are pieces of graph encoded as strings on disk which are added in their entirety to a running application. Partitions are:

- (parts of) a dynamic expressions.
- (parts of) a dynamic types.
- subexpressions shared between dynamic expressions.

In this paper we only present the outline of a naïve partitioning algorithm which colours the *graph* representing the dynamic to be encoded:

- A set of colours is associated with each node of the graph. A unique colour is assigned to each dynamic expression and to each dynamic type.

– If a node is reachable from a dynamic expression or from a dynamic type, then the colour assigned to that dynamic expression or that dynamic type is added to the colour set of that node.

We have chosen a partition to be a set of equally coloured graphs: the colour sets of the graph nodes must all be the same. This *maximizes* the size of a partition to reduce linker overhead. Any other definition of a partition would also do, as long as it contains only equally coloured nodes.

For example, consider the `Producer2` example below. After partitioning the `shared_dynamic` expression, the encoded dynamic consists of seven partitions. There are three dynamics involved. For each dynamic two partitions are created: one partition for the dynamic expression and one partition for its type. An additional partition is created for the shared tail expression.

```
Producer2 :: *World -> *World
Producer2 world = writeDynamic "shared_dynamic" shared_dynamic world
where
    shared_dynamic   = dynamic (first, second)
    first            = dynamic [1 : shared_expr ]
    second           = dynamic [2 : shared_expr ]
    shared_expr      = sieve [3..10000]
```

5.3 Entry Nodes

In general several different nodes within a partition can be pointed to by nodes of other partitions. A node of a partition is called an *entry* node iff it is being pointed to by a node of another partition. For the purpose of sharing, the addresses of entry nodes of constructed partitions have to be retained. The following example shows that a partition can have multiple entry nodes:

```
:: T = Single T | Double T T
f = dynamic (dynamic s1, dynamic s2)
where
    s1 = Single s2
    s2 = Double s1 s2
```

The nodes `s1` and `s2` form one partition because both nodes are reachable from the (nested) dynamics in the `f` function and from each other. Both nodes therefore have the same colour sets. Both nodes are pointed to by the nested dynamics, which makes them both entry nodes. Apart from cyclic references, multiple entry nodes can also occur when dynamics share at least two nodes without one node referencing the other.

5.4 Linking the Function Definitions of a Partition

The dynamic linker takes care of providing the necessary function definitions when evaluation requires a partition to be decoded. The decoding of a partition consists of:

1. *the linking of its* compiled *function definitions*. The references between the compilation units stored in the repositories are *symbolic*. The dynamic linker for Clean resolves these references into *binary* references. This makes the function definitions executable. The linker optimizes by only linking the needed function definitions and its dependencies.
2. *the construction of the graph from its partition*. The graph consists of a set of nodes and each node references a function definition i.e. a Clean function or a data constructor. The *encoded* references to function definitions of each node are resolved in *run-time* references to the earlier linked function definitions.

The dynamic linker has the following additional tasks:

- It checks the equivalence of equally named type definitions. This is used during unification and to preserve the semantics of ordinary pattern matches. The Clean run-time system identifies data constructors by unique addresses in memory. In case of equivalent type definitions, it must be ensured that equally named constructors are all identified by a single unique address. Therefore the dynamic linker guarantees that:
  - There is only a single implementation for equally named and structural equivalent types.
  - All references to data constructors e.g. in dynamic pattern matches, point to that single implementation.
- It presents dynamics to the user as typed files abstracting from the complex representation of a dynamic. Section 8 discusses this topic in more detail.

6 Sharing of Partitions

Partitioned dynamics may lose sharing. Efficiency can be increased by preserving sharing as much as possible. In this section we identify three cases in which sharing needs to be preserved. We conclude by discussing one solution for all cases to prevent loss of sharing.

6.1 Case 1: References between Dynamics on Disk

In this subsection, we show that sharing between dynamics on disk can be preserved. The example below extends the dynamic apply example by using the `readDynamic` and `writeDynamic` functions to perform I/O. The `fun`-dynamic from the file `application` (e.g. your favourite word-processor) and the `arg`-dynamic from the file `document` (e.g. the paper you are writing) are passed to the dynamic apply function `dyn_apply` which returns a new dynamic. The new dynamic is stored in the file result (e.g. a new version of your paper).

```
Start world
    # (fun, world) = readDynamic "application" world
    # (arg, world) = readDynamic "document" world
    = writeDynamic "result" (dyn_apply fun arg) world
```

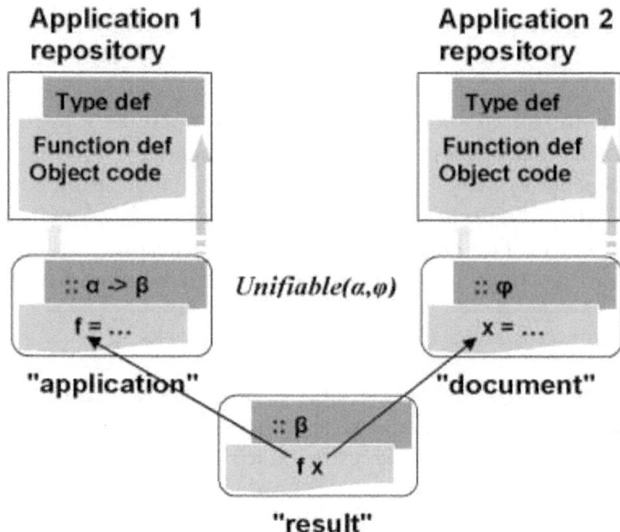

Fig. 2. Sharing between dynamics on disk after the dynamic apply

```
where
    dyn_apply :: Dynamic Dynamic -> Dynamic
    dyn_apply (f :: a -> b) (x :: a) = dynamic (f x) :: b
    dyn_apply else1         else2    = abort "dynamic type error"
```

The function application of `fun` to its argument `arg` *itself* is packed into the dynamic because the dynamic constructor is lazy in its arguments. Since the evaluation of `fun` and `arg` is not required, the system does not read them in at all.

For this example only the first three steps of subsection 5.1 have to be executed to use the dynamic expressions. The reason is that the dynamic expressions `f` and `x` were never required. We preserve the sharing between dynamics on disk by allowing dynamic expressions to be *referenced* from other dynamics on disk.

As figure 2 shows, the dynamic stored in the file `result` contains two references to the `application` and `document` dynamics. To be more precise these references refer to the dynamic expressions of both dynamics. In general a dynamic is distributed over several files. Section 7 abstracts from this internal structure by permitting dynamics to be viewed as typed files.

6.2 Case 2: Sharing within Dynamics at Run-Time

In this subsection, we show that the sharing of partitions at run-time can also be preserved. For example, the `Producer2` function of subsection 5.2 stores the dynamic `shared_dynamic` on disk. The stored dynamic is a pair of the two other dynamics `first` and `second`. The dynamic expressions of these nested dynamics both share the tail of a list called `shared_expr`.

The consumer application reads the dynamic written by the producer application. If the dynamic pattern matches succeed, the function returns the length of both lists.

```
Consumer2 :: *World -> *(Int, *World)
Consumer2 world
# (dyn,world) = readDynamic "shared_dynamic" world
= (g dyn,world)
where
    g :: Dynamic -> Int
    g ( (list1 :: [Int], list2 :: [Int]) :: (Dynamic,Dynamic) )
     = length list1 + length list2
```

The lists stored in the dynamic `shared_dynamic` are lazy: they are independently constructed from each other when evaluation requires one of the lists. The length of `list1` is computed after constructing its head (i.e. `1`) and its tail (which it shares with `list2`). Then the length of the second list is computed after constructing its head (i.e. `2`) and reusing the tail (shared with `list1`). In this manner sharing at run-time can be preserved.

In general, the order in which partitions are constructed is unpredictable because it depends on the evaluation order. Therefore partitions must be constructible in any order.

6.3 Case 3: Sharing and References within Dynamics on Disk

In this subsection, we show that sharing can also be preserved across dynamic I/O. It combines the preservation of sharing discussed in subsections 6.1 and 6.2. In contrast to the dynamic stored in the example of subsection 5.2, the first component of the dynamic stored by the `consumer_producer` function shown below has been completely evaluated. From the second tuple component *only* the tail which `list2` shares with the first component has been constructed. Its head is merely a reference to a partition of the dynamic `shared_dynamic`. Thus the newly created dynamic stores the same expression but in a more evaluated state.

```
consumer_producer :: *World -> *World
consumer_producer world
    # (dyn,world) = readDynamic "shared_dynamic" world
    # (list1,list2) = check dyn
    | length list1 <> 0          // force evaluation of list1
        # list_dynamic
            = dynamic (list1,list2)
        = writeDynamic "partially_evaluated_dynamic" list_dynamic world
where
    check :: Dynamic -> ([Int],[Int])
    check ( (list1 :: [Int], list2 :: [Int]) :: (Dynamic,Dynamic) )
        = (list1,list2)
```

The dynamic named `partially_evaluated_dynamic` is read by an also modified consumer example from the previous subsection. To compute the total length, it should only construct the head of the second list i.e. 2 because the shared tail expression constructed in the slightly modified consumer example of above can be *reused*.

To preserve sharing across dynamic I/O, the `consumer_producer` must also store on disk that the partition for the shared tail has already been constructed. *In this manner sharing within a dynamic can be preserved across dynamic I/O.*

6.4 A Solution to Preserve Sharing during Decoding

In this subsection we explain how dynamic expressions and dynamic types are decoded by inserting so-called decode-nodes for each dynamic expression or dynamic type while preserving sharing. A decode-node reconstructs its dynamic expression or its dynamic type when evaluated.

The decoding of a dynamic expression or a dynamic type may require the decoding of several partitions at once. For example, consider the `Consumer2` function of subsection 6.2: the dynamic expression `list1` extends over two partitions: a partition which contains the head and a partition containing its tail.

We have decided to construct a dynamic expression or a dynamic type in its entirety. For example when the function `length` is about to evaluate the list, the dynamic expression is constructed in its entirety by constructing the head and its tail from its two partitions. The other option would be to construct a partition at a time but this is not discussed in this paper.

Decode-nodes are implemented as *closure*-nodes i.e. a node containing an unevaluated function application to postpone evaluation until really required. Decode-nodes which refer to an entry node of the partition it decodes, are put at the lazy argument positions of the `dynamic`-constructor.
A decode node has the following arguments:

1. *An entry node of the* dynamic *partition.* Dynamic partitions are those partitions which are *directly* referenced from the lazy argument positions of the keyword `dynamic`. All other partitions are called *shared* partitions. An example of a shared partition is the partition for `shared_expr` of subsection 5.2.
2. *The list of entry nodes from already decoded partitions.* This list is used at run-time to preserve sharing within dynamics as discussed in subsection 6.2.

Upon decoding a partition via an entry-node, it is first checked whether the dynamic partition has already been decoded. In this case it is sufficient to return the address of the entry node to preserve sharing (see 6.2). Otherwise the dynamic partition must be decoded. After the shared partitions have been decoded in an appropriate order, the dynamic partition itself is decoded. The entry-nodes of decoded partitions are stored in the list of already decoded partitions. The address of the entry node of the dynamic partition is returned.

We now show how the sharing discussed in subsections 6.1 and 6.3 can be solved. To preserve the sharing of the former subsection, it is already sufficient

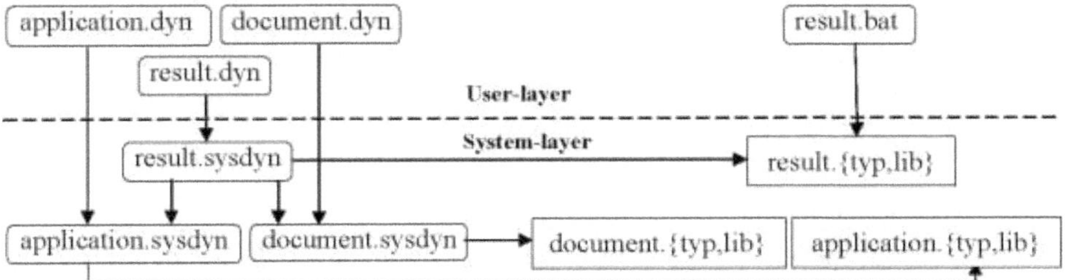

Fig. 3. System organization after executing the dynamic apply

to encode decode-nodes. To preserve the sharing of the latter subsection, the second argument of a decode-node must be encoded in a special way.

The dynamic `partially_evaluated_dynamic` of subsection 6.3 contains the *encoded* decode-node. The second argument of the decode-node only contains the shared tail `shared_expr` because it is shared between `list1` and the not yet decoded `list2`, and both lists are contained in the dynamic `list_dynamic`. In this manner sharing is preserved.

In general after encoding a dynamic *d*, the encoded second arguments of the decode-nodes of a nested dynamic *n* should only contain a subset of the already decoded partitions. This subset can be computed by only including those decoded partitions that are reachable from the decode-nodes of a dynamic *n* and leaving out the partitions which are not *re*-encoded in dynamic *d*. Therefore the list of encoded decode-nodes only contains those partitions which are already used within that newly created dynamic.

7 User View of Dynamics on Disk

The complexity of dynamics is hidden from the user by distinguishing between a user level and a hidden system level. Dynamics are managed as typed files by the users. Only for deletion and copying dynamics to another machine additional tool support is required.

7.1 The System Level

This layer contains the actual system dynamics with the extension *sysdyn* and the executable application repositories with the extensions *typ* and *lib*. A system dynamic may refer to other system dynamics and repositories. These files are all hidden and managed by the dynamic run-time system. User file access is hazardous and therefore not permitted. For example, deleting the system dynamic `document` renders the system dynamic `result` unusable.

All system dynamics and system repositories are stored and managed in a single system directory. This may quickly lead to name clashes; dynamics need to have unique names within the system directory.

We have chosen to solve the unique naming problem by assigning a unique 128-bit identifier to each system dynamic. The *MD5*-algorithm in [12] is used to compute a unique identifier. The generated unique names of system dynamics and repositories are hidden from the user.

7.2 The User Level

The user level merely contains links to the system layer. Links to system dynamics have the *dyn* extension and links to application repositories have the *bat* extension. These files may freely be manipulated (deleted, copied, renamed) by the user. This does not affect the integrity of the (system) dynamics.

Manipulation of user dynamics may have consequences for system dynamics and repositories, however. The following file operations need tool support:

- *The deletion of a user dynamic.* When the user deletes a user dynamic or a dynamic application, system dynamics and repositories may become garbage. These unreferenced dynamics and repositories can safely be removed from the system by a garbage collector. For example first deleting the user dynamic `document` does not create garbage in the system level but deleting the user dynamic `result` makes its system dynamic `result` garbage and also the system dynamic `document`.
- *The copying of a user dynamic to another machine.* When the user copies a user dynamic to another machine, its system dynamic and the other system dynamics and repositories it refers to, need to be copied too. The copying tool takes care of copying a dynamic and its dependencies. Using a network connection, it only copies dynamics and repositories not already present at the other end. The unique MD5-identification of dynamics makes this possible.

8 Related Work

There have been several attempts to implement dynamic I/O in a wide range of programming languages including the strict functional language Objective Caml [6], the lazy functional languages Staple [7] and Persistent Haskell [3], the orthogonal persistent imperative language Napier88 [8], the logic/functional language Mercury [4] and the multiple paradigm language Oz [13]. In standard Haskell only language support for dynamics is provided; it has therefore not been considered. The table below compares the different approaches:

Dynamic	Clean	Ocaml	Staple	Napier88	Mercury	Pers. Haskell	Oz
native code	+	+	−	+	+	+	−
data objects	+	+	+	+	+	+	+
closures/functions	+	−	+	+	−	+	+
application indep.	+	+/−	+	+	+/−	+	+
platform indep.	−	+/−	−	−	+/−	−	+
network	+	+/−	−	−	+/−	−	+
lazy I/O	+	−	−	−	−	−	−

Within the table + and – indicate the presence or the absence of a left column feature for dynamic I/O. A slashed table entry discriminates between data objects on the one hand and closures/functions on the other hand. For reasons of clarity the slashed entries –/– and +/+ are represented by respectively – or +. The table lists the following features:

- *Native code.* The presence of this feature means that dynamics can use compiled function definitions i.e. binary code.
- *Data objects.* The presence of this feature means that data objects i.e. without functions or function applications can be packed into a dynamic and unpacked from a dynamic.
- *Closures/functions.* The presence of this feature means that also function objects and closures i.e. postponed function applications can be packed into a dynamic and unpacked from a dynamic.
- *Application independence.* The presence of this feature means that dynamics can be exchanged between independent applications.
- *Platform independence.* The presence of this feature means that a dynamic has a platform independent representation. This also applies to the representation of (compiled) function definitions it uses.
- *Network.* The presence of this feature means that a dynamic can be exchanged between different machines.
- *Lazy I/O.* The presence of this feature means that a dynamic can be retrieved in pieces when evaluation requires it. Only languages with a run-time mechanism to postpone evaluation can implement this.

Objective Caml restricts dynamic I/O on closures/functions to one particular application provided that it is not recompiled. The Mercury implementation is even more restrictive: it does not support I/O on closures/functions. All other languages support dynamic I/O for closures/functions.

The persistent programming languages Persistent Haskell, Napier88 and Staple do not address the issue of exporting and importing of dynamics between different so called persistent stores. As a consequence the mobility of a dynamic is significantly reduced.

Although the Clean implementation is not yet platform independent, dynamics can be exchanged among different Windows-networked machines. The Mozart programming system offers the language Oz, which supports platform independent dynamics and network dynamics because it runs within a web-browser. However, currently the Oz-language is being interpreted.

Currently only Clean supports lazy dynamic I/O. In non-lazy functional language there is no mechanism to postpone evaluation which makes it impossible to implement lazy I/O in these languages.

9 Conclusions and Future Work

In this paper we have introduced dynamic I/O in the context of the compiled lazy functional language Clean. We have presented the most interesting aspects of the implementation by means of illustrative examples. Our implementation preserves the semantics of the language and in particular laziness and sharing. Acceptable efficiency is one of the main requirements for the design and implementation work and has indeed been realized. The resulting system described in this paper hides its complexity by offering a user-friendly interface. It allows the user to view dynamics as typed files. The resulting system is as far as we know unique in the world.

Dynamic I/O already has some interesting applications. A few examples: our group is working on visualizing and parsing of dynamics using the generic extension of Clean, extendible user-interfaces are created using dynamics, a typed shell which uses dynamics as executables has been created as a first step towards a functional operating system and a Hungarian research group uses dynamics to implement proof carrying code.

The basic implementation of dynamic I/O is nearly complete. However, a lot of work still needs to be done:

- *Increase of performance.* The administration required to add function definitions to a running application is quite large. By sharing parts of repositories e.g. the standard environment of Clean between dynamics, a considerable increase in performance can be realized.
- *Language support.* Several language features are not yet supported. These features include overloading, uniqueness typing, and abstract data types. Especially interesting from the dynamic I/O perspective are unique dynamics which would permit destructive updates of dynamics on disk.
- *Conversion functions.* The rather restrictive definition of type equivalence may result in problems when the required type definition and the offered type definition only differ slightly. For example, if a demanded `Colour`-type is defined as a subset of the offered `Colour`-type, then it would be useful to have a programmer defined conversion function from the offered type to the demanded type. Generics in [2] could help here.
- *Network dynamics.* In order to realize network dynamics both platform independence and the port of the implementation to other platforms are required.
- *Garbage collection of dynamically added function definitions.* This is a generalization of heap-based garbage-collection as used in functional languages. Traditionally only the heap area varies in size at run-time. Dynamic I/O makes also the code/data-areas grow and shrink. To prevent unnecessary run-time errors due to the memory usage of unneeded function definitions, garbage collection is also needed for function definitions.

Acknowledgments

We are grateful to Marco Pil for the more theoretical foundations on which dynamic I/O has been designed and implemented. We would also like to thank the Clean-group for taking part in discussions and for making numerous small changes all over the system, the Hungarian students Mátyás Ivicsics and Zoltan Várnagy for their contributions and the anonymous referees who reviewed this paper.

References

1. M. Abadi, L. Cardelli, B. Pierce, D. Rémy. *Dynamic typing in polymorphic languages*, Journal of Functional Programming 5(1):111-130, Cambridge University Press 1995.
2. A. Alimarine and R. Plasmeijer, *A Generic Programming Extension for Clean*, In Proc. of Implementation of Functional Languages, Älvsjö, Sweden, Arts Th., Mohnen M., Springer-Verlag, LNCS 2312, pages 168-185.
3. T. Davie, K. Hammond, J. Quintela, *Efficient Persistent Haskell*, In: Draft proceedings of the 10th workshop on the implementation of Functional Languages, pp. 183-194, University College London, September 1998.
4. F. Henderson, T. Conway, Z. Somogyi amd D. Jeffery, *The Mercury language reference manual*, Technical Report 96/10, Department of Computer Science, University of Melbourne, Melbourne, Australia, 1996.
5. S. P. Jones and J. Hughes (eds.) (1999), *Report on the Programming Language Haskell 98, A Non-strict Purely Functional Language.*
6. X. Leroy, D. Doligez, J. Garrigue, D. Rémy and J. Vouillon *The Objective Caml system release 3.04 Documentation and user's manual*, December 10, 2001 Institut National de Recherche en Informatique et en Automatique.
7. D. McNally, *Models for Persistence in Lazy Functional Programming Systems*, PhD Thesis, University of St Andrews Technical Report CS/93/9, 1993.
8. R. Morrison, A. Brown, R. Connor, Q. Cutts, A. Dearle, G. Kirby and D. Munro. *Napier88 Reference Manual (Release 2.2.1)*, University of St.Andrews, July 1996.
9. M.R.C. Pil, (1997) *First Class I/O*, In Proc. of Implementation of Functional Languages, 8th International Workshop, Selected Papers, Bad Godesberg, Germany, Kluge Ed., Springer Verlag, LNCS 1268, pp. 233-246.
10. M.R.C.Pil, (1999), *Dynamic types and type dependent functions*, In Proc. of Implementation of Functional Languages, London, UK, Hammond, Davie and Clack Eds. Springer-Verlag, Berlin, Lecture Notes in Computer Science 1595, pp 169-185.
11. R. Plasmeijer, M.C.J.D. van Eekelen (2001), *Language Report Concurrent Clean, Version 2.0 (Draft)* Faculty of mathematics and Informatics, University of Nijmegen, December 2001. Also available at www.cs.kun.nl/ clean/Manuals/manuals.html
12. R.L. Rivest, RFC 1321: *The MD5 Message-Digest Algorithm*, Internet Activities Board, 1992.
13. P. van Roy and S. Haridi, *Mozart: A Programming System for Agent Applications*, International Workshop on Distributed and Internet Programming with Logic and Constraint Languages, Part of International Conference on Logic Programming.

PolyAPM: Parallel Programming via Stepwise Refinement with Abstract Parallel Machines

Nils Ellmenreich and Christian Lengauer

Fakultät für Mathematik und Informatik, Universität Passau, Germany
{nils,lengauer}@fmi.uni-passau.de

Abstract. Writing a parallel program can be a difficult task which has to meet several, sometimes conflicting goals. While the manual approach is time-consuming and error-prone, the use of compilers reduces the programmer's control and often does not lead to an optimal result. With our approach, PolyAPM, the programming process is structured as a series of source-to-source transformations. Each intermediate result is a program for an Abstract Parallel Machine (APM) on which it can be executed to evaluate the transformation. We propose a decision tree of programs and corresponding APMs that help to explore alternative design decisions. Our approach stratifies the effects of individual, self-contained transformations and enables their evaluation during the parallelisation process.

1 Introduction

The task of writing a program suitable for parallel execution consists of several phases: identifying parallel behaviour in the algorithm, implementing the algorithm in a language that supports parallel execution and finally testing, debugging and optimising the parallel program. As this process is often lengthy, tedious and error-prone, languages have been developed that support high-level parallel directives and rely on dedicated compilers to do the low-level work correctly. Taking this approach to an extreme, one may refrain entirely from specifying any parallelism and use instead a parallelising compiler on a sequential program. The price for this ease of programming is a lack of control over the parallelisation process and, as a result, possibly code that is less optimised than its hand-crafted equivalent.

We can view the process of writing a parallel program as a sequence of phases, many of which have alternatives. Selecting a phase from among several alternatives and adjusting it is called a *design decision*.

Both of these opposing approaches – going through the whole parallelisation process manually or leaving the parallelisation to the compiler – are unsatisfactory with respect to the design decisions. Either the programmer has to deal with the entire complexity, which might be too big for a good solution to be found, or one delegates part or all of the process to a compiler which has comparatively little information to base decisions on.

R. Peña and T. Arts (Eds.): IFL 2002, LNCS 2670, pp. 118–133, 2003.

Even if a parallelising compiler honours user preferences to guide the compilation process, it is difficult to identify the effect of every single option on the final program. There is no feasible way of looking into the internals of a compiler and determining the effect of a design decision on the program.

To avoid the aforementioned drawbacks of current parallel program development paradigms, we propose an approach that strikes a balance between manual and automatic parallelisation. To bridge the gap between the algorithm and the final parallel program, we introduce a sequence of *abstract machines* that get more specific and closer to the target machine architecture as the compilation progresses. During the compilation, the program is undergoing a sequence of source-to-source transformations, each of which stands for a particular compilation phase and results in a program designed for a particular APM. This makes the compilation process more transparent since intermediate results become observable by the programmer. The transformations may be performed automatically, by hand or by a mixture of both. The observations made may influence the design decisions the programmer makes as the compilation progresses further. We have implemented simulators for the machines, thus enabling the programmer to evaluate the result of each transformation directly on the executing program. Our experience has been that this result structures parallel program development and that it helps evaluating the effects of a single decision during the parallelisation process.

This paper is organised as follows: Section 2 gives a brief description of the use of APMs in program development. Our PolyAPM approach and the APMs we have designed are presented in Section 3. An example of a parallelisation by using the APMs is given in Section 4. Section 5 describes the experiences we made using APMs. An overview of related work is given in Section 6. The paper is concluded by Section 7.

2 Program Development Using Abstract Machines

The idea of stepwise refinement of specifications has long been prevalent in computer science. Trees are used to represent design alternatives. If we look at the various intermediate specifications that exist between all the transformations of the parallelisation process, we observe an increasing degree of concreteness while we proceed. Thus, the abstract specification is finally transformed into a binary for a target machine. Consider the intermediate steps: on our descent along one path down the tree, we pick up more and more properties of the target architecture. But this also means that, most likely, no existing machine matches the level of abstraction of any intermediate specification. If we employ an abstract machine model that is just concrete enough to cover all the relevant details of our program, we can have it implemented in software and are able to run our intermediate programs on it.

One specific kind of abstract machine has been described by O'Donnell and Rünger in [OR97] as the *Abstract Parallel Machine* (APM). They define it by way of the functional input/output behaviour of a *parallel operation* (ParOp).

Their notion of an APM is closely related to its implementation in the functional language Haskell. The use of Haskell is motivated by its mechanisms for dealing with high-level constructs and by a clearly defined semantics that make proofs of program transformations feasible. However, we would like to model machine characteristics more closely within the APM and will base our work only loosely on [OR97].

3 PolyAPM

Rather than using just one APM in the sense of [OR97] for all transformations, we need to design variations of APMs. The compilation process is a sequence of source-to-source transformations each of which describes one particular step in the generation of a parallel program. Therefore, we need levels of abstraction corresponding to the machines properties assumed by the program transformations. The sequence of programs is associated with a sequence of APMs. In general, there are fewer APMs than programs, since not every transformation introduces new machine requirements.

3.1 The PolyAPM Decision Graph

As discussed above, a single problem specification may lead to a set of possible target programs, mainly because different parallelisation techniques and parameters are used and different target architectures are likely to be encountered. Therefore, the process of deriving a target program is like traversing the tree of design decisions. However, in certain cases, two different branches may lead to the same program, thus making this tree a DAG, the PolyAPM Decision Graph (PDG). Each node in this graph is a transformed program that runs on a dedicated APM. There are two graphs: one for the APMs themselves and one for the APM programs, where each node in the former may correspond to several nodes in the latter. A part of the PDG is given in Figure 1. The transformations depicted in the PDG have been motivated by our experiences with the *polytope model* for parallelisation [Len93] within the LooPo project [GL96], but PolyAPM is not restricted to this model.

The program development process is divided into several phases as follows:

1. Implementation of a problem specification in standard sequential Haskell as a *source program*. There are two main reasons for using Haskell. First, we claim, that for many algorithms that are subject to parallelisation (first of all numerical computations), the Haskell implementation represents a natural "rephrasing" of the problem in just a slightly different language. Second, as we use Haskell to implement the APMs, the APM program's core also is a Haskell function that is being called by the APM interpreter. Crossing an additional language barrier in order to obtain the first APM program should be avoided. However, these reasons make the choice of Haskell only highly suggestive, but not necessary.

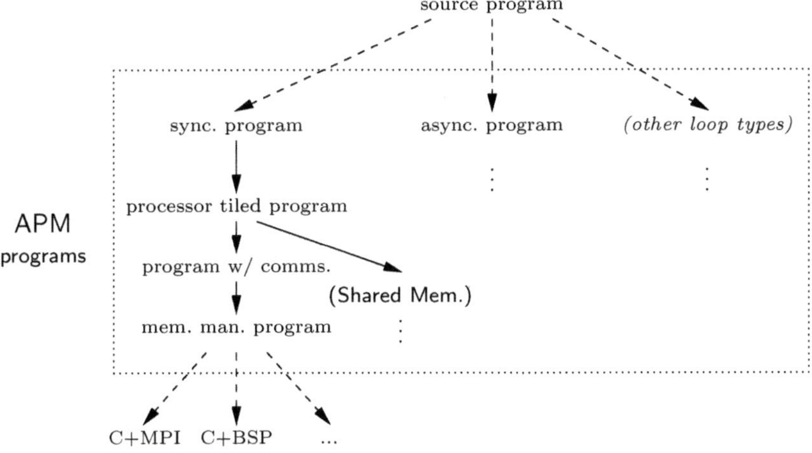

Fig. 1. PolyAPM Decision Graph (PDG), here only a sub-tree

2. Initial parallelisation of the sequential program. This refers to the analysis of the problem to identify independent computations that can be computed in parallel. This process might be done manually (as is the case with our example in Section 4), or with help of a parallelisation tool. We have used LooPo [GL96] for this purpose. In any case, the result of the parallelisation should map each computation to a virtual processor (this mapping is called *allocation*) and to a logical point in time (*schedule*). The granularity of the computation is the choice of the programmer, as the PolyAPM framework will maintain this granularity throughout the process. As the source program will most likely contain recursion or a comprehension, it is often sensible to perform the parallelisation on these and keep the inner computations of the recursion/comprehension *atomic*.
   We assume a one-dimensional processor field so that we have the basic computations, their allocation in *space* (i.e., the processor) and their scheduled computation time. Higher-dimensional allocations can always be transformed to one dimension, although some communication pattern might suffer in performance.
   With these components, the problem has a natural expression as a loop program with two loops, where the processor loop is parallel, the time loop is sequential and the loop body is just our atomic computation. If the outer loop is sequential, we call the program *synchronous*, otherwise *asynchronous*. This motivates the corresponding branches of the PDG in Figure 1. There are other possible types of loop nests, so the even more alternative branches could exist.
3. Based on the parallelisation, the source program is transformed into an APM program, which resembles an imperative loop nest with at least two surrounding loops (there may be additional loops in source program's core computation). The program is subject to several transformations to adapt

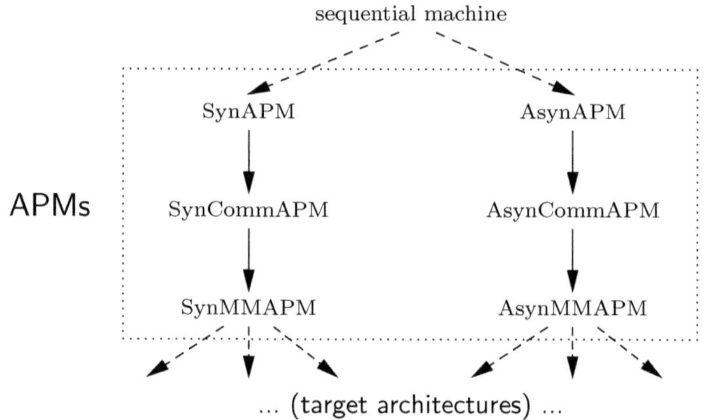

Fig. 2. PolyAPM Machine Tree

it to other APMs. This is the central part of PolyAPM and is discussed in more detail below in Section 3.2.

4. The final result of the compilation, the *target program*, has to be executable on a parallel machine. Therefore the last APM program is transformed into a *target language* for the parallel machine. It is important that the target language exhibits at least as much control as the last APM needs, so that no optimisation of any APM program transformation is lost. Suitable target languages, among others, are C+MPI and C+BSP.

3.2 Abstract Machines and Their Programs

The APMs form a tree, as shown in Figure 2. There is a many-to-one mapping from the programs to APMs. An APM program must reflect the design characteristics of the corresponding APM, e.g., in case of a synchronous program, a loop nest with an outer sequential and an inner parallel loop and a loop body, which may contain more loops. This separates the loops representing the real machine from logical loops.

The synchronous program is subject to a sequence of source-to-source program transformations. Each adds another machine characteristic or optimises a feature needed for execution on a real parallel machine. Assuming that the original parallelisation was done for a number p of processors whose value depends on the input, the p processor's workload has to be distributed on rp real processors of the target machine. This transformation is called *processor tiling*, in contrast to tiling techniques with other purposes.

The next two transformations complete the transition to a distributed memory architecture with communications. This has been deliberately split up into two transformations: First, while still maintaining a shared memory, we'll be generating communication directives. As a second step, the memory is distributed, making the communication necessary for a correct result. The reason for this unusual separation is twofold: one of the aims of PolyAPM is to make each transformation as simple as possible, and both communication generation and memory distribution can get complicated. Furthermore, if we did both transformations in one step and the resulting APM program had an error, it would be more difficult than necessary to isolate the reason for this error. When interpreting an APM program that communicates even in the presence of shared memory, the communications perform identity operations on the shared memory cells. The APM interpreter checks for this identity and issues a warning in case of a mismatch. This way wrong communications will be detected, but missing communications show their effects only after the distribution of memory.

The transformed program will have to run on an APM capable of communications, the SynCommAPM, which provides a message queue and a message delivery system. We assume that each processor stores data in local memory by the *owner-computes rule*. Therefore, data items computed elsewhere have to be communicated, either by point-to-point communications or by collective operations. If we were to employ a different storage management rule, this transformation would have to be adapted accordingly.

The "unnecessary" communications of the SynCommAPM program become crucial when the memory is being distributed for the SynMMAPM-program. This branch of the tree uses the owner-computes rule, making it easy to determine which parts of the global data space are actually necessary to keep in local memory. That completes the minimal necessary set of transformations needed for a synchronous loop program on a distributed-memory machine. The last transformation generates so-called *target code*, i.e., it transforms the SynMMAPM program into non-APM source code that is compilable on the target machine. Possible alternatives include C+MPI and C+BSP.

As outlined in Figure 1, transformation sequences other than the synchronous one are possible. In addition to the corresponding asynchronous one, we have depicted a typical sequence as employed by the tiling community [Wol87].

4 Example/Case Study

As an illustrating example, we chose the one-dimensional finite difference method. We start with an abstract problem specification, and by going through the process of program transformations – each yields a new, interpretable specification – we will eventually obtain an executable program for a specific target platform.

First we need to implement the specification in Haskell and identify the parallelism. The APM program expresses the parallelism as a loop nest with one of the two outermost loops being tagged as "parallel". Then we derive subsequent APM programs until a final transformation to the target language is feasible.

The abstract specification of the one-dimensional finite difference problem (as presented by [Fos95]) describes an iterative process of computing new array elements as a combination of the neighbour values and the previous value at the same location. Formally, the new array a_t with p elements at iteration t is defined as:

$$(\forall i \in \{2 \ldots p-1\} :: a_t[i] := (a_{t-1}[i-1] + 2 * a_{t-1}[i] + a_{t-1}[i+1])/4) \\ a_t[1] := a_{t-1}[1],\ a_t[p] := a_{t-1}[p] \tag{1}$$

The Haskell specification of this problem is given in Figure 3. Note how closely the Haskell program of Figure 3 corresponds to Equation 1. `findiff` represents one iterative step in which a new array is computed from the previous array a, just as Equation 1 requires. Function `findiffn` calls `findiff` as often as the parameter n prescribes. Each call to `findiff` generates a new Haskell array with the updated values. This corresponds to a destructive update of an array using an imperative programming model. In this example, all references to a refer to the previous iteration, so that we need two copies of the array.

We continue with the presentation of transformed `findiff` programs, emphasising the difference to the respective predecessor programs.

```
findiff:: Array Int Float -> Array Int Float
findiff a = listArray (low,up)
              ( a!(low):
                [(a!(i-1)+2*a!(i)+a!(i+1))/4 | i<-[low+1..up-1]] ++[a!(up)])
    where (low,up) = bounds a

findiffn:: Int -> Array Int Float
findiffn n   = f n
    where f:: Int ->Array Int Float
          f 0 = findiff testinput
          f n = findiff (f (n-1))
```

Fig. 3. Sequential Haskell Specification of Finite Differences

4.1 The Synchronous Program

The parallelisation of the source program is done manually. It is obvious that the calculations of the array elements of one particular `findiffn` call are independent, but they all depend on the previous values. Thus, `findiffn` corresponds to an outer, sequential loop, whereas the list comprehension inside `findiff` yields a parallel loop.

To write a SynAPM program for `findiff`, we proceed as follows:

1. We define the memory contents, here: two arrays `a` and `a1` of the same kind as the input array,
2. We set the read-only structure parameter list to n, which describes the size of `a`,
3. We define the loops: one outer sequential loop, arbitrarily set to 21 iterations, and one inner parallel loop, ranging from 0 to $n-1$, and
4. We write a loop body function.

This defines the synchronous loop nest `loop_syn` in Figure 4. The body function of SynAPM has the following type: `BD (e -> b -> e)`, i.e., it takes some *state*,

```
loop_syn = LP [(Seq, \(_,(n:_))->0, \(_,(n:_))->20, 1),
               (Par, \((t:_),(n:_))->0, \((t:_),(n:_))->n, 1)]
              (BD body_syn)

body_syn::((Array Int Float,Array Int Float),[Idx]) -> [Idx]
        -> ((Array Int Float,Array Int Float),[Idx])
body_syn  ((a,a1),splist) (t:p:_)
        | (p == low)||(p == up) = ((a,a1//[(p,a!p)]),splist)
        | (low < p )&&(p <  up) = ((a, stmnt1 a a1 (t,p,n)),splist)
    where stmnt1 a a1 (t, p, n)  = a1 //[(p, (a!(p-1)+2*a!(p)+a!(p+1))/4)]
          (low,up) = bounds a
          (n:_)    = splist
```

Fig. 4. SynAPM version of the Finite Differences

```
loop_til = LP [(Seq, \(_,(n:_))->0, \(_,(n:_))->20, 1),
               (Par, \((t:_),(n:_))->0, \((t:_),(n:_))->physprocs, 1),
               (Seq, \((t:p:_),(n:_))->max (p*(tilesize_p n)) 0,
                     \((t:p:_),(n:_))->min ((p+1)*(tilesize_p n)) n, 1)]
              (BD body_til)
            where tilesize_p:: Int -> Int
                  tilesize_p n = ((n-1) `div` physprocs)+1

body_til::((Array Int Float,Array Int Float),[Idx]) -> [Idx]
        -> ((Array Int Float,Array Int Float),[Idx])
body_til ((a,a1),splist) [t,p,p2]
    | (p2==low)||(p2==up) = ((a,a1//[(p2,a!p2)]),splist)
    | (low< p2)&&(p2< up) = ((a, stmnt1 a a1 (t,p2,n) ),splist)
    where stmnt1 a a1 (t, p, n) = (a1//[(p, (a!(p-1)+2*a!(p)+a!(p+1))/4)])
          (low,up) = bounds a
          (n:_)    = splist
```

Fig. 5. Tiled SynAPM version of the Finite Differences

consisting of memory and structure parameters, and a list of current values of all surrounding loops, to return an updated state. Figure 4 shows the state to be of type `((Array Int Float,Array Int Float),[Idx])`. The first array `a` is the one computed by the last iteration, and `a1` is filled at this time step. Note that the structure parameter list `splist` consists of only one item: the size `n` of the array. As the computation takes place only on the inner array values, we need a case analysis to take care of the border cells.

4.2 The Tiled Program

Figure 5 shows the synchronous `findiff` program after a simple processor tiling transformation. The parallel loop has been partitioned into tiles such that the number of remaining parallel iterations matches the number of physically available processors (as defined by `physprocs`). An additional sequential inner loop

```
body_comm = similar to body_til
loop_comm = similar to loop_til, msg generation after each body

instance Sendable SC_Dom Int Float SCMem where
  generateMsg [t,p,p2] (n:_) (a,a1) =
            [Msg (p2, to_p, t, to_tm, A, p2, a1!p2)|
              to_p <- (case pos_in_tile of
                          pat | pat==low     -> []
                              | pat==up      -> []
                              | pat==0       -> [p-1]
                              | pat==(ts-1) -> [p+1]
                              | True         -> [] ),
              to_tm <- [t+1]
            ]
      where (low,up)    = bounds a
            pos_in_tile = p2 `mod` ts
            ts          = tilesize_comm n

instance Updatable SC_Dom Int Float SCMem where
  updateMem (Msg (from_p, to_p, from_tm, to_tm, dom, idx, val)) (a,a1) =
         if (a1!idx) == val then (a,a1//[(idx,val)])
                            else wrong update
```

Fig. 6. SynCommAPM version of the Finite Differences

$p2$ has been added that enumerates the previously parallel iterations sequentially. Its bounds make sure that the loop variable takes the values previously provided by loop p, so that the relevant parameters of the body now are t and $p2$. Other than that, the function `body_til` is identical to `body_syn`. As the APMs work with an arbitrary but fixed number of processors, the tiled program can still run on SynAPM.

Changes to the Code to Obtain the *Tiled Program*:

- The constant `physprocs` (denoting the number of physical processors on real machine) and the `tilesize` function are added.
- An additional loop in LP with loop variable $p2$ is added.
- The body function takes three loop variables, p is replaced by $p2$.

4.3 The Communicating Program

Loop and body functions are the same as in the tiled program except for the memory type. Whereas in the previous APM programs the memory type could be freely defined, we now require the parameterised type `State` that couples memory and message queue. The parameters are required by context declarations within the SynCommAPM interpreter. See Figure 6. Emphasised font is used for pseudo code that replaces some longer Haskell code. It is meant to shorten the presentation.

New are three additional functions that have to be implemented by the programmer and which are called from inside the interpreter:

- `generateMsg` generates new messages originating from each processor at each time-step;
- `updateMem`, updates the state's memory with values sent by a message;
- `synchronizeMem`, being called after each time-step for possible synchronisation work on all processors. In this case, `synchronizeMem` removes the old array in each processor's state and introduces an empty new one to be filled in by computations in the next time-step. `synchronizeMem` will be omitted in the given code examples as it is just an auxiliary function.

These three functions have to be introduced by class instance declarations because the APM interpreter needs some type information to use the – at this point – undefined functions as stubs. This is because the APM interpreters reside in a separate Haskell module that is being used by different APM program modules. So, for every APM program the specific instances of these three functions are different, yet they need to fit into the APM, and making them instances of multi-parameter type classes guarantees the integration into the APM interpreter.

Function `updateMem` checks before an update whether the memory's and the message's values are identical. If they are not, the interpreter issues a runtime error message because a wrong communication message was generated. This is no method to prove correctness of communications, but testing the SynCommAPM program with a variety of inputs without errors can provide some confidence in the message generation, which belongs to the more error-prone parts of parallel programming. The SynMMAPM will provide further communication checks.

Changes to the Code to Obtain the *Communicating Program*:

- A `State` type combining memory and message queue replaces the memory; types in body and `LP` are adapted accordingly.
- Each call of the body is followed by a call of the message generation function of SynCommAPM, which in turn calls the provided `generateMsg`.
- Instance declarations for `generateMsg`, `updateMem` and `synchronizeMem` are added.

4.4 The Memory-Managed Program

With the paradigm shift from shared to distributed memory, the memory representation in the APM programs has to be adapted. Each processor gets its own chunk of the memory, which in the example in Figure 7 comprises all the data which is computed on this processor and the remotely-owned data that is required for the computation. The values of the latter will be communicated before the computation. So the one-dimensional array is divided into chunks according to the tile size, with an additional element to the left an to the right,

```
data MM_PProcMem = PPM (Array Int Float) (Array Int Float)

body_mm::([Idx],[Idx]) -> MM_PProcState -> (MM_PProcState,[Idx],[Idx])
body_mm (splist, idxlist@[t,p,p2]) (State (PPM a1 a2) msgs)
    | (p2==low)||(p2==up) =
          (State (PPM a1 (a2//[(lidx,a1!lidx)])) msgs,splist,idxlist)
    | (low <p2)&&(p2 <up) =
          (State (PPM a1 (a2//[(lidx,stmnt1)])) msgs,splist,idxlist)
    where stmnt1   = (a1!(lidx-1) + 2*a1!lidx + a1!(lidx+1))/4
          (low,up) = (0,n-1)
          (n:_)    = splist
          lidx     = proc2idx p2 n

The functions loop_mm, generateMsg and updateMem are similar
to before and have only been adjusted to the new memory data type.
```

Fig. 7. SynMMAPM version of the Finite Differences

because each element's computation needs its two neighbours. The body function's indexing into its local array has to be adapted. The index range changed from $\{1 \dots n-1\}$ to $\{1 \dots tilesize-1\}$. Furthermore, all communications within a tile can be eliminated, thus requiring a change in the `generateMsg` function. This program resembles very much an imperative SPMD program with loops as control structure so that the transition to C+MPI is relatively straightforward.

Changes to the Code to Obtain the *Memory-Managed Program*:

- The memory type within the global state changes to an array of local memory types. Body, `generateMsg` and `updateMem` are changed accordingly.
- In LP, just the names of the body/generateMsg functions changes.

4.5 The C+MPI Program

This last transformation leaves the APM realm. Conceptually, nothing interesting happens, but a language barrier has to be crossed. The simpler the body function is, the easier its transformation into a C function gets. The premier area of parallel programming, scientific computation, usually deals with arithmetic operations on arrays. The array as the most frequently used data structure exists in both languages. This is not to say that more general problem domains cannot be handled, but then the target code transformation gets more complicated.

To generate target code, abstract APM communications have to be transformed into MPI calls, the memory data type and its distribution/aggregation function need the imperative equivalent. But all these changes are isolated, and in most cases not difficult, especially if this transformation was taken into account while choosing the appropriate Haskell types.

Changes to the Code to Obtain the *C+MPI Program*:

- A template for an SPMD program in C+MPI for the APM structures is provided.
- The memory type has to be adapted, the message queue is subsumed by MPI.
- The functions `generateMsg`, `updateMem` and `synchronizeMem` are rewritten in C and replace the stubs within the C template.

5 Critical Evaluation

In Section 4 we showed a simple development in a straight sequence of programs. In practise, one will want a choice between sequences, leading to a tree as suggested. An exploration of design alternatives in PolyAPM has been presented elsewhere [EL03]. Still, here is a preliminary evaluation of the PolyAPM approach, based on our sequence example.

5.1 Benefits

In the following, we present some advantages that we see in our approach. In particular, the first two describe benefits of the methodology, whereas the last three emphasise the use of Haskell for implementing PolyAPM.

- Effects of program transformations can be isolated and evaluated, to help deciding for the most suitable transformation path. An example is the communication generation for SynCommAPM. For complex programs, different communication patterns can be tested by executing the different versions of the communicating program. The APM interpreter can output communication statistics to help selecting the most suitable pattern with the smallest total number of communications.
- Building a test environment for program transformations becomes easier, as input and output of each transformation can be executed and compared with other transformations. PolyAPM can be used to construct a compilation system in which not all transformations are automatic, allowing incremental development. Alternatively, the structure of PolyAPM supports parallel compiler research where a complete compilation is not feasible and some transformations are performed manually, which is the case for all transformations in Section 4.
- Using Haskell has the benefit that the definition of the APM programming language as an algebraic data type provides syntax and type checks for free. Because of this, the APM programs and their interpreters can be kept relatively small, as no parsing of APM programs is necessary.
- It is a challenge to split up the Haskell program into the APM interpreter module and APM program modules. The interpreter has to make assumptions about the unknown APM program (especially that the three user-defined functions introduced by SynCommAPM exist and have types of a

certain kind). Haskell's multi-parameter type classes support these assertions.
- A researcher who wants to prove that a transformation of APM programs preserves correctness, can do so with equational reasoning techniques.

5.2 Drawbacks

- It is a lot of effort to write all APM programs (for example four plus one sequential program in Section 4) in order to get one target program if the aim is just a single compilation. PolyAPM is not meant for the development of individual application programs.
- In PolyAPM the loop body has to be a Haskell function to maintain the generality of the approach (i.e., if we devise a special language for array assignments, which could be more easily transformed than a general Haskell function, then we severely restrict the class of applicable problems). The more non-trivial and Haskell-specific code the body function contains, the more problems arise when this code is transferred to an imperative language (see Section 4.5).

5.3 Who May Profit from PolyAPM?

- Researchers who are interested in comparing the effects of transformations. This could be compiler writers or researchers in compilation and parallelisation techniques.
- Programmers who have a PolyAPM compilation systems at their disposal which can perform some transformations automatically. Programming the remaining (if any) transformations manually might be less work than writing the target program directly.
- Programmers who need to compile one source program for different target languages or different machine architectures and who have at least some transformations automated.

6 Related Work

John O'Donnell and Gudula Rünger presented APMs in [OR97] and provided a starting point for others to work on parallel compilation using these.

Joy Goodman has extended the above work [Goo01], included input and output via monads, investigated the decision-making process and formalised the decision making process.

Noel Winstanley also uses the APM methodology in his PEDL system [Win01]. He compiles array-based numerical programs to Single-Assignment C [Sch94]. However, he uses a special restricted language, tailored for his specific problem domain, and focuses on a high degree of optimisation and automation of the compilation. Where Goodman and Winstanley concentrate on the generation of parallel programs with few transformations on restricted input languages,

PolyAPM deals with more general input programs and focuses on the selection and evaluation among many program transformations.

Another effort is Glasgow Parallel Haskell (GPH) [THMJ+96], in which one simply augments a Haskell program with directives that spark subexpressions as independent computations. User control is limited and left to the run time system.

There are many automatic parallel compilation systems with varying degrees of user interaction. Some research systems like SUIF[WFW+94] serve as a compiler's workbench, where some compilation phases may be replaced by custom implementations. The paralleliser LooPo[GL96], developed in our group, also belongs to this category. Other systems like Polaris[BEF+95], Parafrase[PGH+90] and HPF compilers like Adaptor[Bra98] employ a more static view on the parallelisation, in which the selection of transformations is rather fixed.

7 Conclusions

Based on our initial experimental evaluation, we envision the PolyAPM model for specific sub-areas of of parallel program development rather than claiming a general purpose approach.

Structured (parallel) program development: The task of obtaining parallel target code consists of several steps. Current commercial parallelising compilation systems (mainly for HPF) often are only able to perform the compilation in one pass. There is usually no or only restricted influence on the selection of the used algorithms. This static process can be made flexible with a modular system of compilation phases, where single phases can be chosen from a given set of alternatives. A few academic systems use this approach for some phases of their compilation system.

Exploration of design decisions: Each phase in the PolyAPM compilation process is a source-to-source transformation on APM programs. These programs are executable by the respective APM machine interpreter. As a result, the effects of each transformation can be observed directly by looking at the code and executing it.

Rapid prototyping: Researchers with a specialised focus on only one phase of parallel program development can choose an APM at the abstraction level they need and evaluate their work without the need to write a full compiler.

Although, in this paper, program development has only been demonstrated for a single branch of the PDG, the full power of the approach is obtained by making use of a subtree or sub-DAG of the PDG.

Acknowledgements

We thank Paul Feautrier and John O'Donnell for fruitful discussions, the DFG for funding PolyAPM and PROCOPE for supporting the contact with Feautrier.

References

BEF+95. William Blume, Rudolf Eigenmann, Keith Faigin, John Grout, Jay Hoeflinger, David Padua, Paul Petersen, William Pottenger, Lawrence Rauchwerger, Peng Tu, and Stephen Weatherford. Polaris: Improving the effectiveness of parallelizing compilers. In Keshav Pingali, Uptal Banerjee, David Gelernter, Alex Nicolau, and David Padua, editors, *Proceedings of the 7th International Workshop on Languages and Compilers for Parallel Computing*, LNCS 892, pages 141–154. Springer-Verlag, 1995.

Bra98. Thomas Brandes. *ADAPTOR Programmer's Guide, Version 6.0*, June 1998. Available via anonymous ftp from ftp.gmd.de as gmd/adaptor/docs/pguide.ps.

EL03. Nils Ellmenreich and Christian Lengauer. Comparative Parallel Programming with PolyAPM using Abstract Parallel Machines. In Peter Knijnenburg and Paul van der Mark, editors, *Proc. 10th Intl. Worksh. on Compilers for Parallel Computers (CPC 2003)*. Leiden Institute of Advanced Computer Science, January 2003. http://www.infosun.fmi.uni-passau.de/cl/papers/EllLen03.html.

Fos95. Ian Foster. *Design and Building Parallel Programs*. Addison-Wesley, 1995.

GL96. Martin Griebl and Christian Lengauer. The loop parallelizer LooPo. In Michael Gerndt, editor, *Proc. Sixth Workshop on Compilers for Parallel Computers (CPC'96)*, Konferenzen des Forschungszentrums Jülich 21, pages 311–320. Forschungszentrum Jülich, 1996.

Goo01. Joy Goodman. *Incremental Program Transformations using Abstract Parallel Machines*. PhD thesis, Department of Computing Science, University of Glasgow, September 2001.

Len93. Christian Lengauer. Loop parallelization in the polytope model. In Eike Best, editor, *CONCUR'93*, Lecture Notes in Computer Science 715, pages 398–416. Springer-Verlag, 1993.

OR97. John O'Donnell and Gudula Rünger. A methodology for deriving abstract parallel programs with a family of parallel abstract machines. In Christian Lengauer, Martin Griebl, and Sergei Gorlatch, editors, *EuroPar'97: Parallel Processing*, LNCS 1300, pages 662–669. Springer-Verlag, 1997.

PGH+90. Constantine Polychronopoulos, Milind B. Girkar, Mohammad R. Haghighat, Chia L. Lee, Bruce P. Leung, and Dale A. Schouten. The structure of Parafrase-2: An advanced parallelizing compiler for C and Fortran. In David Gelernter, Alex Nicolau, and David Padua, editors, *Languages and Compilers for Parallel Computing (LCPC'90)*, Research Monographs in Parallel and Distributed Computing, pages 423–453. Pitman, 1990.

Sch94. Sven-Bodo Scholz. Single Assignment C – Functional Programming Using Imperative Style. In John Glauert, editor, *Proceedings of the 6th International Workshop on the Implementation of Functional Languages*. University of East Anglia, 1994.

THMJ+96. Phil Trinder, Kevin Hammond, Jim S. Mattson Jr, Andrew Partridge, and Simon Peyton Jones. GUM: A portable parallel implementation of Haskell. In *Proc. of ACM SIPGLAN Conf. on Programming Languages Design and Implementation (PLDI'96)*, pages 79–88. ACM Press, May 1996.

WFW+94. Robert P. Wilson, Robert S. French, Christopher S. Wilson, Saman P. Amarasinghe, Jennifer M. Anderson, Steve W. K. Tjiang, Shih-Wei Liao, Chau-Wen Tseng, Mary W. Hall, Monica S. Lam, and John L. Hennessy. SUIF: An infrastructure for research on parallelizing and optimizing compilers. In *Proc. Fourth ACM SIGPLAN Symp. on Principles & Practice of Parallel Programming (PPoPP)*, pages 31–37. ACM Press, 1994. http://suif.stanford.edu/suif/.

Win01. Noel Winstanley. *Staged Methodologies for Parallel Programming.* PhD thesis, Department of Computing Science, University of Glasgow, April 2001.

Wol87. Michel Wolfe. Iteration space tiling for memory hierarchies. In G. Rodrigue, editor, *Parallel Processing for Scientific Computing*, pages 357–361. SIAM, 1987.

Unboxed Compilation of Floating Point Arithmetic in a Dynamically Typed Language Environment

Tobias Lindahl and Konstantinos Sagonas

Computing Science, Dept. of Information Technology, Uppsala University, Sweden
{Tobias.Lindahl,Konstantinos.Sagonas}@it.uu.se

Abstract. In the context of the dynamically typed concurrent functional programming language ERLANG, we describe a simple static analysis for identifying variables containing floating point numbers, how this information is used by the BEAM compiler, and a scheme for efficient (just-in-time) compilation of floating point bytecode instructions to native code. The attractiveness of the scheme lies in its implementation simplicity. It has been fully incorporated in Erlang/OTP R9, and improves the performance of ERLANG programs manipulating floats considerably. We also show that by using this scheme, Erlang/OTP, despite being an implementation of a dynamically typed language, achieves performance which is competitive with that of state-of-the-art implementations of strongly typed strict functional languages on floating point intensive programs.

1 Introduction

In dynamically typed languages the implementation of built-in arithmetic typically involves runtime type tests to ensure that the calculations which are performed are meaningful, i.e., that one does not succeed in dividing atoms by lists. Some of these tests are strictly necessary to ensure correctness, but the same variable can be repeatedly tested because the type information is typically lost after an operation has been performed. This is a major source of inefficiency. Removing these redundant tests improves execution time both by avoiding their runtime cost and by simplifying the task of the compiler (removing conditional branches simplifies the control flow graphs and allows the compiler to work with bigger basic blocks).

Of course, one way of attempting to solve this problem is to attack it at its root: impose a type system to the language and do (inter-modular) type inference. Doing so *a posteriori* is most often not trivial. More importantly, type systems and powerful static analyses might not necessarily be in accordance with certain features deemed important for intended application domains (e.g., on-the-fly selective code updates that might invalidate the results of previous analyses), design decisions of the underlying implementation (e.g., the ability to selectively compile a *single* function at a time in a just-in-time fashion), or the overall philosophy of the language.

In this paper, rather than changing the basic characteristics of ERLANG, we take a more pragmatic approach to alleviating the downsides that absence of type information has for a (native code) compiler of the language. Specifically, we describe a simple scheme for using *local* type analysis (i.e., the analysis is restricted to a single function) to identify variables containing floating point values. Moreover, we have fully incorporated this

R. Peña and T. Arts (Eds.): IFL 2002, LNCS 2670, pp. 134–149, 2003.

scheme in an industrial-strength implementation of ERLANG (the Erlang/OTP system) and extensively quantify the performance gains that it offers both in execution of virtual machine bytecode and of native code.

To make this paper relatively self-contained, we start with a brief presentation of ERLANG's characteristics (Sect. 2) followed by a brief description of the architecture of the HiPE just-in-time native code compiler (Sect. 3). In Sect. 4 a simple scheme to identify variables containing floating point values is presented, and the floating point aware translation of built-in arithmetic in the BEAM virtual machine instruction set is compared to its older translation. Sect. 5 contains a detailed account of how the HiPE compiler translates floating point instructions of the BEAM from its intermediate representation all the way down to both its SPARC and x86 back-ends, and how the features of the corresponding architectures are effectively utilized. The paper ends with an evaluation of the performance of using the presented scheme both within different implementations of ERLANG and when compared with a state-of-the-art implementation of a strict statically typed functional language.

2 The Erlang Language and Erlang/OTP

ERLANG is a dynamically typed, strict, concurrent functional language. The basic data types include atoms, numbers, and process identifiers; compound data types are lists and tuples. There are no assignments or mutable data structures. Functions are defined as sets of guarded clauses, and clause selection is done by pattern matching. Iterations are expressed as tail-recursive function calls, and ERLANG consequently requires tailcall optimization. ERLANG also has a catch/throw-style exception mechanism. ERLANG processes are created dynamically, and applications tend to use many of them. Processes communicate through asynchronous message passing: each process has a *mailbox* in which incoming messages are stored, and messages are retrieved from the mailbox by pattern matching. Messages can be arbitrary ERLANG values. ERLANG implementations must provide automatic memory management, and the soft real-time nature of the language calls for bounded-time garbage collection techniques.

Erlang/OTP is the standard implementation of the language. It combines ERLANG with the Open Telecom Platform (OTP) middleware, a library with standard components for telecommunications applications. Erlang/OTP is currently used industrially by Ericsson Telecom and other software and telecommunications companies around the world for the development of high-availability servers and networking equipment. Additional information about ERLANG can be found at `www.erlang.org`.

3 The HiPESystem: Brief Overview

HiPE (High Performance Erlang) [5,13] is included in the open source Erlang/OTP system. It consists of a compiler from BEAM virtual machine bytecode to native machine code (currently UltraSPARC or x86), and extensions to the runtime system to support mixing interpreted and native code execution, at the granularity of individual functions.

BEAM. The BEAM intermediate representation is a symbolic version of the BEAM virtual machine bytecode, and is produced by disassembling the functions or module being compiled. BEAM is a register-based virtual machine which operates on a largely implicit heap and call-stack, a set of global registers for values that do not survive function calls (X-registers), and a set of slots in the current stack frame (Y-registers). BEAM is semi-functional: composite values are immutable, but registers and stack slots can be assigned freely.

BEAM to Icode. Icode is an idealized Erlang assembly language. The stack is implicit, any number of temporaries may be used, and all temporaries survive function calls. Most computations are expressed as function calls. All bookkeeping operations, including memory management and process scheduling, are implicit.

BEAM is translated to Icode mostly one instruction at a time. However, function calls and the creation of tuples are sequences of instructions in BEAM but single instructions in Icode, requiring the translator to recognize those sequences. The Icode form is then improved by application of constant propagation, constant folding, and dead-code elimination [11]. Temporaries are also renamed through conversion to a static single assignment form [1], to avoid false dependencies between different live ranges.

Icode to RTL. RTL is a generic three-address register transfer language. RTL itself is target-independent, but the code is target-specific, due to references to target-specific registers and primitive procedures. RTL has tagged registers for proper Erlang values, and untagged registers for arbitrary machine values. To simplify the garbage collector interface, function calls only preserve live tagged registers.

In the translation from Icode to RTL, many operations (e.g., arithmetic, data construction, or tests) are inlined. Data tagging operations are made explicit, data accesses and initializations are turned into loads and stores, etc. Optimizations applied to RTL include common subexpression elimination, constant propagation and folding, and merging of heap overflow tests.

The final step in the compilation is translation from RTL to native machine code of the target back-end (as mentioned, currently SPARC V8+ or IA-32).

4 Identification and Handling of Floats in the BEAM Interpreter

Due to space limitations, we do not present a formal definition of the local static type analysis that we use, but instead explain its basic ideas and how the analysis information is propagated forwards and used in the BEAM interpreter with the following example.

Example 1. Consider the ERLANG code shown in Fig. 1(a). Its translation to BEAM code without taking advantage of the fact that certain operands to arithmetic expressions are floating point numbers is shown in Fig. 1(b). Note that the code uses the general arithmetic instructions of the BEAM. These instructions have to test at runtime that their operands (constants and X-registers in this case) contain numbers, untag and possibly unbox these operands, perform the corresponding arithmetic operation, tag and possibly box the result on the heap, and place a pointer to it in the X-register shown on the left hand side of the arrow. Note that if such an arithmetic operation results in either a type error or an arithmetic exception, execution will continue at the fail label denoted by L_e.

Note however that even though ERLANG is a dynamically typed language, there is enough information in the above ERLANG code to deduce through a simple static analysis

```
-module(example).
-export([f/3]).

f(A,B,C) when is_float(C) ->
    X = A + 3.14,
    Y = B / 2,
    R = C * X - Y.
```

(a) ERLANG code.

```
is_float x2                              Lc
x0 ← arith '+' x0 {float,3.14}          Le
x1 ← arith '/' x1 {integer,2}           Le
x2 ← arith '*' x2 x0                    Le
x0 ← arith '-' x2 x1                    Le
return
```

(b) BEAM instructions for `f/3`.

Fig. 1. Naive translation of floating point arithmetic to BEAM bytecode

```
is_float x2                 Lc
f0 ← fconv  x0
f1 ← fmove  {float,3.14}
fclearerror
f0 ← fadd   f0 f1           Le
f2 ← fconv  x1
f3 ← fconv  {integer,2}
f2 ← fdiv   f2 f3           Le
f4 ← fmove  x2
f4 ← fmul   f4 f0           Le
f0 ← fsub   f4 f2           Le
fcheckerror                 Le
x0 ← fmove f0
return
```

Fig. 2. Floating-point aware translation of `f/3` to BEAM bytecode

that certain arithmetic operations take floating point numbers as operands and return floating point numbers as results. This information can easily be propagated forwards in a function's body. For example, after the type test guard succeeds, it is known that variable `C` (argument register x_2) contains a floating point number. Because of the floating point constant 3.14, if the addition will not result in either a type error or an exception, variable `X` will also be bound to a float. Similarly, because of the use of the floating point division operator, variable `Y` will also be bound to a float if successful, etc.[1] Using the results of such an analysis could allow generation of the more efficient BEAM code shown in Fig. 2. Note that a new set of floating point registers (F-registers) has been introduced to the BEAM. These registers contain untagged floats.

As shown in this example, to exploit the information produced by the local type analysis, in recent versions of the BEAM, a separate set of instructions for handling floating point arithmetic has been introduced. Whenever it can be determined that the type of a variable is indeed a float, a block of floating point operations is created limited

[1] In ERLANG, the type of the result of an arithmetic operation is only determined by the types of the operands. For example, multiplying a float by an integer always results in a float. Not all dynamically typed languages work this way. For example, multiplying anything by the integer 0 can give the integer 0 in Scheme.

Table 1. BEAM floating point instructions

Instruction	Description
fclearerror	Clears any earlier floating point exceptions.
fcheckerror	Checks whether any instruction since the last fclearerror has resulted in a floating point exception. Its implementation can either rely on hardware features (e.g., condition flags), or be more portable (e.g., explicitly check for NaNs).
fconv	Converts a number to a floating point number.
fadd	Performs floating point addition.
fsub	Performs floating point subtraction.
fdiv	Performs floating point division.
fmul	Performs floating point multiplication.
fnegate	Negates a floating point number.
fmove	Moves values between floating point registers and ordinary registers.

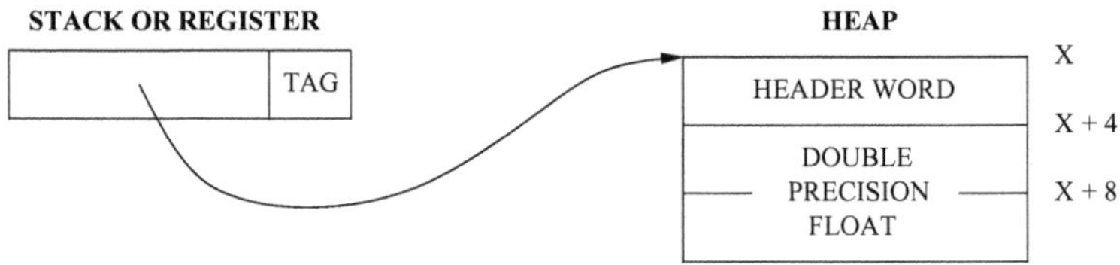

Fig. 3. A boxed float in the BEAM

by fclearerror and fcheckerror instructions. Although not all type tests are eliminated, inside this block no type tests are needed for the variables marked as floats. The complete set of BEAM instructions for handling floats is shown in Table 1.

5 Handling of Floats in the HiPE Native Code Compiler

In the BEAM, whenever it is not known that a particular virtual machine register contains a floating point number, the float value is boxed, i.e., stored on the heap with a header word pointed to by the address kept in the register representing the number. Furthermore the address is tagged to show that the register is bound to a boxed value as shown in Fig. 3. Note that floating point values are not necessarily double word aligned.

Whenever the float is used, the address has to be untagged, the header word has to be examined to find out the type of the variable (because e.g. tuples and bignums are boxed in the same manner), and finally the actual number can be used. Depending on the target architecture, the float is placed in the SPARC's floating point registers or on the x87 floating point stack, the computation takes place and then the result is boxed again and put on the heap. If the result is to be used again, which is typically the case, it has to be unboxed again prior to its use just as described above.

However, inside a basic block that is known to consist of floating point computations, all floating point numbers can be kept unboxed in the F-registers which are loaded either in the floating point unit (e.g., on the SPARC) or on the floating point stack of the machine (e.g., on the x86), thus removing the need of type testing each time the value is used. Furthermore, if a result of a computation is to be used again it can simply remain unboxed instead of being put on the heap and then read into the FPU again.

5.1 Translation to Icode

In the translation from BEAM bytecode to Icode most of the instructions are more or less kept unchanged and just passed on to RTL. The exception is fmove that either moves a value from an ordinary X-register to a floating point one (in which case it corresponds to an untagging operation), or vice versa (in which case it corresponds to a tagging operation). To handle the first case, Icode introduces the operation **unsafe_untag_float** and in the second **unsafe_tag_float**. These Icode operations will be expanded on the RTL-level as described below.

5.2 Translation to RTL

Translation of Boxing and Unboxing. When translating the **unsafe_untag_float** instruction, since it is known that the X-register contains a float, there is no need to examine the header word. The untagging operation can be performed by simply subtracting the float tag which currently is 2; see [12]. As can be seen in Fig. 3 the actual floating point value is stored at an offset of 4 from the untagged address, so instead of being translated to a subtraction of 2 and a **fload** with offset 4, **unsafe_untag_float** is translated to **fload** with offset 2, thus eliminating the actual untagging.

The **unsafe_tag_float** instruction writes the value to the heap, places a header word showing that this is a float, and finally tags the pointer with 2 to show that the value is boxed. Normally the garbage collection test that should be done to ensure that there is space on the heap is handled by a coalesced heap test, but otherwise one is added here.

Translation of Floating Point Conversion. On converting an ERLANG number to its floating point representation it is essential to find out what the old representation was. The legal conversions are from integers, bignums, and possibly other floats. The reason the last case can occur is that the static analysis currently used does not discover all variables containing floats. These do not, of course, need to be converted but implicit in the fconv instruction is also the request to untag the value so this case is turned into an **unsafe_untag_float**.

The conversion from an integer is supported in both back-ends so this operation is kept as an fconv-instruction, but when the value is a bignum the operation is not inlined. Instead the instruction is turned into a call to the **conv_big_to_float** primary operation (primop) that returns a boxed float that needs to be untagged before further processing.

The separate handling of different types of conversion constitutes the only branches in the control flow graph (CFG) where there can be unboxed floats in registers. All functions can branch to a fail label but as discussed below all unboxed floats must be saved on the stack on function calls. Furthermore, if there is a comparison of floats the computational block is ended and the comparison is made on boxed values. Currently, there is no support for unboxed comparison. Adding such support would avoid the unnecessary boxing and increase the live ranges of the unboxed values.

Translation of Error Handling. In BEAM, the instructions fclearerror and fcheckerror are just setting and reading a variable in a C structure of the runtime system. The first translation we tried, implemented these as calls to primops. This turned out to be expensive, not only because a call to a primop is not as cheap as reading the variable, but it also affected the spilling behavior as it required that all floats are spilled on the stack before the primop call. Subsequently, we enhanced HiPE with the ability to access information directly from C variables of the runtime system which opened up the possibility to have a cheap and direct translation of the floating point error handling instructions.

Translation of Floating Point Arithmetic. fadd, fsub, fdiv, and fmul do not have to be treated in any special way. They are just propagated to the back-end. In the SPARC back-end the `fmov` SPARC instruction has a flag telling the processor if the value is to be negated in addition to being moved. The fnegate instruction is therefore translated to a `fmov` which sets that flag.

5.3 Handling of Floats in the SPARC Back-End

Use of the SPARC Floating Point Registers. The SPARC has 32 double precision floating point registers, half of which can instead be used as single precision registers in which case there are 32 single precision and 16 double precision floating point registers. On loading or storing double precision floats the address must be double word aligned, or the operation will result in a fault. Since currently there is no guarantee of such an alignment in neither BEAM nor HiPE, the fact that a double precision register is made up of two single precision ones is used and the instruction is turned into two single precision loads.

If the exclusive double precision registers need to be used, the only way to safely load to them would be to use two scratch single precision registers and then move the double precision value. This is not done, so these 16 registers are not being used.

The register allocation of the pseudo floating point variables to the real registers is handled by a variation of the linear scan register allocation algorithm [14,6]. The algorithm is slightly altered to cater for the needs of floats which require use of two stack positions for spilling rather than one.

Floating Point Numbers on the Native Stack. Floats are spilled to the stack when too many of them are live at the same time, but also whenever they are live over a function call. Since there are no guarantees that the called function does not use the floating point registers, their contents must be saved on the stack and then restored on return from the function. Currently, an extra pass through the CFG removes any redundant stores and loads.

On spilling floats to the native stack it must be ensured that the stack slots are marked as dead since the values are not tagged. (Otherwise, the garbage collector would try to follow and possibly copy the contents of these stack slots which could result in seg-faults or meaningless results.) Fortunately, this is easy to do, as the current version of HiPE generates *stack maps* for all stack frames; see [13].

There is one more case where untagged values are put on the stack. When converting a single word integer to a float the value typically resides in an ordinary register. SPARC handles the conversion by loading the integer value into a single precision floating point register and then converting it into the corresponding double precision register. However, the load instruction cannot use a register as source, so the value is stored on the stack first.

Performing the Operations. When a floating point operation is called all three of its operands must be in floating point registers. The SPARC, unlike the x86, has no support for letting one or more of the operands be a memory reference so two registers need to be available for the case when the two operands reside in memory.

A design decision of the HiPE compiler is to preserve the observable behavior of ERLANG programs. This includes preserving side-effects of arithmetic operations such as floating point exceptions; in ERLANG these can be caught by a `catch` statement. Therefore, even in cases were the result of a floating point arithmetic operation is not needed, the operation can be eliminated only if it can be proved that it will not raise an exception. However, note that when a floating point operation is performed only for its side effects and its result is never used, the latter can safely be left in the register since SPARC does not demand the registers to be empty on leaving a function. If the result is to be used and the pseudo variable tied to the float is spilled, the result is stored in a stack slot. Currently, no test is made to see if the result is the operand of the next floating point operation that needs the scratch registers since this would require another pass through the code. (This would interfere with the JIT nature of the HiPE compiler.)

5.4 Handling of Floats in the x86 Back-end

Use of the x87 Floating Point Unit. On the x86, all floating point operations are performed in the x87 floating point unit. The x87 is used as a stack with eight slots represented by `%st(i)`, $0 \leq$ `i` ≤ 7. In this section, whenever the stack is mentioned the x87 floating point stack is what is meant unless otherwise stated.

On the SPARC the pseudo variables can be globally mapped to floating point registers but because of the stack representation of the x87 the bindings between pseudo variables and stack slots are local to each program point.

Mapping to the x87. The approach of the mapping is based on an improvement of the algorithm proposed in [10]. The main idea is to keep live values on the stack as long as possible while not pushing others when not needed. Each instruction can only have one operand as a memory reference so if both operands are spilled one must be pushed, preferably one that is live out at that point, that is one that is used at a later time. If there is already a spilled value on the stack, it might not be necessary to pop it since there can be room on the stack anyway, but whenever the stack is full and a new value is to be pushed the first spilled value is popped. More specifically, the mapping is performed as follows:

1. As in the SPARC back-end, using a variation of the linear scan register allocation algorithm, the floating point variables are mapped to seven pseudo stack slots. These do not represent the actual slots but this mapping is a way to ensure that at all times the unspilled values and a scratch value fit on the stack.

2. The mapping is done by traversing the CFG trace-wise: Starting from the beginning each successor is handled until the trace either merges with a trace already handled or reaches the CGF's end. In each basic block the instructions are transformed to operate on the actual stack positions and, if needed, to perform appropriate push and pop actions. (For most floating point operations, the x87 has instructions that perform the operation and possibly also pop one of the operands; see [4].) The mapping from pseudo variables to stack positions is propagated to the next basic block.
3. Whenever two traces are merged their mappings are compared. If they differ, the adjoining trace is altered since the basic block and its successors already have been handled. This is done by adding a basic block containing stack shuffling code that synchronizes the mappings.
4. If a floating point instruction branches to a fail label the mapping that is kept at compile time may be corrupt since there is no way of knowing where the error occurred. The stack must then be completely freed so as to assure that it contains no garbage. This is done by calling a primop that restores the stack. Note that this can be done in the same basic block as the fail code since these operations are independent of the predecessor.

Since values that are spilled are not popped right away, there can be inconsistencies between the values on the stack and in the corresponding spill positions, but whenever a spilled value is popped it is written back to the stack slot if it is live out. A value that is not live out is immediately popped without being written back.

Translating the Instructions. To simplify the translation and avoid an extra pass through the intermediate code, a design decision has been made to not use heap positions as memory operands to a floating point instruction. So, initially all values are loaded on the stack using `fld` instructions. The top of the stack is represented by `%st(0)` and this slot is the only one that can interact with memory on loads and stores but also when using a memory cell as an operand. This can at times be inconvenient but an instruction to switch places between the top and an arbitrary position `i` is available, `fxch %st(i)`. When used in conjunction with another floating point operation this instruction is very cheap. Only the source operand (src) of a floating point instruction can be a memory reference, so a spilled src is not pushed prior to its use. The destination operand (dst) must be on the stack so a spilled value can already be on the stack if it has been used as dst in an earlier instruction.

The liveness of each value is known at each point. A value that is not live out is immediately popped, but as described above a value that *is* live out is not necessarily pushed. A spilled value is not written back to its spill position unless it has to be popped. This means that there can be several spilled values on the stack at the same time. When a value is to be pushed and the stack is full a spilled value is popped and written back.

Example 2. Suppose the following calculation is to be performed.

$$X = ((A * B) * (A + C)) + D$$

Using the pseudo variables $\%\mathtt{f}_i$, $\mathtt{i} \in \mathbf{N}$, the calculation corresponds to the following sequence of pseudo RTL instructions:

```
fmov A %f0
fmov B %f1
fmov C %f2
fmov D %f3
fadd %f0 %f2 %f4
fmul %f0 %f1 %f5
fmul %f4 %f5 %f6
fadd %f6 %f3 %f7
fmov %f7 X
```

After register allocation (where the index of $\%\mathtt{f}_i$ has been limited to $0 \leq \mathtt{i} \leq 7$) and translation to the two address code that the x86 uses, the above sequence becomes as the pseudo-x86 code shown in Fig. 4(a). Transforming this into real code for the x87, we get the code shown in Fig. 4(b).

```
fmov A, %f0
fmov B, %f1
fmov C, %f2
fmov D, %f3
fadd %f0, %f2
fmul %f0, %f1
fmul %f1, %f2
fadd %f2, %f3
fmov %f3, X
```

(a) Pseudo-x86 code.

Instruction	Stack
fld A	[A]
fld B	[B,A]
fld C	[C,B,A]
fld D	[D,C,B,A]
fxch %st(3)	[A,C,B,D]
fadd %st(1), %st(0)	[A,A+C,B,D]
fmulp %st(2), %st(0)	[A+C,A*B,D]
fmulp %st(1), %st(0)	[A*B(A+C),D]
faddp %st(1), %st(0)	[A*B(A+C)+D]
fstp X	[]

(b) Generated x86 code and x87 stack.

Fig. 4. Stages of x86 code generation for Example 2. No spilling occurs

Example 3. Again suppose that the calculation $X = ((A * B) * (A + C)) + D$ is to be performed, but for illustration purposes let us now assume that the floating point stack only has three slots. This means only two pseudo variables, $\%\mathtt{f}_0$ and $\%\mathtt{f}_1$ can be used since there might be need of a scratch slot. Instead spill slots denoted by `%sp(i)` are used where `i` is limited by the size of the native stack; see the code in Fig. 5(a). As mentioned, the translation strategy used is a greedy one: leave spill positions that are live out at a certain point on the stack and hope that the new value will not have to leave the stack on account of another spilled value wanting to take its place. Doing so, results in the code shown in Fig. 5(b) which can be improved using a peephole optimization pass.

Some Notes on Precision. The standard precision of floating point values in ERLANG is, as mentioned above, the IEEE double precision. On the x87, however, the precision is 80 bit double extended precision and whenever a floating point value of another type is loaded on the stack it is also converted to this precision.

When the bytecode is interpreted one instruction at a time, as it is in the BEAM interpreter, the operands are pushed to the stack and converted, the operation is performed,

```
fmov A, %f0
fmov B, %f1
fmov C, %sp(0)
fmov D, %sp(1)
fadd %f0, %sp(0)
fmul %f0, %f1
fmul %f1, %sp(0)
fadd %sp(0), %sp(1)
fmov %sp(1), X
```

(a) Pseudo-x86 code.

Instruction	Stack
`fld A`	[A]
`fld B`	[B,A]
`fld C`	[C,B,A]
`fstp %sp(0)`	[B,A]
`fld D`	[D,B,A]
`fstp %sp(1)`	[B,A]
`fld %sp(0)`	[C,A,B]
`fadd %st(0), %st(1)`	[A+C,A,B]
`fxch %st(1)`	[A,A+C,B]
`fmulp %st(2), %st(0)`	[A+C,A*B]
`fmulp %st(1), %st(0)`	[A*B(A+C)]
`fadd %sp(1)`	[A*B(A+C)+D]
`fstp X`	[]

(b) Generated x86 code and x87 stack.

Fig. 5. Stages of x86 code generation for Example 3. Here spilling occurs

and finally the result is popped. The popping involves conversion back to the double precision by rounding the value on the stack.

When using the scheme described above, the results are kept on the x87 stack as long as possible if they are to be used again, which leads to a higher precision in the subsequent computations since no rounding is taking place in between computing an (intermediate) result and using it. This difference in precision can lead to different answers to the same sequence of FP computations depending on which scheme is used. The bigger the block of floating point instructions, the bigger the chance of getting different results. Note however that since less rounding leads to smaller accumulated error, the longer a value stays on the x87 stack, the better the FP precision which is obtained.

6 Performance Evaluation

The following questions are of interest when evaluating the performance of floating point handling in ERLANG.

- How effective is the local type analysis in classifying arithmetic operations that involve floating point values as indeed such?
- How much does the compilation scheme described in this paper improve the performance of ERLANG programs both when running in the BEAM interpreter and in native code?
- Does this scheme make Erlang/OTP competitive with state-of-the-art implementations of other strict functional languages in handling floating point arithmetic? Is the resulting performance competitive with that of statically typed languages?

We address these questions in reverse order below: In Sect. 6.1 the performance of HiPE, and SML/NJ are compared, followed by Sect. 6.2 which contains a performance comparison of different ERLANG implementations. Finally, Sect. 6.3, reports on the effectiveness of the local type analysis.

Table 2. Description of benchmark programs

Benchmark	Lines	Description
float_bm	100	A small synthetic benchmark that tests all floating point instructions; in this benchmark, floating point variables have small live ranges.
float_bm_spill	100	Same as above but variables in the program are kept live; in register-poor architectures spilling occurs.
barnes-hut	171	A floating point intensive multi-body simulator.
fft	257	An implementation of the fast Fourier transform.
wings_subdiv	1802	Wings is a 3D modeler written in ERLANG. This benchmark uses the Catmull-Clark subdivision algorithm to subdivide an initial ball model with 1536 polygons, 3072 edges, and 1538 vertices into a model with 6144 polygons, 12288 edges, and 6146 vertices.
wings_normals	1909	Calculates normals for all vertices of the above initial ball model.
raytracer	2898	A ray tracer tracing a scene with 11 objects (2 of them with textures).
pseudoknot	3310	Computes the 3D structure of a nucleic acid; programs are from [2].

The platforms used to conduct the comparison were a SUN Ultra 30 with a 296 MHz Sun UltraSPARC-II processor and 256 MB of RAM running Solaris 2.7, and a dual processor Intel Xeon 2.4 GHz machine with 1 GB of RAM and 512 KB of cache per processor running Linux. Information about the ERLANG programs used as benchmarks is shown in Table 2.

6.1 Comparing Floating Point Arithmetic in SML/NJ and Erlang/OTP

We have chosen to compare the resulting system against SML since it belongs to the same category of functional languages (namely strict) as ERLANG, it is known to have efficient industrial-strength implementations, and is statically typed so we can see how well our scheme performs against a system whose compiler has exact and complete information about types and absolutely no type tests are performed during runtime. This is not restricted to floats but extends to *all* types. As such, it gives SML/NJ an advantage over Erlang/OTP, but provided that the benchmark programs are floating point intensive, one can expect that the manifestation of this advantage is not so profound.

Two versions of SML/NJ are being used. Version 110.0.7, which is a stable, official release of the compiler, but it is also a bit old (from Sept. 2000). Thus we also included the most recent working version (110.42) of the compiler (from 16 Oct. 2002)[2].

Since SML/NJ generates native code [15], we only present a performance comparison against HiPE which compiles floating point operations to native code using the scheme described in the previous sections. Table 3 contains the results of the comparison in four of the benchmarks[3]. **barnes-hut** shows more or less the same picture on both SPARC

[2] Information about SML/NJ can be found at `cm.bell-labs.com/cm/cs/what/smlnj/`.

[3] Both versions of **float_bm** are small programs and so we wrote equivalent SML versions ourselves; **raytracer** and **wings_*** were too big to also do so. **pseudoknot** and **barnes-hut** are standard benchmark programs of the SML/NJ distribution. The **fft** program typically used as an SML benchmark uses destructive updates and thus does not have the same complexity as the ERLANG one. Unfortunately, **pseudoknot** could not be compiled by SML/NJ version 110.42.

Table 3. Performance comparison between HiPE and SML/NJ versions (times in ms)

Benchmark	HiPE	110.0.7	110.42
float_bm	4040	2660	2860
float_bm_spill	5400	4140	4190
barnes-hut	4280	4390	2230
pseudoknot	1440	620	—

(a) Performance on SPARC.

Benchmark	HiPE	110.0.7	110.42
float_bm	750	790	550
float_bm_spill	1440	1560	1350
barnes-hut	600	870	310
pseudoknot	140	190	—

(b) Performance on the x86.

and x86: HiPE is slightly faster than SML/NJ 110.0.7 and about twice as slow as 110.42; the reason has to do with the precision of the analysis; cf. also Table 5. The picture on the other benchmarks depends on the platform: On the SPARC, SML/NJ is between 30% and 130% faster on the **float_bm** and **pseudoknot** benchmarks. This is partly due to SML/NJ's use of a double word aligned floating point representation, but mostly due to the calling convention used by SML/NJ which passes floating point arguments of function calls in machine registers; HiPE currently does not, and cannot do so without employing a more global analysis. On the x86 where floating point arguments are passed on the stack anyway, the performance gap is significantly smaller for these programs: HiPE achieves a performance which is quite close (or better) to that of SML/NJ. We believe that this also validates the choice of the algorithm sketched in Example 3 for choosing which values to leave on the x87 floating point stack.

6.2 Performance of Float Handling in Implementations of Erlang

In Erlang/OTP R9 the analysis described in this paper is by default part of the BEAM compiler and the floating point instructions of Table 1 part of the BEAM interpreter. However, the compiler can be instructed not to do any analysis so that all floating point arithmetic is performed using generic BEAM instructions operating on boxed values that have to be type tested and unboxed each time the value is used. To study the performance of the presented scheme, a comparison is made using Erlang/OTP R9 both with and without the floating point analysis and finally using the HiPE compiler.

The results of the comparison are shown in Table 4. One can see that the performance of floating point manipulation in Erlang/OTP has improved considerably both as a result of using the analysis in the BEAM interpreter and due to the use of this information by the HiPE compiler. Note that the performance of e.g., **float_bm_spill** has improved up to 4.7 times by using the floating point instructions (on x86) and the performance improvement due to native code compilation of floating point operations ranges from a few percent up to a factor of 4.55, again in the **float_bm_spill** program (on SPARC). It should be clear that the scheme described in this paper is worth its while.

6.3 Effectiveness of the Local Static Analysis

As can be seen in Table 5 the static analysis, despite being local, succeeds in finding most of the floating point arithmetic instructions. This agrees with a statement made in [9, Sect. 5] that local unboxing is most effective on programs that perform a lot of

Table 4. Performance comparison between BEAM R9, and HiPE (times in ms)

	BEAM		HiPE
Benchmark	w/o anal	w anal	w anal
float_bm	39120	14800	4040
float_bm_spill	80630	24610	5400
barnes-hut	11330	10250	4280
fft	19600	16740	8890
wings_subdiv	9270	9520	8970
wings_normals	9070	8310	7370
raytracer	9490	9110	8500
pseudoknot	5200	3110	1440

(a) Performance on SPARC.

	BEAM		HiPE
Benchmark	w/o anal	w anal	w anal
float_bm	8830	1930	750
float_bm_spill	16450	3450	1440
barnes-hut	1830	1510	600
fft	3370	2830	1450
wings_subdiv	1310	1280	1150
wings_normals	1310	1160	850
raytracer	1370	1200	1070
pseudoknot	930	380	140

(b) Performance on x86.

Table 5. Effectiveness of the local static analysis in finding floating point arithmetic operations

Benchmark	FP-operations	Discovered
float_bm	1×10^8	100%
float_bm_spill	2×10^9	100%
barnes-hut	1×10^8	67%
fft	8×10^7	94%
wings_normals	6×10^5	100%
wings_subdivs	3×10^6	100%
raytracer	3×10^7	79%
pseudoknot	8×10^7	100%

floating point computations and for these programs one does not have to propagate type information through the whole compilation chain.

One thing to note is that our analysis technique gets a lot of mileage from the presence of type tests in guards of ERLANG clauses. By adding `is_float` guards in just two of the functions in **barnes-hut**, the percentage of discovered floating point arithmetic operations increased from initially 27% to 67%, which in turn gave a speed-up of 25% on the x86. This is the only program for which source code was modified. The performance on the different versions of **float_bm** is not surprising since they are of a synthetic nature, but considering that **pseudoknot** is a more realistic program, it is noteworthy that the analysis found all of the floating point arithmetics.

7 Discussion and Related Work

Our work is far from being the first or the most sophisticated static analysis for discovering floating point type information and avoiding unnecessary boxing and unboxing operations. Our analysis scheme has been practically rather than theoretically motivated from the start, and we hold that its biggest attractiveness lies in its combination of simplicity and effectiveness. ERLANG is a dynamically typed language and currently the unit of compilation in the HiPE compiler is a single function. One advantage of using a local analysis in our implementation setting is that the analysis is simple enough to be performed even when the compilation starts from bytecode (of a single function) rather than from ERLANG source code, and fast enough so as to be applicable in a just-in-time fashion.

If one decides to relax these constraints, there are more sophisticated analyses which have similar aims as ours that come to mind: Leroy's *representation analysis* [8] for ML-type languages (extended for the ML module system in [15]), or Jones' and Launchbury's analysis [7] for Haskell-like languages. All these analyses have been developed in the context of statically typed languages, are more powerful, but at the same time more expensive. An even more powerful analysis for avoiding unnecessary boxing operations for which optimality results can be established is described in [3]. Experimenting with non-local analysis is an interesting direction for future research. As described in Sect. 5 the back-ends of HiPE — and the x86 back-end in particular — already contain all the necessary ingredients for taking advantage of more powerful analyses. As indicated by the performance results, the implementation technology described in Sect. 5 for exploiting floating point type analysis information is efficient enough to be of interest to other functional programming language implementors independently of the characteristics of the source language.

Acknowledgments

This research has been supported in part by the ASTEC (Advanced Software Technology) competence center with matching funds by Ericsson Development. Sincere thanks to Björn Gustavsson of the Erlang/OTP team for incorporating the floating point type analysis in the BEAM compiler and for sending us the Wings benchmarks.

References

1. R. Cytron, J. Ferrante, B. K. Rosen, M. N. Wegman, and F. K. Zadeck. Efficiently computing static single assignment form and the control dependence graph. *ACM Trans. Prog. Lang. Syst.*, 13(4):451–490, Oct. 1991.
2. P. H. Hartel et al. Benchmarking imlementations of functional languages with "pseudoknot", a float intensive program. *Journal of Functional Programming*, 6(4):621–655, July 1996.
3. F. Henglein and J. Jørgensen. Formally optimal boxing. In *Conference Record of the ACM SIGPLAN-SIGACT Symposium on Principles of Programming Languages*, pages 213–226. ACM Press, Jan. 1994.
4. Intel Corporation. *Intel Pentium 4 and Intel Xeon Processor Optimization Reference Manual*, 2002. Document number 248966-05.
5. E. Johansson, M. Pettersson, and K. Sagonas. HiPE: A High Performance Erlang system. In *Proceedings of the ACM SIGPLAN Conference on Principles and Practice of Declarative Programming*, pages 32–43. ACM Press, Sept. 2000.
6. E. Johansson and K. Sagonas. Linear scan register allocation in a high performance Erlang compiler. In *Practical Applications of Declarative Languages: Proceedings of the PADL'2002 Symposium*, number 2257 in LNCS, pages 299–317. Springer, Jan. 2002.
7. S. L. P. Jones and J. Launchbury. Unboxed values as first class citizens in a non-strict functional language. In J. Hughes, editor, *Proceedings of the 5th ACM Conference on Functional Languages and Computer Architecture*, number 523 in LNCS, pages 636–666. Springer, Aug. 1991.

8. X. Leroy. Unboxed values and polymorphic typing. In *Conference Record of the Nineteenth Annual ACM Symposium on Principles of Programming Languages*, pages 177–188. ACM Press, Jan. 1992.
9. X. Leroy. The effectiveness of type-based unboxing. In *Workshop Types in Compilation'97*, June 1997.
10. A. Leung and L. George. Some notes on the new MLRISC x86 floating point code generator (draft). Unpublished technical report available from: http://cm.bell-labs.com/cm/cs/what/smlnj/compiler-notes/.
11. S. S. Muchnick. *Advanced Compiler Design & Implementation*. Morgan Kaufman Publishers, San Fransisco, CA, 1997.
12. M. Pettersson. A staged tag scheme for Erlang. Technical Report 029, Information Technology Department, Uppsala University, Nov. 2000.
13. M. Pettersson, K. Sagonas, and E. Johansson. The HiPE/x86 Erlang compiler: System description and performance evaluation. In Z. Hu and M. Rodríguez-Artalejo, editors, *Proceedings of the Sixth International Symposium on Functional and Logic Programming*, number 2441 in LNCS, pages 228–244. Springer, Sept. 2002.
14. M. Poletto and V. Sarkar. Linear scan register allocation. *ACM Trans. Prog. Lang. Syst.*, 21(5):895–913, Sept. 1999.
15. Z. Shao and A. W. Appel. A type-based compiler for Standard ML. In *Proceedings of the ACM SIGPLAN '95 Conference on Programming Language Design and Implementation*, pages 116–129. ACM Press, June 1995.

Stacking Cycles: Functional Transformation of Circular Data

Baltasar Trancón y Widemann

Department of Computer Science
Technische Universität Berlin, Germany
bt@cs.tu-berlin.de

Abstract. Functional programming is very powerful when applied to tree-shaped data. Real-world software problems often involve circular graph-shaped data. In this paper, we characterize a class of functions on circular data graphs extending the class of primitively corecursive functions. We propose an abstract, effective implementation technique for these functions under an eager evaluation strategy on standard stack machines. The proposed implementation ensures termination and can be tuned either for exactness or for speed. The latter variant is asymptotically as efficient as standard implementations of algebraic recursion, at the price of suboptimal homomorphic result graphs with decently bounded redundancy.

Keywords: Coalgebra, corecursion, anamorphism, code generation, cycle detection, function memoization

1 Introduction

1.1 On This Paper

In the first section, we discuss the application of coalgebraic functional programming to graph-shaped (circular) data. Then, we characterize a class of corecursive functions on such data and present an algorithm to implement these functions, reconciling eager evaluation and terminating computations on (conceptually) infinite structures. Finally, we examine several optimization techniques that promise to compensate the serious runtime overhead implied by a naïve implementation.

We assume familiarity with the basic concepts and notations of category theory, and especially of categorial algebra and coalgebra. A good introduction can be found in [Rut96]. The basic applications of categorial (co)algebra for functional programming, such as presented in [MFP91], are also presupposed.

1.2 Graphs and Objects

In real-world programming, there are lots of circular data. Especially object-oriented programs, but also semantic networks used for knowledge representation, deal a lot with relational models, represented as graphs of objects. Naturally, objects are represented as memory cells and links to other objects as

R. Peña and T. Arts (Eds.): IFL 2002, LNCS 2670, pp. 150–164, 2003.

pointers to other cells. The rest of a cell (the non-pointers fields) is devoted to the local state of the object (the node label in a graph model).

In a theory of functional programming, circular structures can be captured elegantly by cofree datatypes which are usually modeled as final coalgebras, using corecursion as the primary definition technique. While final coalgebras have numerous nice properties, they fail to represent one central feature of object-orientation: The identity of an object that is discriminable but not a part of its state. This concept is alien to mathematicians, and stems from both philosophical motivations and low-level implementation techniques involving memory cells and pointers. The postulation of identities is the principal paradigmatic difference between cofree datatypes and object systems. As a consequence, the appropriate mathematical model for object systems will be *non-final* coalgebras.

But regardless of coalgebraic or object-oriented interpretations, many functions are defined solely in terms of object state and abstract from identities in their semantics. We shall try to demonstrate in this paper that

1. such functions can be defined by corecursion, and
2. identities are quite relevant for an effective implementation.

There are very well-known standard techniques for implementing algebraic recursive functions on general-purpose stack machines (see, e.g. [ASU86]). Corecursive functions have been much less popular in the history of programming, therefore the corresponding code generation techniques are not as easily found in standard textbooks. Nevertheless, implementing corecursion mainly means implementing recursion and cleverly enforcing termination; either by lazy evaluation and a suitable notion of *productivity* of circular definitions (see [TT97]), or by eager evaluation combined with cycle detection. We will take the latter approach in this paper, since there are already plenty of results for the former.

Algebraic functional programming is essentially about trees. Computations on directed acyclic graphs are possible, though with exponential worst-case complexity if subgraph sharing occurs frequently. The technique of function *memoization* ([Mic68], [Bir80]) can be used to avoid the combinatorial explosion by processing shared subgraphs only once. Cycles, however, cannot be handled gracefully by algebraic functions, even with memoization, because of the algebraic dogma that structures shall be well-founded and processable bottom-up. Implementing coalgebraic functions requires a dual, top-down approach, where the result is (to some degree) initialized before the graph traversal moves on.

1.3 Final Coalgebras

Given some *signature functor* $F : Set \to Set$, an F-coalgebra is a pair $\mathcal{C} = (C, \gamma)$ of a *carrier set* C and an *operation* $\gamma : C \to F(C)$. A set morphism $f : C \to D$ is an F-coalgebra morphism $f : \mathcal{C} \to \mathcal{D} = (D, \delta)$, if $\delta \circ f = F(f) \circ \gamma$. An F-coalgebra $\mathcal{C}$ is called *final*, iff, for any other F-coalgebra $\mathcal{D} = (D, \delta)$, there is exactly one *anamorphism* $[\![\delta]\!] : \mathcal{D} \to \mathcal{C}$. Besides the power of coinductive definition, final coalgebras come with the useful property of *simplicity*; behavioral equivalence of final coalgebra elements (objects) implies their equality. This can be expressed concisely with the help of bisimulations. A bisimulation on two coalgebras $\mathcal{C}$ and $\mathcal{D}$ is a coalgebra relation $\mathcal{B} = (B \subseteq C \times D, \beta)$, such that the projections $\pi_1 : \mathcal{B} \to \mathcal{C}$ and $\pi_2 : \mathcal{B} \to \mathcal{D}$ are coalgebra morphisms. Two objects x, x' are bisimilar ($x \approx x'$), iff a bisimulation including the pair (x, x') exists. If $\mathcal{C}$ is final, then all bisimilar objects are identical. Bisimilarity is the key technique for proving coalgebraic equations.

Examples. Consider the cofree datatype of α-streams (the dual of α-lists). The datatype definition

$$\mathsf{stream}[\alpha] ::= \mathsf{eos} \mid (\mathsf{head} : \alpha, \mathsf{tail} : \mathsf{stream}[\alpha])$$

induces a signature functor

$$\begin{aligned} \mathsf{Str}[\alpha](X) &= 1 + \alpha \times X \\ \mathsf{Str}[\alpha](f) &= \mathsf{id}_1 + \mathsf{id}_\alpha \times f \end{aligned}$$

A final $\mathsf{Str}[\alpha]$-coalgebra models all sorts of α-streams:

1. Finite streams. These are exactly the α-lists. Consider the countdown streams $c_0, c_1, \ldots$ defined by:

$$\mathsf{head}(c_i) = i \qquad \begin{aligned} \mathsf{tail}(c_{i+1}) &= c_i \\ \mathsf{tail}(c_0) &= \mathsf{eos} \end{aligned}$$

   Finite data structures are the supreme domain of classical algebraic functional programming. They are easily defined by induction and processed by recursion.
2. Infinite streams:
   (a) Truly infinite streams. Consider the stream of natural numbers n_0, defined by:

$$\mathsf{head}(n_i) = i \qquad \mathsf{tail}(n_i) = n_{i+1}$$

   (b) Circular streams. Even if a stream (conceptually) has no finite length, the number of *different* states ever reachable may be finite. Consider the alternating streams a_0, a_1 defined by:

$$\begin{aligned} \mathsf{head}(a_0) &= 0 \qquad & \mathsf{tail}(a_0) &= a_1 \\ \mathsf{head}(a_1) &= 1 \qquad & \mathsf{tail}(a_1) &= a_0 \end{aligned}$$

   Circular data structures, representing systems with infinite dynamics and finite state space, are the primary domain of eager coalgebraic functional programming. They can be defined by coinduction and processed effectively by corecursion, though these techniques are neither as widely known nor as well understood as their algebraic duals.

1.4 Intuition of Strict Corecursion

An intuitive grasp on the strict semantics of corecursion is probably best gained by studying a simple example. The example given in this section is quite trivial, but already exceeds the power of both strict and lazy algebraic programming. Given the cofree datatype of natural numbers[1]

$$\mathsf{nat} ::= \big(\mathsf{pred} : \mathsf{optional}[\mathsf{nat}]\big)$$

we can define the length of a stream by corecursion:

$$\begin{aligned} &\mathsf{length} && : \mathsf{stream}[\alpha] \to \mathsf{nat} \\ &\mathsf{pred}\big(\mathsf{length}(\mathsf{eos})\big) && = \mathsf{null} \\ &\mathsf{pred}\big(\mathsf{length}(s)\big) && = \mathsf{length}\big(\mathsf{tail}(s)\big) \end{aligned}$$

At a first glance, this looks like an inside-out notation for the well-known recursive length function on lists. But with the corecursive definition, we are able to compute the "length" of periodical infinite streams as well: Consider the alternating stream of zeroes and ones defined above. By putting $k_0 = \mathsf{length}(a_0)$ and $k_1 = \mathsf{length}(a_1)$, we obtain the cycle

$$\begin{aligned} \mathsf{pred}(k_0) &= \mathsf{length}(a_1) = k_1 \\ \mathsf{pred}(k_1) &= \mathsf{length}(a_0) = k_0 \end{aligned}$$

which is a finite representation for the (correct) result number ω. Note that there is no need for lazy semantics in the corecursive definition. A lazy recursive function could also be used to "compute" the result ω, but this is not quite the same; lazy recursion would compute an unbounded prefix of an infinite representation of ω instead. The effect of this subtle difference is more dramatic than just a loss of efficiency due to thunk construction and evaluation: Inherently strict operations are not supported. E.g., the equality (bisimilarity) relation is decidable on the domain of finitely represented natural numbers, whereas dynamically generated infinite representations cannot be compared in finite time.

1.5 Mostly Final Coalgebras

From a functional viewpoint, we consider the possibility of different objects identities sharing the same observable behavior a weakness of a concrete object system implementation rather than a positive feature. Given some non-final implementation model $\mathcal{C}' = (C', \gamma')$, an application should only observe the represented objects modulo *behavioral equivalence* $\approx$. This relation is the maximal bisimulation on $\mathcal{C}' \times \mathcal{C}'$, manifest as the kernel of $[\![\gamma']\!]$. On the level of implementation infrastructure however, intrinsic object identities are indispensable for actually getting hold on the finite graph representation of system.

[1] This type comprises the algebraic natural numbers plus the value ω, which is characterized by being bisimilar to its predecessor.

If final semantics are to be imposed on object systems and their transformations, e.g., for proving some properties coinductively, then a detrimental effect of object identities is encountered in the non-final models. I.e., a limited degree of homomorphic redundancy of representations ($x \approx y$, but $x \neq y$) is intrinsic and permissible on the infrastructure level, and must be handled gracefully.

The introduction of redundancy is expressed by a semantic (re)*constructor* operation $\tilde{\gamma} : F(C') \to C'$, which is the proper right inverse of operation γ', and its left inverse up to equivalence. I.e., $\gamma' \circ \tilde{\gamma} = \mathsf{id}$ and $[\![\gamma']\!] \circ \tilde{\gamma} \circ \gamma' = [\![\gamma']\!]$ which is the same as $\tilde{\gamma}(\gamma'(x)) \approx x$. Note that this does *not* imply $\tilde{\gamma} \circ \gamma' = \mathsf{id}$, so an implementation of $\tilde{\gamma}$ is free to construct new, redundant representations for objects.

So far, we have identified two different views on coalgebraically modeled systems:

1. On the application level, the power of coinduction is required, implying a final model.
2. On the implementation level, the effects of object identities and redundancy exist (whether beneficial or not), implying a non-final model.

Now, we will try to reconcile these views by giving the specification of our approach in the final model, and the implementation in the non-final model. Then, all properties required by the specification will be met by the implementation only up to $\approx$.

1.6 Objects in Memory

In this section, we will outline our assumptions about the representation of coalgebra elements (called objects for short) in memory in a fairly abstract way. Let S be the space of local object states (some arbitrary interpretation of bits). A memory state is a tuple (A, σ, ψ) where A is a finite set of object identities, $\sigma : A \to S$ computes the local states for the objects in A, and $\psi : A \to A^*$ yields the identities of objects pointed to. Furthermore, the number of pointers an object has shall be determined by its local state, i.e., the following constraint shall hold for all $a, a' \in A$:

$$\sigma(a) = \sigma(a') \Longrightarrow |\psi(a)| = |\psi(a')| \tag{1}$$

This constraint induces a *rank function* $n : S \to \mathbb{N}$, such that, for all $a \in A$, $|\psi(a)| = n(\sigma(a))$. This rank function can be materialized in several ways:

1. by layout information in the cell header, invisible to the application.
2. by application-level type information:
   (a) by dynamic type tagging.
   (b) by static type inference.

2 Mostly Primitive Corecursion

The signature functor for our coalgebraic model of object states is:

$$\mathsf{Obj}(X) = S \times X^*$$
$$\mathsf{Obj}(f) = \mathsf{id}_S \times f^*$$

A final coalgebra $\mathcal{C} = (C, \gamma)$ is known to exist for that functor. A memory state is then a subsystem (A, α) of $\mathcal{C}$, such that $\alpha = \langle \sigma, \psi \rangle$, obeying the rank constraint (1). There shall be a global rank function n that applies uniformly to all subsystems.

Instead of having particular memory state models, and transitions between these by heap operations, we will reason within the whole final coalgebra, assuming that allocation and initialization of cells as needed is performed behind the stages by switching subsystems (no explicit new operator in this paper).

Remember the usual definition of primitive corecursion: Any F-coalgebra $\mathcal{D} = (D, \delta)$ uniquely determines an anamorphism $[\!(\delta)\!] : \mathcal{D} \to \mathcal{C}$, such that:

$$\gamma \circ [\!(\delta)\!] = F([\!(\delta)\!]) \circ \delta$$

Anamorphisms (called *unfolds*, or informally *lenses* due to the weird brackets) are a common and elegant technique to define primitively corecursive functions.

For our special signature, we will modify this technique slightly to what we call mostly primitive corecursion. Given two functions:

$$f_1 : S \times C^* \nrightarrow S \times C^*$$
$$f_2 : S \times C^* \to C^*$$

such that the result of f_1 obeys the rank constraint and f_2 is rank-preserving:

$$f_1(s,p) = \begin{cases} (s',p') \text{ where } |p'| = n(s') & \text{if } |p| = n(s) \\ \text{undefined} & \text{otherwise} \end{cases} \tag{2}$$
$$\big|f_2(s,p)\big| = |p|$$

the corecursive function $[\![_{f_2}, f_1]\!]$ [2] is determined by:

$$\gamma \circ [\![_{f_2}, f_1]\!] = \langle \pi_1, f_2 \rangle \circ \mathsf{Obj}([\![_{f_2}, f_1]\!]) \circ f_1 \circ \gamma \tag{3}$$

This equation reads as follows: First, the initialization stage f_1 is performed on the inner structure of an object; next, the operation follows the links from the current object corecursively; and the finalization stage f_2 rearranges the links of the newly created object, possibly depending on, *but not modifying* the local state. Condition (2) ensures that the result of each stage obeys the successor rank constraint.

Mostly primitive corecursion can be seen as a special case of a coalgebraic hylomorphism, where the second stage (the catamorphism) does not alter the local state of the result. This constraint is of crucial importance for our algorithm, because we can assume the local state, and thus the size of an object, is fixed after the first stage, and actually allocate a cell *before* recurring.

[2] The notation mimics the common hylomorphism notation with a restricted cata part

Note that, on the application level, C is an opaque type (comparable to `void *` in C/C++), so that identities may be passed around by f_1 and f_2, but the state of the corresponding objects cannot be observed. Our implementation relies on this property, passing around references to allocated, but potentially incomplete object cells.

If the second stage is not used, then $[\![_{\pi_2}, f_1]\!] = [\!(f_1 \circ \gamma)\!]$, so the first stage yields just primitive corecursion. Many applications will only use f_1, so mostly primitive corecursion is not a generalization motivated by precise practical requirements, but rather a byproduct of the implementation technique outlined later in this paper. All of the following results hold for purely primitive corecursion as well, yet mostly primitive corecursion has some interesting properties of its own:

Theorem 1. *The construction* $[\![_{f_2}, f_1]\!]$ *is unique.*

Proof. Assume that the morphisms $f, f' : C \to C$ *both satisfy equation (3). Then* $\sigma \circ f = \pi_1 \circ f_1 \circ \gamma = \sigma \circ f'$ *and therefore* $|\psi \circ f| = n \circ \sigma = |\psi \circ f'|$*. Now we define a system* (B, β)*:*

$$
\begin{aligned}
B &= \{(f(x), f'(x)) \mid x \in C\} \\
\beta(x, x') &= \Big(\sigma(x), \mathsf{zip}\big(\psi(x), \psi(x')\big)\Big) \\
\mathsf{zip}(\varepsilon, \varepsilon) &= \varepsilon \\
\mathsf{zip}(x :: w, x' :: w') &= (x, x') :: \mathsf{zip}(w, w')
\end{aligned}
$$

Obviously, $\pi_1^* \circ \mathsf{zip} = \pi_1$ *and* $\pi_2^* \circ \mathsf{zip} = \pi_2$*. We show that* (B, β) *is a bisimulation on* C*, i.e.,* π_1, π_2 *are homomorphisms:*

$$
\begin{aligned}
\mathsf{Obj}(\pi_1) \circ \beta &= (\mathsf{id} \times \pi_1^*) \circ \beta \\
&= (\mathsf{id} \times \pi_1^*) \circ \big\langle \sigma \circ \pi_1, \mathsf{zip} \circ (\psi \times \psi)\big\rangle \\
&= \big\langle \sigma \circ \pi_1, \pi_1^* \circ \mathsf{zip} \circ (\psi \times \psi)\big\rangle \\
&= \big\langle \sigma \circ \pi_1, \pi_1 \circ (\psi \times \psi)\big\rangle \\
&= \langle \sigma, \psi \rangle \circ \pi_1 \\
&= \gamma \circ \pi_1 \\
\mathsf{Obj}(\pi_2) \circ \beta &= (\mathsf{id} \times \pi_2^*) \circ \beta \\
&= (\mathsf{id} \times \pi_2^*) \circ \big\langle \sigma \circ \pi_1, \mathsf{zip} \circ (\psi \times \psi)\big\rangle \\
&= \big\langle \sigma \circ \pi_1, \pi_2^* \circ \mathsf{zip} \circ (\psi \times \psi)\big\rangle \\
&= \big\langle \sigma \circ \pi_1, \pi_2 \circ (\psi \times \psi)\big\rangle \\
&= \sigma \times \psi \\
&= \langle \sigma, \psi \rangle \circ \pi_2 \qquad \textit{since } \sigma\big(f(x)\big) = \sigma\big(f'(x)\big) \\
&= \gamma \circ \pi_2
\end{aligned}
$$

Since C *is final, this implies* $f = f'$ *by coinduction.* □

This result does not imply that a function $[\![f_2, f_1]\!]$ actually *exists*. Instead of a general proof of existence, we will take a pragmatic approach and provide an algorithm implementing mostly primitive corecursion as a computable function on finite-state circular data. The general case of corecursive functions on infinite systems, which has to be evaluated lazily to retain any kind of "computability", is outside the scope of this paper.

Examples

All of the following examples deal with streams. In order to fit the stream signature on the cell signature Obj, assume there is one special state $\mathsf{eos} \in S$, such that $n(\mathsf{eos}) = 0$, and other states s denote stream elements, with $\sigma = \mathsf{head}$ and $\psi = \mathsf{tail}$.

The first examples are all instances of primitive corecursions (with $f_2 = \pi_2$). These are given as an introduction to the reader unfamiliar with corecursion.

1. **Mapping a stream.** This is the traditional corecursive map function applying a function g to each stream element. Assume g is *rank-homomorphic*, i.e., $n(s) = n\big(g(s)\big)$:
$$f_1(s,p) = \big(g(s), p\big)$$
2. **Cutting a stream.** The following function terminates a stream right before the first occurrence of element z, i.e., it maps z homomorphically to eos:
$$f_1(s,p) = \begin{cases} (\mathsf{eos}, \varepsilon), & \text{if } s = z \\ (s,p), & \text{otherwise} \end{cases}$$
3. **Unfolding a stream.** Assume there are two special objects x_0, x_1 with $\sigma(x_i) = i$ and $\psi(x_i) = \varepsilon$. Then we can construct infinitely alternating streams of zeroes and ones with $[\![f_2, f_1]\!]$:
$$f_1(i, \varepsilon) = (i, x_{1-i})$$
4. **Counting the elements of a stream.** Assume there are additionally two states $\mathsf{succ}, \mathsf{zero}$ for natural numbers, such that $n(\mathsf{succ}) = 1$ and $n(\mathsf{zero}) = 0$.
$$\begin{aligned} f_1(\mathsf{eos}, \varepsilon) &= (\mathsf{zero}, \varepsilon) \\ f_1(s,p) &= (\mathsf{succ}, p) \quad \text{otherwise} \\ f_2(s,p) &= p \end{aligned}$$
Even for non-terminating streams that iterate a finite sequence of k elements periodically, the "correct" length is calculated: The resulting cycle of k mutual successors is easily recognizable as a representation of ω.
5. **Repeating each element of a stream twice.** This example is quite hard to express in terms of purely primitive corecursion:
$$\begin{aligned} f_1(s,p) &= (s,p) \\ f_2(\mathsf{eos}, \varepsilon) &= \varepsilon \\ f_2(s,p) &= \tilde{\gamma}(s,p) \quad \text{otherwise} \end{aligned}$$

3 Implementation

3.1 Corecursion = Recursion + Cycle Detection

Our implementation technique for corecursion is based on cycle detection by means of the call stack only. It combines well with heap-based function memoization handling non-circular data sharing. We believe that the duality of sharing and cycles in graphs is reflected properly in the duality of respectively heap and stack employed in their detection.

3.2 Constraints on Calling Conventions

We assume that the following standard information is available for each stack frame:

1. the identity of the called function.
2. the parameter values of the call.
3. the enclosing stack frame.

Furthermore, we assume that there is an extra slot in the stack frame for storing the *result*. Our algorithm will fill that slot with the identity of a newly allocated cell, before any recursive calls are made, so as an invariant, the result slots of enclosing stack frames are all initialized, albeit with incomplete objects.

3.3 The Algorithm

The implementation of $[\![{}_{f_2}, f_1]\!](x)$ works as follows:

1. (Scan) Scan the stack for a frame incarnating the same function with the same argument node. If found, return the result value stored in that frame; otherwise continue.
2. (Init) Compute $x' := (\tilde{\gamma} \circ f_1 \circ \gamma)(x)$. Store x' in the result slot for this stack frame, so that nested calls can retrieve it. The object identified by x' is not yet fully constructed (still pointing to original nodes). The application is not allowed to observe its temporary state.
   Note that we are not reasoning on the final coalgebra; the implementation of $\tilde{\gamma}$ is required to be aggressively non-final and construct a new cell instead of reusing an equivalent one. As a consequence, $f_1 = \mathsf{id}$ will clone all nodes, unless preempted by memoization.
3. (Recur) Compute $p := [\![{}_{f_2}, f_1]\!]^*(\psi(x'))$. This is where corecursion actually takes place. Note that, when nested calls do stack scanning, all relevant enclosing stack frames are past step 2.
4. (Complete) Compute $p' := f_2(\sigma(x), p)$.
5. (Update) Store p' in x'. This is a destructive update. It is safe only because x' is known to be a new cell, and that $\psi(x')$ has not been observed so far. Now x' is complete and may be exposed to the application.
6. (Memo) If function memoization is turned on, then store the completed object x' now as the result for $[\![{}_{f_2}, f_1]\!](x)$.
7. (Return) Return the content of the result slot (i.e., x').

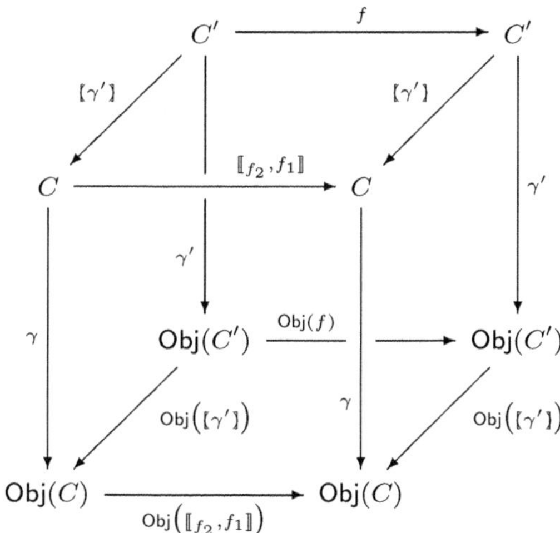

Fig. 1. Soundness of the Implementation

Note that our implementation works on a non-final coalgebra C', whereas the specification of mostly primitive corecursion is based on the final coalgebra $\mathcal{C}$. The function actually implemented is some loosely determined $f : C' \to C'$, such that the final semantics function $(\!|\gamma'|\!)$ of our infrastructural model is a transformation from the implementation f to the specification $[\![f_2, f_1]\!]$:

$$(\!|\gamma'|\!) \circ f = [\![f_2, f_1]\!] \circ (\!|\gamma'|\!) \tag{4}$$

4 Optimizations

Obviously, brute-force stack scanning incurs an overhead of the worst-case complexity of $\mathcal{O}(n^2)$, where n is the number of function calls. This is far from acceptable in general, but can be improved substantially by some optimizations.

4.1 Function-Based Optimization

It is obviously not feasible that the whole stack of the running program be scanned for cycle detection. In some cases, however, there is compile-time evidence that stack scanning need not proceed beyond a particular frame, because there can be no enclosing call to the same function. Then, a slightly different call sequence can be generated. The back pointer of the frame created for the called function is tagged somehow (or even set to *null* if not needed for other purposes) to indicate a barrier for stack scanning.

Static call graph analysis works fine, as long as the program does not rely too heavily on dynamic *apply*-style operators, i.e., higher-order functions that take closures as their arguments and invoke them. For such functions, only a conservative guess at what they might possibly call can be made, based on type information.

Under the assumption that corecursive computations are utility code that is called at deeply nested points in an application, and calls only other equally low-level functions, call analysis is strongly required to prevent expensive and useless scanning of the enclosing stack frames of higher application levels. It is even possible to require the special calling conventions mentioned above only for the corecursion-aware parts of code confined, e.g., in a library. Other parts of an application need not adhere to this calling convention, as long as it is guaranteed that the corresponding stack frames are never scanned.

Function-based optimization can benefit from other simplifications of the call graph. In some settings there are no mutually (co)recursive functions, i.e., a function recurs either directly or not at all. This may be the case

1. in systems where general recursion is not supported, and (co)recursive functions are constructed by some limited means such as (ana-/)catamorphisms, or
2. because exhaustive function inlining has been performed.

Then, stack scanning always can be limited to those immediately enclosing stack frames belonging to the same function.

4.2 Data-Based Optimization

Another potential for optimization, and a much more fine-grained one due to its completely dynamic nature, lies in the layout of the data graphs. We assume a spare tag bit for each pointer in a cell. Then we can postulate some invariants:

1. Each cycle in a data graph shall contain at least one tagged edge. (Mandatory)
2. The number of tagged edges in a data graph shall be as small as possible. (Supplementary; loss of time efficiency if violated, but not of correctness)
3. In each cycle, the path from the entry point of the cycle to the target of the tagged edge shall be as short as possible, optimally both being the same node. (Supplementary; loss of space efficiency if violated, but not of correctness)

The algorithm is changed slightly:

1. Stack scanning is only performed when traversing a tagged edge in the original graph.
2. A newly constructed edge is tagged, if (and only if) its target results from cycle detection. This strategy preserves Constraint (1).

Constraint (1) is necessary for the termination of the relaxed algorithm. Constraints (2) and (3) express quality criteria for the optimization. Note that the presented algorithm always yields results that are optimal with respect to both (2) and (3), thus optimizing the data layout for subsequent calls to corecursive transformations. This means that the composition of arbitrary many corecursive functions will have literally the same space overhead characteristics (no scaling).

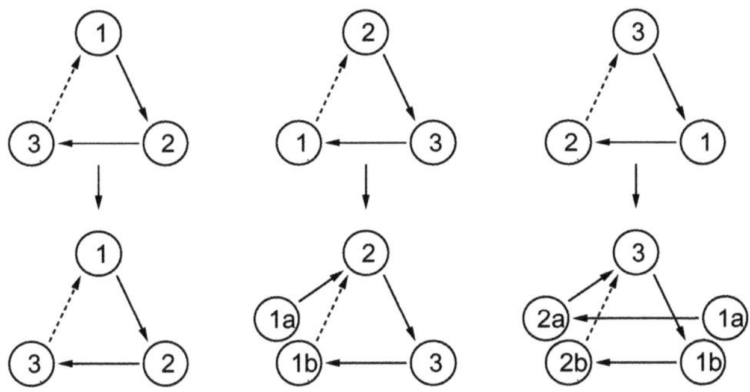

Fig. 2. Optimal and Suboptimal Tagging

Only if the root node of a data graph is changed between successive transformations, then (3) might fail.

If (2) is violated, then there will some superfluous stack scanning. If (3) is violated, then stack scanning will be triggered at an inconvenient point in time. As a result, some cycles may be detected somewhere between one and two full turns, resulting in a target structure containing more redundancy than necessary. However, the increase in data size is strongly bounded (see below), and the impact on computation speed is great: Cycle-free data is processed without any stack scanning, i.e., with no significant overhead compared to implementations of purely algebraic recursion.

Examples. Have a look at the three examples depicted in figure 2. The clone operation $[\![\pi_2, \mathsf{id}]\!]$ is applied to a simple circular graph, starting at different root nodes. The numbers indicate the order of traversal of the original graph. Tagged edges are rendered as dashed arrows.

The optimal result (left column) is achieved, if the tagged edge points to the first visited node. In this case, the cycle is mapped one-to-one, with no redundancy added, but just one instead of three stack scans. Every cycle member that has been visited *before* the target of the tagged edge will be duplicated, because there is no matching stack frame yet when the tagged edge is traversed for the first time, and the stack scan fails. This can amount to $(n-1)$ duplicated nodes in a cycle of size n (right column).

The example in figure 3 shows the interaction with memoization. Additional edge numbers are provided to indicate the order of construction. Memoization mappings are rendered as dotted arrows.

Most remarkable in this figure is edge 7. After edge 4 has been computed, the result nodes 1b and 2 are completed and memoized, so that when re-ascending to node 1a, the result node 2 can be reused for edge 7.

Another interesting fact is that there are two possible memoized results for node 1. If memoization is implemented to overwrite, then edge 8 will supersede edge 5. Otherwise, if the first entry wins, then edge 5 will persist. In the latter

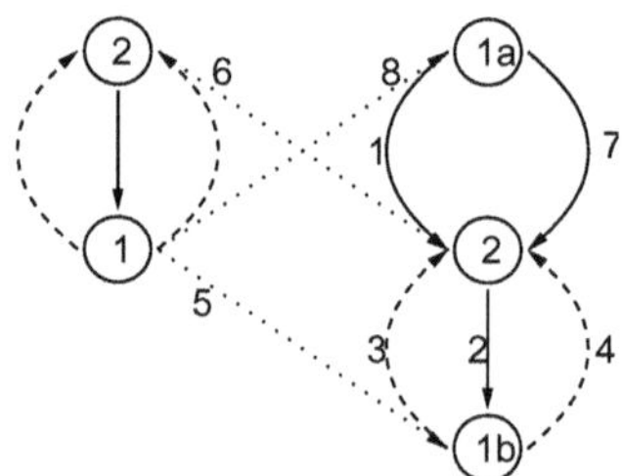

Fig. 3. Memoized Corecursion

case, node 1a will not be reused by subsequent memo lookups, and become unreachable (and reclaimable) presumably earlier in program execution time.

In general terms, an overwriting strategy for memoization will optimize placement of tagged edges, whereas a non-overwriting strategy will favor smaller sets of live nodes.

4.3 Tail Recursion Optimization

Because of the result slot, tail recursion optimization cannot be applied straightforwardly to mostly corecursive functions. However, if $f_2 = \pi_2$, i.e., the applied function is a purely primitive corecursion, the elimination of tail calls would be desirable.

Let us assume that the information whether a node is *pointed to* by a tagged edge is available, e.g., by dedicating a flag bit in the cell header. Then, a node will only ever be encountered on stack scanning if this flag is set. All other result slots need not persist, so all stack frames incarnated for unflagged nodes can be immediately reused for a tail call. As a consequence, cycle-free linear (sub)structures are processed not only without time overhead for stack scanning, but also on constant stack space.

4.4 Cell Reuse Optimization

Lastly, mostly final corecursion combines with destructive updating. If data-flow analysis statically or dynamically determines that the argument cell x is not used anymore after the computation, it might be reused as x', an optimization available in some high-performance implementations of functional languages, e.g. OPAL[Pep91].

5 Conclusion

We have presented two layers of coalgebraic models for finite circular data: A signature functor, together with a final coalgebra for modeling the semantic properties, and non-final coalgebras for the syntactical representation in memory. These two layers are related accurately by the corresponding anamorphisms.

We have specified a straightforward effective implementation for a class of eagerly computable corecursive functions on such data. This implementation imposes a nontrivial time overhead for cycle detection, which can be significantly improved, especially, but not exclusively for cycle-free subgraphs, by a trade-off against space overhead, namely some homomorphic redundancy in the result graph.

5.1 Implementation Status

The abstract algorithm presented above has been instantiated prototypically for some corecursive functions in a proof-of-concept hand-coding style using C and C++ as implementation languages. Since some control over the stack is required, the mechanism cannot be ported directly to "safe" stack machines, such as the Java or .NET VMs.

5.2 Related Work

A type theory of dynamically infinite data based on non-well founded algebra rather than on coalgebra has been proposed in [TT97].

An implementation of primitive corecursion given by unfold morphisms can be found, e.g., in the programming language charity [CF92]. The implementation of charity is based on graph rewriting in an abstract machine rather than on traditional code generation.

A detailed treatment of graph algorithms in functional programming, though without the connection to coalgebras, can be found in [Erw01].

The idea of tagging certain pointers in cycles has been explored in the context of reference-counting memory management by several authors ([Bro85], [Sal87], [PvEP88]). See [JL96] for a summary.

5.3 Open Issues

1. A formal proof of the correctness of the basic algorithm (equation 4).
2. Some hard numbers (and a proof) for the worst-case space behavior of the optimized algorithm.
3. Extension of the mostly primitive corecursion scheme to more than one argument (product coalgebras).
4. Extension of the class of covered functions towards general hylomorphisms.
5. Thorough comparison to lazy-evaluation approaches to circular data.
6. A feasible front-end syntax for defining mostly primitive corecursive functions.
7. Integration of the coding scheme into a real compiler.
8. Significant benchmarking.

Acknowledgments

Thanks to Markus Lepper and Jacob Wieland, Technische Universität Berlin, for valuable discussions.

References

ASU86. A.V. Aho, R. Sethi, and J.D. Ullman. *Compilers: Principles, Techniques, and Tools.* Addison-Wesley, 1986.

Bir80. R.S. Bird. Tabulation Techniques for Recursive Programs. *ACM Comp. Surv.*, 12(4):403–417, 1980.

Bro85. D.R. Brownbridge. Cyclic reference counting for combinator machines. In *LNCS*, volume 201. Springer, 1985.

CF92. R. Cockett and T. Fukushima. About Charity. Technical Report 92/480/18, University of Calgary, 1992.

Erw01. M. Erwig. Inductive graphs and functional graph algorithms, 2001.

JL96. R. Jones and R. Lins. *Garbage Collection.* Wiley, Chichester, 1996.

MFP91. E. Meijer, M. Fokkinga, and R. Paterson. Functional programming with bananas, lenses, envelopes and barbed wire. In *Proceedings of the ACM FPCA'91, LNCS*, volume 523. Springer, 1991.

Mic68. D. Michie. "Memo" functions and machine learning. *Nature*, 218:19–22, 1968.

Pep91. P. Pepper. The Programming Language OPAL (5th corrected edition). Technical Report 91–10, TU Berlin, June 1991.

PvEP88. E.J.H. Pepels, M.C.J.D. van Eekelen, and M.J. Plasmeijer. A cyclic reference counting algorithm and its proof. Technical Report 88–10, Computing Science Department, University of Nijmegen, 1988.

Rut96. J.J.M.M. Rutten. *Universal Coalgebra: a Theory of Systems, Technical Report CS-R9652.* CWI, Amsterdam, 1996.

Sal87. J.D. Salkild. Implementation and analysis of two reference counting algorithms. Master's thesis, University College, London, 1987.

TT97. A. Telford and D. Turner. Ensuring streams flow. In *Algebraic Methodology and Software Technology*, pages 509–523, 1997.

Transforming Haskell for Tracing

Olaf Chitil, Colin Runciman, and Malcolm Wallace

The University of York, UK

Abstract. Hat is a programmer's tool for generating a trace of a computation of a Haskell 98 program and viewing such a trace in various different ways. Applications include program comprehension and debugging. A new version of Hat uses a stand-alone program transformation to produce self-tracing Haskell programs. The transformation is small and works with any Haskell 98 compiler that implements the standard foreign function interface. We present general techniques for building compiler independent tools similar to Hat based on program transformation. We also point out which features of Haskell 98 caused us particular grief.

1 Introduction

A tracer gives the programmer access to otherwise invisible information about a computation. It is a tool for understanding how a program works and for locating errors in a program [2]. Tracing a computation with Hat consists of two phases, trace generation and trace viewing:

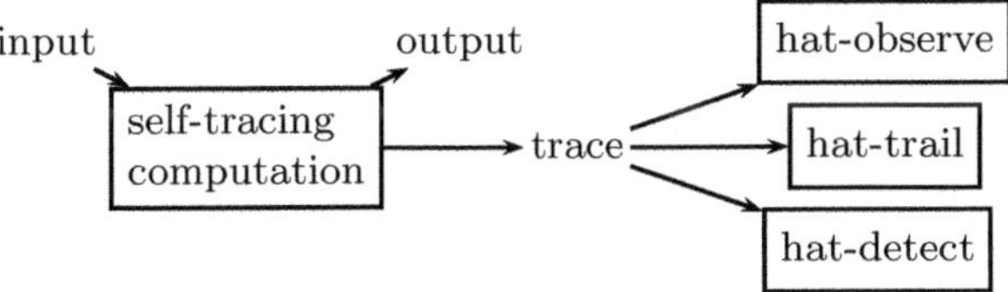

First, a special version of the program runs. In addition to its normal input/output behaviour it writes a trace into a file. Second, after the program has terminated, the programmer studies the trace with a collection of viewing tools. The trace as concrete data structure liberates the views from the time arrow of the computation. The trace and the viewing tools are described in [9].

Until recently the production of the self-tracing executable was integrated into the Haskell compiler nhc98[1]. Although the implementation consisted mostly of a single transformation phase [7], many small but crucial modifications had been made in the remainder of the compiler. We have now separated Hat from its host Haskell compiler. The new program HAT-TRANS transforms the original Haskell program into a Haskell program that, when compiled and linked with a library provided with Hat, is self-tracing:

[1] http://www.cs.york.ac.uk/fp/nhc98/

R. Peña and T. Arts (Eds.): IFL 2002, LNCS 2670, pp. 165–181, 2003.

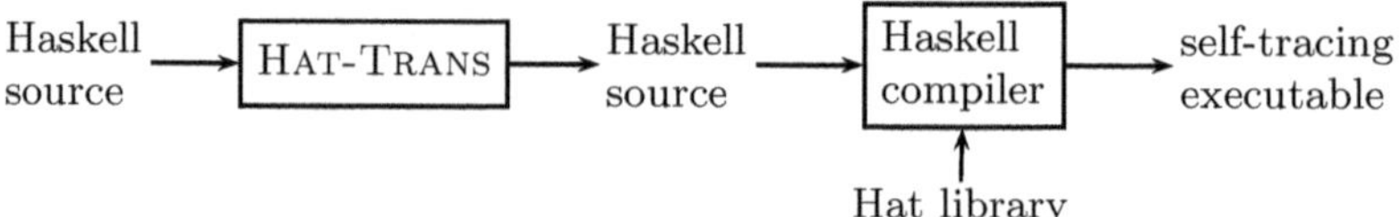

The separation between Hat and the compiler has the following advantages:

- HAT-TRANS and the Hat library together capture the essence of tracing.
- The small size of HAT-TRANS and the library minimised the implementation effort and ease experimental changes in the course of research.
- The future life of Hat is not tied to the future life, that is, continued support, of a specific compiler.
- Hat can be combined with Haskell compilers that have different characteristics, for example with respect to availability on certain computing platforms, compilation speed, or optimisation for speed or space.
- Hat is more easily accepted by programmers who wish to continue using a familiar compiler.

Obviously HAT-TRANS has to duplicate some work of a Haskell compiler, for example parsing. However, we will show that this duplicate work can be kept to a minimum and the implementation of nearly all duplicated phases can be shared between HAT-TRANS and nhc98 without compromises.

Tools such as profilers, tracers and debuggers are essential for wider adoption of functional programming languages [8]. It is our belief that most of these tools can be implemented for a functional language through the use of program transformation. Thus these tools can be separate from any specific compiler or interpreter, with all the advantages we just listed specifically for Hat. The new Hat proves that such an implementation can be done. In this paper we discuss a number of points that we had to take into consideration and problems we faced. We describe several techniques that we developed for the implementation of Hat in the hope that they will be useful for other people who build similar tools. In addition, we also point out features of Haskell that made our job particularly hard. These observations may be taken into consideration in the future development of Haskell or similar languages.

The new Hat using the compiler-independent program transformation has been publicly released as Hat 2.0 (http://www.cs.york.ac.uk/fp/hat).

2 How Tracing Works

In previous work, we described Hat's trace [9] and how a transformed program generates it [7] (the latter is partially outdated). To get a general idea here, let us consider an example.

The Trace of a Reduction. A trace is a complex graph. Figure 1 shows several intermediate stages of the trace during the reduction of the term `f True`, using the definition `f x = g x`. Initially (a) there is the representation of the term as one application and two atom nodes. The first entry of each node points to a representation of the parent, the creator of the expression. Because our computation starts with `f True`, the parent is just a special node Root. In stage (b) the redex `f True` is "entered"; the result pointer of the application node changes from a null value to $\perp$. In stage (c) the representation of the reduct has been generated in the trace. The application node of the redex is the parent of all new nodes of the reduct (the application node and the atom node for `g`). Finally (d) the result pointer of the redex is updated to point to its reduct.

A trace with its parent, subexpression and result pointers is a complex graph that is traversed by Hat's viewing tools. The "entered" mark $\perp$ is essential information when a computation aborts with an error. In general, several redexes may be "entered" at one time, because pattern matching forces the evaluation of arguments before a reduction can be completed.

Augmented Expressions. The central idea for the tracing transformation is that every expression is augmented with a pointer to its description in the trace. Thus expression and its description "travel together" throughout the computation, so that when expressions are plumbed together by application, the corresponding descriptions can also be plumbed together to create the description of the application.

We transform an expression of type T into an expression of type `R` T, where

```
data R a = R a RefExp
```

A value of type `RefExp` is a pointer to a trace graph node. The trace graph structure is linearised to a file. Hence a pointer to a node is represented as the integer offset of the node in the trace file.

Transformed Program. Figure 2 shows the result of transforming our example, including additional definitions used. We assume `f` came with type signature `Bool -> Bool`. The program has been simplified for explanatory purposes.

In the first argument of `f`, respectively `g`, a pointer to its parent is passed. The original type constructor `->` is replaced by the new type constructor `Fun`. A self-tracing function needs to take an augmented argument and return an augmented result. The pointer to the parent of the right-hand side of the function definition, the redex, also needs to be passed as argument. Hence this definition of `Fun`.

The tracing combinator `ap` realises execution and tracing of an application. The primitive tracing combinators `mkAt`, `mkApp`, `entRedex` and `entResult` write to the trace file. They are side-effecting C-functions used via the standard Foreign Function Interface (FFI) for Haskell [1].

Tracing a Reduction. Figure 3 shows the reduction steps of the transformed program that correspond to the original reduction `f True` $\Rightarrow$ `g True`. The first line shows the result of transforming `f True`. The surrounding `case` and `let` are there, because it is the initial expression of the computation. The arrows indicate sharing of subexpressions, which is essential for tracing to work. Values of `RefExp`

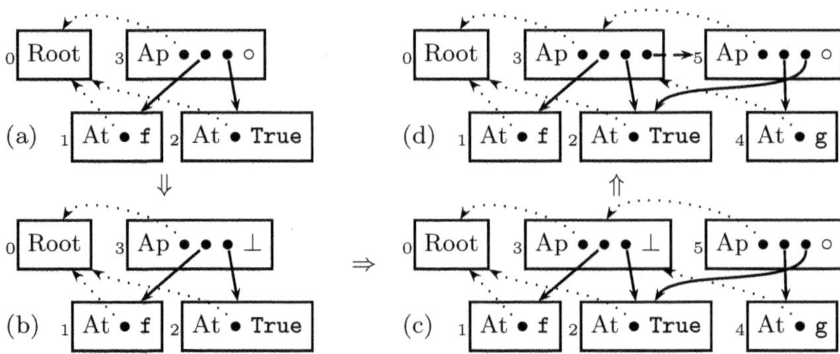

Fig. 1. Trace generation for a reduction step

```
f :: RefExp -> Fun Bool Bool
f p = R (Fun (\x r -> ap r (g r) x)) (mkAt p "f")
g p = R (...) (mkAt p "g")

newtype Fun a b = Fun (R a -> RefExp -> R b)
ap :: RefExp -> R (Fun a b) -> R a -> R b
ap p (R (Fun f) rf) a@(R _ ra) =
  let r = mkAp p rf ra
  in R (entRedex r `seq` case f a r of R y ry -> updResult r ry `seq` y) r
```

Fig. 2. Transformed program with additional definitions

```
    case (let p=mkRoot in ap p (f p) (R True (mkAt p "True"))) of R x _ -> x
⇒*  case (ap • (R (...) (mkAt • "f")) (R True (mkAt • "True")) of R x _ -> x
                                                              mkRoot
⇒*  entRedex • `seq` case ((\x r->ap r (g r) x) (R True •) •) of
                   R y ry -> updResult • ry `seq` y
                                                       mkAp • • •
                     mkAt • "f"    mkAt • "True"                  mkRoot
(a)
⇒*  entRedex 3 `seq` case ((\x r->ap r (g r) x) (R True 2) 3) of
                   R y ry -> updResult 3 ry `seq` y
(b)
⇒*  case ((\x r->ap r (g r) x) (R True 2) 3) of
      R y ry -> updResult 3 ry `seq` y
⇒*  case (ap 3 (R (...) (mkAt 3 "g")) (R True 2)) of
      R y ry -> updResult 3 ry `seq` y
⇒*  updResult 3 • `seq` (entRedex • `seq` ...)
(c)                                    mkAp 3 • 2        mkAt 3 "g"
⇒*  updResult 3 5 `seq` (entRedex 5 `seq` ...)
(d)
⇒*  entRedex 5 `seq` ...
```

Fig. 3. Evaluation of self-tracing expression

are the same integers as used in Figure 1. The reduction steps perform the original reduction and write the trace in parallel. In the sequence of reductions we can see at (a) how strictness of `entRedex` forces recording of the redex in the trace, at (b) the redex is "entered", at (c) strictness of `updResult` forces recording of the reduct, and at (d) the result pointer of the redex is updated.

Properties of the Tracing Scheme. The transformed program mostly preserves the structure of the original program. Trace-writing via side effects enables this preservation of structure. It ensures that the Haskell compiler determines the evaluation order, not Hat. Otherwise Hat would not be transformation-based but would need to implement a full Haskell interpreter. In a few places the order of evaluation is enforced by `seq` and by the fact that the primitive trace-writing combinators are strict in all arguments. The evaluation order of the original and the transformed program agree to the degree that the definition of Haskell fixes the evaluation order.

To simplify the transformation, `RefExp` is independent of the type of the wrapped expression. The correctness of the transformation ensures that the trace contains only representations of well-typed expressions.

The new function type constructor `Fun` is defined specially, different from all other types, because reduction of function applications is the essence of a computation and its trace. The transformation naturally supports arbitrary higher-order functions.

All meta-information that is needed for the creation of the trace, such as identifier names, is made available by the transformation as literal values (cf. `mkAt p "f"` and `mkAt p "True"`). Thus Hat does not require any reflection features in the traced language.

3 The Hat Library

The Hat library includes two categories of combinators: primitive combinators such as `entRedex` and `mkApp1` that write the trace file, and high-level combinators such as `ap1` and `ap2` that manipulate augmented expressions. The high-level combinators structure and simplify the transformation. The transformation enlarges a program by a factor of 5-10. For the development of Hat it is useful that a transformed program is readable and most changes to the tracing process only require changes to the combinator definitions, not to the transformation.

Haskell demands numerous combinators to handle all kinds of values and language constructs, from floating point numbers to named field update. Figure 4 shows an excerpt of the real Hat library. The types `RefAtom`, `RefSrcPos` and `RefExp` indicate that there are different sorts of trace nodes. The trace contains references to positions in the original program source. The combinators `fun`n allow a concise formulation of function definitions of arity n. The combinators `wrapReduction` and `pap1` are just helper functions.

```
fun1 :: RefAtom -> RefSrcPos -> RefExp  -> (R a -> RefExp -> R z)
     -> R (Fun a z)
fun1 var sr p f = R (Fun f) (mkValueUse p sr var)

ap1 :: RefSrcPos -> RefExp -> R (Fun a z) -> R a -> R z
ap1 sr p (R (Fun f) rf) a@(R _ ra) =
  let r = mkApp1 p sr rf ra in  wrapReduction (f a r) r

fun2 :: RefAtom -> RefSrcPos -> RefExp -> (R a -> R b -> RefExp -> R z)
     -> R (Fun a (Fun b z))
fun2 var sr p f = R (Fun (\a r -> R (Fun (f a)) r) (mkValueUse p sr var)

ap2 :: RefSrcPos -> RefExp -> R (Fun a (Fun b z)) -> R a -> R b -> R z
ap2 sr p (R (Fun f) rf) a@(R _ ra) b@(R _ rb) =
  let r = mkApp2 p sr rf ra rb
  in  wrapReduction (pap1 sr p r (f a r) b) r

pap1 :: RefSrcPos -> RefExp -> RefExp -> R (Fun a z) -> R a -> R z
pap1 sr p r wf@(R (Fun f) rf) a = if r == rf then f a r else ap1 sr p wf a

wrapReduction :: R a -> RefExp -> R a
wrapReduction x r =
  R (entRedex r `seq` case x of R y ry -> updResult r ry `seq` y) r
```

Fig. 4. Examples of combinators from the Hat library

***N*-ary Applications.** The combinator ap2 for an application with two arguments could be defined in terms of ap1, but then two application nodes would be recorded in the trace. For efficiency we want to record n-ary application nodes as far as possible. We have to handle partial and oversaturated applications explicitly. The pap1 combinator recognises when its first wrapped argument is a saturated application by comparing its parent with the parent passed to the function of the application. The fun$n$ combinators are defined so that a partial application just returns the passed parent. If the function of ap2 has arity one, then pap1 uses ap1 to record the application of the intermediate function to the last argument.

The fact that the function has arity one can only be recognised after recording the oversaturated application in the trace. Therefore the ap2 combinator does not record the desired nested two applications with one argument each. Instead it constructs an application with two arguments whose reduct is an application with one argument. Because both applications have the same parent, the viewing tools can recognise applications of this sort in the trace and patch them for correct presentation to the user.

Often the function in an n-ary application is a variable f that is known to be of arity n. In that case the construction of Fun values and their subsequent destruction is unnecessary; the wrapped function can be used directly. A similar and even simpler optimisation applies to data constructors; their arity is always known and they cannot be oversaturated.

Further Optimisations. Preceding the transformation, list and string literals could be desugared into applications of `:` and `[]`. Such desugaring would however increase size and compile time of the transformed programs. Instead, special combinators perform the wrapping of these literals at runtime.

There is still considerable room left for further optimising combinators, which have not been the main focus in the development of Hat.

4 The Transformation Program Hat-Trans

The tracing transformation Hat-Trans parses a Haskell module, transforms the abstract syntax tree, and pretty prints the abstract syntax in concrete syntax. Hat-Trans is purely syntax-directed. In particular, Hat-Trans does *not* require the inclusion of a type inference phase which would contradict our aim of avoiding the duplication of any work that is performed by a Haskell compiler. Figure 5 shows the phases of Hat-Trans.

To enable separate transformation of modules, an interface file is associated with every module, similar to the usual `.hi`-file. Haskell already requires for complete parsing of a module some sort of interface file that contains the user defined associativities and priorities of imported operators. Hat interface files also associate various other sorts of information with exported identifiers, for example its arity in case of a function identifier. Hat-Trans does not use the `.hi`-files of its collaborating compiler, because, first, this would always require

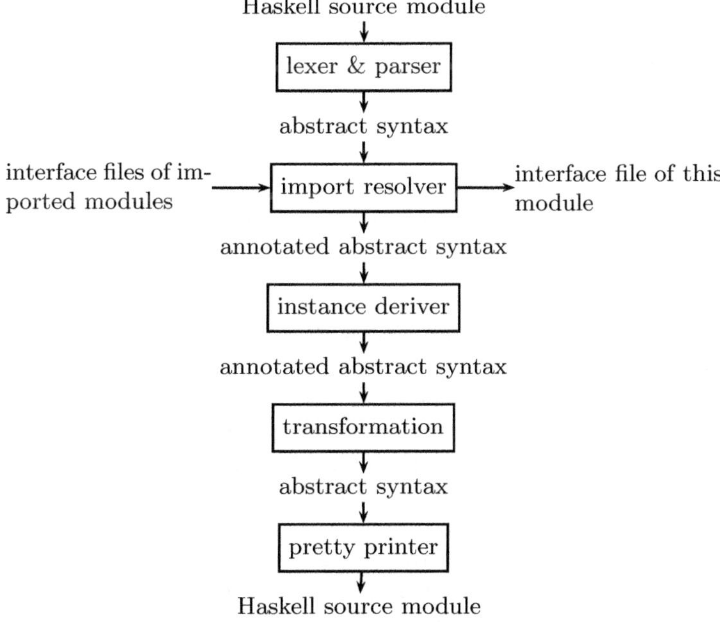

Fig. 5. Phases of Hat-Trans

the compilation of the original program before the tracing compilation and, second, every compiler uses a different format for its `.hi`-files. HAT-TRANS also does not generate its interface files in a format used by any compiler, because `.hi`-files always contain the type of every exported variable but Hat does not have these types.

The import resolver uses the import declarations of a module to determine for each identifier from where it is imported. This phase also finalises the parsing of operator chains and augments every occurrence of an identifier with the information which for imported identifiers is obtained from the interface files and otherwise is obtained syntactically by a traversal of the syntax tree. Whereas the import resolution phase of the nhc98 compiler qualifies each identifier with the identifier of the module in which it is *defined*, HAT-TRANS leaves identifiers unchanged to ensure that pretty printing will later create a well-formed module.

The instance deriver replaces the **`deriving`** clause of a type definition by instances of the listed standard classes for the defined type. These derived instances need to be transformed (cf. Section 8) and obviously a Haskell compiler cannot derive instances of the transformed classes. To determine the context of a derived instance, Haskell requires full type inference of the instance definition. Because HAT-TRANS does not perform type inference, it settles on generating a canonical context, that is, for an instance $C(Ta_1 \ldots a_n)$ it generates the context $(Ca_1, \ldots, Ca_n)$. In principle, if this canonical context is incorrect, the Hat user has to write the correct instance by hand. But in practice we have not yet come across this problem.

The implementations of the lexer and parser and of the pretty printer are reused from nhc98. The import resolver and instance deriver have similarities with the corresponding phases of nhc98, but had to be implemented specially for HAT-TRANS.

5 The Transformation

The transformation is implemented through a single traversal of the annotated abstract syntax tree.

Namespace. The transformation leaves class, type, type variable and data constructor identifiers unchanged. Only special identifiers such as `(,)` and `:` have to be replaced by new identifiers such as `TPrelBase.Tuple2` and `TPrelBase.Cons`, qualified to avoid name clashes. Because many new variables are needed in the transformed program, every variable identifier is prefixed by a single letter. Different letters are used to associate several new identifiers with one original identifier, for example the definition of `rev` is transformed into definitions of `grev`, `hrev` and `arev`. All names of a transformed modules are prefixed by the letter "T"; the Hat combinator library is imported qualified as "T" and qualified identifiers are used to avoid name clashes. As a result the development of Hat profits from readable transformed programs.

Types. Because every argument of a data constructor has to be augmented with a description, type definitions need to be transformed. For example:

```
    data Point = P Integer Integer
⇝   data Point = P (T.R Integer) (T.R Integer)
```

Predefined types such as `Char`, `Integer` and `Bool` can be used unchanged, because the definition of an enumeration type does not change.

Type signatures require only replacement of special syntactic forms and additional parent and source position arguments. For example:

```
    sort :: Ord a => [a] -> [a]
⇝   gsort :: Ord a => T.RefSrcPos -> T.RefExp -> T.R (Fun (List a) (List a))
```

The transformation has to accept any Haskell program and yield a well-formed Haskell program. Because partially applied type constructors can occur in Haskell programs, a transformation for the full language cannot just replace types of kind `*`, but has to replace type constructors. On the other hand, Haskell puts various restrictions on types that occur in certain contexts. For example, a type occurring in a qualifying context has to be a type variable or a type variable applied to types; a type in the head of an instance declaration has to be a type constructor, possibly applied to type variables. So it is important that the transformation does not change the form of types, in particular it maps type variables to type variables.

Type Problems. In the last example the `Ord` in the transformed type refers to a different class than the `Ord` in the original type. The method definitions in the instances of `Ord` have to be transformed for tracing and hence also the class `Ord` needs to be transformed to reflect the change in types. Sadly the replacement of classes by new transformed classes means that the defaulting mechanism of Haskell cannot resolve ambiguities of numeric expressions in the transformed program. Defaulting applies only to ambiguous type variables that appear only as arguments of Prelude classes. Hence Hat requires the user to resolve such ambiguities. In practice, if an ambiguity error occurs when compiling the transformed program, a good tactic for the user is to add the declaration `default ()` to the original program and compile it to obtain a meaningful ambiguity error message. The ambiguities in the original program can then be resolved by type signatures or applications of `asTypeOf`.

The transformation of type definitions cannot preserve the strictness of data constructors. The transformation

```
    data RealFloat a => Complex a = !a :+ !a
⇝   data RealFloat a => Complex a = !(T.R a) :+ !(T.R a)
```

would not yield the desired strictness for `:+`. Ignoring this strictness issue only yields programs that are possibly less space efficient but it does not introduce semantic errors. Nonetheless, the transformation can achieve correct strictness by replacing all use occurrences of `:+` by a function that is defined to call `:+` but uses `seq` to obtain the desired strictness.

```
rev :: [a] -> [a] -> [a]
rev [] ys = ys
rev (x:xs) ys = rev xs (x:ys)
```

Fig. 6. Original definition of list reversal

```
grev :: T.RefSrcPos -> T.RefExp -> T.R (Fun (List a) (Fun (List a) (List a)))
grev p j = T.fun2 arev p j hrev

hrev :: T.R (List a) -> T.R (List a) -> T.RefExp -> T.R (List a)
hrev (T.R Nil _) fys j = T.projection p3v13 j fys
hrev (T.R (Cons fx fxs) _) fys j =
  T.ap2 p4v17 j (grev p4v17 j) fxs (T.con2 p4v26 j Cons aCons fx fys)

arev = T.mkVariable tMain 3 1 3 2 "rev" TPrelBase.False

tMain = T.mkModule "Main" "Reverse.hs" TPrelBase.True

p3v13 = T.mkSrcPos tMain 3 13
p4v17 = T.mkSrcPos tMain 4 17
p4v26 = T.mkSrcPos tMain 4 26
```

Fig. 7. Transformed definition of list reversal

Expression and Function Definitions. Figures 6 and 7 show the original and the transformed definition of a list reversal function `rev`. Each equation of `rev` is transformed into an equation of the new function `hrev`. The argument variables `x`, `xs` and `ys` turn into `fx`, `fxs` and `fys`. The transformation wraps the patterns with the `R` data constructor to account for the change in types. In the first equation the combinator `projection` is applied to the variable `fys` to record an indirection node (cf. [6]). In the second equation `ap2` basically applies `grev` to `fxs` and the constructor application (`con2`) of `Cons` (renamed `(:)`) to `fx` and `fys`. The type of `hrev` still contains the standard function type constructor instead of the tracing function type constructor `Fun`. The function `grev` is the fully augmented tracing version of `rev`. The remaining new variables refer to meta-information about variables and expressions, for example `p3v13` refers to a position in line 3 column 13 of the original program.

Tricky Language Constructs. Most of Haskell can be handled by a simple, compositionally defined transformation, but some language constructs describing a complex control flow require a context-sensitive transformation.

A guard cannot be transformed into another guard. The problem is that the trace of the reduct must include the history of the computation of *all* guards that were evaluated for its selection, including all those guards that failed. Hence a sequence of guards is transformed into an expression that uses continuation passing to be able to pass along the trace of all evaluated guards.

The pattern language of Haskell is surprisingly rich and complex. Matching on numeric literals and $n + k$ patterns causes calls to functions such as `fromInteger`, `==` and `-`. The computation of these functions needs to be recorded in the trace, in particular when matching fails. In general it is not even easy to move the test from a pattern into a guard, because Haskell specifies a left-to-right matching of function arguments.

An irrefutable pattern may never be matched within a computation but all the variables within the pattern may occur in the right hand side of the equation and need a sensible description in the trace. For variables that are proper subexpressions of an irrefutable pattern, that is those occurring within the scope of a `~` or the data constructor of a newtype, the standard transformation does not yield any description, because the `R` wrappers are not matched. We do not present the transformation of arbitrary patterns here, because it is the most complex part of the transformation.

Preservation of Complexity. Currently a transformed program is about 60 times slower with nhc98 and 130 times slower with GHC[2] (with `-O`) than the original program. This factor should be improved, but it is vital that it is only a constant factor. We have to pay attention to two main points to ensure that the transformation preserves the time and space complexity of the original program.

Although by definition Haskell is only a non-strict language, all compilers implement a lazy semantics and thus ensure that function arguments and constants (CAFs) are only evaluated once with their values being shared by all use contexts. To preserve complexity, constants have to remain constants in the transformed program. Hence the definition of a constant is transformed differently from the definition of a function. In Haskell not every variable defined without arguments is a constant; the variable may be overloaded. Fortunately the monomorphism restriction requires that an explicit type signature is given for such non-constant variables without arguments. Thus such cases can be detected without having to perform type inference.

Figures 6 and 7 demonstrate that a tail recursive definition is transformed into a non-tail recursive definition. Although the transformation does not preserve tail recursion, the stack usage of the tracing program is still proportional to the stack usage of the original program. This is, because the `ap2` combinator, which makes the transformed definition non-tail recursive, calls `wrapReduction`. That combinator immediately evaluates to an `R` wrapper whose first argument is returned after a single reduction step — not full evaluation.

6 Error Handling

Because debugging is the main application of Hat, programs that abort with an error or are interrupted by Control-C must still record a valid trace. An error message, a pointer to the trace node of the redex that raised the error, and some buffers internal to Hat need to be written to the trace file before it can be closed.

[2] http://www.haskell.org/ghc/

Catching Errors. Because Haskell lacks a general exception handling mechanism, Hat combines several techniques to catch errors:

- To catch failed pattern matching all definitions using pattern matching are extended by an equation (or case clause) that always matches and then calls a combinator which finalises the trace.
- The Prelude functions `error` and `undefined` are implemented specially, so that they finalise the trace.
- The C signalling mechanism catches interruption by Control-C and arithmetic errors.
- The transformed `main` function uses the Haskell exception mechanism to catch any IO exceptions.
- Variants of the Hat library for nhc98 and GHC catch all remaining errors, in particular blackholes and out-of-memory errors. These variants take advantage of the extended exception handling mechanism of GHC (which does not catch all errors) and features of the runtime systems.

The Trace Stack. The redex that raised an error is the last redex that was "entered" but whose result has not yet been updated. Most mechanisms for catching an error do not provide a pointer to the trace node of this redex. In these cases the pointer is obtained from the top of an internal trace stack.

The trace stack contains pointers to the trace nodes of all redexes that have been "entered" but not yet fully reduced. Instead of writing to the trace, `entRedex` r puts r on the trace stack. Later `updResult` r ry pops this entry from the stack and updates the result of r in the trace (cf. Section 2). The trace stack and the Haskell runtime stack grow and shrink synchronously. Besides a successful reduction, an IO exception also causes shrinking of the runtime stack. To detect the occurrence of a (caught) IO exception, `updResult` r ry compares its first argument with the top of the stack and keeps popping stack elements until the entry for the description r is popped.

The stack not only enables the location of the redex that caused an error, it also saves the time of marking each "entered" application in the trace file. Only when an error occurs must all redexes on the stack be marked as "entered" in the trace file. Because sequential writing of a file is considerably more efficient than random access, `updResult` does not perform its update immediately but stores it in a buffer. When the buffer is full all updates are performed at once. The use of stack and buffer nearly halves the runtime of the traced program.

7 Connecting to Untraced Code

For some functions a self-tracing version cannot be obtained through transformation, because no definition in Haskell is available. This is the case for primitive functions on types that are not defined in Haskell: for example, addition of `Int`s, conversion between `Int`s and `Char`s, IO operations and operations on `IOError`.

We need to define self-tracing versions of such functions in terms of the original functions instead of by transformation. In other words, we need to lift the original function to the tracing types with its R-wrapped values.

Calling Primitive Haskell Functions. HAT-TRANS (mis)uses the foreign function interface notation to mark primitive functions. For example:

```
foreign import haskell "Char.isUpper" isUpper :: Char -> Bool
```

⇝
```
gisUpper :: T.RefSrcPos -> T.RefExp -> T.R (Fun Char Bool)
gisUpper p j = T.ufun1 aisUpper p j hisUpper

hisUpper :: T.R Char -> T.RefExp -> R Bool
hisUpper z1 k = T.fromBool k (Char.isUpper (T.toChar k z1))

aisUpper = T.mkVariable tPrelude 8 3 3 1 "isUpper" Prelude.False
```

The variant `ufun1` of the combinator `fun1` ensures that exactly the application of the primitive function and its result are recorded in the trace, no intermediate computation.

Type Conversion Combinators. The definition of combinators such as

```
toChar :: T.RefExp -> T.R Char -> Prelude.Char
fromBool :: T.RefExp -> Prelude.Bool -> T.R Bool
```

that convert between wrapped and unwrapped types is mostly straightforward.

For a type constructor that takes types as arguments, such as the list type constructor, the conversion combinator takes additional arguments. The conversion combinators are designed so that they can easily be combined:

```
toList :: (T.RefExp -> T.R a -> b) -> T.RefExp -> T.R (List a) -> [b]

toString :: T.RefExp -> T.R String -> Prelude.String
toString = toList toChar
```

Some types have to be handled specially:

- No values can be recorded for abstract types such as `IO`, `IOError` or `Handle`. Instead of a value only the type is recorded and marked as abstract.
- For primitive higher-order functions such as `>>=` of the IO monad we also need combinators that convert functions. When a wrapped higher-order function calls a traced function, the latter has to be traced and connected to the trace of the whole computation.
  The function type is not only abstract but it is also contravariant in its first argument. The contravariance shows up in the types of the first arguments of the combinators. Because `toFun` needs a `RefExp` argument, all unwrapping combinators take a `RefExp` argument.

```
toFun :: (T.RefExp -> c -> T.R a) -> (T.RefExp -> T.R b -> d)
      -> T.RefExp -> T.R (Fun a b) -> (c -> d)
toFun from to r (T.R (Fun f) _) = to r . f r . from r
```

```
fromFun :: (T.RefExp -> T.R a -> b) -> (T.RefExp -> c -> T.R d)
        -> T.RefExp -> (b -> c) -> T.R (Fun a d)
fromFun to from r f = T.R (Fun (\x _ -> (from r . f . to r) x))
                          (T.mkValueUse r T.mkNoSrcPos aFun)

aFun = T.mkAbstract "->"
```

IO Actions. Although a value of type IO is not recorded in the trace, the output produced by the execution of an IO-action is. Primitive IO functions such as `putChar` are wrapped specially, so that their output is recorded and connected to the trace of the IO expression that produced it.

8 Trusting

Hat allows modules to be marked as trusted. The internal workings of functions defined in a trusted module are not traced. Thus Hat saves recording time, keeps the size of the trace smaller and avoids unnecessary details in the viewing tools. By default the Prelude and the standard libraries are trusted.

No (Un)Wrapping for Trusting. An obvious idea is to access untransformed trusted modules with the wrapping mechanism described in the previous section. Thus the functions of trusted modules could compute at the original speed and their source would not even be needed, so that internally they could use extensions of Haskell that are not supported by Hat. However, this method cannot be used for the following reasons:

- It can increase the time complexity. Regard the list append function `++`: In evaluation `++` traverses its first argument but returns its second argument as part of the result without traversing it. However, the wrapped version of `++` has to traverse both arguments to unwrap them and finally traverse the whole result list to wrap it. Therefore the computation time for `xs ++ (xs ++ ... (xs ++ xs)...)` is linear in the size of the result for the original version but quadratic for the lifted version. Also the information that part of the result was not constructed but passed unchanged is lost.
- Overloaded functions cannot be lifted. For example, the function `elem` uses the standard `Eq` class, but its wrapped version `gelem` has to use the transformed `Eq` class. No combinator can change the class of a function, because it cannot access the implicitly passed instance (dictionary). Instances are not first class citizens in Haskell.

Combinators for Trusting. So trusted modules have to be transformed as well. The same transformation is applied, only different combinators are used. The computation of trusted code is not traced, but the combinators have to record in the trace for each traced application of a trusted function its call, the computations of any traced functions called by it, and its result.

In our first implementation of trusting, combinators did not record any reductions in trusted code, but all constructions of values. The disadvantage of this implementation is that not only the result value of a trusted function but also all intermediate data structures of the trusted computation are recorded.

Our current implementation takes advantage of lazy evaluation to only record those values constructed in trusted code that are *demanded* from traced code. Thus no superfluous values are recorded. However, sadly also values that are first demanded by trusted code and later demanded by traced code are not recorded either. It seems impossible to change this behaviour without losing the ability to record cyclic data structures, for example the result of the standard function `repeat`. The limitations of the current implementation of trusting are acceptable for tracing most programs, but not all.

The result values of trusted functions may contain functions. These functions are currently only recorded as abstract values, because otherwise they could show arbitrary large subexpressions of trusted code. The connection between trusting and abstraction barriers needs to be studied further.

9 Conclusions

We described the design and implementation of Hat's program transformation for tracing Haskell programs.

Compiler Independence. We have used the new Hat together with both nhc98 and GHC (the standard foreign function interface is not supported by hbc[3] and only by the latest release of Hugs[4] that appeared very recently). Compiling a self-tracing program with both compilers and running the executables does not yield an identical trace file, because side effects of the trace recording combinators are performed at different times. However, manual comparison of small traces shows the *graph structure* of these traces to be the same. The size of large trace files differs by about 0.001 %, proving that sometimes different structures are recorded. We will have to build a tool for comparing trace structures to determine the cause of these differences. Semantic-preserving eager evaluation may cause structural differences, but otherwise the trace structure is fully defined by the program transformation, not the compiler.

Haskell Characteristics. The implementation of tracing through program transformation owes much to the expressibility of Haskell. Higher-order functions and lazy evaluation allowed the implementation of a powerful combinator library, describing the process of tracing succinctly.

Nonetheless we also faced a number of problems with Haskell. The source-to-source transformation exposed several irregularities and exceptions in the language design. The limited exception handling mechanism, the limited defaulting

[3] http://www.cs.chalmers.se/ augustss/hbc/hbc.html

[4] http://www.haskell.org/hugs/

mechanism, the fact that class instances are not first class citizens, and the fact that instance deriving requires full type inference, all forced us to make some compromises with respect to our aims of full coverage of the language and compiler independence. In contrast, the generally disliked monomorphic restriction proves to be useful. Many other language features such as guards, the complex pattern language and the strictness of data constructors increase the complexity of HAT-TRANS substantially. In general, the sheer size of Haskell makes life hard for the builder of a tool such as Hat. Most language constructs can be translated into a core language, but because traces must refer to the original program, the program transformation has to handle every construct directly.

Related Work. Hat demonstrates that program transformation techniques are also suitable for implementing tools that give access to operational aspects of program computation. Which alternatives exist?

The related work sections of [4, 5, 10] list a large number of research projects on building tracers for lazy higher-order functional languages. Very few arrived at an implementation of a practical system for a full-size programming language.

The Haskell tracing tool Hood [3] consists of a library only. Hence its implementation is much smaller and it can even trace programs that use various language extensions without having to be extended itself. Hood's architecture is actually surprisingly similar to that of Hat: the library corresponds to Hat's combinator library and Hood requires the programmer to annotate their program with Hood's combinators and add specific class instances, so that the program uses the library. Hat's trace contains far more information than Hood's and hence requires a more complex transformation with which the programmer cannot be burdened.

On the other end of the design space is the algorithmic debugger Freja [4], a compiler developed specially for the purpose of tracing. Its self-tracing programs are very fast. However, implementing and maintaining a full Haskell compiler is a major undertaking. Freja only supports a subset of Haskell and runs only under Solaris.

Extending an existing compiler would also require major modifications, because all existing Haskell compilers translate a program into a core language in early phases, but a trace must refer to all constructs of the original program. The implementation of a tracing Haskell interpreter would require more work than the implementation of HAT-TRANS, and achieving similar or better trace times would still be hard. Finally HAT-TRANS yields unsurpassable modularity.

Current Status and Future Work. An improved version of Hat is about to be released as Hat 2.02. Hat is an effective tool for locating errors in programs. We use it to locate errors in the nhc98 compiler and recently people outside York located subtle bugs in complex programs with Hat.

Although trusting of modules works mostly well in practice, the current choice of which information is recorded is unsatisfactory. Additionally, a trusted module should run close to the speed of the original module. This paper already indicates that the design space for a trusting mechanism is large. Improved trusting and further optimisations of the Hat library will reduce the current slowdown factor of 60–130 of traced programs with respect to the original.

A trace contains a wealth of information; we are still far from exploiting it all. We have several ideas for tools that present trace information in new ways. We intend to develop a combinator library so that Haskell can be used as a query language for domain specific investigation of a trace. We have plans for tools that compare multiple traces and finally we want to link trace information with profiling information. We believe that these future developments will benefit from Hat's modular design and portable implementation.

Acknowledgements

The work reported in this paper was supported by the Engineering and Physical Sciences Research Council of the United Kingdom under grant GR/M81953.

References

1. M. Chakravarty et al. The Haskell 98 foreign function interface 1.0: An addendum to the Haskell 98 report. http://www.haskell.org/definition/, 2002.
2. K. Claessen, C. Runciman, O. Chitil, J. Hughes, and M. Wallace. Testing and tracing lazy functional programs using QuickCheck and Hat. 4th Summer School in Advanced Functional Programming, Oxford, to appear in LNCS, 2002.
3. A. Gill. Debugging Haskell by observing intermediate data structures. *Electronic Notes in Theoretical Computer Science*, 41(1), 2001. 2000 ACM SIGPLAN Haskell Workshop.
4. H. Nilsson. *Declarative Debugging for Lazy Functional Languages.* PhD thesis, Linköping, Sweden, May 1998.
5. A. Penney. *Augmenting Trace-based Functional Debugging.* PhD thesis, University of Bristol, UK, September 1999.
6. J. Sparud and C. Runciman. Complete and partial redex trails of functional computations. In C. Clack, K. Hammond, and T. Davie, editors, *Selected papers from 9th Intl. Workshop on the Implementation of Functional Languages (IFL'97)*, pages 160–177. Springer LNCS Vol. 1467, Sept. 1997.
7. J. Sparud and C. Runciman. Tracing lazy functional computations using redex trails. In H. Glaser, P. Hartel, and H. Kuchen, editors, *Proc. 9th Intl. Symposium on Programming Languages, Implementations, Logics and Programs (PLILP'97)*, pages 291–308. Springer LNCS Vol. 1292, Sept. 1997.
8. P. Wadler. Functional programming: Why no one uses functional languages. *SIGPLAN Notices*, 33(8):23–27, Aug. 1998. Functional programming column.
9. M. Wallace, O. Chitil, T. Brehm, and C. Runciman. Multiple-view tracing for Haskell: a new Hat. In *Preliminary Proceedings of the 2001 ACM SIGPLAN Haskell Workshop*, UU-CS-2001-23. Universiteit Utrecht, 2001.
10. R. D. Watson. *Tracing Lazy Evaluation by Program Transformation.* PhD thesis, Southern Cross, Australia, Oct. 1996.

Axis Control in SAC

Clemens Grelck[1] and Sven-Bodo Scholz[2]

[1] University of Lübeck
Institute of Software Technology and Programming Languages
grelck@isp.uni-luebeck.de
[2] University of Kiel
Institute of Computer Science and Applied Mathematics
sbs@informatik.uni-kiel.de

Abstract. High-level array processing is characterized by the composition of generic operations, which treat all array elements in a uniform way. This paper proposes a mechanism that allows programmers to direct effects of such array operations to non-scalar subarrays of argument arrays without sacrificing the high-level programming approach. A versatile notation for axis control is presented, and it is shown how the additional language constructs can be transformed into regular SAC code. Furthermore, an optimization technique is introduced which achieves the same runtime performance regardless of whether code is written using the new notation or in a substantially less elegant style employing conventional language features.

1 Introduction

SAC (Single Assignment C) [19] is a purely functional programming language, which allows for high-level array processing in a way similar to APL [11]. Programmers are encouraged to construct application programs by composition of basic, generic, shape- and dimension-invariant array operations, typically via multiple intermediate levels of abstraction. As an example take a SAC implementation of the L2 norm:

```
double L2Norm( double[*] A)
{
  return( sqrt( sum( A * A)));
}
```

The argument type `double[*]` refers to double precision floating point number arrays of any shape, i.e., arguments to `L2Norm` can be vectors, matrices, higher-dimensional arrays, or even scalars, which in SAC like in APL or J are considered 0-dimensional arrays. The same generality applies to the main building blocks `*`, `sum`, and `sqrt`. While `*` refers to the element-wise multiplication of arrays, `sum` computes the sum of all elements of an argument array. Although in the example `sqrt` is applied to a scalar only, `sqrt` in general is applicable to arbitrarily shaped arrays as well.

Such a composite programming style has several advantages. Programs are more concise because error-prone explicit specifications of array traversals are

R. Peña and T. Arts (Eds.): IFL 2002, LNCS 2670, pp. 182–198, 2003.

hidden from that level of abstraction. The applicability of operations to arrays of any shape in conjunction with the multitude of layers of abstraction allows for code reuse in a way that is not possible in scalar languages. However, when it comes to applying such universal operations to parts of an array only, a more sophisticated notation is required [19].

This paper is concerned with the special but frequently occurring situation where an operation is to be performed on certain axes of arrays only. As an example, Fig. 1 illustrates the various possible applications of `L2Norm` to different axes of a 3-dimensional array.

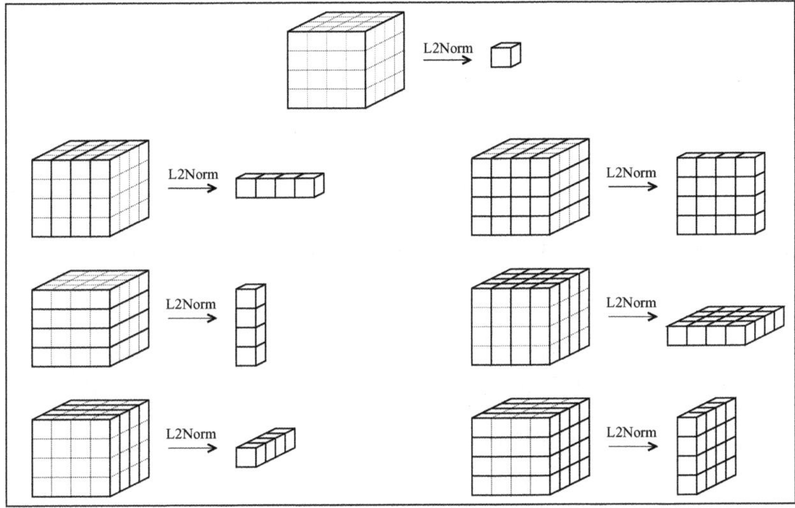

Fig. 1. Different views of an array.

In the standard case, as shown at the top of Fig. 1, `L2Norm` is applied to all elements and, hence, reduces the whole cube into a single scalar. However, the same cube may also be interpreted as a vector of matrices, as on the left hand side of Fig. 1. In this case, we would like to apply a reduction operation like `L2Norm` to each of the submatrices individually, yielding a vector of results. Similarly, the cube may also be regarded as a matrix of vectors. This view should result in applying `L2Norm` to individual subvectors yielding an entire matrix of results, as shown on the right hand side of Fig. 1. To add further complexity to the issue, the latter two views additionally offer the choice between three different orientations each.

In principle, such a mapping of an operation to parts of arrays in SAC can be specified by means of so-called WITH-loops, the central language construct for defining array operations in SAC. However, their expressiveness by far exceeds the functionality required in this particular situation because the design of WITH-loops aims at a much broader range of application scenarios. Rather cumbersome specifications may be the consequence when this generality is not needed, as for example in the cases shown in Fig. 1.

One approach to improve this situation without a language extension seems to be the creation of a large set of slightly different abstractions. However, continuously "re-inventing" minor variations of more general operations runs counter the idea of generic, high-level programming. Providing all potentially useful variations in a library is also not an option because this number explodes with an increasing number of axes and is unlimited in principle. Moreover, coverage of one operation still does not solve the problem for any other.

Another potential solution may be found in additional format parameters. Unfortunately, the drawbacks of this solution are manifold. Format arguments may have to be interpreted at runtime, which mostly prevents code optimizations. Many binary operations are preferably written in infix notation, which does not allow for an additional parameter. Last but not least, additional format parameters once again must be implemented for any operation concerned, although the problem itself is independent of individual operations.

What is needed instead is a more general mechanism that — independent of concrete operations — provides explicit control over the choice of axes of argument arrays to which an operation is actually applied. In this paper we propose such a mechanism, which fits well into the framework of generic, high-level array programming. It consists of a syntactical extension, called *axis control notation*, a compilation scheme, which transforms occurrences of the new notation into existing SAC code, and tailor-made code optimization facilities.

The remainder of the paper is organized as follows. Section 2 provides a very brief introduction into SAC for those who are not yet familiar with the language. In Section 3, we present the axis control notation. The compilation of axis control constructs into existing SAC code is outlined in Section 4, while optimization issues specific to the new mechanism are discussed in Sections 5 and 6. Finally, some related work is sketched out in Section 7, and Section 8 draws conclusions.

2 SAC

The core language of SAC is a functional subset of C, extended by n-dimensional arrays as first class objects. Despite the different semantics, a rule of thumb for SAC code is that everything that looks like C also behaves as in C. Arrays are represented by two vectors, a shape vector that specifies an array's extent wrt. each of its axes, and a data vector that contains all its elements. Array types include arrays of fixed shape, e.g. `int[3,7]`, arrays with a fixed number of dimensions, e.g. `int[.,.]`, and arrays with any number of dimensions, i.e. `int[*]`.

In contrast to other array languages, e.g. FORTRAN-95, APL, or later versions of SISAL [7], SAC provides only a very small set of built-in operations on arrays. Basically, they are primitives to retrieve data pertaining to the structure and contents of arrays, e.g. an array's number of dimensions (`dim(`*array*`)`), its shape (`shape(`*array*`)`), or individual elements of an array (*array*`[`*index-vector*`]`), where the length of *index-vector* is supposed to meet the number of dimensions or axes of *array*.

All basic aggregate array operations which are typically built-in in other array languages in SAC are specified in the language itself using powerful mapping and folding operations, the so-called WITH-loops. As a simple example take the definition of the element-wise `sqrt` function:

```
double[*] sqrt ( double[*] A)
{
  res = with (. <= iv <= .)
        genarray( shape( A), sqrt( A[iv]) );
  return( res);
}
```

This function takes an array `A` of any shape as argument and computes a new array `res` by means of a simple WITH-loop. The WITH-loop consists of two parts, a so-called *generator* (preceded by the keyword `with`) and an *operation* (preceded by the keyword `genarray`). The basic functionality is defined in the operation part. In the given example, an array of the same shape as the array `A` is to be generated (first expression within the operation part), and an element at index position `iv` is computed by applying `sqrt`[1] to the corresponding element of `A` (second expression within the operation part). The generator part specifies an index set to which the given element computation actually applies. The dot symbols used within the generator part of the example are a shortcut notation for the lowest and for the highest legal index vector, respectively. Hence, the generator in fact covers the entire index range of `A`.

WithLoopExpr	⇒	**with** (*Generator*) [*AssignBlock*] *Operation*
Generator	⇒	*Expr RelOp IdVec RelOp Expr* [*Filter*]
RelOp	⇒	< | <=
Operation	⇒	**genarray** (*Expr* , *Expr*) | ...

Fig. 2. Syntax of with-loop expressions.

As indicated by the (simplified) syntax of WITH-loops presented in Fig. 2, WITH-loops in general are more flexible. The generator set can be refined to rectangular index ranges specified by arbitrary lower and upper bounds, which in turn can be further restricted by optional filters. This inherently introduces the notion of a default definition for all those elements of the result array that are not covered by the generator. Furthermore, several variants of mapping and folding are available as operation parts, and an optional assignment block between the two parts allows more complex element definitions within the operation part to be abstracted out into local variables. However, in the context of this paper this flexibility is not required. A more detailed introduction into SAC can be found in [19]; a case study on a non-trivial problem investigating both the programming style and the resulting runtime performance is presented in [8].

---

[1] This seeming recursion is resolved by the type system of SAC; cf. [19].

3 Axis Control Notation

Having a closer look at the L2 norm example used to motivate the need for axis control, it turns out that the desired behaviour basically is a 3-step process.

1. Split the argument array along selected axes into uniform subarrays.
2. Apply the operation, e.g. `L2Norm`, to each subarray individually.
3. Laminate the array of subresults to form the overall result.

Fig. 3 illustrates this 3-step process for the L2 norm example and a 1-dimensional (top) as well as a 2-dimensional (bottom) splitting operation.

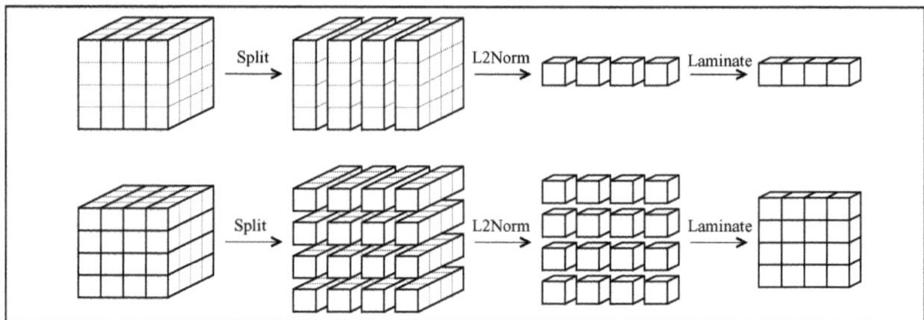

Fig. 3. Axis control as a 3-step process.

As a first step towards notational support for axis control we introduce a generalized selection facility. As outlined in the previous section, array element selection in SAC is specified as *array*[*index-vector*], where the length of *index-vector* is supposed to meet the number of dimensions or axes of *array*. This selection facility is generalized by allowing index values in one or several dimensions to be left unspecified. Substituting elements of *index-vector* by single dots allows for selection of all elements of *array* along the corresponding axes. As illustrated in Fig. 4, the number of dimensions of the resulting value is identical to the number of dots in *index-vector*. Leaving all dimensions unspecific makes the selection facility an identity function. Of course, dots are only permitted in array selections, not in expressions in general. These syntactical extensions and their limitations are formally defined in Fig. 5.

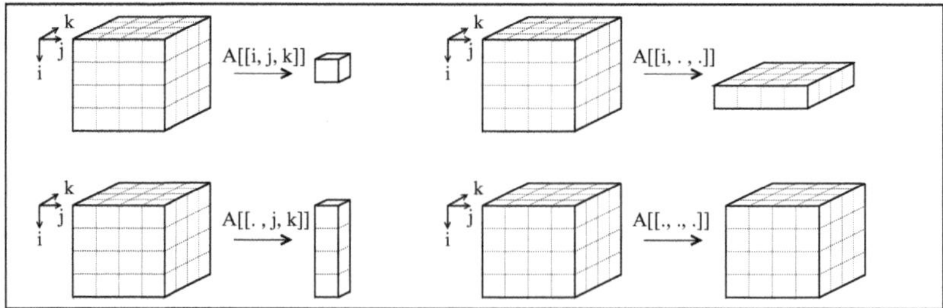

Fig. 4. Generalized array selection facility.

As a second step, we introduce a notation for lamination of subarrays, which includes the replicated application of operations prior to the lamination itself.

The new notation is based on expressions of the form { *idvec* `->` *expr*(*idvec*) }. Basically, such set expressions define a function from indices, represented by a so-called *frame vector* of identifiers (*idvec*), to values defined by the subsequent expression. In some sense, the set notation resembles a ZF-expression without a range specification or — in terms of SAC — a WITH-loop without a generator. This observation raises the question of how the range of indices is determined in the absence of an explicit specification. In fact, it is implicitly derived from the (mandatory) occurrence of each element of the frame vector in a selection operation within the subsequent expression. The shape of the array involved then defines the range for this particular index.

Associating the frame vector with these ranges yields a set of index vectors. For each element of this set the expression is evaluated and the resulting values are laminated according to the frame vector. Hence, the overall result and value of the entire set expression is characterized by a rank which equals the sum of the the frame vector's length and the rank of the expression.

Generalized selection facility and set notation form our *axis control notation* since in conjunction they offer a concise solution to the problem of axis control. For example, applications of `L2Norm` to submatrices of a cube can be written as simple as { `[j] -> L2Norm( A[[.,j,.]])` }; applying `L2Norm` to subvectors is as straightforward as { `[i,k] -> L2Norm( A[[i,.,k]])` }.

In both examples, the elements of the frame vector naturally occur in a selection operation within the expression. Hence, the range can easily be derived from the shape of the argument array `A`. The observation also illustrates why we use the term *notation* in this context. The axis control notation allows for shorter, more concise specifications in all those simple though frequent cases where a range *can* be derived from corresponding selections and, hence, the notational power of a full-fledged WITH-loop is not required.

As a reduction operation `L2Norm` reduces any subarray to a scalar. In general, any relationship between the shapes of argument and result subarrays may occur. The only restriction to the choice of operations here is uniformity, i.e., suitable operations must map all argument subarrays to result subarrays of identical shape. Otherwise, the subsequent lamination step would have to create an array with non-rectangular shape, which is not supported by SAC.

Examples which benefit from the new axis control notation are manifold, e.g., matrix transposition may be written as { `[i,k] -> Matrix[[k,i]]` }, matrix multiplication as { `[i,k] -> sum( MatrixM[[i,.]] * MatrixN[[.,k]])` }. Also purely structural array operations often benefit from axis control, e.g., the row-wise concatenation of a matrix with a vector can simply be written as { `[i] -> Matrix[[i,.]] ++ Vector` } based on the vector concatenation operator `++`.

If row-wise matrix-vector concatenation can be written easily, what about column-wise matrix-vector concatenation? Here, a limitation of axis control, as described so far, becomes apparent. In all cases examined so far, lamination used to be along the leftmost axis. However, column-wise matrix-vector concatenation requires lamination along the second axis. To cover this and similar cases we further extend our axis control notation by the free choice of lamination axes. This is accomplished by allowing dot symbols to be used in the frame vector of the set notation. As a consequence, column-wise matrix-vector concatenation can be specified as { `[., j] -> Matrix[[., j]] ++ Vector` }.

Expr	⇒ ...
	| [*Expr* [, *Expr*]*]
	| *Expr* [*Expr*]
	| *Expr* [*SelVec*]
	| { *FrameVec* − > *Expr* }
SelVec	⇒ [*DotOrExpr* [, *DotOrExpr*]*]
DotOrExpr	⇒ . | *Expr*
FrameVec	⇒ [*DotOrId* [, *DotOrId*]*]
DotOrId	⇒ . | *Id*

Fig. 5. Syntactical extensions for axis control notation.

Fig. 5 summarizes the various syntactical extensions introduced with the axis control notation and clarifies where dots may occur in program texts and where not. However, there are restrictions on the use of set notations which cannot elegantly be expressed by means of syntax. In all the examples presented so far, each identifier introduced by the frame vector occurs exactly once within the expression, which is directly in a selection operation. Consequently, ranges can be determined without ambiguity. In general, restrictions are less severe. First, the emphasis is on *direct* occurrence in a selection operation. For example, in the set expression { `[i, j] -> M[[i, N[[j]]]]` } ranges for `i` and `j` are clearly determined by the shapes of `M` and `N`, respectively. The indirect occurrence of `j` in the selection on `M` is not considered harmful. Similarly, additional occurrences outside of selection operations as in { `[i, j] -> M[[i, j]] + i * j` } are ignored. Multiple direct occurrences in selections on different arrays as in { `[i, j] -> M[[i, j]] + N[[j, i]]` } can easily be resolved by taking the minimum over all potential ranges. This ensures legality of selection indices with respect to the shapes of all arrays involved.

Only those set expressions in which elements of the frame vector do not directly occur in any selection operation have to be rejected. For example, in { `[i] -> M[[ fun( i)]]` } deriving a range specification from the shape of `M` would require to compute the inverse of `fun`, which usually is not feasible. Even simpler set expressions like { `[i] -> M[[ i - 1]]` } are ruled out because their meaning is not obvious: Legal values for `i` would be in the range from `1` up to and including `shape(M)[[0]]`. However, this contradicts to the rule that indexing in SaC always starts at zero.

These observations lead to the rule: A set notation that is constructed according to the syntax presented in Fig. 5 is considered legal, iff each identifier of the frame vector occurs at least once directly within an array selection.

4 Translating Axis Control Notation into WITH-loops

The reason why the two new language features — generalized selection and set notation — are referred to as "notations" stems from the observation that they are hardly more than syntactic sugar for particular forms of WITH-loops. In fact, their translation into WITH-loops can be implemented as part of a preprocessing phase mapping full SAC into core SAC.

4.1 Translating Generalized Selections

Generalized selections directly correspond to WITH-loops over ordinary (dot-less) selections. For example, the selection of the third column of a two-dimensional array `A`, specified as `A[[.,2]]`, can be implemented as

```
with (. <= [ tmp_0] <= .)
genarray( [ shape(A)[[0]] ], A[[tmp_0,2]])
```

The shape of the result equals the extent of `A` along the first axis, i.e., the number of rows of `A`, and the elements are selected from all rows of `A` at column position 2 which refers to the third element each.

In general, an expression of the form *expr* `[`*iv*`]` can be translated into a WITH-loop that ranges over as many axes as dot symbols are found in *iv*. The shape of the resulting array is determined by the corresponding components of the shape of the expression *expr*. A formalization of this transformation is presented in Fig. 6. The transformation of an expression *expr* into an expression *expr'* is

$$\mathcal{AC}[\![expr\,\texttt{[}iv\texttt{]}]\!] = \left\{ \begin{array}{l} \texttt{with(. <= } ds \texttt{ <= .)} \\ \texttt{genarray(} shp\texttt{, } expr\,\texttt{[}idx\texttt{])} \end{array} \right.$$

where

$$< ds\ ,\ shp\ ,\ idx > \ = \ DeCon\ iv\ 0$$

$$\begin{array}{l}
DeCon\ \texttt{[]}\ i \\
\quad = < \texttt{[]}\ ,\ \texttt{[]}\ ,\ \texttt{[]} > \\
DeCon\ \texttt{[}\ \ \texttt{.}\ ,\ e_1,\ \ldots,\ e_n\texttt{]}\ i \\
\quad = < \texttt{[tmp_}i\texttt{]} +\!\!+\ ds\ ,\ \texttt{[shape(}expr\texttt{)[[}i\texttt{]]]} +\!\!+\ shp\ ,\ \texttt{[tmp_}i\texttt{]} +\!\!+\ idx > \\
\qquad \text{where} \\
\qquad\quad < ds\ ,\ shp\ ,\ idx > \ = \ DeCon\ \texttt{[}e_1,\ \ldots,\ e_n\texttt{]}\ i+1 \\
DeCon\ \texttt{[}\ expr_0,\ e_1,\ \ldots,\ e_n\texttt{]}\ i \\
\quad = < ds\ ,\ shp\ ,\ \texttt{[}expr_0\texttt{]} +\!\!+\ idx > \\
\qquad \text{where} \\
\qquad\quad < ds\ ,\ shp\ ,\ idx > \ = \ DeCon\ \texttt{[}e_1,\ \ldots,\ e_n\texttt{]}\ i+1
\end{array}$$

Fig. 6. Compiling array decomposition into WITH-loops.

denoted by $\mathcal{AC}[\![expr]\!] = expr'$. It is assumed that this transformation is applied to all subexpressions where axis control notation is used without explicitly applying $\mathcal{AC}$ recursively to all potential subexpressions. SAC program code and meta variables that represent arbitrary SAC expressions are distinguished by means of different fonts: `teletype` is used for explicit SAC code, whereas *italics* refer to arbitrary expressions.

The transformation rule is based on the computation of the three vectors *ds*, *shp*, and *idx*, which determine the generator variable, the shape vector, and the modified index vector of the generated WITH-loop, respectively. All three vectors are computed from the index vector *iv* by means of a recursive function *DeCon*. It traverses the given index vector and looks for dot symbols. Whenever a dot symbol is encountered, new components are inserted into the generator variable and the shape expression. Furthermore, the dot symbol of the index expression is replaced with the freshly generated generator variable component. The additional parameter i is needed for keeping track of the position within the original index vector *iv* only.

4.2 Translating Set Notations

As shown in Section 3, the multiplication of two matrices `M` and `N` can be specified as `{ [i,j] -> sum( M[[i,.]] * N[[.,j]]) }`. Basically, this expression can be translated into a WITH-loop by turning the frame vector, i.e. `[i,j]`, into an index generator variable and by turning the right hand side expression into the body of a WITH-loop:

```
with (. <= [i,j] <= .)
genarray( [ shape(M)[[0]], shape(N)[[1]] ],
          sum( M[[i,.]] * N[[.,j]]) );
```

As explained in the previous section, the difficulty involved here is the determination of the result shape, i.e., `[ shape(M)[[0]], shape(N)[[1]] ]`. It has to be derived from the direct occurrences of `i` and `j` within array selections on the right hand side of the set notation. Since `M[[i,.]]` selects the $\mathtt{i}^{th}$ row of `M`, its maximum range is determined by the extent of `M` in the leftmost axis, i.e., `shape(M)[[0]]`. Likewise, the selection of the $\mathtt{j}^{th}$ column of `N` limits the range of `j` by `shape(N)[[1]]`.

A formalization of this approach towards the compilation of the set notation into WITH-loops is presented in Fig. 7. Two functions *FindSels* and *CompExt* are used for computing the components s_j of the result shape from the right hand side expression *expr*. *FindSels* expects two arguments: an expression *expr*

$$\mathcal{AC}[\![\{\ \texttt{[}var_0\texttt{,}\ \ldots\texttt{,}\ var_n\texttt{]}\ \texttt{->}\ expr\ \}]\!] = \begin{cases}\texttt{with(. <= [}var_0\texttt{,}\ldots\texttt{,}var_n\texttt{] <= .)}\\ \texttt{genarray([}s_0\texttt{,}\ \ldots\texttt{,}\ s_n\texttt{],}\ expr\texttt{)}\end{cases}$$

where

$\forall j \in \{0,\ldots,n\} : s_j = CompExt\ (\ FindSels\ var_j\ expr\ )$

$FindSels\ var\ \dashv \ldots expr'\texttt{[[}e_0\texttt{,}\ldots\texttt{,}e_{i-1}\texttt{,}\ var\texttt{,}\ e_{i+1}\texttt{,}\ldots\texttt{,}e_m\texttt{]]}\ldots\vdash$
$= [\texttt{shape(}\ expr'\texttt{)[[}i\texttt{]]}]$
$+\!\!+\ (\ FindSels\ var\ \dashv \ldots expr'\texttt{[[}e_0\texttt{,}\ldots\texttt{,}e_{i-1}\texttt{,}\ \texttt{0}\texttt{,}\ e_{i+1}\texttt{,}\ldots\texttt{,}e_m\texttt{]]}\ldots\vdash\ )$

$FindSels\ var\ expr$
$= []$

$CompExt\ [] = ERROR$
$CompExt\ [ext_0] = ext_0$
$CompExt\ [ext_0\texttt{,}\ldots\texttt{,}ext_k] = \texttt{min(}\ ext_0\texttt{,}\ CompExt\ [ext_1\texttt{,}\ldots\texttt{,}ext_k]\ \texttt{)}$

Fig. 7. Compiling array construction into WITH-loops.

and a variable name *var*. It locates subexpressions of *expr* that consist of array selections containing the given variable *var*. This is indicated by a pseudo pattern notation $\dashv \ldots expr'$ `[`$expr''$`]`$\ldots \vdash$ which is meant to match arbitrary expressions that contain a subexpression of the form $expr'$`[`$expr''$`]`. For each array selection that contains the variable *var*, an according shape component selection is put into a resulting list of expressions. Note here, that for each component of the result shape such a list is computed. In the matrix multiplication example, all these lists do contain a single element only.

The function *CompExt* finally creates the expressions of the shape components from such lists. Empty lists indicate illegal programs as the corresponding variables are not used directly within array selections at all. If a list contains a single element only, this can be taken directly, as in the example. Multiple list entries require to guarantee that none of the corresponding selections violates array boundaries. To do so expressions are created that compute the minimum of all list components at runtime.

So far, it has been assumed that the frame vectors contain variables only. As a consequence, non-scalar right hand side expressions always constitute the rightmost axes of the result arrays. Now, the scheme has to be extended to cope with dot symbols in frame vectors. As these serve only one purpose, namely to place the right hand side expressions freely within the result, set expressions that contain dot symbols in their frame vectors can be transformed into nestings of two dot-free set expressions: one for computing the results and another one for accomplishing the intended transpose operation.

Applying this idea to the column-wise matrix-vector concatenation example, the original specification { `[.,i] -> M[[.,i]] ++ v` } first is transformed into { `[i] -> M[[.,i]] ++ v` } which inserts the prolongated column vectors as leftmost axis, i.e. as rows, of the result. Subsequently, the modified computation is embedded into a simple matrix transpose which leads to an expression of the form { `[tmp_0,i] ->` { `[i] -> M[[.,i]] ++ v` } `[[i,tmp_0]]` }.

The transformation of set notations that contain dot symbols in the frame vector into a nesting of dot-free ones can be formalized as shown in Fig. 8. As-

```
AC[{ iv -> expr }] = { lhs -> { vs -> expr }[ vs ++ ds ] }
where
  < lhs , vs , ds > = Perm iv 0

  Perm [] i
    = < [] , [] , [] >
  Perm [ . , v1, ..., vn] i
    = < [tmp_i] ++ lhs , vs , [tmp_i] ++ ds >
      where
        < lhs , vs , ds > = Perm [v1, ..., vn] i+1
  Perm [ var, v1, ..., vn] i
    = < [var] ++ lhs , [var] ++ vs , ds >
      where
        < lhs , vs , ds > = Perm [v1, ..., vn] i+1
```

Fig. 8. Resolving dot symbols on the left hand side of array constructions.

suming that the frame vector *iv* contains at least one dot symbol, a set notation { *iv* -> *expr* } first is turned into an expression { *vs* -> *expr* } where *vs* is obtained from *iv* by stripping off the dot symbol(s). This expression is embedded into a transpose operation { *lhs* -> { ...}[*vs* ++*ds*] }. The frame vector *lhs* in this set notation equals a version of *iv* whose dots have been replaced by temporary variables named `tmp_`*i* with *i* indicating the position of the temporary variable in *lhs*. The selection vector consists of a concatenation of the "dot stripped" version *vs* and a vector *ds* that contains a list of the temporary variables that have been inserted into the left hand side. This guarantees that all axes referred to by the dot symbols of *iv* are actually taken from the leftmost axes of { *vs* -> *expr* } and inserted correctly into the result.

5 Compilation Intricacies

As can be seen from applying the compilation scheme $\mathcal{AC}$ to the few examples on axis control notation given so far, intensive use of the new notation typically leads to deep nestings of WITH-loops. This contrasts strongly with the typical structure of SAC programs so far. The effect of this change in programming style can be observed when comparing the runtimes of direct specifications versus specifications that make use of axis control notation. A comparison of a direct specification of the row-wise matrix-vector concatenation with the axis control notation based solution on a SUN ULTRASPARC I for a 2000 x 2000 element matrix and a 500 element vector shows a slowdown by about 50%. For the column-wise matrix-vector concatenation (same extents) the slowdown even turns out to be a factor of 14! Since runtime performance is a key issue for SAC, this observation calls the entire approach in question. Performance figures, which have been found competitive even to low-level imperative languages [9,8,19], could only be achieved without using axis control notation.

A closer examination of the compilation process shows that the nestings of WITH-loops generated by the transformation are not particularly apt to the optimizations incorporated into the SAC compiler implementation `sac2c`[2] so far. The problems involved can be observed nicely with the column-wise matrix-vector concatenation example. Starting with the expression

```
{ [.,i] -> M[[.,i]] ++ v }
```

the transformation scheme $\mathcal{AC}$ first eliminates the dots of the frame vector:

```
{ [tmp_0,i] -> { [i] -> M[[.,i]] ++ v }[[i,tmp_0]] }          .
```

Then, both set notations are transformed into WITH-loops:

```
with (. <= [tmp_0,i] <= .) {
  inner = with ( . <= [i] <= .)
            genarray( [ shape(M)[[1]] ], M[[.,i]] ++ v);
} genarray( ..., inner[[i, tmp_0]])                           .
```

[2] See <http://www.sac-home.org/>.

Note here, that the temporary variable `inner` is introduced for presentation purposes only. It represents the value of the inner set notation.

Finally, yet another WITH-loop is substituted for the column selection. For clarity of code, we again introduce a temporary variable `col` that holds the selected column(s):

```
with (. <= [tmp_0,i] <= .) {
  inner = with ( . <= [i] <= .) {
            col = with ( . <= [tmp_0] <= .)
                    genarray( [ shape(M)[[0]] ], M[[tmp_0,i]]);
          } genarray( [ shape(M)[[1]] ], col ++ vect);
} genarray( ..., inner[[i, tmp_0]])                                  .
```

During optimization the WITH-loop-invariant computation of `inner` is lifted out of the body of the outer WITH-loop and the WITH-loop-based implementation of the concatenation operation `++` is inlined, which leads to a code structure of the form:

```
inner = with (... [i] ...) {
            col = with (... [tmp_0] ...)        // col = M[[.,i]]
                    genarray( ... M[[tmp_0, i]] ...);
            res = with (... [j] ...)            // res = col ++ v
                    genarray( ... col[[j]] ...  v[[j]] ...);
        } genarray( ... , res);
  res = with (... [tmp_0,i] ...)                // transpose
        genarray( ... inner[[i,tmp_0]] ...);                       .
```

At this stage, WITH-LOOP-FOLDING [18], a SAC-specific optimization that allows consecutive WITH-loops to be folded into single ones, is applied. It condenses the column selection and the concatenation operation into a single WITH-loop:

```
inner = with (... [i] ...) {
            res = with (... [j] ...)            // res = M[[.,i]] ++ v
                    genarray( ... M[[j, i]] ... v[[j]] ...);
        } genarray( ... , res);
  res = with (... [tmp_0,i] ...)                // transpose
        genarray( ... inner[[i,tmp_0]] ...);                       .
```

Unfortunately, the remaining WITH-loops cannot be folded any further, as `[i]` is a 1-dimensional generator, whereas `[tmp_0,i]` is a 2-dimensional one. This leads to the generation of C code which copies all array elements three times. First, the individual vectors that represent the prolongated columns are built by the inner WITH-loop. Then, these vectors are copied into the transpose of the result, as represented by `inner`. Finally, the last WITH-loop realizes the transpose required.

The major hindrance of further optimizations is the nesting of WITH-loops as it resulted from the expression `M[[.,i]] ++ v` within the set notation. If this nesting was converted into a single WITH-loop that operates on scalars, all copying could be avoided. Rewriting the nesting as a single WITH-loop, we obtain

```
inner = with (... [i,j] ...)
        genarray( ... M[[j, i]] ... v[[j]] ... );
  res = with (... [tmp_0,i] ...)
        genarray( ... inner[[i,tmp_0]] ...);                       ,
```

which can be folded into

```
res = with (... [tmp_0,i] ...)
        genarray( ... M[[tmp_0, i]] ... v[[tmp_0]] ...);
```
.

As the resulting WITH-loop is identical to a direct specification, the runtime overhead inflicted by the use of axis control notation is eliminated entirely.

6 Scalarization of WITH-loops

The observation that WITH-loops operating on scalars are compiled into more efficient code than nested WITH-loops gives raise to a new optimization technique, called WITH-LOOP-SCALARIZATION. It systematically transforms nested WITH-loops into non-nested ones. Fig. 9 presents the basic transformation scheme $\mathcal{SC}$. The pattern which has to be looked for is a WITH-loop whose body is entirely

```
    [[ with (lb1 <= iv1 < ub1) {                    ]]     ( with (lb1++lb2 <= iv < ub1++ub2) {
    [[  v1 = with (lb2 <= iv2 < ub2) {              ]]     (  iv1 = take( shape( lb1), iv );
 SC [[         v2 = expr( iv1,iv2);                 ]]  = <   iv2 = drop( shape( lb1), iv );
    [[       } genarray( shp2, v2);                 ]]     (  v = expr( iv1,iv2);
    [[ } genarray( shp1, v1)                        ]]     ( } genarray( shp1++shp2, v);
```

if $iv_1 \notin FV(lb_2) \wedge iv_1 \notin FV(ub_2)$

Fig. 9. Simple WITH-LOOP-SCALARIZATION scheme.

made up of another WITH-loop. The transformation itself turns out to be rather simple: the vectors for the shape of the result and the bounds of the index generator have to be concatenated. The body of the resulting WITH-loop basically is identical to the body of the inner WITH-loop. It only requires the two index vectors of the original WITH-loop nesting (iv_1 and iv_2 in Fig. 9) to be derived from the new index generator variable by splitting it up accordingly.

However, an application of the transformation is not appropriate for all kinds of WITH-loop nestings that match the given pattern. The problem involved here is the fact that the bounds of the inner WITH-loop, i.e. lb_2 and ub_2, are lifted out of the scope of iv_1. Therefore, the transformation can only be applied if neither lb_2 nor ub_2 depends on iv_1.

Code generated from applications of our axis control notation typically match the nesting pattern of Fig. 9. For example, both row-wise as well as column-wise matrix-vector concatenation, as discussed in Section 3, benefit tremendously from WITH-LOOP-SCALARIZATION. In both cases, WITH-LOOP-SCALARIZATION is the key to compiling specifications based on axis control notation into codes which are equivalent to direct implementations of the problems. As a consequence, the performance degradations caused by using the axis control notation reported in Section 5 — factors of 1.5 and 14 — are eliminated entirely.

Although the new axis control notation is a major source for nested WITH-loops, these or similar intermediate code representations may occur for many reasons. Hence, WITH-LOOP-SCALARIZATION as an optimization technique is independent of axis control. However, hand-coded WITH-loop nestings often have slightly different forms. To enhance the applicability of this transformation, the

```
SC [[ with (lb1 <= iv1 < ub1) {
        var = expr1( iv1);
        v1 = with (lb2 <= iv2 < ub2) {
               v2 = expr2( iv1,iv2,var);
             } genarray( shp2, v2);
      } genarray( shp1, v1) ]]

  =  with (lb1 <= iv1 < ub1) {
        v1 = with (lb2 <= iv2 < ub2) {
               var = expr1( iv1);
               v2 = expr2( iv1,iv2,var);
             } genarray( shp2, v2);
     } genarray( shp1, v1)
```

```
SC [[ v1 = with (lb2 <= iv2 < ub2) {
             v2 = expr( iv2);
           } genarray( shp2, v2);

      r = with (lb1 <= iv1 < ub1)
          genarray( shp1, v1); ]]

  =  with (lb1 <= iv1 < ub1) {
        v1 = with (lb2 <= iv2 < ub2) {
               v2 = expr( iv2);
             } genarray( shp2, v2);
     } genarray( shp1, v1)
```

Fig. 10. Enhancing the applicability of WITH-LOOP-SCALARIZATION.

$\mathcal{SC}$ scheme is accompanied by additional rules for deriving the desired nesting pattern from others. Two transformations to this effect are shown in Fig. 10. The upper transformation rule moves assignments that precede the inner WITH-loop into its body. The lower part demonstrates how entire WITH-loops can be moved into others for generating WITH-loop nestings that can be scalarized.

In contrast to the basic scheme, which guarantees an improvement of the code generated, these two transformations may introduce considerable overhead as the computation of the expressions that are moved into the WITH-loop bodies is duplicated. Whether or not this overhead actually leads to any runtime degradation depends on the concrete code it is applied to. If the transformation does trigger further optimizations such as WITH-LOOP-FOLDING, the amount of overhead may be easily amortized by the effect of these optimizations. Otherwise, if the code remains almost unmodified, the back-end of the compiler may detect the loop-invariant portions of the code and lift them back out again during the final code generation phase.

7 Related Work

APL [11], the origin of all array languages, addresses the issue of axis control only in a very restricted way. Certain built-in operators provide an additional optional parameter which allows selection of exactly one axis. For example, the reduction operator / by default reduces the rightmost axis of an argument array A using an appropriate binary built-in operation α: α/A. Reduction along the second axis, provided that A is of suitable rank, can be written as α/[2]A. Although this language feature of APL is sometimes erroneously called *dimension operator*, it clearly lacks the desired generality as it is limited to certain built-in operators as well as to the selection of exactly one axis.

These shortcomings have been addressed in the further development of APL. IBM's APL-2, which largely influenced the current APL standard [12], introduced the notion of *nested arrays* [4]. Whereas arrays in APL originally were multidimensional data structures based on scalar elements, nested arrays impose additional structure. Entire arrays can be "wrapped" by means of the new *enclose* operator and behave just as scalars afterwards, i.e., they hide their internal structure. A complementary *disclose* operator allows for "unwrapping" previously enclosed arrays.

The array language NIAL [14,15] also uses the notion of nested arrays, but comes without an explicit *enclose/disclose* mechanism. Instead the nesting of arrays simply follows their construction. Full support for recursion allows for elegantly traversing multiple nesting levels of arrays. Since the effect of normal operations is limited to the outermost level, careful manipulation of nesting levels may achieve similar effects as our axis control notation. However, repeated re-organization of data structures for this purpose may be tedious and time-consuming both in terms of programmer time as well as in terms of execution time.

As an alternative to nested arrays, Sharp-APL [2] and later J [13] proposed the idea of *function rank* [5,10]. Rather than extending the data structure of arrays, they introduced the *rank operator* (or *rank conjunction* in J terminology). Basically, the rank conjunction is a built-in higher-order function, denoted by the infix operator "`"`", which provides a uniform and general concept for directing effects of any operation to a given number of either leading or trailing dimensions. For example, `L2Norm"2 A` would apply `L2Norm` to each 2-dimensional subarray of `A` individually and laminate the results. Provided that `L2Norm` is defined as its SAC counterpart, this operation would be equivalent to the SAC axis control expression `{[i] -> L2Norm( A[[i,.,.]])}`. Compared with our approach the rank conjunction is limited in two aspects. First, it only allows to address consecutive leading and trailing axes of argument arrays. Any other choice of axes requires explicit transposition of arguments beforehand. Second, it does not allow for permutation of axes as axes are not identified by names.

So far, we have only sketched out work related to axis control. WITH-LOOP-SCALARIZATION does not find its counterpart in conventional loop optimizations (For surveys see [3,1].) as the setting is rather different. Conventional loops correspond to a single axis of an array each, whereas the whole issue discussed in Section 5 arises because by means of WITH-loops SAC does provide an inherently multi-dimensional loop construct. Only this feature provides the opportunity to merge nested loops into a single construct, whereas conventional languages do not offer means to express multi-dimensional loops other than by nesting.

An example of a multidimensional loop construct other than WITH-loops are the FOR-loops of SISAL [16]. However, according to [6] no optimizations similar to WITH-LOOP-SCALARIZATION are performed by the SISAL compiler. One reason may be the fact that SISAL 1.2 represents multidimensional arrays as nested vectors. Although this data representation has its flaws [17], it helps here because it avoids data copying of subarrays to a large extent.

8 Conclusions

This paper presents axis control notation as a general means for controlling the application of generic array operations in a dimension-specific manner. Axis control notation gives explicit control over the axes to which operations are applied as well as allowing the programmer to choose arbitrary dimensions for placing the results of such applications. The advantages of this approach are demonstrated in the context of the array programming language SAC. It is shown, that despite the enhanced flexibility – when compared to well-known concepts such as the rank conjunction in J – it can be implemented as a simple preprocessing step rather than requiring support for a built-in higher-order operator.

Unfortunately, these appealing properties do not come for free. Both notations, generalized selection and set notation, impose some syntactical restrictions which may be considered not very intuitive. The dot symbols used for generalized selection are put within the index vectors rather than being attached to the selection operator. Although this elegantly allows for indicating the axes to be selected, it may wrongly insinuate that dot symbols are legal vector entities. In a similar fashion, liberating the programmer from the burden to specify the index range of set notations leads to the restriction that the identifiers of frame vectors have to be used literally within array selections. However, in the context of axis control, these restrictions do not become apparent. Only if the axis control notation is "misused" for specifying more sophisticated functionalities, these restrictions may force the programmer to use WITH-loops instead.

As an offspring of the implementation of axis control notation, a new compiler optimization called WITH-LOOP-SCALARIZATION is proposed. It transforms nested WITH-loops into non-nested ones, which allows programs that make use of the new notation to be compiled into code that is identical to direct specifications that do without. This discloses another benefit of the proposed approach. Since the new notation is transformed into ordinary WITH-loops, WITH-LOOP-SCALARIZATION as an optimization technique is not specific to axis control notation, but it improves arbitrary SAC programs that contain nested WITH-loops.

Acknowledgements

We would like to thank Sébastien de Menten de Horne who inspired the development of the axis control notation by his ideas on active and passive indices. Furthermore, we are grateful to the people who helped improving this paper, in particular to Robert Bernecky for sharing his APL expertise, and to the four anonymous referees.

References

1. R. Allen and K. Kennedy. *Optimizing Compilers for Modern Architectures.* Morgan Kaufmann Publishers, 2001. ISBN 1-55860-286-0.

2. I.P Sharp & Associates. *SHARP APL Release 19.0 Guide for APL Programmers.* I.P Sharp & Associates, Ltd., 1987.
3. D.F. Bacon, S.L. Graham, and O.J. Sharp. Compiler Transformations for High-Performance Computing. *ACM Computing Surveys*, 26(4):345–420, 1994.
4. J.P. Benkard. Nested Arrays and Operators — Some Issues in Depth. In *Proceedings of the International Conference on Array Processing Languages (APL'92), St.Petersburg, Russia*, APL Quote Quad, pages 7–21. ACM Press, 1992.
5. R. Bernecky. An Introduction to Function Rank. In *Proceedings of the International Conference on Array Processing Languages (APL'88), Sydney, Australia*, volume 18 of *APL Quote Quad*, pages 39–43. ACM Press, 1988.
6. D.C. Cann. *The Optimizing SISAL Compiler: Version 12.0.* Lawrence Livermore National Laboratory, Livermore, California, 1993. part of the SISAL distribution.
7. J.T. Feo, P.J. Miller, S.K.Skedzielewski, S.M. Denton, and C.J. Solomon. Sisal 90. In A.P.W. Böhm and J.T. Feo, editors, *Proceedings of the Conference on High Performance Functional Computing (HPFC'95), Denver, Colorado, USA*, pages 35–47. Lawrence Livermore National Laboratory, Livermore, California, USA, 1995.
8. C. Grelck. Implementing the NAS Benchmark MG in SAC. In *Proceedings of the 16th International Parallel and Distributed Processing Symposium (IPDPS'02), Fort Lauderdale, Florida, USA*. IEEE Computer Society Press, 2002.
9. C. Grelck and S.-B. Scholz. HPF vs. SAC — A Case Study. In A. Bode, T. Ludwig, W. Karl, and R. Wismüller, editors, *Proceedings of the 6th European Conference on Parallel Processing (Euro-Par'00), Munich, Germany*, volume 1900 of *Lecture Notes in Computer Science*, pages 620–624. Springer-Verlag, Berlin, Germany, 2000.
10. R.K.W. Hui. Rank and Uniformity. In *Proceedings of the International Conference on Array Processing Languages (APL'95), San Antonio, Texas, USA*, APL Quote Quad, pages 83–90. ACM Press, 1995.
11. International Standards Organization. International Standard for Programming Language APL. ISO N8485, ISO, 1984.
12. International Standards Organization. Programming Language APL, Extended. ISO N93.03, ISO, 1993.
13. K.E. Iverson. *Programming in J.* Iverson Software Inc., Toronto, Canada, 1991.
14. M.A. Jenkins and J.I. Glagow. A Logical Basis for Nested Array Data Structures. *Computer Languages Journal*, 14(1):35–51, 1989.
15. M.A. Jenkins and W.H. Jenkins. *The Q'Nial Language and Reference Manual.* Nial Systems Ltd., Ottawa, Canada, 1993.
16. J.R. McGraw, S.K. Skedzielewski, S.J. Allan, R.R. Oldehoeft, et al. Sisal: Streams and Iteration in a Single Assignment Language: Reference Manual Version 1.2. M 146, Lawrence Livermore National Laboratory, Livermore, California, USA, 1985.
17. R.R. Oldehoeft. Implementing Arrays in SISAL 2.0. In *Proceedings of the 2nd SISAL Users Conference, San Diego, California, USA*, pages 209–222. Lawrence Livermore National Laboratory, 1992.
18. S.-B. Scholz. With-loop-folding in SAC — Condensing Consecutive Array Operations. In *Proc. 9th International Workshop on Implementation of Functional Languages (IFL'97), St. Andrews, Scotland, UK, selected papers*, volume 1467 of *LNCS*, pages 72–92. Springer, 1998.
19. S.-B. Scholz. Single Assignment C — Efficient Support for High-Level Array Operations in a Functional Setting. *Journal of Functional Programming*, 2003. Accepted for publication.

Thread Migration in a Parallel Graph Reducer

André Rauber Du Bois[1], Hans-Wolfgang Loidl[2], and Phil Trinder[1]

[1] School of Mathematical and Computer Sciences
Heriot-Watt University, Riccarton, Edinburgh EH14 4AS, UK
{dubois,trinder}@macs.hw.ac.uk
[2] Ludwig-Maximilians-Universität München
Institut für Informatik, D-80538 München, Germany
hwloidl@informatik.uni-muenchen.de

Abstract. To support high level coordination, parallel functional languages need effective and automatic work distribution mechanisms. Many implementations distribute potential work, i.e. sparks or closures, but there is good evidence that the performance of certain classes of program can be improved if current work, or threads, are also distributed. Migrating a thread incurs significant execution cost and requires careful scheduling and an elaborate implementation.
This paper describes the design, implementation and performance of thread migration in the GUM runtime system underlying Glasgow parallel Haskell (GPH). Measurements of nontrivial programs on a high-latency cluster architecture show that thread migration can improve the performance of data-parallel and divide-and-conquer programs with low processor utilisation. Thread migration also reduces the variation in performance results obtained in separate executions of a program. Moreover, migration does not incur significant overheads if there are no migratable threads, or on a single processor. However, for programs that already exhibit good processor utilisation, migration may increase performance variability and very occasionally reduce performance.

1 Introduction

The potential of functional languages to support parallelism with minimal programmer intervention has been long recognised [31], but has only recently been realised using sophisticated language implementations, e.g. [4,9,29]. Parallel functional languages typically generate massive, but fine-grained, parallelism and a successful implementation must have effective mechanisms to distribute work across the parallel machine. In many models potential work is easily and cheaply distributed, e.g. in graph reduction a *spark* is simply a reference to an unevaluated closure in the graph. On receiving a potential work item an idle processor will create a *thread* to perform the computation, and the thread has an execution state, typically including stack(s) and a set of registers.

It is well known that the performance of certain classes of programs can be improved if, in addition to potential work, threads can be distributed. These are programs with poor load balance leading to under utilisation of some processors:

R. Peña and T. Arts (Eds.): IFL 2002, LNCS 2670, pp. 199–214, 2003.

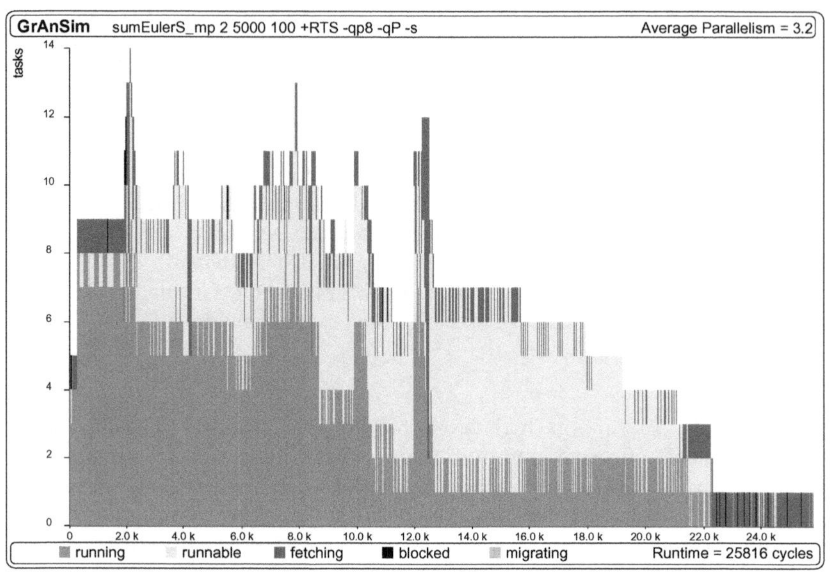

Fig. 1. Activity Profile of sumEuler, a Program with Migratable Threads

some processors are idle while others have several threads to execute. Many data parallel programs are vulnerable to this, especially those that generate parallelism only at the start of execution. Like software developers in other parallel languages, we have encountered poor load balance in large-scale GPH programs [19]. As a simple example, Figure 1 shows an overall activity profile of the sumEuler program discussed in section 4. The profile is recorded on 8 processors and shows execution time on the X-axis and the number of threads on the Y-axis. The shades of gray in the figure represent the different states of the threads, and the key states are *running*, i.e. currently executing and *runnable*, i.e. could be executed but residing on a processor currently executing another thread. For much of the execution there are idle processors and runnable threads simultaneously. If these threads can be *migrated* from a heavily-loaded processor to a lightly-loaded processor, runtime can be reduced.

Although conceptually simple, engineering effective thread migration in a sophisticated compiled parallel language implementation is challenging. The execution state of a thread has an elaborate representation that must be carefully packed, communicated and unpacked for execution to resume. Moreover the sharing of data and computations by the thread with other threads on the source and destination processors must be preserved. A further consequence is that migrating threads is not only expensive but also destroys any locality of reference the thread enjoyed on the source processor. In consequence thread migration must be carefully scheduled, to be used only when other load balancing mechanisms have failed. It is salutary that relatively few systems have been constructed, examples include [3] and [10]. This paper describes the implementation of thread migration in the GUM runtime system [29] supporting GPH [28].

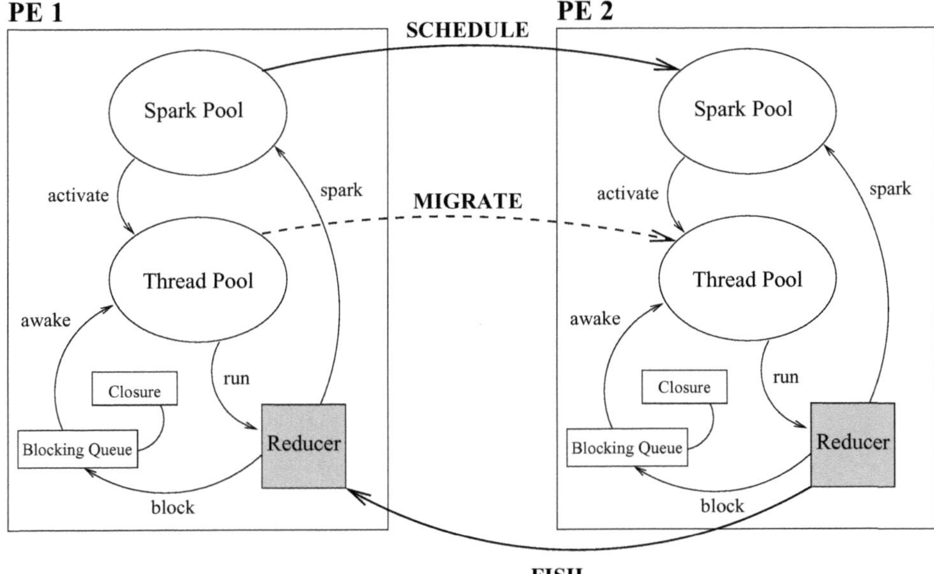

Fig. 2. Interaction of the Components of a GUM PE

The remainder of the paper is structured as follows. Section 2 describes GPH and its associated GUM runtime system, including existing work distribution mechanisms. Section 3 presents the design and implementation of the new thread migration mechanism. Section 4 gives preliminary performance measurements. Section 5 covers related work and Section 6 concludes.

2 GpH and GUM

2.1 GpH

GPH(*Glasgow Parallel Haskell*) [28] is a modest and conservative extension of Haskell 98, using the parallel combinator `par` to specify parallel evaluation. The expression `` p `par` e `` (here we use Haskell's infix operator notation) has the same value as `e`. Its dynamic effect is to indicate that `p` could be evaluated by a new parallel thread, with the parent thread continuing evaluation of `e`. Higher-level coordination is provided using *evaluation strategies*: higher-order polymorphic functions that use `par` and `seq` combinators to introduce and control parallelism [28].

2.2 GUM Parallel Virtual Machine

Figure 2 summarises the main components of GUM. Potential parallelism is represented as "sparks", i.e. pointers to graph structures in the heap, which are collected in a spark pool. Sparks are generated by executing the `par` primitive. Threads are generated on a processing element (PE), consisting of a CPU and

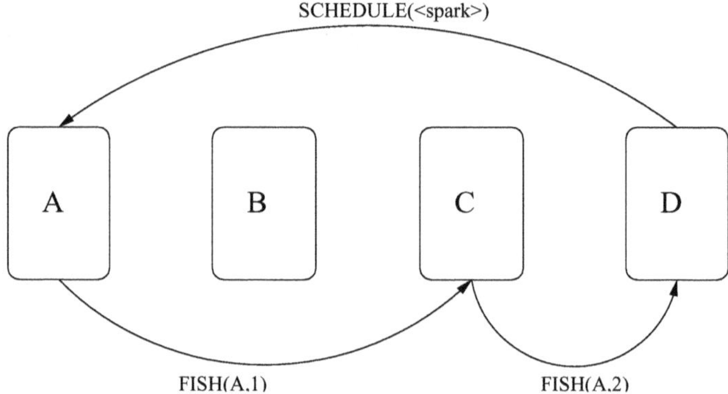

Fig. 3. Spark Distribution in GUM

local memory, if it is idle, i.e. if its thread pool is empty. More threads are added from blocking queues when the required data becomes available. By design the generation of sparks is very cheap, while threads are far more heavy-weight (although still light compared to usual OS threads). Both spark and thread pools are managed as FIFO queues. To create a new thread the PE activates one of its sparks, generating a Thread State Object (TSO), which holds essential information such as registers and a stack pointer. The scheduler then determines how to choose one of the threads from the thread pool to run on the graph reduction engine (Reducer). If a running thread blocks on unavailable data, it is added to the blocking queue of that node. A blocked thread is added to the thread pool when the required data becomes available, either because a local thread produces it or the data arrives from another processor.

Figure 3 illustrates the communications induced by the existing spark distribution mechanism, a *work stealing* scheme. A FISH message requests work and specifies the PE requesting work as well as an age limit, i.e. the maximum number of PEs to visit, in the form `FISH(Source, Age)`. Initially all PEs except for the main PE are idle and without sparks. Idle PEs send a `FISH` message to a PE chosen at random, and only ever have one outstanding FISH: in our case PE A sends to PE C. If a FISH recipient has an empty spark pool it increases the age and forwards the FISH to another PE chosen at random, in our case PE D. If a FISH recipient has a spark it sends it to the source PE as a SCHEDULE message: in our case PE D sends to PE A. The age limit of a FISH is used to avoid swamping a lightly loaded machine with FISH messages: if the age reaches this limit (a tunable system parameter) the FISH is returned to the source PE which delays before reissuing another FISH.

3 Implementing Thread Migration

3.1 Scheduler

A central component in GUM is the scheduler, which determines which thread to execute next. To implement thread migration the following scheduling policy is

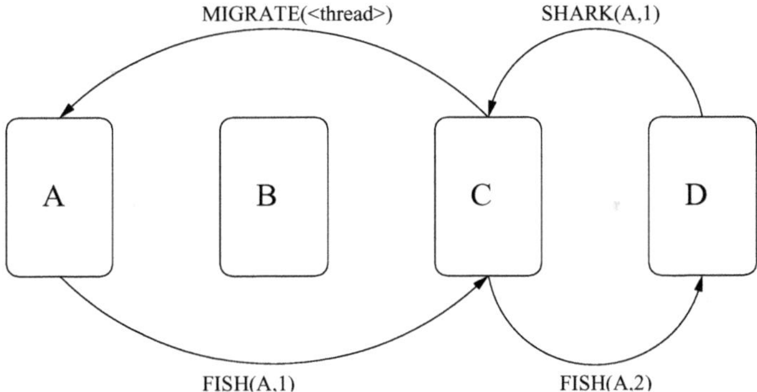

Fig. 4. Thread Migration in GUM

used. It attempts thread migration only if other cheaper work location schemes fail. The new policy is an extension of the existing policy and has been tested for simulated parallel execution [16], but hasn't previously been available in GUM.

1. execute another runnable thread, if available;
2. turn a spark into a thread if no runnable threads are available;
3. try to acquire a remote spark if the processor has no local sparks;
4. try to **migrate** another runnable thread if no remote sparks can be found;

Several scheduling alternatives are possible. Currently the TSO of a migrated thread is added at the end of the (FIFO) runnable queue. Migrated threads could be preferred by inserting at the front of the runnable queue, or more generally by distinguishing them in the queue.

3.2 Communication Protocol

The communication protocol in GUM is very simple and consists of only 6 classes of messages [29]. Thread migration introduces two new messages, both variants of existing messages: a SHARK which is a hungry variant of the FISH message; and MIGRATE which is a variant of the SCHEDULE message and transmits a thread and an associated graph structure between PEs.

Figure 4 illustrates the communications induced by the new thread migration mechanism. As before, a FISH seeks to locate a spark, and in our example the FISH visits PEs C and D unsuccessfully. Now, however, when a FISH reaches its age limit instead of returning to its source PE, it becomes a SHARK message with age 1 and is forwarded to a random PE. When a SHARK arrives, if the PE has a spark it is sent to the source PE in a SCHEDULE message; otherwise if the PE has a runnable thread it is sent to the source PE in a MIGRATE message; otherwise the PE increases the age and forwards the SHARK at random. SHARKs and FISHes have the same age limit, and a SHARK reaching this age limit is returned to the source PE. In the example the SHARK finds a thread, but no spark on PE C, and migrates it to PE A.

At the moment GUM does not propagate load information between PEs. One potential improvement of the load balancing mechanism would be to carry information about spark and thread pool sizes of the visited PEs as part of a FISH message. In our experience even the naive, but cheap mechanism of randomly choosing the target of a FISH works well for most applications. In the presence of thread migration the additional overhead might be justified, though, because in general runnable threads are much rarer than available sparks. Similarly, information about the granularity of threads would be useful in order to choose the largest thread. However, such information is not directly available and hard to obtain automatically [15].

3.3 Graph Packing

The main modification to enable thread migration is to provide mechanisms to pack and unpack threads for communication between PEs. This entails packing a TSO and its associated stack. Since a TSO is a (slightly special) heap object, we simply extend the cases for packing a graph node, to include a case for a TSO. Packing most of the entries in the TSO is uncomplicated, since they are static data rather than pointers. The exceptions are the pointers in the stack that have to be adjusted when unpacking the TSO.

GUM is a parallel extension of the STG-machine [26] and the TSO and stack layout is unchanged. Figure 5 summarises the transfer of a thread, represented as a TSO, from PE 1 to PE 2 (note, that the stack grows downwards). The TSO can be partitioned into a header, containing mostly non-pointer data, and the stack. The stack consists of a continuous sequence of variable sized activation records. Each record starts with one of 4 possible frame types (named in Figure 5): an update frame, a stop frame, a seq frame or an exception frame. The most common type is an update frame, which contains a pointer into the heap, pointing to a graph structure that will be updated with the result of the current evaluation. As shown in Figure 5, the type of the updatee will be either BH, a "black hole" representing a graph structure under evaluation, or a BH_BQ, a "black hole blocking queue" which additionally contains a list of TSOs waiting for the result of this evaluation. An exception frame contains a pointer to the code that has to be executed when catching an exception. A seq frame contains a pointer to the code corresponding to the second part of a sequential composition (the `y` in a `x 'seq' y` construct). A stop frame can only occur at the bottom of the stack and indicates the end of the computation for this thread. All frames are linked together, with one thread register pointing to the top-of-stack frame. The layout of an activation record itself is specified by a bitmask immediately after the update frame, with 1 representing data and 0 a pointer entry. Since this layout is similar to the one of a partial application closure we can treat the elements of one activation record on the stack in the same way as the available arguments in a partially applied function when packing the stack.

During packing, the overall structure of the stack is maintained, but some modifications are made. As with all graph structures, global addresses (GAs) have to be allocated for pointers, in order to ensure that thunks, or unevaluated

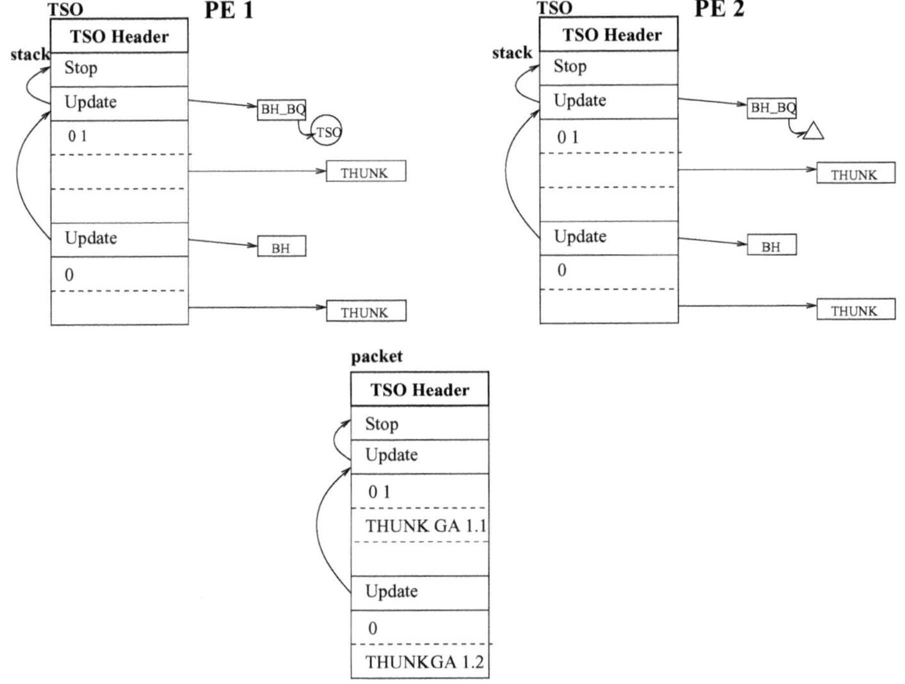

Fig. 5. Transfer of a Thread (TSO) between PEs

closures, are uniquely identified in the virtual shared heap. This can be seen in the packet in Figure 5 where the two thunks are packed with new global addresses GA 1.1 and GA 1.2. As with ordinary graph structures, a mapping of old GAs on the source PE, to new GAs on the target PE, is sent back as a reply to the communication shown here and the BH and BH_BQ closures on PE 1 are converted into FetchMe (FM) and FetchMe blocking queue (FM_BQ) closures. If a thread on PE 1 demands a thunk being evaluated by the migrated TSO, a FETCH request will be sent to PE 2 upon entering the FM or FM_BQ closure.

Note that when unpacking the black hole blocking queue (BH_BQ) on PE 2, a different kind of closure has to be used to represent the TSO that is blocked on the black hole on PE 1. This closure is a "blocked fetch" closure, which already exists in GUM. It normally represents a fetch request from another PE, and contains information about the requesting PE and TSO, so that upon updating the BH_BQ closure, a message with the result data is sent to the original PE. By this mechanism the TSO on PE 1 will continue as soon as the migrated TSO updates the BH_BQ on PE 2.

4 Performance Measurements

The measurements in this section are performed on a high-latency cluster: a Beowulf [27] consisting of Linux RedHat 6.2 workstations with a 533MHz Celeron

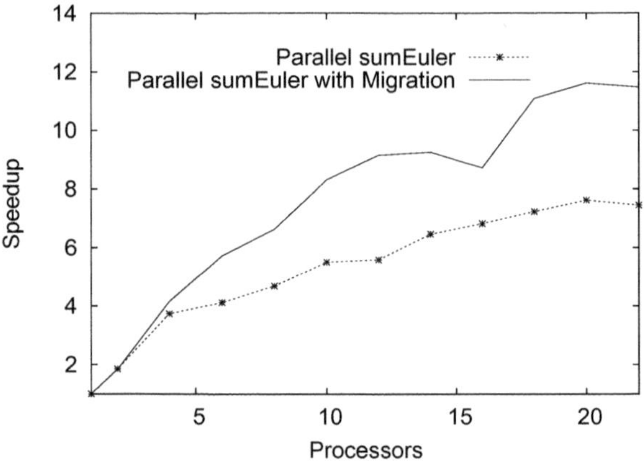

Fig. 6. Speedups for sumEuler

processor, 128kB cache, 128MB of DRAM and 5.7GB of IDE disk. The workstations are connected through a 100Mb/s fast Ethernet switch with a latency of 142μs, measured under PVM 3.4.2.

4.1 Performance Improvement

Experience has shown that many GPH programs have migratable threads and some under-utilised processors [19], and four programs from two parallel paradigms are discussed in this section.

The first program, sumEuler, is data parallel: computing the sum of the Euler totient function over an integer list [18]. Figure 6 shows mean speedup curves for sumEuler with and without migration calculated from five executions of the program. The speedups reported here and throughout the paper are *relative*, i.e. improvement over the single-PE parallel execution. Table 1 shows, for varying numbers of PEs: the mean, minimum and maximum runtimes, the average number of threads migrated in each execution, the range of runtimes as a percentage of the mean runtime and the percentage reduction in mean runtime.

The sumEuler results show that thread migration improves runtime for all numbers of PEs measured. For small numbers of PEs the improvement is limited by the small numbers of migratable threads, but between 6 and 22 PEs the improvement is approximately 30% with a single exception. The improvement is variable, as discussed in the next section, with the greatest improvement being 39% on 12 PEs.

The second program, Maze, uses a divide-and-conquer algorithm to search a maze for an exit [8]. Figure 7 shows the mean speedup curves and table 2 the performance improvements. The results show that thread migration improves performance on all numbers of PEs; from 4 PEs onwards improvements of approximately 13% are achieved with two exceptions. The improvement is variable with the greatest improvement being 21% on 16 PEs.

Table 1. SumEuler Runtimes(s) with/without Migration

	Mean Runtime		Min. Runtime		Max. Runtime		Avg No Thr Mig	% Range		Performance Improvement
No PEs	**Mig.**	No Mig.	**Mig.**	No Mig.	**Mig.**	No Mig.		**Mig.**	No Mig.	
1	**97.5**	97.5	**97.3**	97.4	**97.7**	97.6	0	**0.4%**	0.2%	0%
2	**51.9**	52.5	**50.2**	50.1	**54.2**	55.4	1	**7.7%**	10%	1.1%
4	**23.5**	26.1	**20.5**	21.4	**26.3**	31.7	4.2	**24.6%**	39.4%	10%
6	**17.0**	23.7	**15.66**	20.4	**18.8**	27.3	3	**18.4%**	29.1%	28%
8	**14.7**	20.8	**12.8**	14.9	**17.8**	27.5	4.0	**34%**	60.5%	29%
10	**11.7**	17.7	**9.5**	14.7	**12.9**	20.2	3.4	**29%**	31%	33%
12	**10.6**	17.5	**9.0**	12.6	**11.9**	20.8	3.4	**27.3%**	46.8%	39%
14	**10.5**	15.1	**8.1**	11.8	**11.8**	19.7	4.6	**35.2%**	52.3%	30%
16	**11.2**	14.3	**9.8**	8.4	**12.5**	19.0	5.2	**24.1%**	74.1%	21%
18	**8.8**	13.5	**7.9**	11.2	**9.2**	14.8	3.4	**14.7%**	26.6%	34%
20	**8.4**	12.8	**5.3**	9.0	**11.1**	14.9	4	**69%**	46.3%	34%
22	**8.5**	13.1	**5.7**	10.9	**11.4**	17.6	4.6	**67%**	51%	35%

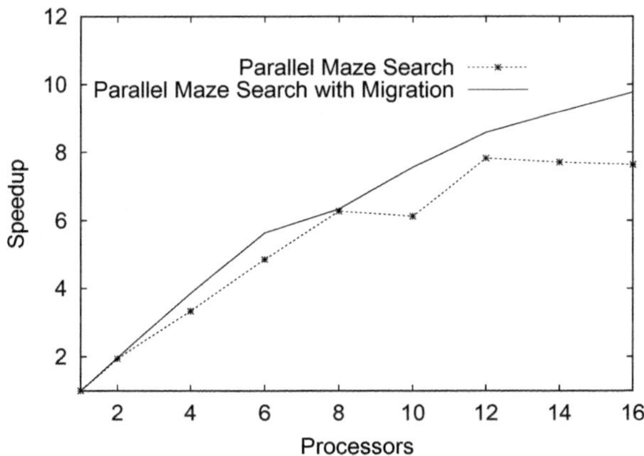

Fig. 7. Speedups for Maze

A third program, Raytracer, is data parallel: constructing a scene from objects and a viewpoint [11,17]. Space precludes a full presentation of Raytracer results, but as with the previous programs they show that thread migration improves performance on all numbers of PEs; from 3 PEs onwards improvements of approximately 20% are achieved. The improvement is variable with the greatest improvement being 34% on 5 PEs.

The fourth program, Queens, is data parallel: placing chess pieces on a board. Figure 8 shows the mean speedup curves and table 3 the performance improvements. The results show that while thread migration improves performance on most configurations, it degrades it on two; the 4-PE and 8-PE configurations. There is an enormous amount of variability in the improvement, with a maximum of 37% and minimum of -10%.

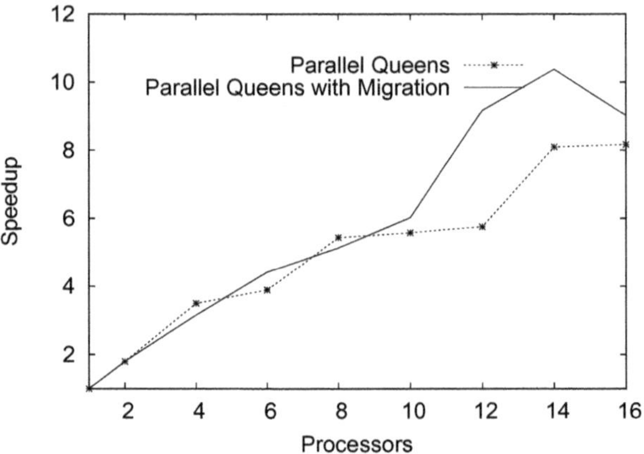

Fig. 8. Speedups for Queens

Table 2. Maze Runtimes(s) with/without Migration

	Mean Runtime		Min. Runtime		Max. Runtime		Avg No Thr Mig	% Range		Performance Improvement
No PEs	**Mig.**	No Mig.	**Mig.**	No Mig.	**Mig.**	No Mig.		**Mig.**	No Mig.	
1	**162.9**	162.0	**162.6**	159.7	**163.7**	163.5	0	**0.6%**	0 %	0%
2	**82.7**	83.5	**82.5**	83.3	**82.9**	83.5	1	**0.4%**	0.2%	0.9%
4	**42.2**	48.5	**40.4**	43.1	**44.1**	58.2	0.8	**8.7%**	31.1%	13%
6	**28.9**	33.3	**27.9**	30.8	**30.3**	35.1	2	**8.3%**	12.9 %	13%
8	**25.7**	25.8	**23.8**	24.9	**28.3**	29.1	5.8	**17.5%**	16.2%	0%
10	**21.5**	26.4	**19.8**	24.5	**24.1**	29.6	2.4	**20%**	19.3%	18%
12	**18.9**	20.7	**16.3**	16.7	**22.0**	24.6	4.2	**30.1%**	38.1%	8%
14	**17.7**	21.0	**16.0**	18.0	**20.3**	24.7	4	**24.2%**	31.9%	15%
16	**16.6**	21.2	**12.2**	16.4	**20.3**	25.3	4.4	**48.7%**	41.9%	21%

Thread migration does not consistently or significantly improve the performance of either Queens or Maze up to 8 PEs because both have excellent processor utilisation, achieving a speedup of approximately 6 in each case. If the default GUM work distribution mechanism is achieving good utilisation, it is hard for the more expensive migration mechanism to improve on it. Indeed results for Queens show that the additional communication introduced may reduce performance (e.g. at 4 and 8 PEs), and increase variability. In contrast migration delivers significant and consistent improvements when utilisation is low, e.g. on 8 PEs sumEuler without migration has a speedup of just 4.7 and migration delivers a 29% improvement. Likewise on 7 PEs Raytracer has a speedup of just 4 and migration delivers a 21% improvement. In a similar way, migration improves the performance of both Queens and Maze at higher numbers of PEs as the utilisation delivered by the default load balancing mechanism falls.

In summary, thread migration always improves the runtime of programs with migratable threads and low processor utilisation, like sumEuler, Maze and Ray-

Table 3. Queens Runtimes(s) with/without Migration

	Mean Runtime		Min. Runtime		Max. Runtime		Avg No Thr Mig	% Range		Performance Improvement
No PEs	**Mig.**	No Mig.	**Mig.**	No Mig.	**Mig.**	No Mig.		**Mig.**	No Mig.	
1	**405.4**	405.6	**405.3**	405.2	**405.7**	405.9	0	**0.0%**	0.1%	0%
2	**225.0**	227.8	**219.6**	227.8	**227.7**	227.9	0	**3.6%**	0.0%	1%
4	**128.4**	116.7	**114.9**	116.6	**169.6**	116.8	1.5	**42.6%**	0.1%	-10%
6	**91.7**	104.9	**78.03**	103.1	**117.6**	108.7	4.8	**43.1%**	5.3%	12%
8	**78.9**	75.1	**72.2**	74.9	**102.1**	75.3	2.5	**37.8%**	0.5%	-5%
10	**67.3**	73.2	**63.2**	67.1	**68.8**	103.0	1.33	**8.3%**	49%	8%
12	**44.2**	70.9	**38.8**	62.9	**70.8**	73.1	1.33	**72.3%**	14.3%	37%
14	**39.0**	50.5	**39.0**	38.9	**39.1**	78.9	0.84	**0.2%**	79.2%	22%
16	**44.9**	50.0	**38.9**	39.0	**73.9**	72.3	1.6	**77.9%**	66.6%	10%

tracer. Thread migration often improves but may degrade programs with migratable threads and good processor utilisation, like Queens. In both cases the runtimes and improvements achieved are variable. The improvements are achieved by migrating a relatively small number of threads: typically around 4. This indicates that the migration policy described in section 3 works adequately, striking a balance between good data locality and even load distribution.

4.2 Variability

We hypothesised that thread migration would reduce the variability in runtimes, as it allows a poor initial distribution of sparks to PEs to be rectified. The '% Range' column in tables 1 and 2 together with measurements of the Raytracer show that migration reduces the range of performance results for programs with low utilisation, like sumEuler, Maze and Raytracer. However, table 3 shows that migration may increase the variability of some programs with good utilisation, like Queens on small numbers of processors. In these cases, we have observed increased communication in programs with migration and suspect the variability is due to both increased communication and potential blocking after having migrated threads. Depending on the amount of sharing with other graphs on the original PE, threads on a PE may send data requests and become blocked, thereby reducing the gain in performance due to migration. However, none of the programs with poor utilisation seems to suffer from an increased amount of data transfer caused by migration.

A second factor is that programs with a short runtime allow little time for migration to correct a poor initial load distribution. This can be seen in the relatively high variability of sumEuler on 20 and 22 PEs in table 1. However, migration still helps even in these cases: the mean, minimum and maximum runtimes are always smaller than for the program without migration.

4.3 Overheads

To investigate the overheads of thread migration two simple programs without migratable threads have been measured: one data-parallel the other divide-and-

Table 4. Migration Overheads

Program Name	Paradigm	Mean Runtime		Avg No	% Change
		With Migration	Without Mig.	Thr Mig	in Runtime
ParFib 35	Div & Conq.	**5.6**	5.7	0	+2%
ParMap	Data Par.	**25.2**	25.3	0	+1%

conquer. For each program table 4 reports the paradigm, the mean runtime with and without migration, the average number of threads migrated in each execution and the percentage change in runtime, all measured on 7 PEs. The results show that the migration mechanism has no significant overhead if there are no migratable threads. Moreover, tables 1, 2 and 3 together with measurements of the Raytracer demonstrate that execution with migration enabled on a single PE does not incur significant additional overheads compared to parallel execution without migration.

5 Related Work

Thread migration suffered from bad press due to early news of excessive overhead. Therefore, comparable systems that provide light-weight, and typically fine-grained, threads tend to avoid migration [5,7,13,14].

In the context of earlier versions of parallel graph reducers, early experiments on the GRIP system, implemented on a special-purpose distributed memory machine, indicated, that despite the availability of several sparking strategies to control and balance parallelism, thread migration is still needed for some applications to guarantee high utilisation [10].

The Cid system [24] extends C with primitives for creating ("forking") new threads and synchronising ("joining") them on shared variables, managed in a virtual shared heap. The Cid systems holds runnable threads in two different queues: one for the threads that must be executed on the current processor, one for threads that might be migrated to another processor. The cost for handling the messages is reduced by using the technique of active messages [30] where the message carries a pointer to a function, the "handler", that is called when receiving the message. The effectiveness of Cid's load balancing and latency tolerance mechanisms is assessed in [25].

Cilk [3] is similar to Cid, in that it extends C with constructs for creating and synchronising light-weight threads. Its processors also use a sophisticated work-stealing scheduler to obtain new parallelism. While Cilk provides thread migration, it is optimised for local execution of a thread, since that is the most common case. Thus, still high overhead is associated with migration.

The Filaments system [20] is in many aspects similar to our system: it emphasises fine-grained parallelism on a distributed shared heap, with dynamic and implicit management of work and data; the programmer is only required to expose parallelism. It is implemented as an extension of C. Two levels of threads can be distinguished: filaments, with a code pointer and arguments but without a stack, and server threads, with an attached stack, acting as a scheduler over a set of filaments. In balancing the load of the system, it employs a sophisticated adaptive data placement mechanism, that tries to minimise access to remote data and uses information gained from dynamic monitoring of data access. Overall, the system focuses on the placement of data rather than threads.

The Ariadne Threads system [21] is C-based and implements user-level threads and explicit thread migration on shared and distributed memory machines. In contrast to Filaments, placement decisions focus on threads, rather than data, by migrating a thread to the location of its data, rather than vice versa.

The Amber system [6] uses a virtual shared memory model, implemented on the Topaz operating system and is programmed in C++. It provides library calls to realise dynamic clustering of threads at runtime, via explicit thread migration. In contrast to Ariadne it puts limitations on the total number of threads per node, but gains reduced packing and thread management overhead.

Another virtual shared memory system focusing on thread migration is Millipede [12]. It uses kernel-threads and is very flexible, allowing explicit migration at almost any point in the execution. It uses dynamic mechanisms migrating both threads and data to maximise data locality. Stack packing is simplified by guaranteeing that stacks will occupy the same place on all processors. This reduces packing costs but wastes some memory space.

A lot of research was done on process migration in the area of operating systems in the late 70s [23]. The objective of introducing process migration into an operating system was to improve load balancing and fault tolerance. Thus, process migration should be transparent to the user and is not under the control of the programmer. Many operating systems were designed to support process migration, some well known examples are Mach [2] and MOSIX [1].

We are primarily interested in thread migration as a way to obtain even load balance and thereby improve performance in a system for parallel computation. Alternative applications of this technique, with different design requirements, are the use of migration in persistent systems [22] and for mobile computing [23].

6 Conclusions

We have presented a design and implementation of thread migration for the GUM runtime system underlying GPH. The design exploits the uniform representation of heap objects in the STG-machine: the packing of a TSO and its stack only requires an extension of the default packing mechanism to handle a new kind of heap closure. The design also makes minimal extensions to the relatively simple GUM communication protocol, adding only two new kinds of messages. Here we profit from both data and threads being represented by heap objects.

Performance measurements of six programs on a high-latency Beowulf cluster show that thread migration in GUM can improve the performance, and reduce the variability in performance, of data-parallel and divide-and-conquer programs with low processor utilisation. In summary: sumEuler is 35% faster on 22 PEs, Maze is 21% faster on 16 PEs, Raytracer is 21% faster on 7 PEs, and Queens is 10% faster on 16 PEs. Measurements of these and two other programs show that migration does not incur significant overheads if there are no migratable threads, or on a single PE. However, it is hard for migration to improve programs that already have good utilisation, and migration may both increase variability and occasionally reduce performance. For example neither Maze nor Queens is significantly improved by migration until 10 or more PEs are used.

In future work it may be possible to better characterise programs and architectures where thread migration may be beneficial. GUM's thread migration mechanism and load management policies could easily be improved, e.g. replacing the random targeting of FISH and SHARK messages with a more focused approach; and possibly recording partial load information in all messages to maintain a time-stamped partial load information on each PE.

Acknowledgements

The authors would like to thank the following funding agencies for supporting this research: UK's EPSRC council (grant GR/R88137), the Austrian Academy of Sciences (fellowship APART 624), the European Community (IST-2001-33149) and the UK CVCP ORS Scheme.

References

1. A. Barak and O. La'adan. The MOSIX Multicomputer Operating System for High-Performance Cluster Computing. *Future Generation Computer Systems*, 13(4–5):361–372, 1998.
2. R. Baron, R. Rashid, E. Siegel, A. Tevanian, and M. Young. Mach-1: An Operating Environment for Large-Scale Multiprocessor Applications. *IEEE Software*, 2(4):65–67, July 1985.
3. R.D. Blumofe, C.F. Joerg, C.E. Leiserson, K.H. Randall, and Y. Zhou. Cilk: An Efficient Multithreaded Runtime System. In *PPoPP'95 — Symp. on Principles and Practice of Parallel Programming*, pages 207–216, Santa Barbara, USA, 1995.
4. S. Breitinger, R. Loogen, Y. Ortega Mallén, and R. Peña Marí. Eden — The Paradise of Functional Concurrent Programming. In *EuroPar'96 — European Conf. on Parallel Processing*, LNCS 1123, pages 710–713, Lyon, France, 1996. Springer.
5. T. Bülck, A. Held, W. Kluge, S. Pantke, C. Rathsack, S-B. Scholz, and R. Schröder. Experience with the Implementation of a Concurrent Graph Reduction System on an nCUBE/2 Platform. In *CONPAR'94 — Conf. on Parallel and Vector Processing*, LNCS 854, pages 497–508. Springer, 1994.
6. J.S. Chase, F.G Amador, E.D. Lazowska, H.M Levy, and R.J. Littlefield. The Amber System: Parallel Programming on a Network of Multiprocessors. In *Symp. on Operating Systems Principles*, pages 147–158, Litchfield Park, AZ, USA, 1989.
7. D.E. Culler, S.C. Goldstein, K.E. Schauser, and T. von Eicken. TAM — A Compiler Controlled Threaded Abstract Machine. *J. of Parallel and Distributed Computing*, 18:347–370, June 1993.

8. A. R. Du Bois, R. Pointon, H-W. Loidl, and P. W. Trinder. Implementing Declarative Parallel Bottom-Avoiding Choice. In *14th Symposium on Computer Architecture and High Performance Computing*, pages 82–89, Vitoria, Brazil, october 2002. IEEE Press.
9. K. Hammond and S.L. Peyton Jones. Some Early Experiments on the GRIP Parallel Reducer. In *IFL'90 — Intl. Workshop on the Parallel Implementation of Functional Languages*, pages 51–72, Nijmegen, The Netherlands, June 1990.
10. K. Hammond and S.L. Peyton Jones. Profiling Scheduling Strategies on the GRIP Multiprocessor. In *IFL'92 — Intl. . Workshop on the Parallel Implementation of Functional Languages*, pages 73–98, RWTH Aachen, Germany, September 1992.
11. Impala. Impala – (IMplicitly PArallel LAnguage Application Suite). <URL:`http://www.csg.lcs.mit.edu/impala/`>, July 2001.
12. A. Itzkovitz, A. Schuster, and L. Shalev. Thread Migration and its Applications in Distributed Shared Memory Systems. *J. of Systems and Software*, 42(1):71–87, 1998.
13. M. H. G. Kesseler. *The Implementation of Functional Languages on Parallel Machines with Distributed Memory*. PhD thesis, Wiskunde en Informatica, Katholieke Universiteit van Nijmegen, The Netherlands, 1996.
14. H. Kingdon, D.R. Lester, and G. Burn. The HDG-machine: a Highly Distributed Graph-Reducer for a Transputer Network. *Computer Journal*, 34(4):290–301, 1991.
15. H-W. Loidl. *Granularity in Large-Scale Parallel Functional Programming.* PhD thesis, University of Glasgow, March 1998.
16. H-W. Loidl and K. Hammond. Making a Packet: Cost-Effective Communication for a Parallel Graph Reducer. In *IFL'96 — Intl. Workshop on the Implementation of Functional Languages*, LNCS 1268, pages 184–199, Bonn/Bad-Godesberg, Germany, September 1996. Springer.
17. H-W. Loidl, U. Klusik, K. Hammond, R. Loogen, and P.W. Trinder. GpH and Eden: Comparing Two Parallel Functional Languages on a Beowulf Cluster. In *SFP'00 — Scottish Functional Programming Workshop*, volume 2 of *Trends in Functional Programming*, pages 39–52, University of St Andrews, Scotland, July 2000. Intellect.
18. H-W. Loidl, P.W. Trinder, and C. Butz. Tuning Task Granularity and Data Locality of Data Parallel GpH Programs. *Parallel Processing Letters*, 11(4):471–486, December 2001.
19. H-W. Loidl, P.W. Trinder, K. Hammond, S.B. Junaidu, R.G. Morgan, and S.L. Peyton Jones. Engineering Parallel Symbolic Programs in GPH. *Concurrency — Practice and Experience*, 11:701–752, 1999.
20. D.K. Lowenthal, V.W. Freeh, and G.R. Andrews. Using Fine-Grain Threads and Run-Time Decision Making in Parallel Computing. *J. of Parallel and Distributed Computing*, 37:42–54, 1996.
21. E. Mascarenhas and V. Rego. Ariadne: Architecture of a Portable Threads System Supporting Thread Migration. *Software — Practice and Experience*, 26(3):327–356, March 1996.
22. B. Mathiske, F. Matthes, and J.W. Schmidt. On Migrating Threads. In *Intl. Workshop on Next Generation Information Technologies and Systems*, Naharia, Israel, June 1995.
23. D. Milojicić, F. Douglis, and R. Weeler. *Mobility: Processes, Computers, and Agents.* Addison-Wesley, Reading, MA, USA, 1999.
24. R.S. Nikhil. Parallel Symbolic Computing in Cid. In *Workshop on Parallel Symbolic Computing*, LNCS 1068, pages 217–242, Beaune, France, Oct. 1995. Springer.

25. R.S. Nikhil and A. Singla. Automatic Granularity Control and Load-Balancing in Cid. Technical report, DEC Research Labs, December 1994.
26. S.L. Peyton Jones. Implementing Lazy Functional Languages on Stock Hardware: the Spineless Tagless G-machine. *J. of Functional Programming*, 2(2):127–202, July 1992.
27. D. Ridge, D. Becker, P. Merkey, and T. Sterling. Beowulf: Harnessing the Power of Parallelism in a Pile-of-PCs. In *IEEE Aerospace Conference*, pages 79–91, 1997.
28. P.W. Trinder, K. Hammond, H-W. Loidl, and S.L. Peyton Jones. Algorithm + Strategy = Parallelism. *J. of Functional Programming*, 8(1):23–60, January 1998.
29. P.W. Trinder, K. Hammond, J.S. Mattson Jr., A.S. Partridge, and S.L. Peyton Jones. GUM: a Portable Parallel Implementation of Haskell. In *PLDI'96 — Conf. on Programming Language Design and Implementation*, pages 79–88, Philadephia, USA, May 1996.
30. T. von Eicken, D.E. Culler, S.C. Goldstein, and K.E. Schauser. Active Messages: a Mechanism for Integrated Communication and Computation. In *ISCA'92 — Intl. Symp. on Computer Architecture*, pages 256–266, Gold Coast, Australia, May 1992. ACM Press.
31. P. Wegner. *Programming Languages, Information Structures and Machine Organisation.* McGraw-Hill, New York, 1971.

Towards a Strongly Typed Functional Operating System*

Arjen van Weelden and Rinus Plasmeijer

Computer Science Institute
University of Nijmegen
Toernooiveld 1, 6525 ED Nijmegen, The Netherlands
{arjenw,rinus}@cs.kun.nl

Abstract. In this paper, we present Famke. It is a prototype implementation of a strongly typed operating system written in Clean. Famke enables the creation and management of independent distributed Clean processes on a network of workstations. It uses Clean's dynamic type system and its dynamic linker to communicate values of any type, e.g. data, closures, and functions (i.e. compiled code), between running applications in a type safe way. Mobile processes can be implemented using Famke's ability to communicate functions. We have built an interactive shell on top of Famke that enables user interaction. The shell uses a functional-style command language that allows construction of new processes, and it type checks the command line before executing it. Famke's type safe run-time extensibility makes it a strongly typed operating system that can be tailored to a given situation.

1 Introduction

Functional programming languages like Haskell [1] and Clean [2,3] offer a very flexible and powerful static type system. Compact, reusable, and readable programs can be written in these languages while the static type system is able to detect many programming errors at compile time. But this works only within a single application.

Independently developed applications often need to communicate with each other. One would like the communication of objects to take place in a type safe manner as well. And not only simple objects, but objects of any type, including functions. In practice, this is not easy to realize: the compile time type information is generally not kept inside a compiled executable, and therefore cannot be used at run-time. In real life therefore, applications often only communicate simple data types like streams of characters, ASCII text, or use some ad-hoc defined (binary) format. Although more and more applications use XML to communicate data together with the definitions of the data types used, most programs do not support run-time type unification, cannot use previously unknown data types or cannot exchange functions (i.e. code) between different programs in a

* This work was supported by STW as part of project NWI.4411.

R. Peña and T. Arts (Eds.): IFL 2002, LNCS 2670, pp. 215–231, 2003.

type safe way. This is mainly because the used programming language has no support for such things.

In this paper, we present a prototype implementation of a micro kernel, called *Famke* (emphfunctional micro kernel experiment). It provides explicit non-deterministic concurrency and type safe message passing for all types to processes written in Clean. By adding servers that provide common operating system services, an entire strongly typed, distributed operating system can be built on top of Famke.

Clearly, we need a powerful dynamic type system [4] for this purpose and a way to dynamically extend a running application with new code. Fortunately, the new Clean system offers some of the required basic facilities: it offers a hybrid type system with static as well as dynamic typing (*dynamics*) [5], including run-time support for *dynamic linking* [6] (currently on Microsoft Windows only). To achieve type safe communication, Famke uses the above mentioned facilities offered by Clean to implement *lightweight threads*, *processes*, *exception handling* and *type safe message passing* without requiring additional language constructs or run-time support.

It also makes use of an underlying operating system to avoid some low-level implementation work and to integrate better with existing software (e.g. resources such as the console and the file system). With Famke, we want to accomplish the following objectives without changing the Clean compiler or run-time system.

- Present an interface (API) for Clean programmers with which it is easy to create (distributed) processes that can communicate expressions of any type in a type safe way;
- Present an interactive shell with which it is easy to manage, apply and combine (distributed) processes, and even construct new processes interactively. The shell should type check the command line before executing it in order to catch errors early;
- Achieve a modular design using an extensible micro kernel approach;
- Achieve a reliable system by using static types where possible and, if static checking cannot be done (e.g. between different programs), dynamic type checks;
- Achieve a system that is easy to port to another operating system (if the Clean system supports it).

We will introduce the static/dynamic hybrid type system of Clean in section 2. Sections 3 and 4 present the micro kernel of Famke, which provides cooperative thread scheduling, exception handling, and type safe communication. It also provides an interface to the preemptively scheduled processes of the underlying operating system. These sections are very technical, but necessary to understand the interesting sections that follow. On top of this micro kernel an interactive shell has been implemented, which we describe in section 5. During these sections the crucial role of dynamics will become apparent. Related work is discussed in section 6 and we conclude and mention future research in section 7.

2 Dynamics in Clean

Clean has recently been extended with a polymorphic dynamic type system [4,5,6] in addition to its static type system. Here, we will give a small introduction to dynamics in Clean. A dynamic is a value of type `Dynamic` which contains a value as well as a representation of the type of that value.

```
dynamic 42 :: Int
```
[1]

Dynamics can be formed (i.e. lifted from the static to the dynamic type system) using the keyword `dynamic` in combination with the value and an optional type (otherwise the compiler will infer the type), separated by a double colon.

```
:: Maybe a = Nothing | Just a
```
[2]

```
matchInt :: Dynamic -> Maybe Int
matchInt (x :: Int) = Just x
matchInt  other     = Nothing
```

Values of type `Dynamic` can be matched in function alternatives and case patterns to bring them from the dynamic back into the static type system. Such pattern matches consist of an optional value pattern and a type pattern. In the example above, `matchInt` returns `Just` the value contained inside the dynamic if it has type `Int`; and `Nothing` if it has any other type. The compiler translates type pattern matches into run-time type unifications. If the unification fails, the next function alternative is tried, as in a common pattern match.

```
dynamicApply :: Dynamic Dynamic -> Dynamic
dynamicApply (f :: a -> b) (x :: a) = dynamic f x :: b
dynamicApply  _             _       = dynamic "Error: cannot apply"
```
[3]

A type pattern can contain type variables which, if the run-time unification is successful, are bound to the offered type. In the example above, `dynamicApply` tests if the type of the function `f` inside its first argument can be unified with the type of the value `x` inside the second argument. If this is the case then `dynamicApply` can safely apply `f` to `x`. The result of this application has type `b`. At compile time it is generally unknown what this type `b` will be. The result can be wrapped into a dynamic (and only a dynamic) again, because the type variable `b` will be instantiated by the run-time unification.

```
matchDynamic :: Dynamic -> Maybe t | TC t
matchDynamic (x :: t^) = Just x
matchDynamic  other    = Nothing
```
[4]

Type variables in dynamic patterns can also relate to a type variable in the static type of a function. Such functions are called type dependent functions. A

[1] Numeric literals are not overloaded in Clean, hence 42 has type `Int` instead of Haskell's `(Num a) => a`.

[2] A `::`, instead of the `data` keyword of Haskell, precedes a type definition in Clean.

[3] Function types in Clean separate arguments by white space instead of `->`.

[4] Clean denotes overloading in a class `K` as: `a | K a`, whereas Haskell uses `(K a) => a`.

carrot (^) behind a variable in a pattern associates it with the type variable with the same name in the static type of the function. The static type variable then becomes overloaded in the predefined `TC` (type code) class [5]. In the example above, the static type `t` will be determined by the static context in which it is used, and will impose a restriction on the actual type that is accepted at run-time by `matchDynamic`. It yields `Just` the value inside the dynamic (if the dynamic contains a value of the required context dependent type) or `Nothing` (if it does not).

The new dynamic run-time system of Clean [6] supports writing dynamics to disk and reading them in again, possibly in another program or during another execution of the same program.

```
writeDynamic :: String Dynamic *World -> (Bool, *World)
readDynamic :: String *World -> (Bool, Dynamic, *World)
```
[5]

The dynamic will be read in lazily after a successful run-time unification (triggered by a pattern match on the dynamic). The amount of data and code that the dynamic linker will link in, is therefore determined by the amount of evaluation of the value inside the dynamic. Dynamics written by a program can be safely read by any other program, providing a form of persistence and a rudimentary means of communication.

The ability of Clean, as well as other functional languages, to construct new functions (e.g. currying and higher-order functions) in combination with Clean's new support for run-time linking, enables us to extend a running application with new code that can be type checked after which it is guaranteed to fit.

3 Threads in Famke

Here we show how a programmer can construct concurrent programs in Clean, using Famke's thread management and exception handling primitives.

Currently, Clean offers only very limited library support for process management and communication.

Old versions of Concurrent Clean [7] did offer sophisticated support for parallel evaluation and lightweight processes, but no support for exception handling. Concurrent Clean was targeted at deterministic, implicit concurrency, but we want to build a system for distributed, non-deterministic, explicit concurrency.

Porting Concurrent Clean to Microsoft Windows is a lot of work and still would not give us exactly what we want. Although Microsoft Windows offers threads to enable multi-tasking within a single process, there is no run-time support for making use of these preemptive threads in Clean. We could emulate threads using the preemptive processes that Microsoft Windows provides by multiple incarnations of the same Clean program, but this would make the

[5] The `*` in front of `World` is a uniqueness attribute. It indicates that the (state of the) world will be passed around in a unique/single-threaded way. Clean's type checker allows destructive updates, but reject sharing, of such unique objects. Clean's `World` type corresponds to the hidden state of Haskell's `IO` monad.

threads unacceptably heavyweight, and it would prevent them from sharing the Clean heap, and we still would not have exception handling.

Therefore, Famke does her own scheduling of threads in order to keep them lightweight and to provide exception handling.

3.1 Thread Implementation

In order to implement cooperative threads we need a way to suspend running computations and to resume them later. Wand [8] shows that this can be done using continuations and the call/CC construct offered by Scheme and other functional programming languages. We copy this approach using first class continuations in Clean. Because Clean has no call/CC construction, we have to write the continuation passing explicitly. Our approach closely resembles Claessen's concurrency monad [9], but our primitives operate directly on the kernel state using Clean's uniqueness typing, and we have extended the implementation with easily extendable exception handling (see section 3.2).

```
:: Thread a :== (a -> KernelOp) -> KernelOp[6]
:: KernelOp :== Kernel -> Kernel

threadExample :: Thread a
threadExample = \cont kernel -> cont x kernel‘
where
  x = ...                 //[7] calculate argument for cont
  kernel‘ = ...kernel... // operate on the kernel state
```

A function of the type `Thread`, such as the example function above, gets the tail of a computation (named `cont`; of type `a -> KernelOp`) as its argument and combines that with a new computation step, which calculates the argument (named `x`) for the tail computation, to form a new function (of type `KernelOp`). This function returns, when evaluated on a kernel state (named `kernel`; of type `Kernel`), a new kernel state.

```
:: ThreadId  // abstract thread id

:: *Kernel[8] = {currentId  :: ThreadId, newId :: ThreadId,
                 ready :: [ThreadState], world :: *World}

:: ThreadState = {thrId :: ThreadId, thrCont :: KernelOp}

:: Void = Void  // written more elegantly as () in Haskell
```

The kernel state (of type `Kernel`) is a record that contains the information required to do the scheduling of the threads. It contains information like the current running thread (named `currentId`), the threads that are ready to be

[6] Clean uses `:==` to indicate a type synonym, whereas Haskell uses the `type` keyword.

[7] This is a single line comment in Clean, Haskell uses `--`

[8] Record types in Clean are surrounded by { and }. The `*` before `Kernel` indicates that the record must always be unique. Therefore, the `*` can then be omitted in the rest of the code.

scheduled (in the `ready` list), and the `world` state which is provided by the Clean run-time system. Clean's uniqueness type system makes these types a little more complicated, but we will not show this in the examples in order to keep them readable.

```
newThread :: (Thread a) -> Thread ThreadId
newThread thread = \cont k=:{newId, ready}⁹ ->
  cont newId {k & newId = inc newId, ready = [threadState:ready]}¹⁰
where
  threadState = {thrId = newId, thrCont = thread (\_ k -> k)}

threadId :: Thread ThreadId
threadId = \cont k=:{currentId} -> cont currentId k
```

The `newThread` function starts the given thread concurrently with the other threads. Threads are evaluated for their effect on the kernel and the world state. They therefore do not return a result, hence the polymorphically parameterized `Thread a` type. It relieves our system from the additional complexity of returning the result to the parent thread. The communication primitives that will be introduced later enable programmers to extend the `newThread` primitive to deliver a result to the parent. Threads can obtain their thread identification with `threadId`.

Scheduling of the threads is done cooperatively. This means that threads must occasionally allow rescheduling using `yield`, and should not run endless tight loops. The `schedule` function then evaluates the next ready thread. `StartFamke` can be used like the standard Clean `Start` function to start the evaluation of the main thread.

```
yield :: KernelOp Kernel -> Kernel
yield cont k=:{currentId, ready} = {k & ready = ready ++ [threadState]}
where
  threadState = {thrId = currentId, thrCont = cont}

schedule :: Kernel -> Kernel
schedule k=:{ready = []} = k  // nothing to schedule
schedule k=:{ready = [{thrId, thrCont}:tail]} =
  let k` = {k & ready = tail, currentId = thrId}
      k`` = thrCont k`  // evaluate the thread until it yields
  in schedule k``

StartFamke :: (Thread a) *World -> *World
StartFamke mainThread world = (schedule kernel).world
where
  firstId = ...  // first thread id
  kernel = {currentId = firstId, newId = inc firstId,
```

[9] `r=:{f}` denotes the (lazy) selection of the field `f` in the record `r`. `r=:{f = v}` denotes the pattern match of the field `f` on the value `v`.

[10] `{r & f = v}` denotes a new record value that is equal to `r` except for the field `f`, which is equal to `v`.

```
            ready = [threadState], world = world}
  threadState = {thrId = firstId, thrCont = mainThread (\_ k -> k)}
```

The thread that is currently being evaluated returns directly to the scheduler whenever it performs a `yield` action, because `yield` does not evaluate the tail of the computation. Instead, it stores the continuation at the back of the ready queue (to achieve round-robin scheduling) and returns the current kernel state. The scheduler then uses this new kernel state to evaluate the next ready thread.

Programming threads using a continuation style is cumbersome, because one has to carry the continuation along and one has to perform an explicit yield often. Therefore, we added thread-combinators resembling a more common monadic programming style. Our `return`, `>>=` and `>>` functions resemble the monadic `return`, `>>=` and `>>` functions of Haskell[11]. Whenever a running thread performs an atomic action, such as a return, control is voluntarily given to the scheduler using `yield`.

```
return :: a -> Thread a
return x = \cont k -> yield (cont x) k

(>>=) :: (Thread a) (a -> Thread b) -> Thread b
(>>=) l r = \cont k -> l (\x -> r x cont) k

(>>) l r = l >>= \_ -> r

combinatorExample = newThread (print ['h', 'e', 'l', 'l', 'o']) >>
                    print ['w', 'o', 'r', 'l', 'd']
where
    print []     = return Void
    print [c:cs] = printChar c >> print cs
```

The `combinatorExample` above starts a thread that prints "`hello`" concurrent with the main thread that prints "`world`". It assumes a low-level print routine `printChar` that prints a single character. The output of both threads is interleaved by the scheduler, and is printed as "`hweolrllod`".

3.2 Exceptions and Signals

Thread operations (e.g. `newThread`) may fail because of external conditions such as the behavior of other threads or operating system errors. Robust programs quickly become cluttered with lots of error checking code. An elegant solution for this kind of problem is the use of exception handling.

There is no exception handling mechanism in Clean, but our thread continuations can easily be extended to handle exceptions. Because of this, exceptions can only be thrown or caught by a thread. This is analogous to Haskell's `ioError` and `catch` functions, with which exceptions can only be caught in the `IO` monad.

In contrast to Haskell exceptions, we do not want to limit the set of exceptions to system defined exceptions and strings, but instead allow any value. Exceptions

[11] Unfortunately, Clean does not support Haskell's do-notation for monads, which would make the code even more readable.

are therefore implemented using dynamics. This makes it possible to store any value in an exception and to easily extend the set of exceptions at compile-time or even at run-time. To provide this kind of exception handling, we extend the `Thread` type with a continuation argument for the case that an exception is thrown.

```
:: Thread a :== (SucCnt a) -> ExcCnt -> KernelOp
:: SucCnt a :== a -> ExcCnt -> KernelOp
:: ExcCnt   :== Exception -> KernelOp

:: Exception :== Dynamic

throw :: e -> Thread a | TC e
throw e = \sc ec k -> ec (dynamic e :: e^) k

rethrow :: Exception -> Thread a
rethrow exception = \sc ec k -> ec exception k

try :: (Thread a) (Exception -> Thread a) -> Thread a
try thread catcher =
  \sc ec k -> thread (\x _ -> sc x ec) (\e -> catcher e sc ec) k
```

The `throw` function wraps a value in a dynamic (hence the `TC` context restriction) and throws it to the enclosing `try` clause by evaluating the exception continuation (`ec`). `rethrow` can be used to throw an exception without wrapping it in a dynamic again. The `try` function catches exceptions that occur during the evaluation of its first argument (`thread`) and feeds it to its second argument (`catcher`). Because any value can be thrown, exception handlers must match against the type of the exception using dynamic type pattern matching.

The kernel provides an outermost exception handler (not shown here) that aborts the thread when an exception remains uncaught. This exception handler informs the programmer that an exception was not caught by any of the handlers and shows the type of the occurring exception.

```
return :: a -> Thread a
return x = \sc ec k -> yield (sc x ec) k

(>>=) :: (Thread a) (a -> Thread b) -> Thread b
(>>=) l r = \sc ec k -> l (\x -> r x sc) ec k
```

The addition of an exception continuation to the thread type also requires small changes in the implementation of the `return` and `bind` functions. Note how the `return` and `throw` functions complement each other: `return` evaluates the success continuation while `throw` evaluates the exception continuation. This implementation of exception handling is relatively cheap, because there is no need to test if an exception occurred at every bind or return. The only overhead caused by our exception handling mechanism is the need to carry the exception continuation along.

```
:: ArithErrors = DivByZero | Overflow
```

```
exceptionExample = try (divide 42 0) handler

divide x 0 = throw DivByZero
divide x y = return (x / y)

handler (DivByZero :: ArithErrors) = return 0  // or any other value
handler  other                     = rethrow other
```

The `divide` function in the example throws the value `DivByZero` as an exception when the programmer tries to divide by zero. Exceptions caught in the body of the `try` clause are handled by `handler`, which returns zero on a `DivByZero` exception. Caught exceptions of any other type are thrown again outside the try, using `rethrow`.

In a distributed or concurrent setting, there is also a need for throwing and catching exceptions between different threads. We call this kind of inter-thread exceptions *signals*. Signals allow threads to throw kill requests to other threads. Our approach to signals, or *asynchronous exceptions* as they are also called, follows the semantics described by Marlow et. al. in an extension of Concurrent Haskell [11]. We summarize our interface for signals below.

```
throwTo :: ThreadId e -> Thread Void | TC e
signalsOn :: (Thread a) -> Thread a
signalsOff :: (Thread a) -> Thread a
```

Signals are transferred from one thread to the other by the scheduler. A signal becomes an exception again when it arrives at the designated thread, and can therefore be caught in the same way as other exceptions. To prevent interruption by signals, threads can enclose operations in a `signalsOff` clause, during which signals are queued until they can interrupt. Regardless of any nesting, `signalsOn` always means interruptible and `signalsOff` always means non-interruptible. It is, therefore, always clear whether program code can or cannot be interrupted. This allows easy composition and nesting of program fragments that use these functions. When a signal is caught, control goes to the exception handler and the interruptible state will be restored to the state before entering the try.

The try construction allows elegant error handling. Unfortunately, there is no automated support for identifying the exceptions that a function may throw. This is partly because exception handling is written in Clean and not built in the language/compiler, and partly because exceptions are wrapped in dynamics and can therefore not be expressed in the type of a function. Furthermore, exceptions of any type can be thrown by any thread, which makes it hard to be sure that all (relevant) exceptions are caught by the programmer. But the same can be said for an implementation that uses user defined strings, in which non-matching strings are also not detected at compile-time.

4 Processes in Famke

In this section we will show how a programmer can execute groups of threads using processes on multiple workstations, to construct distributed programs in Clean.

Famke uses Microsoft Windows processes to provide preemptive task switching between groups of threads running inside different processes. Once processes have been created on one or more computers, threads can be started in any one of them. First we introduce Famke's message passing primitives for communication between threads and processes. The dynamic linker plays an essential role in getting the code of a thread from one process to another.

4.1 Process and Thread Communication

Elegant ways for type-safe communication between threads are Concurrent Haskell's M-Vars [10] and Concurrent Clean's lazy graph copying [7].

Unfortunately, M-Vars do not scale very well to a distributed setting because of two problems, described by Stolz and Huch in [12]. The first problem is that M-Vars require distributed garbage collection because they are first class objects, which is hard in a distributed or mobile setting. The second problem is that the location of the M-Var is generally unknown, which complicates reasoning about them in the context of failing or moving processes. Automatic lazy graph copying allows processes to work on objects that are distributed over multiple (remote) heaps, and suffers from the same two problems.

Distributed Haskell [13,12] solves the problem by implementing an asynchronous message passing system using ports. Famke uses the same kind of ports. Ports in Famke are channels that vanish as soon as they are closed by a thread, or when the process containing the creating thread dies. Accessing a closed port results in an exception. Using ports as the means of communication, it is always clear where a port resides (at the process of the creating thread) and when it is closed (explicitly or because the process died). In contrast with Distributed Haskell, we do not limit ports to a single reader (which could be checked at compile-time using Clean's uniqueness typing). The single reader restriction also implies that the port vanishes when the reader vanishes but we find it too restrictive in practice.

```
:: PortId msg  // abstract port id
:: PortExceptions = UnregisteredPort | InvalidMessageAtPort | ...

newPort   :: Thread (PortId msg)         | TC msg
closePort :: (PortId msg) -> Thread Void | TC msg

writePort :: (PortId msg) msg -> Thread Void | TC msg
writePort port m = windowsSend port (dynamicToString (dynamic m :: msg^))

readPort :: (PortId msg) -> Thread msg | TC msg
readPort port = windowsReceive port >>= \maybe ->
                case maybe of
```

```
                Just s  -> case stringToDynamic s of
                                  (True, (m :: msg^)) -> return m
                                  other -> throw InvalidMessageAtPort
                Nothing -> readPort port  // make it appear blocking

registerPort :: (PortId msg) String -> Thread Void | TC msg
lookupPort   :: String -> Thread (PortId msg)      | TC msg

dynamicToString :: Dynamic -> String
stringToDynamic :: String -> (Bool, Dynamic)
```

All primitives on ports operate on typed messages. The `newPort` function creates a new port and `closePort` removes a port. `writePort` and `readPort` can be used to send and receive messages. The dynamic run-time system is used to convert the messages to and from a dynamic. Because we do not want to read and write files each time we want to send a message to someone, we will use the low-level `dynamicToString` and `stringToDynamic` functions from the dynamic run-time system library. These functions are similar to Haskell's `show` and `read`, except that they can (de)serialize functions and closures. They should be handled with care, because they allow you to distinguish between objects that should be indistinguishable (e.g. between a closure and its value). The actual sending and receiving of these strings is done via simple message (string) passing primitives of the underlying operating system. The `registerPort` function associates a unique name with a port, by which the port can be looked up using `lookupPort`.

Although Distributed Haskell and Famke both use ports, our system is capable of sending and receiving functions (and therefore also closures) using Clean's dynamic linker. The dynamic type system also allows programs to receive, through ports of type `(PortId Dynamic)`, previously unknown data structures, which can be used by polymorphic functions or functions that work on dynamics such as the `dynamicApply` functions in section 2. An asynchronous message passing system, such as presented here, allows programmers to build other communication and synchronization methods (e.g. remote procedure calls, semaphores and channels).

Here is a skeleton example of a database server that uses a port to receive functions from clients and applies them to the database.

```
:: DBase = ...  // list of records or something like that

server :: Thread Void
server = openPort >>= \port ->
         registerPort port "MyDBase" >>
         handleRequests emptyDBase
where
  emptyDBase = ... // create new data base
  handleRequests db = readPort port >>= \f ->
                      let db‘ = f db in  // apply function to data base
                      handleRequests db‘

client :: Thread Void
```

```
client = lookupPort "MyDBase" >>= \port ->
         writePort port mutateDatabase
where
  mutateDatabase :: DBase -> DBase
  mutateDatabase db = ...  // change the database
```

The server creates, and registers, a port that receives functions of type `DBase -> DBase`. Clients send functions that perform changes to the database to the registered port. The server then waits for functions to arrive and applies them to the database `db`. These functions can be safely applied to the database because the dynamic run-time system guarantees that both the server and the client have the same notion of the type of the database (`DBase`), even if they reside in different programs. This is also an example of a running program that is dynamically extended with new code.

4.2 Process Management

Since Microsoft Windows does the preemptive scheduling of processes, our scheduler does not need any knowledge about multiple processes. Instead of changing the scheduler, we let our system automatically add an additional thread, called the *management thread*, to each process when it is created. This management thread is used to handle signals from other processes and to route them to the designated threads. On request from threads running at other processes, it also handles the creation of new threads inside its own process. This management thread, in combination with the scheduler and the port implementation, form the micro kernel that is included in each process.

```
:: ProcId                  // abstract process id
:: Location :== String

newProc :: Location -> Thread ProcId
newThreadAt :: ProcId (Thread a) -> Thread ThreadId
```

The `newProc` function creates a new process at a given location and returns its process id. The creation of a new process is implemented by starting a pre-compiled Clean executable, the *loader*, which becomes the new process. The loader is a simple Clean program that starts a management thread. The `newThreadAt` function starts a new thread in another process. The thread is started inside the new process by sending it to the management thread at the given process id via a typed port. When the management thread receives the new thread, it starts it using the local `newThread` function. The dynamic linker on the remote computer then links in the code of the new thread automatically.

Here is an example of starting a thread at a remote process and getting the result back to the parent.

```
:: *Remote a = Remote (PortId a)

remote :: ProcId (Thread a) -> Thread (Remote a) | TC a
remote pid thread = newPort >>= \port ->
```

```
                    newThreadAt pid (thread >>= writePort port) >>
                    return (Remote port)

join :: (Remote a) -> Thread a | TC a
join (Remote port) = readPort port >>= \result ->
                     closePort port >>
                     return result
```

The `remote` function creates a port to which the result of the given thread must be sent. It then starts a child thread at the remote location `pid` that calculates the result and writes it to the port, and returns the port enclosed in a `Remote` node to the parent. When the parent decides that it wants the result, it can use `join` to get it and to close the port.

The extension of our system with this kind of heavyweight process enables the programmer to build distributed concurrent applications. If one wants to run Clean programs that contain parallel algorithms on a farm of workstations, this is a first step. However, non-trivial changes are required to the original program to fully accomplish this. These changes include splitting the program code into separate threads and making communication between the threads explicit. The need for these changes is unfortunate, but our system was primarily designed for explicit distributed programs (and eventually mobile programs), not to speedup existing programs by running them on multiple processors.

This concludes our discussion of the micro kernel and its interface that provides support for threads (with exceptions and signals), processes and type-safe communication of values of any type between them. Now it is time to present the first application that makes use of these strongly typed concurrency primitives.

5 Interacting with Famke: The Shell

In this section we introduce our shell that enables programmers to construct new (concurrent) programs interactively.

A shell provides a way to interact with an operating system, usually via a textual command line/console interface. Normally, a shell does not provide a complete programming language, but it does enable users to start pre-compiled programs. Although most shells provide simple ways to combine multiple programs, e.g. pipelining and concurrent execution, and support execution-flow controls, e.g. if-then-else constructs, they do not provide a way to construct new programs. Furthermore, they provide very limited error checking before executing the given command line. This is mainly because the programs mentioned at the command line are practically untyped because they work on, and produce, streams of characters. The intended meaning of these streams of characters varies from one program to the other.

Our view on pre-compiled programs differs from common operating systems in that they are dynamics that contain a typed function, and not untyped executables. Programs are therefore typed and our shell puts this information to good use by actually type checking the command line before performing the specified actions. For example, it could test if a printing program (`:: WordDocument -> PostScript`) matches a document (`:: WordDocument`).

The shell supports function application, variables, and a subset of Clean's constant denotations. The shell syntax closely resembles Haskell's do-notation, extended with operations to read and write files.

Here follow some command line examples with an explanation of how they are handled by the shell.

```
> map (add 1) [1..10]
```

The names `map` and `add` are unbound (do not appear in the left hand side of a let of lambda expression) in this example and our shell therefore assumes that they are names of files (dynamics on disk). All files are supposed to contain dynamics, which together represent a typed file system. The shell reads them in from disk, practically extending its functionality with these functions, and inspects the types of the dynamics. It uses the types of `map` (let us assume that the file `map` contains the type that we expect: `(a -> b) [a] -> [b]`), `add` (let us assume: `Int Int -> Int`) and the list comprehension (which has type: `[Int]`) to type-check the command line. If this succeeds, which it should given the types above, the shell applies the partial application of `add` with the integer one to the list of integers from one to ten, using the `map` function. The application of one dynamic to another is done using the `dynamicApply` function from Section 2, extended with better error reporting. With the help of the `dynamicApply` function, the shell constructs a new function that performs the computation `map (add 1) [1..10]`. This function uses the compiled code of `map`, `add`, and the list comprehension. Our shell is a hybrid interpreter/compiler, where the command line is interpreted/compiled to a function that is almost as efficient as the same function written directly in Clean and compiled to native code. Dynamics are read in before executing the command line, so it is not possible to change the meaning of a part of the command line by overwriting a dynamic.

```
> inc <- add 1; map inc [2,4..10]
```

Defines a variable with the name `inc` as the partial application of the `add` function to the integer one. Then it applies the `map` function using the variable `inc` to the list of even integers from two to ten. The dynamic linker detects that `map` and `add` are already linked in, and reuses their code.

```
> inc <- add 1; map inc ['a'..'z']
```

Defines the variable `inc` as in the previous example, but applies it, using the `map` function, to the list of all the characters in the alphabet. This obviously fails with the usual type error: `Cannot unify [Int] with [Char]`.

```
> write "result" (add 1 2); x <- read "result"; x
> add 1 2 > result; x < result; x
```

Both the above examples do the same thing, because the `<` (read file) and `>` (write file) shell operators can be expressed using predefined `read` and `write` functions. The sum of one and two is written to the file with the name `result`. The variable `x` is defined as the contents of the file with the name `result`, and the final result of the command line is the contents of the variable `x`. In contrast to the add and map functions, which are read from disk by the shell before type checking and executing the command line, result is read in during the execution of the command line.

```
> newThread server;
> p <- lookupPort "MyDBase"; writePort p (insertDBase MyRecord)
```

The first line in the example above creates a new thread that executes the server from section 4.1. Let us assume that we have two dynamics on disk: one with the name insertDBase containing a function that can insert a record into a database, and one with the name MyRecord containing a record for the database. In the second line, we get the port of the server by looking it up using the name MyDBase. We send the function insertDBase applied to MyRecord to the server by writing the closure to the port. This example shows how we can interactively communicate with threads in a type safe way.

6 Related Work

There are concurrent versions of both Haskell and Clean. Concurrent Haskell [10] offers lightweight threads in a single UNIX process and provides M-Vars as the means of communication between threads. Concurrent Clean [7] is only available on multiprocessor Transputers and on a network of single-processor Apple Macintosh computers. Concurrent Clean provides support for native threads on Transputer systems. On a network of Apple computers, it ran the same Clean program on each processor, providing a virtual multiprocessor system. Concurrent Clean provided lazy graph copying as the primary communication mechanism. Both concurrent systems cannot easily provide type safety between different programs or between multiple incarnations of a single program.

Another difference between Famke and the concurrent versions of Haskell and Clean is the choice of communication primitives. Neither lazy graph copying nor M-Vars scale very well to a distributed setting because they require distributed garbage collection. This issue has led to a distributed version of Concurrent Haskell [13] that also uses ports. However, its implementation does not allow functions or closures to be sent over ports, because it cannot serialize functions. Support for this could be provided by a dynamic linker for Concurrent Haskell.

Both Cooper [14] and Lin [15] have extended Standard ML with threads (implemented as continuations using call/CC) to form a small functional operating system. Both systems implement the basics needed for a stand-alone operating system. However, none of them support the type-safe communication of any value between different computers.

Erlang [16] is a functional language specifically designed for the development of concurrent processes. It is completely dynamically typed and primarily uses interpreted byte-code, while Famke is mostly statically typed and executes native code generated by the Clean compiler. A simple spelling error in a token used during communication between two processes is often not detected by Erlang's dynamic type system, sometimes causing deadlock.

Back et al. [17] built two prototypes of a Java operating system. Although they show that Java's extensibility, portable byte code and static/dynamic type system provides a way to build an operating system where multiple Java programs can safely run concurrently, Java lacks the power of polymorphic and higher-order functions and closures (to allow laziness) that our functional approach offers.

Haskell provides exception handling, while remaining pure and lazy. In [11] support for asynchronous exceptions has been added to Concurrent Haskell. Our implementation of signals closely follows their approach.

The Scheme Shell [18] integrates a shell into the programming language in order to enable the user to use the full expressiveness of Scheme. Es [19] is a shell that supports higher-order functions and allows the user to construct new functions at the command line. Neither shell provides a way to read and write typed objects from and to disk, and they cannot provide type safety because they operate on untyped executables.

7 Conclusions and Future Work

In this paper, we presented the basics of our prototype functional operating system called Famke. Famke is written entirely in Clean and provides lightweight threads, exceptions and heavyweight processes, and a type safe communication mechanism, using Clean's dynamic type system and dynamic linking support. Furthermore, we have built an interactive shell that type checks the command line before executing it. With the help of these mechanisms it becomes feasible to build distributed concurrent Clean programs running on a network. Programs can easily be extended with new code at run-time using the dynamic run-time system of Clean.

We can extend our kernel in a modular way by putting all extensions in separate dynamics, which would allow us to tailor our system (at run-time) to a given situation. Nevertheless, there remain issues that need further research.

We would like to give the programmer more information about what exceptions a function may throw. Unfortunately, we have not yet found a way to do this without compromising the flexibility of our approach.

The implementation of ports given in this paper does not check if the name is unique (when registering) or even exists (when looking up), entrusting this responsibility upon the programmer. Fortunately, this situation will be detected at run-time because it causes an exception at the receiving end. We intend to repair it in a more mature implementation.

The current focus of further research on Famke is to increase the power and usability of the shell.

References

1. S. Peyton Jones and J. Hughes et al. *Report on the programming language Haskell 98*. University of Yale, 1999. http://www.haskell.org/definition/

2. M. J. Plasmeijer and M. C. J. D. van Eekelen. *Functional Programming and Parallel Graph Rewriting.* Addison Wesley, 1993.
3. M. van Eekelen and R. Plasmeijer. *Concurrent CLEAN Language Report (version 2.0, draft).* University of Nijmegen, December 2001. http://www.cs.kun.nl/~clean.
4. M. Abadi, L. Cardelli, B. Pierce, and G. Plotkin. Dynamic Typing in a Statically Typed Language. *ACM Transactions on Programming Languages and Systems*, 13(2):237–268, April 1991.
5. M. Pil. Dynamic Types and Type Dependent Functions. In T. Davie K. Hammond and C. Clack, editors, *Proceedings of the 10th International Workshop on the Implementation of Functional Languages*, volume 1595 of *Lecture Notes in Computer Science*, pages 171–188. Springer-Verlag, 1998.
6. M. Vervoort and R. Plasmeijer. Lazy Dynamic Input/Output in the Lazy Functional Language Clean. In R. Peña and T. Arts, editors, *Proceedings of the 14th International Workshop on the Implementation of Functional Languages*, Lecture Notes in Computer Science. Springer-Verlag, 2002.
7. E.G.J.M.H. Nocker, J.E.W. Smetsers, M.C.J.D. van Eekelen, and M.J. Plasmeijer. Concurrent Clean. In E.H.L. Aarts, J. van Leeuwen, and M. Rem, editors, *PARLE '91: Parallel Architectures and Languages Europe, Volume II*, volume 506 of *Lecture Notes in Computer Science*, pages 202–219. Springer, 1991.
8. M. Wand. Continuation-Based Multiprocessing. In J. Allen, editor, *Conference Record of the 1980 LISP Conference*, pages 19–28, Palo Alto, CA, 1980. The Lisp Company.
9. K. Claessen. A Poor Man's Concurrency Monad. *Journal of Functional Programming*, 9, May 1999.
10. S. Peyton Jones, A. Gordon, and S. Finne. Concurrent Haskell. In *Conference Record of POPL '96: The* 23rd *ACM SIGPLAN-SIGACT Symposium on Principles of Programming Languages*, pages 295–308, St. Petersburg Beach, Florida, 21–24 1996.
11. S. Marlow, S.L. Peyton Jones, A. Moran, and J.H. Reppy. Asynchronous Exceptions in Haskell. In *SIGPLAN Conference on Programming Language Design and Implementation*, pages 274–285, 2001.
12. V. Stolz and F. Huch. Implementation of Port-based Distributed Haskell, 2001. http://www-i2.informatik.rwth-aachen.de/Research/distributedHaskell/ ifl2001.ps.gz.
13. F. Huch and U. Norbisrath. Distributed Programming in Haskell with Ports. In M. Mohnen and P.W.M. Koopman, editors, *Implementation of Functional Languages, 12th International Workshop, IFL 2000*, volume 2011 of *Lecture Notes in Computer Science*, pages 107–121. Springer, September 2000.
14. E.C. Cooper and J.G. Morrisett. Adding Threads to Standard ML. Technical Report CMU-CS-90-186, Pittsburgh, PA, 1990.
15. A.C. Lin. *Implementing Concurrency For An ML-based Operating System.* PhD thesis, Massachusetts Institute of Technology, February 1998.
16. J. Armstrong, R. Virding, C. Wikström, and M. Williams. *Concurrent Programming in Erlang.* Prentice-Hall, second edition, 1996.
17. G. Back, P. Wullmann, L. Stoller, W. C. Hsieh, and J. Lepreau. Java Operating Systems: Design and Implementation. Technical Report UUCS-98-015, 6, 1998.
18. O. Shivers. A Scheme Shell. Technical Report MIT/LCS/TR-635, 1994.
19. P. Haahr and B. Rakitzis. Es: A shell with higher-order functions. In *USENIX Winter*, pages 51–60, 1993.

Cost Analysis Using Automatic Size and Time Inference

Álvaro J. Rebón Portillo[1], Kevin Hammond[1], Hans-Wolfgang Loidl[2], and Pedro Vasconcelos[1]

[1] School of Computer Science, University of St Andrews
St Andrews, KY16 9SS, UK
{alvaro,kh,pv}@dcs.st-and.ac.uk
[2] Ludwig-Maximilians-Universität München
Institut für Informatik, D-80538 München, Germany
hwloidl@informatik.uni-muenchen.de

Abstract. Cost information can be exploited in a variety of contexts, including parallelizing compilers, autonomic GRIDs and real-time systems. In this paper, we introduce a novel type and effect system – the *sized time system* that is capable of determining upper bounds for both time and space costs, and which we initially intend to apply to determining good granularity for parallel tasks. The analysis is defined for a simple, strict, higher-order and polymorphic functional language, $\mathcal{L}$, incorporating arbitrarily-sized list data structures. The inference algorithm implementing this analysis constructs cost- and size-terms for $\mathcal{L}$-expressions, plus constraints over free size and cost variables in those terms that can be solved to produce information for higher-order functions. The paper presents both the analysis and the inference algorithm, providing examples that illustrate the primary features of the analysis.

1 Introduction

Good cost information is useful or even vital to a large number of application areas. Examples range from small-scale real-time embedded systems through databases and parallel systems to large-scale *autonomic* GRID computations. We are especially concerned with the issue of determining appropriate task granularity, which is highly important to the efficient execution of parallel programs [1]: excessively fine granularity introduces high overheads; conversely, excessively coarse granularity can lead to poor load balance and starvation. This paper introduces a novel static cost analysis for automatically determining upper bound cost information in the presence of higher-order, polymorphic but non-recursive functions.

Our static analysis is defined as a *type and effect system* [2], a modern approach that uses standard type inference mechanisms to perform static analysis. A type system defines upper bound costs and sizes for expressions in a simple, strict, higher-order and polymorphic functional language, $\mathcal{L}$. Types include size- and cost-annotations, which are related by a subtyping relation [3]. The

R. Peña and T. Arts (Eds.): IFL 2002, LNCS 2670, pp. 232–247, 2003.

corresponding inference algorithm yields cost and size terms for $\mathcal{L}$-expressions, plus constraints over cost and size variables. These constraints are resolved in a separate constraint solver and combined with the cost and size terms to yield closed forms of those terms. These closed forms can be used to solve the costs of function applications.

While our focus is on cost rather than size information, we also infer a restricted form of size information primarily in order to obtain cost information in common cases where cost depends on input sizes. Our analysis is defined for both scalar and compound data structures. We have illustrated the approach with reference to recursive lists, the primary data structure used in functional languages. It should be straightforward to extend the analysis to other recursive data structures such as binary trees, or to arbitrary non-recursive data structures such as vectors or tuples.

The design of our analysis is guided by the intended use of the information it can provide. Although it is desirable to produce quality cost information, precise cost information is not absolutely essential for scheduling parallel tasks: it is sufficient to be able to identify tasks that are *potentially* large enough to be worth executing in parallel. We have structured our system so as to generate strict upper bounds on size and cost information.

2 A Sized Time System for $\mathcal{L}$

$\mathcal{L}$ is a very simple functional language, intended solely as a vehicle to explore static analysis for cost determination. $\mathcal{L}$ is strict, polymorphic, and higher-order; with lists as its only compound data type. The abstract syntax of $\mathcal{L}$ is given below. For simplicity, variables, $v \in \mathbf{Var}$, and constants, $k \in \mathbf{Const}$, are required to be disjoint and all names are unique. Boolean values, $b \in \{\mathsf{true}, \mathsf{false}\}$, and natural numbers, $n \in \mathbb{N}$, are both in **Const**.

$$e \;:=\; v \;\mid\; k \;\mid\; \lambda v.e \;\mid\; e_1\, e_2 \;\mid\; \mathsf{if}\ e_1\ \mathsf{then}\ e_2\ \mathsf{else}\ e_3 \;\mid\; \mathsf{let}\ v = e_1\ \mathsf{in}\ e_2\,.$$

Local bindings (let) are non-recursive. An $\mathcal{L}$ program is defined to be an $\mathcal{L}$ expression.

2.1 The Type Language

$\mathcal{L}$ uses *sized types* [4], a small extension to standard Hindley-Milner polymorphic types: each type, other than function and boolean types, has a superscript specifying an upper bound for its size. For function types, a *latent cost* [5] is attached to the function arrow. The latent cost of a function type is an upper bound for the cost of evaluating the function body. In the following syntax of type expressions, α represents a type variable:

$$\tau \;:=\; \alpha \;\mid\; \mathsf{Bool} \;\mid\; \mathsf{Nat}^z \;\mid\; \mathsf{List}^z\tau \;\mid\; \tau_1 \xrightarrow{z} \tau_2\,.$$

Size and latent cost expressions are specified by z-expressions:

$$z \;:=\; l \;\mid\; n \;\mid\; z_1 + z_2 \;\mid\; z_1 - z_2 \;\mid\; z_1 \times z_2 \;\mid\; \max(z_1, z_2) \;\mid\; \omega\,.$$

In these z-expressions, n is a constant natural number and l is a z-variable. The ω symbol is used to express an unbounded size. For sizes less than ω, the arithmetic operators $+$, $-$, $\times$ and max behave as usual over natural numbers ($-$ is subtraction over naturals, with $a - b = 0$, for $a < b$). When one of the operands is ω the result is ω, too; with the exception of $l - \omega$ which is 0 for $l \neq \omega$, and ω otherwise. The $\leq$ relation, which will be used later, is defined over natural numbers with $l \leq \omega$ for all l.

Polymorphism is achieved in the usual way by quantifying over all free type and size variables of a let-bound expression. The general structure of type schemes is:

$$\sigma \ := \ \tau \ \mid \ \forall x.\sigma \ ,$$

with x representing either a type or a size variable.

Since sizes are attached to types, and these may be embedded within other types, it is possible to describe the sizes of the elements of a structure as well as the structure itself, e.g.: $\mathsf{List}^5 \left(\mathsf{Nat}^{10}\right)$ denotes a list whose length is at most 5 with natural numbers no larger than 10 as elements, and the type of the built-in constant $\mathsf{nil} \in$ **Const** is: $\forall\alpha.\mathsf{List}^0\alpha$.

2.2 The Type System

Figure 1 shows our extended type system. A judgment $\Gamma \vdash e : \tau \ \$ \ z$ reads: "under the type assumptions Γ the expression e has type τ and z is an upper bound for the cost of its evaluation." The assumption set Γ contains bindings of variables, of constants, and of primitive operations to type schemes (of the form $v : \sigma$). There can be at most one binding of any name in an assumption set. Assumption sets are combined using set union. The construct $\tau[\tau'/\alpha]$ is used to denote a substitution of all free occurrences of α in τ by τ'. It extends to vectors, written as $\tau[\bar{\tau}_i'/\bar{\alpha}_i]$, by performing all substitutions simultaneously. Similarly, we allow size expression substitutions of the forms $\tau[z/l]$ and $\tau[\bar{z}_i/\bar{l}_i]$. For convenience, we will often combine type substitutions or size expression substitutions in a single substitution.

The cost model expressed in the system is parameterized through constants representing costs for elementary computations: c_{nat} and c_{bool} are the costs associated with evaluating naturals and booleans; c_{var} is the cost of accessing a variable from the environment; c_{abs} and c_{app} are the cost for creating a lambda-abstraction and executing an application step, respectively; c_{if} is the cost of executing a conditional and c_{let} is the cost of creating a let-binding.

With the exception of the $[\mathit{weak}_{st}]$ rule, the system represents a straightforward extension of the standard Hindley-Milner rules. The $[\mathit{weak}_{st}]$ rule allows weakening, i.e. relaxing the upper bounds on sizes. It makes use of the subtyping relation, $\trianglelefteq$, defined in Figure 2, which produces a set of inequalities over z-expressions. Note that with this definition of $\trianglelefteq$, the relation $\tau_1 \trianglelefteq \tau_2$ does not by itself imply that $\mathsf{List}^{z_1}\tau_1 \trianglelefteq \mathsf{List}^{z_2}\tau_2$, i.e. the subtype system is not structural. This is because there needs to be no relationship between the sizes of a structure and the elements of that structure.

$$\frac{}{\Gamma \vdash n : \mathsf{Nat}^n \ \$ \ c_{\mathsf{nat}}}[nat_{st}] \qquad \frac{\tau' = \tau[\bar{\tau}_i/\bar{x}_i], \quad \mathrm{FV}(\bar{\tau}_i) \cap (\mathrm{FV}(\tau) \cup \mathrm{FV}(\Gamma)) = \emptyset}{\Gamma \cup \{v : \forall \bar{x}_i \tau\} \vdash v : \tau' \ \$ \ c_{\mathsf{var}}}[var_{st}]$$

$$\frac{\Gamma \cup \{v : \tau_1\} \vdash e : \tau_2 \ \$ \ z}{\Gamma \vdash \lambda v.e : \tau_1 \xrightarrow{z} \tau_2 \ \$ \ c_{\mathsf{abs}}}[abs_{st}] \qquad \frac{\Gamma \vdash e_1 : \tau_1 \xrightarrow{z} \tau_2 \ \$ \ z_1 \quad \Gamma \vdash e_2 : \tau_1 \ \$ \ z_2}{\Gamma \vdash e_1\, e_2 : \tau_2 \ \$ \ c_{\mathsf{app}} + z + z_1 + z_2}[app_{st}]$$

$$\frac{}{\Gamma \vdash b : \mathsf{Bool} \ \$ \ c_{\mathsf{bool}}}[bool_{st}] \qquad \frac{\Gamma \vdash e_1 : \mathsf{Bool} \ \$ \ z_1 \quad \Gamma \vdash e_2 : \tau \ \$ \ z \quad \Gamma \vdash e_3 : \tau \ \$ \ z}{\Gamma \vdash \mathsf{if}\ e_1\ \mathsf{then}\ e_2\ \mathsf{else}\ e_3 : \tau \ \$ \ c_{\mathsf{if}} + z_1 + z}[if_{st}]$$

$$\frac{\Gamma \vdash e_1 : \tau_1 \ \$ \ z_1 \quad \Gamma \cup \{v : \forall \bar{x}_i \tau_1\} \vdash e_2 : \tau_2 \ \$ \ z_2 \quad \bar{x}_i = \mathrm{FV}(\tau_1) \backslash \mathrm{FV}(\Gamma)}{\Gamma \vdash \mathsf{let}\ v\ =\ e_1\ \mathsf{in}\ e_2 : \tau_2 \ \$ \ c_{\mathsf{let}} + z_1 + z_2}[let_{st}]$$

$$\frac{\Gamma \vdash e : \tau \ \$ \ z \quad \tau \trianglelefteq \tau' \quad z \leq z'}{\Gamma \vdash e : \tau' \ \$ \ z'}[weak_{st}]$$

Fig. 1. A sized time system for $\mathcal{L}$

$$\frac{}{\tau \trianglelefteq \tau}[\mathrm{reflex}_\trianglelefteq] \qquad \frac{\tau_1 \trianglelefteq \tau_2 \quad \tau_2 \trianglelefteq \tau_3}{\tau_1 \trianglelefteq \tau_3}[\mathrm{trans}_\trianglelefteq] \qquad \frac{\tau_1 \trianglelefteq \tau_1' \quad \tau_2' \trianglelefteq \tau_2 \quad l' \leq l}{\tau_1' \xrightarrow{l'} \tau_2' \trianglelefteq \tau_1 \xrightarrow{l} \tau_2}[\mathrm{abs}_\trianglelefteq]$$

$$\frac{z_1 \leq z_2}{\mathsf{Nat}^{z_1} \trianglelefteq \mathsf{Nat}^{z_2}}[\mathrm{nat}_\trianglelefteq] \qquad \frac{z_1 \leq z_2 \quad \tau_1 \trianglelefteq \tau_2}{\mathsf{List}^{z_1}\tau_1 \trianglelefteq \mathsf{List}^{z_2}\tau_2}[\mathrm{list}_\trianglelefteq]$$

Fig. 2. Subtyping relation

The $[abs_{st}]$ rule infers the cost of evaluating the body of a lambda abstraction as a latent cost. The cost for the abstraction itself is just the parameter c_{abs}.

In the $[app_{st}]$ rule we add the latent cost z to the costs of obtaining the function and argument. Note that in this rule the type of the function's domain must match exactly the type of the argument. Since types can be weakened by relaxing their size bounds, this means that the size bound of the argument must be no greater than the size given in the type of the function's domain.

As an example, consider the application of a function, f, of type $\mathsf{Nat}^5 \xrightarrow{1} \mathsf{Nat}^{10}$ to an expression, e, of type Nat^3. To type the expression $(f\, e)$ we have to use the $[weak_{st}]$ rule in either of the following two ways: 1) weaken the type of f to $\mathsf{Nat}^3 \xrightarrow{1} \mathsf{Nat}^{10}$; or 2) weaken the type of e to Nat^5. Then we can apply the $[app_{st}]$ rule to infer Nat^{10} as the type of $(f\, e)$.

A problem arises when e.g. f is of type $\mathsf{Nat}^3 \xrightarrow{1} \mathsf{Nat}^{10}$ and e is of type Nat^5. There is no way, using the subtyping relation defined in Figure 2, to weaken either of these two types (or even both) so that it matches the other one in the way described in the $[app_{st}]$ rule. The type system, therefore, rejects the

$$\frac{\Gamma \vdash e_1 : \tau_1 \xrightarrow{z} \tau_2 \ \$ \ z_1 \quad \Gamma \vdash e_2 : \tau_1' \ \$ \ z_2 \quad \mathrm{L}(\tau_1) = \mathrm{L}(\tau_1')}{\Gamma \vdash e_1\, e_2 : \mathrm{L}(\tau_2) \ \$ \ \omega} \ [app'_{st}]$$

$$\begin{array}{lll} \mathrm{L} \quad :: \tau \to \tau & \mathrm{L}(\mathsf{Bool}) = \mathsf{Bool} & \mathrm{L}(\mathsf{List}^z \tau) \quad = \mathsf{List}^\omega \mathrm{L}(\tau) \\ \mathrm{L}(\alpha) = \alpha & \mathrm{L}(\mathsf{Nat}^z) = \mathsf{Nat}^\omega & \mathrm{L}(\tau_1 \xrightarrow{z} \tau_2) = \mathrm{L}(\tau_1) \xrightarrow{\omega} \mathrm{L}(\tau_2) \end{array}$$

Fig. 3. Extra rule for application

expression as badly typed, although it has a well-formed Hindley-Milner type, i.e. Nat. Since, for pragmatic reasons, the analysis must not fail on any legitimate program, such behavior is not acceptable.

A variant of the application rule must therefore be introduced (see Figure 3). The new rule infers the correct Hindley-Milner type for the result of the application, but loses all the invalid size information. The auxiliary function L recursively loses all the size information in the result type, by replacing it with the unbounded value ω.

Since $[app'_{st}]$ discards all size information, it is preferable to use a combination of the $[weak_{st}]$ rule plus the normal $[app_{st}]$ rule wherever these are applicable, i.e. when $\tau_1' \trianglelefteq \tau_1$. The $[app'_{st}]$ should be restricted to situations when the Hindley-Milner types are identical but the subtyping relation on sized types doesn't hold.

3 The Inference Algorithm

In this section we discuss an inference algorithm that yields cost and size expressions plus an associated set of constraints for all top level function definitions in $\mathcal{L}$. The constraint set is solved in the implementation via a separate constraint solver.

In order to simplify the presentation and without loss of generality, we will describe the algorithm specialized for one specific cost model, namely the one that calculates (an upper bound on) the *number of applications* that are required for the reduction of an $\mathcal{L}$-expression. This is achieved by setting the values of the cost parameters as $c_{\mathsf{app}} = 1$ and $c_{\mathsf{nat}} = c_{\mathsf{bool}} = c_{\mathsf{var}} = c_{\mathsf{if}} = c_{\mathsf{abs}} = c_{\mathsf{let}} = 0$. The algorithm can be modified for other cost models by choosing different values for these parameters; alternatively, by leaving the parameters as free variables, we would obtain a constraint set representing a *parametric cost model.*

A key question in designing a type reconstruction algorithm for our type system is where to apply the weakening rule, as all other rules are both structural and exhaustive. Our algorithm uses weakening at precisely one location: the conditional case, in order to find a super-type of the types of both branches [4], that is in order to obtain an upper bound on the costs of the conditional branches. It also uses *domain matching* in order to construct a correct subtyping relation between the type of a concrete argument to a function and that function's domain. Both of these uses are described below.

In contrast to classical type inference algorithms, the algorithm presented here returns a constraint set as part of the output [4]. The idea behind this is to simplify the weakening process by dealing only with variables in the type, maintaining the full, complex expressions only in the set of constraints. The two types of constraints we allow are as follows:

$$\begin{aligned} C &::= c \mid cC \\ c &::= z_1 \leq z_2 \mid z_1 = z_2 \,, \end{aligned}$$

with z_i being z-expressions.

With this idea of allowing only size variables to appear in a type expression, the syntax for type schemes has to be changed to:

$$\sigma := (\tau, C) \mid \forall x.\sigma \,,$$

with C representing the constraints for the size variables involved in τ. As an example, the type scheme $\forall m.\mathsf{Nat}^m \xrightarrow{1} \mathsf{Nat}^{m+1}$ is now written as

$$\forall m \forall n \forall k.(\mathsf{Nat}^m \xrightarrow{k} \mathsf{Nat}^n, \{n = m + 1, k = 1\}) \,.$$

Substitutions over types are denoted by θ, whereas substitutions over z-expressions are denoted by ϑ. Notationally, the application of a substitution to a type expression is denoted by juxtaposition, as is also the composition of two or more substitutions. To shorten the notation, we abbreviate the substitution composition $\theta_{i+n}\theta_{i+n-1}\ldots\theta_i$ as Θ_i^{i+n}.

Figure 4 specifies a size reconstruction algorithm in the same inference style that has been used for the type system of $\mathcal{L}$. The arguments to the algorithm are a type environment Γ and the expression to be analyzed. The result of the algorithm is a 4-tuple $\langle \tau, \theta, z, C \rangle$, where τ is the type of the expression, θ is a substitution on types, z is the cost of the expression and C is the constraint set, i.e. a set of inequalities over z-expressions. The algorithm is similar to that developed by Reistad and Gifford [5] for the cost reconstruction of FX programs.

As the $[nat_{st}]$ case indicates, the algorithm maintains the invariant that size annotations in sized types are always variables. Thus, an explicit constraint $l = n$ has to be added to the constraint set in the $[nat_{st}]$ case rather than just using Nat^n as in the sized type system.

The $[if_{st}]$ case shows how the unification and weakening algorithms are used to guarantee that both branches have the same type. Note here that the substitution obtained from weakening, ϑ, is not part of the second component of the output tuple. This is because applications of the weakening rule are not propagated beyond the scope of the conditional, so avoiding over-weakening of the collected size information. The example in Section 4 illustrates the use of this rule.

The $[app_{st}]$ case deals with the first variant of application described in the type system. Applications requiring the alternative $[app'_{st}]$ rule in the type system will generate an inconsistent result constraint set.

Since the weakening algorithm cannot be used directly, a new function, $\mathcal{D}$ (see Figure 5), is therefore introduced. This function constructs the set of constraints needed for the argument type to match (be a subtype of) the type of

$$\frac{}{\Gamma \vdash n : \langle \mathsf{Nat}^l, [], 0, \{l = n\}\rangle}\ [nat_{st}] \qquad \frac{\vartheta = [\bar{l}'_i/\bar{l}_i] \quad \theta = [\bar{\alpha}'_i/\bar{\alpha}_i] \quad \text{fresh } \bar{l}'_i, \bar{\alpha}'_i}{\Gamma \cup \{v : \forall \bar{l}_i \bar{\alpha}_i(\tau, C)\} \vdash v : \langle \vartheta\theta\tau, [], 0, \vartheta C\rangle}\ [var_{st}]$$

$$\frac{}{\Gamma \vdash b : \langle \mathsf{Bool}, [], 0, \emptyset\rangle}\ [bool_{st}] \qquad \frac{\Gamma \cup \{v : (\alpha, \emptyset)\} \vdash e : \langle \tau, \theta, z, C\rangle, \quad \text{fresh } \alpha, l}{\Gamma \vdash \lambda v.e : \langle \theta\alpha \xrightarrow{l} \tau, \theta, 0, \{l = z\} \cup C\rangle}\ [abs_{st}]$$

$$\frac{\begin{array}{c}\Gamma \vdash e_1 : \langle \tau_1, \theta_1, z_1, C_1\rangle \quad \theta_1\Gamma \vdash e_2 : \langle \tau_2, \theta_2, z_2, C_2\rangle \\ \theta = \mathcal{U}(\theta_2\tau_1, \tau_2 \xrightarrow{l} \alpha) \quad C_3 = \mathcal{D}(\theta\theta_2\tau_1, \theta(\tau_2 \xrightarrow{l} \alpha)) \quad \text{fresh } \alpha, l\end{array}}{\Gamma \vdash e_1\, e_2 : \langle \theta\alpha, \theta\Theta_1^2, 1{+}l{+}z_1{+}z_2, \bigcup_{i=1}^3 C_i\rangle}\ [app_{st}]$$

$$\frac{\begin{array}{c}\Gamma \vdash e_1 : \langle \tau_1, \theta_1, z_1, C_1\rangle \quad \theta_1\Gamma \vdash e_2 : \langle \tau_2, \theta_2, z_2, C_2\rangle \quad \Theta_1^2\Gamma \vdash e_3 : \langle \tau_3, \theta_3, z_3, C_3\rangle \\ \theta_4 = \mathcal{U}(\Theta_2^3\tau_1, \mathsf{Bool}) \quad \theta_5 = \mathcal{U}(\Theta_3^4\tau_2, \theta_4\tau_3) \quad \langle \vartheta, C_4\rangle = \mathcal{W}(\Theta_3^5\tau_2, \Theta_4^5\tau_3)\end{array}}{\Gamma \vdash \mathsf{if}\ e_1\ \mathsf{then}\ e_2\ \mathsf{else}\ e_3 : \langle \vartheta\Theta_4^5\tau_3, \Theta_1^5, z_1{+}\max(z_2, z_3), \bigcup_{i=1}^4 C_i\rangle}\ [if_{st}]$$

$$\frac{\begin{array}{c}\Gamma \vdash e_1 : \langle \tau_1, \theta_1, z_1, C_1\rangle \\ \theta_1\Gamma \cup \{v : \forall \bar{l}_i \forall \bar{\alpha}_i(\tau_1, C_1)\} \vdash e_2 : \langle \tau_2, \theta_2, z_2, C_2\rangle \\ \bar{\alpha}_i = \mathrm{FTV}(\tau_1)\backslash\mathrm{FTV}(\theta_1\Gamma) \quad \bar{l}_i = (\mathrm{FZV}(\tau_1) \cup \mathrm{FZV}(C_1))\backslash\mathrm{FZV}(\theta_1\Gamma)\end{array}}{\Gamma \vdash \mathsf{let}\ v\ =\ e_1\ \mathsf{in}\ e_2 : \langle \tau_2, \Theta_1^2, z_1{+}z_2, \bigcup_{i=1}^2 C_i\rangle}\ [let_{st}]$$

Fig. 4. A sized time reconstruction algorithm for $\mathcal{L}$

$$\begin{array}{lll}
\mathcal{D} & :: \tau \to \tau \to C & \mathcal{D}(\mathsf{Nat}^{l_1}, \mathsf{Nat}^{l_2}) = \{l_1 \le l_2\} \\
\mathcal{D}(\alpha, \alpha) & = \emptyset & \mathcal{D}(\mathsf{List}^{l_1}\tau_1, \mathsf{List}^{l_2}\tau_2) = \{l_1 \le l_2\} \cup \mathcal{D}(\tau_1, \tau_2) \\
\mathcal{D}(\mathsf{Bool}, \mathsf{Bool}) & = \emptyset & \mathcal{D}(\tau_1 \xrightarrow{l} \tau_2, \tau'_1 \xrightarrow{l'} \tau'_2) = \{l \le l'\} \cup \mathcal{D}(\tau'_1, \tau_1) \cup \mathcal{D}(\tau_2, \tau'_2)
\end{array}$$

Fig. 5. Domain matching test

the function's domain, according to the subtyping relation previously presented in Figure 2. The types given as arguments must share the same underlying Hindley-Milner structure.

The unification algorithm presented in Figure 6 outputs a substitution over types which, when applied to each of its arguments, makes them identical under Hindley-Milner, but perhaps containing different size information. The auxiliary operator ν is used to achieve this.

A separate function, $\mathcal{W}$, is used to weaken two types, computing a pair consisting of a substitution over z-expressions and a set of constraints which collectively make the two types equal. This function and its dual, strengthening, $\mathcal{S}$, which is needed because of the contravariance present in the subtyping relation for functional types, are shown in Figure 7. As with the function $\mathcal{D}$, both of these algorithms require their arguments to share the same underlying Hindley-Milner structure.

$$
\begin{array}{ll}
\mathcal{U} & :: \tau \to \tau \to \theta \\
\mathcal{U}(\alpha, \tau) & = [\nu(\tau)/\alpha] \\
\mathcal{U}(\mathsf{Bool}, \mathsf{Bool}) & = [] \\
\mathcal{U}(\mathsf{Nat}^{l_1}, \mathsf{Nat}^{l_2}) & = [] \\
\mathcal{U}(\mathsf{List}^{l_1}\tau_1, \mathsf{List}^{l_2}\tau_2) & = \mathcal{U}(\tau_1, \tau_2) \\
\mathcal{U}(\tau_1 \xrightarrow{l} \tau_2, \tau_1' \xrightarrow{l'} \tau_2') & = \mathcal{U}(\theta\tau_2, \theta\tau_2')\theta \\
\quad \text{where } \theta = \mathcal{U}(\tau_1, \tau_1') &
\end{array}
\qquad
\begin{array}{lll}
\nu & :: \tau \to \tau & \\
\nu(\alpha) & = \alpha & \\
\nu(\mathsf{Bool}) & = \mathsf{Bool} & \\
\nu(\mathsf{Nat}^{l}) & = \mathsf{Nat}^{l'}, & \text{fresh } l' \\
\nu(\mathsf{List}^{l}\tau) & = \mathsf{List}^{l'}\nu(\tau), & \text{fresh } l' \\
\nu(\tau_1 \xrightarrow{l} \tau_2) & = \nu(\tau_1) \xrightarrow{l'} \nu(\tau_2), & \text{fresh } l'
\end{array}
$$

Fig. 6. Unification algorithm

$$
\begin{array}{ll}
\mathcal{W} & :: \tau \to \tau \to \langle \vartheta, C \rangle \\
\mathcal{W}(\alpha, \alpha) & = \langle [], \emptyset \rangle \\
\mathcal{W}(\mathsf{Bool}, \mathsf{Bool}) & = \langle [], \emptyset \rangle \\
\mathcal{W}(\mathsf{Nat}^{l_1}, \mathsf{Nat}^{l_2}) & = \langle [l/l_1, l/l_2], \\
 & \quad \{l_1 \le l, l_2 \le l\} \rangle \\
\quad l \text{ is fresh} & \\
\mathcal{W}(\mathsf{List}^{l_1}\tau_1, \mathsf{List}^{l_2}\tau_2) & = \langle [l/l_1, l/l_2]\vartheta, \\
 & \quad \{l_1 \le l, l_2 \le l\} \cup C \rangle \\
\quad l \text{ is fresh} & \\
\quad \langle \vartheta, C \rangle = \mathcal{W}(\tau_1, \tau_2) & \\
\mathcal{W}(\tau_1 \xrightarrow{l'} \tau_2, \tau_1' \xrightarrow{l''} \tau_2') & = \langle \vartheta, C \rangle \\
\quad l \text{ is fresh} & \\
\quad \vartheta = [l/l', l/l'']\vartheta_2\vartheta_1 & \\
\quad C = \{l' \le l, l'' \le l\} C_1 \cup C_2 & \\
\quad \langle \vartheta_1, C_1 \rangle = \mathcal{S}(\tau_1, \tau_1') & \\
\quad \langle \vartheta_2, C_2 \rangle = \mathcal{W}(\tau_2, \tau_2') &
\end{array}
\qquad
\begin{array}{ll}
\mathcal{S} & :: \tau \to \tau \to \langle \vartheta, C \rangle \\
\mathcal{S}(\alpha, \alpha) & = \langle [], \emptyset \rangle \\
\mathcal{S}(\mathsf{Bool}, \mathsf{Bool}) & = \langle [], \emptyset \rangle \\
\mathcal{S}(\mathsf{Nat}^{l_1}, \mathsf{Nat}^{l_2}) & = \langle [l/l_1, l/l_2], \\
 & \quad \{l \le l_1, l \le l_2\} \rangle \\
\quad l \text{ is fresh} & \\
\mathcal{S}(\mathsf{List}^{l_1}\tau_1, \mathsf{List}^{l_2}\tau_2) & = \langle [l/l_1, l/l_2]\vartheta, \\
 & \quad \{l \le l_1, l \le l_2\} \cup C \rangle \\
\quad l \text{ is fresh} & \\
\quad \langle \vartheta, C \rangle = \mathcal{S}(\tau_1, \tau_2) & \\
\mathcal{S}(\tau_1 \xrightarrow{l'} \tau_2, \tau_1' \xrightarrow{l''} \tau_2') & = \langle \vartheta, C \rangle \\
\quad l \text{ is fresh} & \\
\quad \vartheta = [l/l', l/l'']\vartheta_2\vartheta_1 & \\
\quad C = \{l \le l', l \le l''\} C_1 \cup C_2 & \\
\quad \langle \vartheta_1, C_1 \rangle = \mathcal{W}(\tau_1, \tau_1') & \\
\quad \langle \vartheta_2, C_2 \rangle = \mathcal{S}(\tau_2, \tau_2') &
\end{array}
$$

Fig. 7. Weakening and strengthening algorithms

4 Examples

We now present three examples to illustrate the inference algorithm just described: one using conditionals, one using lists and one using higher-order functions.

Example 1: Conditionals

Figure 8 depicts an inference for

$$\Gamma = \{\, inc : \sigma_{inc},\ p : (\mathsf{Bool}, \emptyset) \,\} \overset{?}{\vdash} \lambda v.\mathsf{if}\ p\ \mathsf{then}\ v\ \mathsf{else}\ inc\ v$$

where $\sigma_{inc} = \forall m \forall n \forall c.(\mathsf{Nat}^{m} \xrightarrow{c} \mathsf{Nat}^{n}, \{n = m + 1, c = 0\})$. We use e to denote the sub-expression '$\mathsf{if}\ p\ \mathsf{then}\ v\ \mathsf{else}\ inc\ v$'.

We are interested in the final type and cost for the expression, therefore we solve the resulting set of constraints:

$$\{m' \le a, n' \le a, n = m + 1, c = 0, m' \le m, n \le n', c \le l, d = \max(0, 1 + l)\}\,.$$

$$\left.\mathcal{W}(\mathsf{Nat}^{m'},\mathsf{Nat}^{n'}) = \langle [a/m', a/n'], C_6 = \{m' \le a, n' \le a\}\rangle\right\} (6)$$
$$\left.\mathcal{U}(\mathsf{Nat}^{m'},\mathsf{Nat}^{n'}) = []\right\} (5)$$
$$\left.\mathcal{U}(\mathsf{Bool},\mathsf{Bool}) = []\right\} (4)$$

$$(3.1)\left\{\frac{}{\Gamma' \vdash inc : \langle \mathsf{Nat}^m \xrightarrow{c} \mathsf{Nat}^n, [], 0, C_{3.1} = \{n = m+1, c = 0\}\rangle}[var_{st}]\right.$$
$$(3.2)\left\{\frac{}{\Gamma' \vdash v : \langle \alpha, [], 0, \emptyset\rangle}[var_{st}]\right.$$
$$(3.3)\left\{\theta_{3.3} = \mathcal{U}(\mathsf{Nat}^m \xrightarrow{c} \mathsf{Nat}^n, \alpha \xrightarrow{l} \beta) = [\mathsf{Nat}^{m'}/\alpha, \mathsf{Nat}^{n'}/\beta]\right.$$
$$(3.4)\left\{C_{3.4} = \mathcal{D}(\mathsf{Nat}^m \xrightarrow{c} \mathsf{Nat}^n, \mathsf{Nat}^{m'} \xrightarrow{l} \mathsf{Nat}^{n'}) = \{m' \le m, n \le n', c \le l\}\right.$$

$$\left.\frac{(3.1) \quad (3.2) \quad (3.3) \quad (3.4)}{\Gamma' \vdash inc\ v : \langle \mathsf{Nat}^{n'}, \theta_{3.3}, 1 + l, C_3 = C_{3.1} \cup C_{3.4}\rangle}[app_{st}]\right\} (3)$$
$$\left.\frac{}{\Gamma' \vdash v : \langle \alpha, [], 0, \emptyset\rangle}[var_{st}]\right\} (2)$$
$$\left.\frac{}{\Gamma' \vdash p : \langle \mathsf{Bool}, [], 0, \emptyset\rangle}[var_{st}]\right\} (1)$$

$$\frac{\dfrac{(1) \quad (2) \quad (3) \quad (4) \quad (5) \quad (6)}{\Gamma' = \Gamma \cup \{v : (\alpha, \emptyset)\} \vdash e : \langle \mathsf{Nat}^a, \theta_{3.3}, \max(0, 1+l), C_3 \cup C_6\rangle}[if_{st}]}{\Gamma = \{\ inc : \sigma_{inc},\ p : (\mathsf{Bool}, \emptyset)\ \} \vdash \lambda v.e : \langle \mathsf{Nat}^{m'} \xrightarrow{d} \mathsf{Nat}^a, \theta_{3.3}, 0, C_3 \cup C_6 \cup \{d = \max(0, 1+l)\}\rangle}[abs_{st}]$$

Fig. 8. A type reconstruction for '$\lambda v.$if p then v else $inc\ v$'

As the type we obtain is the abstraction $\mathsf{Nat}^{m'} \xrightarrow{d} \mathsf{Nat}^a$, we need the least upper bounds for a and d, for a given m'. These are, according to the set of constraints, $m' + 1$ and 2, respectively. Thus the type for the expression is

$$\mathsf{Nat}^{m'} \xrightarrow{1} \mathsf{Nat}^{m'+1}$$

and the cost of evaluating it is zero, since it is a lambda abstraction (Section 3).

Example 2: Lists

In this example we show how the system deals with lists, adding the types of the primitive constant *nil* and the primitive operator *cons* to the initial environment. The inference for

$$\Gamma = \{\ nil : \sigma_{nil},\ \ cons : \sigma_{cons}\ \} \overset{?}{\vdash} \lambda v.cons\ v\ nil$$

with

$$\sigma_{nil} = \forall m \forall \alpha.(\mathsf{List}^m \alpha, \{m = 0\}),$$
$$\sigma_{cons} = \forall m \forall n \forall c \forall d \forall \alpha.(\alpha \xrightarrow{c} \mathsf{List}^m \alpha \xrightarrow{d} \mathsf{List}^n \alpha, \{n = m+1, c = 0, d = 0\}),$$

$$C_4 = \mathcal{D}(\mathsf{List}^e\beta \xrightarrow{f} \mathsf{List}^g\beta, \mathsf{List}^h\delta \xrightarrow{l} \mathsf{List}^i\beta) = \{f \leq l, h \leq e, g \leq i\}\Big\} \; (4)$$

$$\theta_3 = \mathcal{U}(\mathsf{List}^e\beta \xrightarrow{f} \mathsf{List}^g\beta, \mathsf{List}^h\delta \xrightarrow{l} \epsilon) = [\beta/\delta, \mathsf{List}^i\beta/\epsilon]\Big\} \; (3)$$

$$\left.\frac{}{\Gamma' \vdash \mathit{nil} : \langle \mathsf{List}^h\delta, [], 0, C_2 = \{h = 0\}\rangle}\,[\mathit{var}_{st}]\right\} \; (2)$$

$$(1.4)\left\{\begin{array}{l} C_{1.4} = \mathcal{D}(\beta \xrightarrow{a} \mathsf{List}^b\beta \xrightarrow{c} \mathsf{List}^d\beta, \beta \xrightarrow{k} \mathsf{List}^e\beta \xrightarrow{f} \mathsf{List}^g\beta) \\ \quad\;\; = \{a \leq k, e \leq b, c \leq f, d \leq g\} \end{array}\right.$$

$$(1.3)\left\{\theta_{1.3} = \mathcal{U}(\beta \xrightarrow{a} \mathsf{List}^b\beta \xrightarrow{c} \mathsf{List}^d\beta, \alpha \xrightarrow{k} \gamma) = [\beta/\alpha, \mathsf{List}^e\beta \xrightarrow{f} \mathsf{List}^g\beta/\gamma]\right.$$

$$(1.2)\left\{\frac{}{\Gamma' \vdash v : \langle \alpha, [], 0, \emptyset\rangle}\,[\mathit{var}_{st}]\right.$$

$$(1.1)\left\{\frac{}{\Gamma' \vdash \mathit{cons} : \langle \beta \xrightarrow{a} \mathsf{List}^b\beta \xrightarrow{c} \mathsf{List}^d\beta, [], 0, C_{1.1} = \{d = b + 1, a = 0, c = 0\}\rangle}\,[\mathit{var}_{st}]\right.$$

$$\left.\frac{(1.1) \quad (1.2) \quad (1.3) \quad (1.4)}{\Gamma' \vdash \mathit{cons}\;\; v : \langle \mathsf{List}^e\beta \xrightarrow{f} \mathsf{List}^g\beta, \theta_1 = \theta_{1.3}, 1 + k, C_1 = C_{1.1} \cup C_{1.4}\rangle}\,[\mathit{app}_{st}]\right\} \; (1)$$

$$\frac{\dfrac{(1) \qquad (2) \qquad (3) \qquad (4)}{\Gamma' = \Gamma \cup \{v : (\alpha, \emptyset)\} \vdash e : \langle \mathsf{List}^i\beta, \theta_3\theta_1, 2 + k + l, C_1 \cup C_2 \cup C_4\rangle}\,[\mathit{app}_{st}]}{\begin{array}{l}\Gamma = \{\, \mathit{nil} : \sigma_{nil},\; \mathit{cons} : \sigma_{cons}\,\} \vdash \lambda v.e : \langle \beta \xrightarrow{m} \mathsf{List}^i\beta, \theta_3\theta_1, 0, \\ \qquad\qquad\qquad\qquad\qquad\qquad\qquad C_1 \cup C_2 \cup C_4 \cup \{m = 2 + k + l\}\rangle\end{array}}\,[\mathit{abs}_{st}]$$

Fig. 9. A type reconstruction for '$\lambda v.$ *cons v nil*'

is developed in figure 9, where e has been used to denote the sub-expression '*cons v nil*'. The set of constraints obtained is

$$\{d = b + 1, a = 0, c = 0, a \leq k, e \leq b, c \leq f, d \leq g, h = 0, f \leq l, h \leq e, g \leq i\}\,,$$

from which the least upper bounds for k, l and i can be inferred as 0 ($0 = a \leq k$), 0 ($0 = c \leq f \leq l$) and 1 ($0 = h \leq e \leq b$, $b + 1 = d \leq g \leq i$), respectively. We can consequently express the final type for '$\lambda v.\mathit{cons}\; v\; \mathit{nil}$' as

$$\beta \xrightarrow{2} \mathsf{List}^1\beta\,.$$

Example 3: Higher-Order Functions

Finally, in order to illustrate the application of our analysis to programs using higher-order functions and to demonstrate its usefulness even without being able to infer costs for recursive definitions, we present a cost inference for a function that sums a list of naturals using partial application of the standard left-fold function over lists:

$$\mathit{sum} \;=\; \mathit{foldl}\,(+)\,0$$

$$(1.1)\left\{\begin{array}{l}\overline{\Gamma \vdash \mathit{foldl} : \langle(\alpha \xrightarrow{c_1} \beta \xrightarrow{c_2} \alpha) \xrightarrow{c_3} \alpha \xrightarrow{c_4} \mathsf{List}^k \beta \xrightarrow{c_5} \alpha, [], 0, C_{1.1}\}\rangle}\;[\mathit{var}_{st}] \\ \quad\quad \text{where } C_{1.1} = \{c_3 = 0, c_4 = 0, c_5 = k(2 + c_1 + c_2)\}\end{array}\right.$$

$$(1.2)\left\{\overline{\Gamma \vdash (+) : \langle \mathsf{Nat}^n \xrightarrow{d_1} \mathsf{Nat}^m \xrightarrow{d_2} \mathsf{Nat}^p, [], 0, C_{1.2} = \{d_1 = 0, d_2 = 0, p = n + m\}\rangle}\;[\mathit{var}_{st}]\right.$$

$$(1.3)\left\{\begin{array}{l}\theta_{1.3} = \mathcal{U}((\alpha \xrightarrow{c_1} \beta \xrightarrow{c_2} \alpha) \xrightarrow{c_3} \alpha \xrightarrow{c_4} \mathsf{List}^k \beta \xrightarrow{c_5} \alpha,\; (\mathsf{Nat}^n \xrightarrow{d_1} \mathsf{Nat}^m \xrightarrow{d_2} \mathsf{Nat}^p) \xrightarrow{d_3} \gamma) = \\ \quad = [\mathsf{Nat}^{n_1}/\alpha,\; \mathsf{Nat}^{m_1}/\beta,\; (\mathsf{Nat}^{n_2} \xrightarrow{d_4} \mathsf{List}^{k_1} \mathsf{Nat}^{m_2} \xrightarrow{d_5} \mathsf{Nat}^{p_1})/\gamma]\end{array}\right.$$

$$(1.4)\left\{\begin{array}{l}C_{1.4} = \mathcal{D}(\theta_{1.3}((\alpha \xrightarrow{c_1} \beta \xrightarrow{c_2} \alpha) \xrightarrow{c_3} \alpha \xrightarrow{c_4} \mathsf{List}^k \beta \xrightarrow{c_5} \alpha), \\ \quad\quad \theta_{1.3}((\mathsf{Nat}^n \xrightarrow{d_1} \mathsf{Nat}^m \xrightarrow{d_2} \mathsf{Nat}^p) \xrightarrow{d_3} \gamma)) = \{n_1 \leq n,\, p \leq n_1,\, n_1 \leq p_1 \ldots\}\end{array}\right.$$

$$\left.\frac{(1.1)\qquad (1.2)\qquad (1.3)\qquad (1.4)}{\Gamma \vdash \mathit{foldl}\,(+) : \langle \mathsf{Nat}^{n_2} \xrightarrow{d_4} \mathsf{List}^{k_1} \mathsf{Nat}^{m_2} \xrightarrow{d_5} \mathsf{Nat}^{n_3}, \theta_{1.3}, 1, C_{1.1} \cup C_{1.2} \cup C_{1.4}\rangle}\;[\mathit{app}_{st}]\right\}(1)$$

$$\left.\frac{}{\Gamma \vdash 0 : \langle \mathsf{Nat}^z, [], 0, \{z = 0\}\rangle}\;[\mathit{nat}_{st}]\right\}(2)$$

$$\left.\theta_3 = \mathcal{U}(\mathsf{Nat}^{n_2} \xrightarrow{d_4} \mathsf{List}^{k_1} \mathsf{Nat}^{m_2} \xrightarrow{d_5} \mathsf{Nat}^{p_1},\; \mathsf{Nat}^z \xrightarrow{d_6} \delta) = [(\mathsf{List}^{k_2} \mathsf{Nat}^{m_3} \xrightarrow{d_7} \mathsf{Nat}^{p_2})/\delta]\right\}(3)$$

$$\left.\begin{array}{l}C_4 = \mathcal{D}(\mathsf{Nat}^{n_2} \xrightarrow{d_4} \mathsf{List}^{k_1} \mathsf{Nat}^{m_2} \xrightarrow{d_5} \mathsf{Nat}^{p_1},\; \mathsf{Nat}^z \xrightarrow{d_6} \mathsf{List}^{k_2} \mathsf{Nat}^{m_3} \xrightarrow{d_7} \mathsf{Nat}^{p_2}) = \\ \quad = \{p_1 \leq p_2 \ldots\}\end{array}\right\}(4)$$

$$\frac{(1)\qquad (2)\qquad (3)\qquad (4)}{\Gamma \vdash \mathit{foldl}\,(+)\,0 : \langle \mathsf{List}^{k_2} \mathsf{Nat}^{m_3} \xrightarrow{d_7} \mathsf{Nat}^{p_2}, \theta_3\theta_{1.3}, 2, C_{1.1} \cup C_{1.2} \cup C_{1.4} \cup C_4\rangle}\;[\mathit{app}_{st}]$$

Fig. 10. A type reconstruction for *sum*

Figure 10 shows the inference for the sized-time type of the function body,

$$\Gamma = \{+ : \sigma_{plus},\, \mathit{foldl} : \sigma_{foldl}\} \overset{?}{\vdash} \mathit{foldl}\,(+)\,0$$

assuming suitable types for $(+)$ and *foldl*:

$$\sigma_{plus} = \forall n \forall m \forall p \forall c_1 \forall c_2 .\, (\mathsf{Nat}^n \xrightarrow{c_1} \mathsf{Nat}^m \xrightarrow{c_2} \mathsf{Nat}^p,\; \{c_1 = 0, c_2 = 0, p = n + m\})$$
$$\sigma_{foldl} = \forall \ldots\; ((\alpha \xrightarrow{c_1} \beta \xrightarrow{c_2} \alpha) \xrightarrow{c_3} \alpha \xrightarrow{c_4} \mathsf{List}^k \beta \xrightarrow{c_5} \alpha, \{c_3 = 0, c_4 = 0, c_5 = k(2 + c_1 + c_2)\})$$

Our assumption σ_{foldl} captures the fact that *foldl* must apply its argument function k times (where k is the length of the list) to two separate arguments. Since we are using λ-calculus style binary function application, each use of the argument function thus requires two distinct applications in addition to the latent cost for evaluating the function body. The quantifier ranges over all free type and cost variables.

Looking at just three constraints from $C_{1.1}$ and $C_{1.4}$ we can infer that $p = n + m \wedge n_1 \leq n \wedge p \leq n_1 \Rightarrow n = p = \omega$ because the constraints must hold for values of $m > 0$. Simplifying the remainder of the constraint set (not shown), we obtain the following type for the function:

$$\sigma_{sum} = \mathsf{List}^k \mathsf{Nat}^m \overset{2k}{\rightarrow} \mathsf{Nat}^\omega$$

As we would expect, the number of applications for executing *sum* is precisely twice the number of elements in the list because (+) incurs no additional latent costs. Unfortunately, in this case the system is unable to infer any useful size information for the result of the *sum*. Is is not difficult to see that the best upper-bound size for *sum* would be

$$\sigma'_{sum} = \mathsf{List}^k \mathsf{Nat}^m \overset{2k}{\rightarrow} \mathsf{Nat}^{km}$$

The size we obtain is indeed a super-type of this type, and is therefore a safe approximation. Moreover, our type system will not even accept σ'_{sum} as a valid type for *sum*, and we are therefore unable to derive this using our inference algorithm. Informally, the reason for this is that the argument function to *foldl* must have the same polymorphic type α both for its first argument and for its result. The sharing that is introduced in this way implies an *aliasing on size annotations* in the argument and result types. When the (+) is supplied as an argument to *foldl*, this aliasing can only be resolved by substituting ω in both places.

This loss of size-information limits the quality of the analysis we can infer because further composition of *sum* with other functions will inevitably yield ω-sizes and costs. However, this unhappy situation only occurs with certain high-order functions: fold-type functions are essentially a "worst-case scenario" and our prototype implementation has demonstrated that the inference algorithm does preserve useful result sizes with applications of standard *map*, *filter* and *compose* functions, for example.

5 Experimental Results

This section describes experimental results obtained from the prototype implementation of our cost analysis. The inference algorithm was written as a Haskell program that takes as input a $\mathcal{L}$-expression together with a type environment that includes hand-written cost annotation for builtin and library functions such as +, *foldl* etc.

The output of the analysis is a sized-time type together with a set of constraints over the cost and size variables that appear in that type. These constraints are then simplified using a specially constructed solver written in a version of Prolog that includes *constraint handling rules* [6]. In the past we have experimented with other constraint solvers, including the Mozart implementation of the Oz constraint programming language [7].

Our experiment was conducted as follows: we took a representative set of non-recursive function definitions involving only naturals, booleans and lists from the Haskell language standard prelude [8] and coded them as $\mathcal{L}$-expressions. We then added a type environment containing hand-written sized-time types for all necessary primitive operations (e.g. arithmetic and boolean operations) and for those library functions involving recursive definitions (e.g. *foldl/r*, *map* and

Function	Inferred type	Cost?	Size?
max	$\mathsf{Nat}^n \xrightarrow{0} \mathsf{Nat}^m \xrightarrow{2} \mathsf{Nat}^{\max(n,m)}$	√	√
min	$\mathsf{Nat}^n \xrightarrow{0} \mathsf{Nat}^m \xrightarrow{2} \mathsf{Nat}^{\max(n,m)}$	√	×
even	$\mathsf{Nat}^n \xrightarrow{4} \mathsf{Bool}$	√	√
odd	$\mathsf{Nat}^n \xrightarrow{6} \mathsf{Bool}$	√	√
compose	$(\gamma \xrightarrow{z_1} \beta) \xrightarrow{0} (\alpha \xrightarrow{z_2} \gamma) \xrightarrow{0} \alpha \xrightarrow{z_1+z_2+2} \beta$	√	√
flip	$(\alpha \xrightarrow{z_1} \beta \xrightarrow{z_2} \gamma) \xrightarrow{0} \beta \xrightarrow{0} \alpha \xrightarrow{z_1+z_2+2} \gamma$	√	√
subtract	$\mathsf{Nat}^n \xrightarrow{0} \mathsf{Nat}^m \xrightarrow{2} \mathsf{Nat}^m$	√	√
concat	$\mathsf{List}^n(\mathsf{List}^m \alpha) \xrightarrow{n(2m+2)} \mathsf{List}^\omega \alpha$	√	×
reverse	$\mathsf{List}^k \alpha \xrightarrow{4k} \mathsf{List}^\omega \alpha$	√	×
and, or	$\mathsf{List}^k \mathsf{Bool} \xrightarrow{2k} \mathsf{Bool}$	√	√
any, all	$(\alpha \xrightarrow{z_1} \mathsf{Bool}) \xrightarrow{3} \mathsf{List}^k \alpha \xrightarrow{k(z_1+5)+2} \mathsf{Bool}$	√	√
elem	$\alpha \xrightarrow{5} \mathsf{List}^k \alpha \xrightarrow{5k+2} \mathsf{Bool}$	√	√
sum, product	$\mathsf{List}^k \mathsf{Nat}^n \xrightarrow{2k} \mathsf{Nat}^\omega$	√	×

Fig. 11. Summary of prototype implementation results

++). All higher-order functions that can be expressed directly in $\mathcal{L}$ (e.g. *compose* and *flip*) were defined explicitly through let-bindings and their costs were inferred automatically using our analysis. Finally, wherever necessary, Haskell's overloaded operators were specialized to $\mathcal{L}$ monotypes (e.g. arithmetic functions were specialized to naturals).

The definitions for these examples, complete with the sized-type assumptions for the library functions used in the analysis, are available for download from the following URL: `http://www-fp.dcs.st-and.ac.uk/publications.html`.

Figure 11 summarizes the results obtained: the first column gives the name(s) of the function(s) that were analysed while the second column shows the sized-time type generated by the analysis. The third and fourth columns present a qualitative appreciation of the costs and sizes that were obtained by the analysis: a '√' indicates that the approximation obtained is *accurate* (i.e. the best that can be expressed using z-expressions), and an '×' indicates a safe but inaccurate answer. The table shows that our analysis computes accurate cost information in all 16 cases, and accurate size information in 11 of these cases. Four cases where size information is inaccurate represent applications of folds, where all size information is lost. The remaing case is the *min* function, where a finite size is infered but it is larger than need be.

Some of the types that are derived may seem counter-intuitive, and thus require more detailed explanations. For example, the size of the result for *subtract* (the function that subtracts its first argument from its second argument) must be identical to that of its second argument because the first argument may be zero. The *concat* function is defined as by folding ++ over a list: each application of ++ requires $2m$ function application steps, and the fold itself incurs two extra applications for each element of the outer list. The *reverse* function is defined as a fold of '*flip* (:)' costing two applications each; the fold itself costs two applications for each list element, totaling $4k$ application. Finally, the functions *any*, *all* and *elem* have non-zero costs on the first arrow because they are partial applications of higher-order functions.

6 Related Work

The work described in this paper extends our earlier work [9,10] in the following way. The ω-relaxation operator allows sizes to be given for function applications that would have been rejected in the earlier system. In the type reconstruction algorithm, unification has been separated from weakening, and substitutions on cost/size variables have been separated from those on type variables. These changes allow weakening to be restricted in the $[if_{st}]$ rule, preventing incorrect weakening of cost/size variables outside the scope of conditionals. Strengthening handles the contravariance of the subtype relation for function types.

Most closely related to our granularity analysis is the system by Reistad and Gifford [5] for the cost analysis of Lisp expressions. This system introduces the notion of "latent costs", partially based on the "time system" by Dornic et al. [11], annotating the function type with a cost expression representing its computation cost, thereby enabling the system to treat higher-order functions. Rather than trying to extract closed forms for general recursive functions, however, they require the use of higher-order functions with known latent costs.

Hughes, Pareto and Sabry [4] have developed "sized types" and a type checking algorithm for a simple higher-order, non-strict functional language, which influenced our design. This type system checks upper bounds for the size of arbitrary algebraic data types, and is capable of dealing with recursive definitions. Like our own system, Hughes et al. produce sets of linear constraints that are resolved by an external constraint solver. Unlike our system, however, sized types are restricted to type checking, which is sufficient to provide type security, as is their goal, but inadequate for a use as an analysis.

The technique used by Grobauer [12] for extracting cost recurrences out of a Dependent ML (DML) program is in several aspects similar to ours: size-annotated types are used to capture size information; the analysis is based on type inference and a cost extraction algorithm is outlined. The main differences to our work are that size inference is not attempted, DML is first-order rather than higher-order, and no attempt is made at finding closed forms for the extracted recurrences.

Chin and Khoo [13] describe a type-inference based algorithm for computing size information expressed in terms of Presburger formulae, for a higher-order, strict, functional language with lists, tuples and general non-recursive data constructors. Like the other work described here, however, this work does not cover cost analysis involving cost and size inference from unannotated source expressions.

In the context of *complexity analysis* Le Métayer [14] uses program transformation via a set of rewrite rules to derive complexity functions for FP programs. A database of known recurrences is used to produce closed forms for some recursive functions. Rosendahl [15] first uses abstract interpretation to obtain size information and then program transformation to generate a time bound program for first-order Lisp programs. Flajolet et al. [16] obtain average-case complexity functions for functional programs using the Maple computer algebra system to solve recurrences. Several systems elaborate on the *dynamic use of cost information* for parallel execution. Huelsbergen et al. [17] define an abstract interpretation of a higher-order, strict language using dynamic estimates of the size of data.

Finally, systems for granularity analysis in parallel logic programs [18,19] typically combine the compile-time derivation of a cost bound, with a run-time evaluation of the cost estimate to throttle the generation of parallelism. Such systems are restricted to first-order programs.

7 Conclusions

This paper has introduced a novel type-based analysis of the computation costs in a simple strict polymorphic higher-order functional language. Formally the analysis is presented as an extension to a conventional Hindley-Milner type system, a *sized time system*. Its implementation combines a cost reconstruction algorithm, based on subtyping, with a separate constraint solver for checking type correctness and producing upper-bound cost information that is aimed at guiding parallel computation. To the best of our knowledge our sized time system is the first attempt to construct a static analysis that exploits size information to *automatically infer* upper bound time costs of polymorphic higher-order functions. This is significant since it allows the immediate application of our analysis to a wide range of non-recursive functional programs. By using standard techniques such as cost libraries for known higher-order functions [5], we can, in principle, analyze costs for a range of programs that do not directly use recursion.

We are in the process of extending our work in a number of ways. Firstly, we have successfully prototyped a system to generate constraints that capture cost and size information for certain recursive definitions. This work has not yet been formalized, however.

Although we have not provided proofs of soundness and completeness, similar results on sized types suggest these can be constructed for our own work. A full comparison of the effectiveness of our approach is also pending.

References

1. Hammond, K., Michaelson, G.: Parallel Functional Programming. Springer (2000)
2. Nielson, F., Nielson, H.R., Hankin, C.: Principles of Program Analysis. Springer (1999)
3. Mitchell, J.C.: Subtyping and Related Concepts. In: Foundations for Programming Languages. MIT Press (1996)
4. Hughes, R., Pareto, L., Sabry, A.: Proving the Correctness of Reactive Systems using Sized Types. In: POPL'96, St Petersburg, FL (1996)
5. Reistad, B., Gifford, D.: Static Dependent Costs for Estimating Execution Time. In: LFP'94, Orlando, FL (1994) 65–78

6. Frühwirth, T.: Theory and practice of constraint handling rules. Journal of Logic Programming 37 (1998)
7. Smolka, G.: The Oz Programming Model. In: Computer Science Today. LNCS 1000. Springer (1995) 324–343
8. Jones, S.P., Hughes, J., Augustsson, L., Barton, D., Boutel, B., Burton, W., Fasel, J., Hammond, K., Hinze, R., Hudak, P., Johnsson, T., Jones, M., Launchbury, J., Meijer, E., Peterson, J., Reid, A., Runciman, C., Wadler, P.: Haskell 98: A Non-Strict, Purely Functional Language. (1999)
9. Loidl, H.W., Hammond, K.: A Sized Time System for a Parallel Functional Language. In: Glasgow Workshop on Functional Programming, Ullapool (1996)
10. Loidl, H.W.: Granularity in Large-Scale Parallel Functional Programming. PhD thesis, Department of Computing Science, University of Glasgow (1998)
11. Dornic, V., Jouvelot, P., Gifford, D.: Polymorphic Time Systems for Estimating Program Complexity. ACM Letters on Prog. Lang. and Systems 1 (1992) 33–45
12. Grobauer, B.: Cost Recurrences for DML Programs. In: ICFP'01, Florence, Italy, ACM Press (2001)
13. Chin, W.N., Khoo, S.C.: Calculating sized types. Higher-Order and Symbolic Computing 14 (2001)
14. Le Métayer, D.: ACE: An Automatic Complexity Evaluator. TOPLAS 10 (1988)
15. Rosendahl, M.: Automatic Complexity Analysis. In: FPCA'89. (1989) 144–156
16. Flajolet, P., Salvy, B., Zimmermann, P.: Automatic Average-Case Analysis of Algorithms. Theoretical Computer Science 79 (1991) 37–109
17. Huelsbergen, L., Larus, J., Aiken, A.: Using Run-Time List Sizes to Guide Parallel Thread Creation. In: LFP'94, Orlando, FL (1994) 79–90
18. Debray, S., Lin, N.W., Hermenegildo, M.: Task Granularity Analysis in Logic Programs. In: PLDI'90. SIGPLAN Notices 25(6), ACM Press (1990) 174–188
19. Tick, E., Zhong, X.: A Compile-Time Granularity Analysis Algorithm and its Performance Evaluation. New Generation Computing 11 (1993) 271–295

Author Index

Lecture Notes in Computer Science

For information about Vols. 1–2575

please contact your bookseller or Springer-Verlag

Vol. 2576: S. Cimato, C. Galdi, G. Persiano (Eds.), Security in Communication Networks. Proceedings, 2002. IX, 365 pages. 2003.

Vol. 2577: P. Petta, R. Tolksdorf, F. Zambonelli (Eds.), Engineering Societies in the Agents World III. Proceedings, 2002. X, 285 pages. 2003. (Subseries LNAI).

Vol. 2578: F.A.P. Petitcolas (Ed.), Information Hiding. Proceedings, 2002. IX, 427 pages. 2003.

Vol. 2580: H. Erdogmus, T. Weng (Eds.), COTS-Based Software Systems. Proceedings, 2003. XVIII, 261 pages. 2003.

Vol. 2581: J.S. Sichman, F. Bousquet, P. Davidsson (Eds.), Multi-Agent-Based Simulation II. Proceedings, 2002. X, 195 pages. 2003. (Subseries LNAI).

Vol. 2582: L. Bertossi, G.O.H. Katona, K.-D. Schewe, B. Thalheim (Eds.), Semantics in Databases. Proceedings, 2001. IX, 229 pages. 2003.

Vol. 2583: S. Matwin, C. Sammut (Eds.), Inductive Logic Programming. Proceedings, 2002. X, 351 pages. 2003. (Subseries LNAI).

Vol. 2584: A. Schiper, A.A. Shvartsman, H. Weatherspoon, B.Y. Zhao (Eds.), Future Directions in Distributed Computing. X, 219 pages. 2003.

Vol. 2585: F. Giunchiglia, J. Odell, G. Weiß (Eds.), Agent-Oriented Software Engineering III. Proceedings, 2002. X, 229 pages. 2003.

Vol. 2586: M. Klusch, S. Bergamaschi, P. Edwards, P. Petta (Eds.), Intelligent Information Agents. VI, 275 pages. 2003. (Subseries LNAI).

Vol. 2587: P.J. Lee, C.H. Lim (Eds.), Information Security and Cryptology – ICISC 2002. Proceedings, 2002. XI, 536 pages. 2003.

Vol. 2588: A. Gelbukh (Ed.), Computational Linguistics and Intelligent Text Processing. Proceedings, 2003. XV, 648 pages. 2003.

Vol. 2589: E. Börger, A. Gargantini, E. Riccobene (Eds.), Abstract State Machines 2003. Proceedings, 2003. XI, 427 pages. 2003.

Vol. 2590: S. Bressan, A.B. Chaudhri, M.L. Lee, J.X. Yu, Z. Lacroix (Eds.), Efficiency and Effectiveness of XML Tools and Techniques and Data Integration over the Web. Proceedings, 2002. X, 259 pages. 2003.

Vol. 2591: M. Aksit, M. Mezini, R. Unland (Eds.), Objects, Components, Architectures, Services, and Applications for a Networked World. Proceedings, 2002. XI, 431 pages. 2003.

Vol. 2592: R. Kowalczyk, J.P. Müller, H. Tianfield, R. Unland (Eds.), Agent Technologies, Infrastructures, Tools, and Applications for E-Services. Proceedings, 2002. XVII, 371 pages. 2003. (Subseries LNAI).

Vol. 2593: A.B. Chaudhri, M. Jeckle, E. Rahm, R. Unland (Eds.), Web, Web-Services, and Database Systems. Proceedings, 2002. XI, 311 pages. 2003.

Vol. 2594: A. Asperti, B. Buchberger, J.H. Davenport (Eds.), Mathematical Knowledge Management. Proceedings, 2003. X, 225 pages. 2003.

Vol. 2595: K. Nyberg, H. Heys (Eds.), Selected Areas in Cryptography. Proceedings, 2002. XI, 405 pages. 2003.

Vol. 2596: A. Coen-Porisini, A. van der Hoek (Eds.), Software Engineering and Middleware. Proceedings, 2002. XII, 239 pages. 2003.

Vol. 2597: G. Păun, G. Rozenberg, A. Salomaa, C. Zandron (Eds.), Membrane Computing. Proceedings, 2002. VIII, 423 pages. 2003.

Vol. 2598: R. Klein, H.-W. Six, L. Wegner (Eds.), Computer Science in Perspective. X, 357 pages. 2003.

Vol. 2599: E. Sherratt (Ed.), Telecommunications and beyond: The Broader Applicability of SDL and MSC. Proceedings, 2002. X, 253 pages. 2003.

Vol. 2600: S. Mendelson, A.J. Smola, Advanced Lectures on Machine Learning. Proceedings, 2002. IX, 259 pages. 2003. (Subseries LNAI).

Vol. 2601: M. Ajmone Marsan, G. Corazza, M. Listanti, A. Roveri (Eds.) Quality of Service in Multiservice IP Networks. Proceedings, 2003. XV, 759 pages. 2003.

Vol. 2602: C. Priami (Ed.), Computational Methods in Systems Biology. Proceedings, 2003. IX, 214 pages. 2003.

Vol. 2603: A. Garcia, C. Lucena, F. Zambonelli, A. Omicini, J. Castro (Eds.), Software Engineering for Large-Scale Multi-Agent Systems. XIV, 285 pages. 2003.

Vol. 2604: N. Guelfi, E. Astesiano, G. Reggio (Eds.), Scientific Engineering for Distributed Java Applications. Proceedings, 2002. X, 205 pages. 2003.

Vol. 2606: A.M. Tyrrell, P.C. Haddow, J. Torresen (Eds.), Evolvable Systems: From Biology to Hardware. Proceedings, 2003. XIV, 468 pages. 2003.

Vol. 2607: H. Alt, M. Habib (Eds.), STACS 2003. Proceedings, 2003. XVII, 700 pages. 2003.

Vol. 2609: M. Okada, B. Pierce, A. Scedrov, H. Tokuda, A. Yonezawa (Eds.), Software Security – Theories and Systems. Proceedings, 2002. XI, 471 pages. 2003.

Vol. 2610: C. Ryan, T. Soule, M. Keijzer, E. Tsang, R. Poli, E. Costa (Eds.), Genetic Programming. Proceedings, 2003. XII, 486 pages. 2003.

Vol. 2611: S. Cagnoni, J.J. Romero Cardalda, D.W. Corne, J. Gottlieb, A. Guillot, E. Hart, C.G. Johnson, E. Marchiori, J.-A. Meyer, M. Middendorf, G.R. Raidl (Eds.), Applications of Evolutionary Computing. Proceedings, 2003. XXI, 708 pages. 2003.

Vol. 2612: M. Joye (Ed.), Topics in Cryptology – CT-RSA 2003. Proceedings, 2003. XI, 417 pages. 2003.

Vol. 2613: F.A.P. Petitcolas, H.J. Kim (Eds.), Digital Watermarking. Proceedings, 2002. XI, 265 pages. 2003.

Vol. 2614: R. Laddaga, P. Robertson, H. Shrobe (Eds.), Self-Adaptive Software: Applications. Proceedings, 2001. VIII, 291 pages. 2003.

Vol. 2615: N. Carbonell, C. Stephanidis (Eds.), Universal Access. Proceedings, 2002. XIV, 534 pages. 2003.

Vol. 2616: T. Asano, R. Klette, C. Ronse (Eds.), Geometry, Morphology, and Computational Imaging. Proceedings, 2002. X, 437 pages. 2003.

Vol. 2617: H.A. Reijers (Eds.), Design and Control of Workflow Processes. Proceedings, 2002. XV, 624 pages. 2003.

Vol. 2618: P. Degano (Ed.), Programming Languages and Systems. Proceedings, 2003. XV, 415 pages. 2003.

Vol. 2619: H. Garavel, J. Hatcliff (Eds.), Tools and Algorithms for the Construction and Analysis of Systems. Proceedings, 2003. XVI, 604 pages. 2003.

Vol. 2620: A.D. Gordon (Ed.), Foundations of Software Science and Computation Structures. Proceedings, 2003. XII, 441 pages. 2003.

Vol. 2621: M. Pezzè (Ed.), Fundamental Approaches to Software Engineering. Proceedings, 2003. XIV, 403 pages. 2003.

Vol. 2622: G. Hedin (Ed.), Compiler Construction. Proceedings, 2003. XII, 335 pages. 2003.

Vol. 2623: O. Maler, A. Pnueli (Eds.), Hybrid Systems: Computation and Control. Proceedings, 2003. XII, 558 pages. 2003.

Vol. 2625: U. Meyer, P. Sanders, J. Sibeyn (Eds.), Algorithms for Memory Hierarchies. Proceedings, 2003. XVIII, 428 pages. 2003.

Vol. 2626: J.L. Crowley, J.H. Piater, M. Vincze, L. Paletta (Eds.), Computer Vision Systems. Proceedings, 2003. XIII, 546 pages. 2003.

Vol. 2627: B. O'Sullivan (Ed.), Recent Advances in Constraints. Proceedings, 2002. X, 201 pages. 2003. (Subseries LNAI).

Vol. 2628: T. Fahringer, B. Scholz, Advanced Symbolic Analysis for Compilers. XII, 129 pages. 2003.

Vol. 2631: R. Falcone, S. Barber, L. Korba, M. Singh (Eds.), Trust, Reputation, and Security: Theories and Practice. Proceedings, 2002. X, 235 pages. 2003. (Subseries LNAI).

Vol. 2632: C.M. Fonseca, P.J. Fleming, E. Zitzler, K. Deb, L. Thiele (Eds.), Evolutionary Multi-Criterion Optimization. Proceedings, 2003. XV, 812 pages. 2003.

Vol. 2633: F. Sebastiani (Ed.), Advances in Information Retrieval. Proceedings, 2003. XIII, 546 pages. 2003.

Vol. 2634: F. Zhao, L. Guibas (Eds.), Information Processing in Sensor Networks. Proceedings, 2003. XII, 692 pages. 2003.

Vol. 2636: E. Alonso, D, Kudenko, D. Kazakov (Eds.), Adaptive Agents and Multi-Agent Systems. XIV, 323 pages. 2003. (Subseries LNAI).

Vol. 2637: K.-Y. Whang, J. Jeon, K. Shim, J. Srivastava (Eds.), Advances in Knowledge Discovery and Data Mining. Proceedings, 2003. XVIII, 610 pages. 2003. (Subseries LNAI).

Vol. 2638: J. Jeuring, S. Peyton Jones (Eds.), Advanced Functional Programming. Proceedings, 2002. VII, 213 pages. 2003.

Vol. 2639: G. Wang, Q. Liu, Y. Yao, A. Skowron (Eds.), Rough Sets, Fuzzy Sets, Data Mining, and Granular Computing. Proceedings, 2003. XVII, 741 pages. 2003. (Subseries LNAI).

Vol. 2642: X. Zhou, Y. Zhang, M.E. Orlowska (Eds.), Web Technologies and Applications. Proceedings, 2003. XIII, 608 pages. 2003.

Vol. 2643: M. Fossorier, T. Høholdt, A. Poli (Eds.), Applied Algebra, Algebraic Algorithms and Error-Correcting Codes. Proceedings, 2003. X, 256 pages. 2003.

Vol. 2644: D. Hogrefe, A. Wiles (Eds.), Testing of Communicating Systems. Proceedings, 2003. XII, 311 pages. 2003.

Vol. 2645: M.A. Wimmer (Ed.), Knowledge Management in Electronic Government. Proceedings, 2003. XI, 320 pages. 2003. (Subseries LNAI).

Vol. 2646: H. Geuvers, F. Wiedijk (Eds.), Types for Proofs and Programs. Proceedings, 2002. VIII, 331 pages. 2003.

Vol. 2648: T. Ball, S.K. Rajamani (Eds.), Model Checking Software. Proceedings, 2003. VIII, 241 pages. 2003.

Vol. 2649: B. Westfechtel, A. van der Hoek (Eds.), Software Configuration Management. Proceedings, 2003. VIII, 241 pages. 2003.

Vol. 2653: R. Petreschi, Giuseppe Persiano, R. Silvestri (Eds.), Algorithms and Complexity. Proceedings, 2003. XI, 289 pages. 2003.

Vol. 2656: E. Biham (Ed.), Advances in Cryptology – EUROCRPYT 2003. Proceedings, 2003. XIV, 649 pages. 2003.

Vol. 2663: E. Menasalvas, J. Segovia, P.S. Szczepaniak (Eds.), Advances in Web Intelligence. Proceedings, 2003. XII, 350 pages. 2003. (Subseries LNAI).

Vol. 2665: H. Chen, R. Miranda, D.D. Zeng, C. Demchak, J. Schroeder, T. Madhusudan (Eds.), Intelligence and Security Informatics. Proceedings, 2003. XIV, 392 pages. 2003.

Vol. 2667: V. Kumar, M.L. Gavrilova, C.J.K. Tan, P. L'Ecuyer (Eds.), Computational Science and Its Applications – ICCSA 2003. Proceedings, Part I. 2003. XXXIV, 1060 pages. 2003.

Vol. 2668: V. Kumar, M.L. Gavrilova, C.J.K. Tan, P. L'Ecuyer (Eds.), Computational Science and Its Applications – ICCSA 2003. Proceedings, Part II. 2003. XXXIV, 942 pages. 2003.

Vol. 2669: V. Kumar, M.L. Gavrilova, C.J.K. Tan, P. L'Ecuyer (Eds.), Computational Science and Its Applications – ICCSA 2003. Proceedings, Part III. 2003. XXXIV, 948 pages. 2003.

Vol. 2670: R. Peña, T. Arts (Eds.), Implementation of Functional Languages. Proceedings, 2002. X, 249 pages. 2003.

Vol. 2692: P. Nixon, S. Terzis (Eds.), Trust Management. Proceedings, 2003. X, 349 pages. 2003.

GPSR Compliance

The European Union's (EU) General Product Safety Regulation (GPSR) is a set of rules that requires consumer products to be safe and our obligations to ensure this.

If you have any concerns about our products, you can contact us on ProductSafety@springernature.com

In case Publisher is established outside the EU, the EU authorized representative is:

Springer Nature Customer Service Center GmbH
Europaplatz 3
69115 Heidelberg, Germany

Batch number: 09474024

Printed by Printforce, the Netherlands